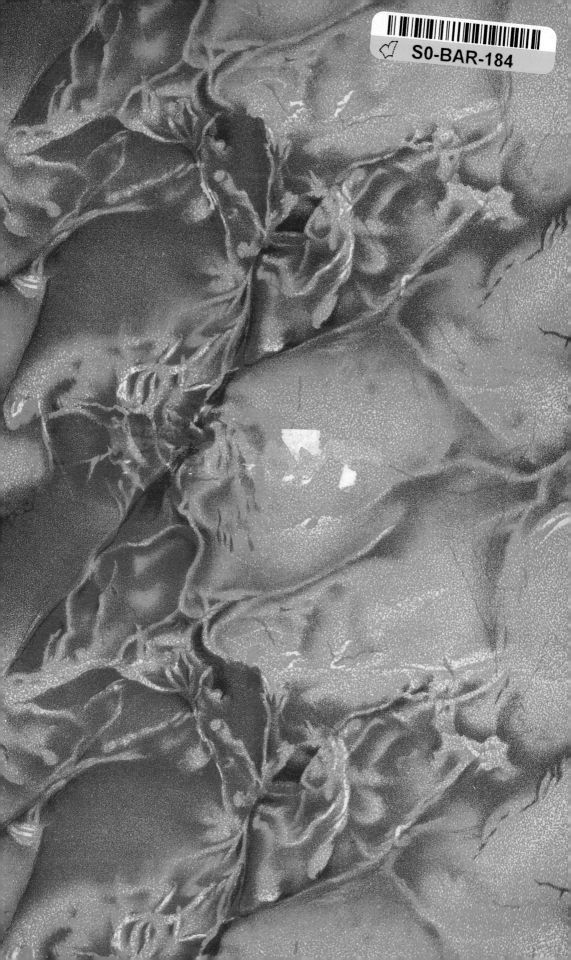

Philip Alexander Bruce

VIRGINIA

REBIRTH OF THE OLD DOMINION

BY

PHILIP ALEXANDER BRUCE, LL. B., LL. D.

Centennial Historian of UNIVERSITY OF VIRGINIA
and
Late Corresponding Secretary of the
Virginia Historical Society

———

VIRGINIA BIOGRAPHY
By Special Staff of Writers

———

Issued in Five Volumes
VOLUME I

———

ILLUSTRATED

———

THE LEWIS PUBLISHING COMPANY
CHICAGO AND NEW YORK

1929

CONTENTS

v

CONTENTS

CHAPTER XV

III—THE COLONIAL PERIOD, 1700-1776

CHAPTER I

CHAPTER II

CHAPTER III

CHAPTER IV

CHAPTER V

CHAPTER VI

CHAPTER VII

CHAPTER VIII

IV—THE FEDERAL PERIOD, 1776-1861

VOLUME II

V—SECESSION AND POST-BELLUM PERIODS, 1860-1876

CHAPTER V

VI—POLITICAL RECONSTRUCTION AND ITS
AFTERMATH

CHAPTER I

CHAPTER II

CHAPTER III

CHAPTER IV

CHAPTER V

VII—REBIRTH OF THE OLD DOMINION—DEVELOPMENT
AFTER 1876

CHAPTER I

CHAPTER II

CHAPTER III

CHAPTER IV

CHAPTER V

CHAPTER VI

CHAPTER VII

CHAPTER VIII

VIII—THE WORLD WAR AND ITS SEQUENCE

CHAPTER I

CHAPTER II

CHAPTER III

CHAPTER IV

CHAPTER V

CONTENTS xi

INDEX

Philip Alexander Bruce

VIRGINIA

REBIRTH OF THE OLD DOMINION

BY

PHILIP ALEXANDER BRUCE, LL. B., LL. D.

Centennial Historian of UNIVERSITY OF VIRGINIA
and
Late Corresponding Secretary of the
Virginia Historical Society

———

VIRGINIA BIOGRAPHY
By Special Staff of Writers

———

Issued in Five Volumes
VOLUME I

———

ILLUSTRATED

———

THE LEWIS PUBLISHING COMPANY
CHICAGO AND NEW YORK

1929

CONTENTS

VOLUME I

I—THE LAND AND THE PEOPLE

II—THE COLONIAL PERIOD, 1607-1700

v

CONTENTS

CONTENTS

CONTENTS xi

INDEX

xiii

PREFACE

The two great constructive periods in the history of Virginia are, (1) the interval between 1607 and 1700; and (2) the interval between 1876 and 1927. Both were periods of foundation. Each was preeminently the beginning of new conditions; destined, in the one case, to last, with some important modifications, down to the War for Southern Independence; and in the other, apparently destined to last indefinitely.

The general plantation organization of the first century really continued,—in the spirit, at least,—to exist for one hundred and sixty years after 1700. The system of labor of that century remained unaltered until slavery was abolished in 1865. Agriculture, during that long interval, was still restricted in the main to the production of maize, tobacco, and wheat. The Established Church only perished with the Revolution. Some features of the legal administration were protracted even into the Twentieth Century. The militia muster disappeared only with the opening of the War in 1861. The political administration was only broken by the change in the form of government which followed the rupture with Great Britain. The system of education in the Seventeenth Century, with the College of William and Mary at the top and tutors and private schools below, was harmoniously succeeded in the early Nineteenth Century by the system of education which was represented at the top by the University of Virginia, and below by tutors and private academies.

Without a complete understanding of the conditions to be found in Virginia before 1700, we would be unable to form an accurate conception of the conditions to be found there throughout the whole of the Eighteenth Century, and the greater part of the Nineteenth. It is for this reason that, in the present work,

1

we have described the various aspects of the Seventeenth Century in so much detail. Here we find the germ of nearly all the conditions that prevailed down to the opening of the War in 1861.

With the abolition of slavery in 1865, a revolution began which has made the period since the close of the War for Southern Independence radically different from the periods which preceded that date. The emancipation of the negro destroyed the former plantation system by disintegrating the old system of labor. It undermined the foundations on which the old social life of the State rested. It quickened the growth of cities, while it tended to retard the growth of the rural districts. It encouraged the creation and expansion of manufactures. It increased the volume of wealth. It fostered the spirit of cooperation by nourishing the community spirit. It diminished the provincial isolation of the people by bringing them more into contact with the world at large; and it widened the scope of their educational and intellectual interests. Above all, it raised up new opportunities for the improvement of the lower class of the inhabitants, who had languished under the weight of the slave system.

In short, there could not be a greater contrast between two periods in Virginia History than the one which exists between the period of the Seventeenth Century, on the one hand, and the period of the Twentieth on the other. It is this remarkable contrast which we have endeavored to bring out in the contents of these two volumes; and it is for that reason, that we have presented them both with so much fullness.

PHILIP ALEXANDER BRUCE.

University, Va., September 1, 1929

To

LYON GARDINER TYLER

Scholar, Historian, Loyal American, Ardent Virginian

This book is affectionately dedicated by his friend
and co-worker for forty years
the Author

FOREWORD

No adequate conception of the industrial, educational, and other achievements of the Virginia people since 1876, the real date of the rebirth of their Commonwealth, can be formed without a very full knowledge, (1) of the devastation caused within the boundaries of the State by the War of 1861-65; (2) the deep discouragement that accompanied the Period of Reconstruction; and (3) the paralyzing confusion which followed the controversy over the Public Debt. The protracted and malignant consequences of all these events had to be overcome before the process of real development could begin. When that development did once start, nothing could permanently scotch its progress. The far greater part of the present volume is devoted to the growth in every province of the State's interests in the course of the last fifty years. My principal authorities for this division of my narrative are the Reports of the State officials, filling some sixty odd large volumes, an invaluable collection of material for the description of this period. I am also indebted to the numerous documents issued by the Chambers of Commerce representing the different cities and towns of Virginia. Additional information has been obtained through the kindness of Professors Gee and Snavely of the University of Virginia, President Eggleston, of Hampden-Sidney College, Dr. Ennion G. Williams, of the State Board of Health, Hon. George W. Koiner, State Commissioner of Agriculture, and Hon. J. B. Fishburn, of Roanoke. I am indebted to *Heatwole's* History of Education in Virginia for important facts.

5

I

THE LAND AND THE PEOPLE

CHAPTER I

WHY VIRGINIA WAS SETTLED

It is a fact of remarkable interest that the State, which, of all the States in the American Union, has had the most romantic history is the one that had its origin, as a colony, in the most practical business motives. It is true that, back in the minds of the organizers of the London Company, there was a thoroughly sincere desire to improve the moral condition of the Indian tribes inhabiting the region on the Chesapeake Bay, by converting them to Christianity, but not even colonization itself was, in the beginning, an object of the first importance to the members of the company, except as the best means of making the most of those natural advantages of the country which could be employed as a source of profit in the great markets of that age in England and in Continental Europe. Indeed, it was not until the prospect of material returns in a quickly transferable form darkened, that the interest in colonization, as an end, rather than as a means, in itself, assumed an aspect of permanent significance.

Long, however, before Captain Newport and his followers landed at Cape Henry, a perfectly distinct hope existed in the minds of the English traders, and the English statesmen also, that Virginia, in her natural products, as first revealed by the enterprise of Sir Walter Raleigh, would supply nearly all those deficiencies in indispensable articles which were then only furnished to the households, factories, and shops of England by the merchants of the European continent.

But first in importance in itself, and most influential in stimulating an organized exploitation of the natural resources of

9

Virginia was the burning hope that gold would be discovered in the soil of the region that abutted on the shores of the Chesapeake Bay. The English traders and merchants were not men who would be content to look on at the passage, almost in sight of the seaward slopes of Devonshire and Cornwall, of the Spanish galleons, which, year after year, poured into the lap of the Spanish treasury the dazzling heaps of the precious metals obtained from the inexhaustible mines of Mexico and Peru. That was a spectacle which might well have aroused the keen cupidity, and the deep envy also, of such an enterprising people as the Englishmen of that adventurous period; nor were they likely to be satisfied, for any length of time, to limit their aspiration to secure a share in the enormous metallic wealth of America to the daring raids of a few sea-rovers, like Drake and Hawkins, who, from year to year, swooped down on the Spanish silver fleets as they were sailing homeward through the southern seas.

The English merchants desired to use a more legitimate means than this of acquiring possession of a part of the output of the western Golconda. And such means became imperative after the death of Elizabeth, who had turned a deaf ear to the clamor of the Spanish Government when her bold sea-captains pounced down on their Spanish quarry, although their acts were really not better than the acts of pirates, since Spain and England were not at war.

James, timid by nature, was so much disposed to exaggerate the Spanish power, and so anxious to avoid all cause of quarrel with it, that he punished with severity any of his subjects whose intrusion into the colonial seas of Spain had occasioned displeasure at Madrid. It was under the influence of this resentment that Raleigh had been brought by him to the block. But that strange mixture of foolishness and uncanniness was perfectly ready to encourage his subjects to spy out the possible existence of the precious metals along the banks of the Powhatan in Virginia. And that gold was really to be found there in abundance was the belief of all classes in England at that time. "I tell thee," exclaimed one of the characters in the play of Eastward Ho, "gould is more plentiful in Virginia than copper is with us; and for as much redde copper as I can bring, I will have thrice the weight in gould. All their dripping pans and chamber potts are pure gould, and all the chains with which they chaine up their streets are massie gould; all the prisoners they take are fettered in gould; and for rubies and diamonds, they goe forth in holidays and gather them by the seashore to hang on their children's coates, and stick in their children's caps, as commonly as our children wear saffron gilt broaches and groates with hoales in them."

The poet Drayton, inspired, no doubt, by what he had heard of the wealth of Peru, urged the voyagers of 1606 to continue their search in Virginia until "they had found the pearl and gold," which was then associated with the whole of the new world; and the council was so certain of the presence of these precious objects there that they instructed Captain Newport to send out men with picks to prospect just as soon as hills were sighted on the Powhatan. And so eagerly did the members of the expedition nurse the hope of discovering in these high lands the glittering particles of the precious metals, that they easily deceived themselves into thinking that any sparkle in the dirt there indicated that their feverish quest had been rewarded with success.

After the first exploration of the Powhatan, when their thirst seemed to be on the point of being satisfied, the Council at Jamestown urged the authorities in England to hasten the Second Supply so that the people now present in Virginia could be sufficiently reinforced to prevent the "all-devouring Spaniard from laying his ravenous hands" upon the "gold-showing mountains" that rose along the banks of the principal river.

Captain Newport, on his first return to England, was clearly aware that no report of what he had seen would stimulate the Company to such vigorous support of the enterprise as the announcement that silver and gold mines had been really discovered. But there is no reason to think that, in stating this to be a fact, he was consciously exaggerating his own convictions for a purpose. Nor can he be charged with insincerity for bringing back a great quantity of what he held out as precious ore, since he frankly offered it for examination as a proof of the accuracy of his assertion; but its assay only revealed the groundlessness of his hopes. Nevertheless, the officers of the company refused to allow themselves to be discouraged. When Newport again set sail for Jamestown, he was accompanied by two goldsmiths, two refiners, and one jeweler. They must have understood their callings but poorly, for, when the heap of presumptive ore which Newport carried back to England, was tested, it turned out to be worthless dirt.

When Newport sailed for Virginia in the autumn of 1608, he had orders from the company to remain there until he had unearthed a nugget of virgin gold, or obtained a clue to a new route by water to the South Sea. The discovery of both was sought in an expedition which he made after reaching Jamestown to the region lying west of the Falls of the Powhatan. Among those who took part in this expedition was Faldo, a Dutchman, who, wandering away from his companions among the hills, reported, on his rejoining the main body, that, in prospecting, he had run upon indications of a genuine mine. He was permitted to sail with Newport when the vessels of the Second Supply set out for England because it was expected that his testimony to the presence of the precious metals in Virginia would stimulate the merchants of London to contribute to the stores of the Third Supply; and this it was successful in doing.

The hope of finding gold and silver in the soil of the colony persisted until Delaware's arrival at Jamestown. It then grew still more ardent, owing to his encouragement, although it found even less substantial basis to rest upon than before. Captain John Smith alone among the councillors showed impatience with the loss of time which followed from the diversion of attention from more practical ways of advancing the welfare of the new settlement. He boldly censured Captain Martin for his expressed purpose of loading his ship with a cargo of spangled dirt, instead of filling it with cedar and other products that would be useful for English manufactures.

But even the sensible Smith was disposed to share the impression that a route to the South Sea could be found through the forests back of the Chesapeake Bay. It was ostensibly for the purpose of discovering this route that he obtained permission to explore the waters of the Chickahominy River. That stream at the point where it entered the Powhatan spread over a considerable surface, and as this part of it was the only part known to the English when Smith's voyage began, he might naturally enough have thought that this mouth was really the gateway to a strait which extended westward until the waters of the South Sea were reached.

At that time, there was a belief that the distance from the Atlantic to the Pacific, even in Virginia, was not great. This delusion had probably been suggested by the narrowness of the Isthmus of Panama. There was no reason apparently why the same physical condition should not exist in the region of Virginia. If Smith, in guiding his boat into the mouth of the Chickahominy, was influenced more by the possibility of finding the South Sea than by a mere love of exploration of strange scenes, then he was soon dispossessed of the expectation, for the river, after a while, narrowed to the width of a moderate stream, which grew more shallow and more contracted in its windings as the land was more deeply penetrated.

One of the keenest desires of the English merchants of that age was to shorten the route to the East. Expeditions had already been dispatched to the ocean north of Sweden and Norway, in the hope that a path by sea to China and Japan could be found in that direction, but the vast ice fields and the terrible snow storms had soon put a permanent end to this expectation, as it was to put to the like expectation which attended the explorations of Frobisher and others west of Greenland. Cape

Horn was in the possession of Spain, and Cape of Good Hope in that of Portugal. The overland highway through Asia Minor and Syria was controlled by the Turks, and was exposed also to the incursions of the wild tribes of the desert. The demand for the silks, spices, and other luxurious articles of the East had grown to be enormous, and the profits of the trade had been in proportion. Had Smith succeeded in passing from the watershed of the Atlantic to that of the Pacific by the natural canal of the Chickahominy—in short, could he have proved, by actual investigation of its width and length, that this short and insignificant stream was really a strait between the two oceans—he would have come down to us as one of the greatest explorers of the English race; and one of the greatest benefactors of English trade who ever lived.

The immediate effect of a discovery of a route through Virginia to the South Sea would have been very stimulating to the colony's prosperity, as this discovery would have converted the Powhatan into one of the most frequented highways of the world in those times. Ships would have been constantly passing through the strait at all seasons of the year. The advantages of the Virginian soil, products, and climate, would have become generally known, and the stream of immigration which this fact would have created would have been further increased by the lower cost of transportation which the great number of vessels that would have followed this channel would have certainly brought about.

The first actual knowledge which the English colonists acquired of the presence of vast bodies of water far behind the Falls of the Powhatan was obtained by them from the Indians. The information which the latter imparted was, however, very indefinite. It was evident that they had in mind both the Gulf of Mexico and the Great Lakes, which were described in such language as to convey to the eager listeners the impression that a mighty ocean was intended, such as the Englishmen were

aware of in the existence of the Pacific, which had already been
explored as far as California by Admiral Drake.

The hope of finding a passage to the South Sea lingered in
the hearts of the colonists long after the company in London
had ceased to make an organized effort to discover it. When
about 1616 there was reason to think that a permanent peace
with the Indians had been established, it was thought that one
of its most satisfactory features was that now an opportunity
would be open for further explorations of the rivers to show
whether one of them did not run back to the Pacific, or, at least,
connect with a great lake that emptied a part of its waters
through another stream flowing westward to that ocean. As
late as 1623, George Sandys, the treasurer of Virginia, offered
to lead an expedition towards the mountains in the west, in the
hope that, from the crest of one of the peaks, the grand mass of
water forming the sea so ardently sought for, would become
plainly visible on the horizon.

Even in 1669, Berkeley organized a band of volunteers who
were ready to follow him westward until the shores of the East
India Sea should be sighted. "If the distance to it by land," he
wrote in his report to the English authorities, "be not too great
for traffic or commerce, nothing would be more advantageous to
the wealth of England." How little he was aware of the real
extent of that distance was revealed in the fact that he calculated
that it would not take more than thirty days to complete the
journey to and fro. It is one of the triumphs of modern invention that, although the space between the two oceans exceeds by
thousands of miles Berkeley's utmost imagination, yet the time
now taken to traverse it falls short of nearly one-half of the
span which the old colonial governor had allowed for the journey
in both directions.

As a matter of fact, the hope of finding gold and silver in
Virginia, and discovering a passage to the Pacific by water
through its wooded hills and plains, was always more or less
visionary, for both were at best mere conjectures, but the pros-

pect that the forests, fields, and waters of the virgin land would supply the English merchant and artisan with a great quantity of raw materials was perfectly substantial, for had not those forests been actually inspected by the explorers of the new country? Had they not sent back a minute report on the products of that fertile soil and those teeming seas?

The London Company was sanguine that the market for all these articles in England would never fall away. For many years, the Muscovy Company had been importing from Russia and Poland, tar, pitch, rosin, flax, cordage, masts, yards, timber, glass, and soap ashes. Copper from Sweden was constantly unloaded at the London docks for distribution by sale. From France came to the same great port cargoes of wine, salt, and canvas; from Italy, silk and velvets; from Spain, iron and steel, figs and raisins.

These supplies of valuable and popular commodities were never sure of unobstructed arrival from year to year. In reality, their flow to English ports was subject to numerous casualties and interruptions. The intercourse with Russia was likely either to be broken up altogether by bad seasons, or made unprofitable by the tax impositions of the Danish Government on the right of entry into the Baltic Sea. The trade with Italy had to run the gauntlet of the Algerian pirates in the Mediterranean; and it was also burdened with heavy custom duties both on imports and on exports after the harbors of the peninsula were reached. In the commercial exchanges with Spain and Italy, there was also a constant danger that these countries would seize the semi-annual English trading fleets and all their cargos on some flimsy pretext, or no pretext at all. Moreover, in the intercourse with these Catholic countries, the English sailors were exposed to the risk of being imprisoned and forced to change their Protestant faith by the threat of the Inquisition.

Was it not natural, in the light of all these drawbacks, that the hope should be entertained that Virginia would supply the articles then only procurable from distant, and openly or secretly

hostile, peoples on the European continent? But, at the same
time, it was perfectly clear that, without colonization, the resources of the new region could not be utilized to the fullest
extent, in spite of their natural abundance. Especially was this
so in the case of iron ore and furs, flax and hemp, silk, and the
various fruits. Among the first artisans to be brought out to
Virginia were eight Dutchmen and Poles, who had been trained
in Europe to the manufacture of glass, pitch, tar, and soap-
ashes; and the production of these commodities in the colony by
them demonstrated the feasibility of turning to account all its
other natural resources.

How extravagant were the anticipations of the abundance of
merchantable articles to be furnished by the new land was disclosed in the words of Daniel Price, who asserted his belief that
Virginia was, in time, to be "equal to Tyrus for colors, Bason
for woods, Persia for oils, Arabia for spices, Spain for silks,
Narsis for shipping, Netherlands for fish, Bonoma for fruits,
and by tillage, Babylon for corn."

That the country along the Chesapeake and its tributaries
would ultimately have fulfilled many of these expectations, there
is no good reason to doubt had not tobacco been found to be easily cultivated in the fresh soil of that region, and after transportation to England, quickly and profitable marketable. James
the First and his son, the first Charles, might denounce the weed
as both worthless for practical purposes and noxious to health,
but the commerce in this supposed baleful commodity never
ceased, after once started, until, in the end, it diverted the colonists' attention from the production of every other natural object of barter.

Another reason for the English traders' desire to find substitutes in Virginia for the merchandise imported from the continent was that, when brought to England, they would not have
to be paid for in coin, as had to be done there with the like articles from Russia and other countries in Europe, but simply by
accepting them in return for all sorts of domestic goods manu-

factured in London and other English towns. At that time, it was believed by economists that the balance of trade against England in settling for these continental commodities indicated a dangerous condition, because, apparently, it meant that the kingdom was being steadily drained of its metallic money. The country, it was supposed, was only saved from disaster by the specie which flowed into it from the sale of East India goods to the kingdoms of Europe. These goods had been first brought to England by the ships of the East India Company.

With Virginia producing the articles which the English merchants and manufacturers needed, that colony, it was expected, would become, as its population increased, the special promoter, from year to year, of the English trades of clothier, woolman, carder, spinner, weaver, fuller, shearman, dyer, draper, capper, and hatter. This character it did assume in time. The vessels crossed the ocean eastward, loaded down with cargos of tobacco, and they returned westward equally burdened with all those household articles which the Virginians found it difficult, if not impossible, to manufacture on their side of the water.

It followed, as a corollary, that this enormous exchange of the natural products of the Virginian soil for the artificial products of English handiwork would encourage the expansion of English shipping. A new school for the professional training of English seamen would also be created, which signified that the number of capable defenders of the English shores would be vastly increased. Before Virginia could develop into a great school for English sailors, loud complaint was to be constantly heard that young Englishmen were continuously being drawn away into the service of the merchant marine of other kingdoms. Holland was the principal ocean carrier of that age, and the inducements which she offered filled her merchant ships with sailors from every land of Europe. Where England could show one hundred stout vessels in the international trade, Holland could show three thousand. It was only in commercial intercourse with her own colony in Virginia, and her later colonies situated towards the north, that the mother country was finally able to raise such restrictions as first dimished, and then practically destroyed, the competition of the Dutch. During many decades, however, England was unsuccessful in creating a barrier, but, under the operation of the Navigation Acts, the carrying trade between Holland and Virginia gradually fell off to the point virtually of extinction.

Another reason for the encouragement of the colonization of Virginia was that it would furnish an asylum for thousands of people in England whose hope of bread depended upon the prices of a fluctuating wheat market and small wages, and who too often were forced to turn to parish alms for temporary, if not permanent, relief. These people transported to another region, where, it was afterwards said, only labor was dear, would find ample employment ready to hand in the cultivation of the fields; and after the close of their indentures, would have the choice of becoming the possessors of small homesteads of their own. Many immigrants in this station in life did, in subsequent years, rise to the proprietorship of good estates and the enjoyment of high political honors.

Such in mere outline were the practical reasons which governed the first step taken to establish a colony on the banks of the Powhatan. One of these reasons alone was based on a delusion. It is true that the first settlers' attention was diverted for a time by the certainty which they felt that the precious metals existed in the neighboring hills. But this was a natural expectation on their part, for had not the whole world, during this period, been put agog by the reports of the wealth which Spain was gathering up from the mines scattered through her dominions in Central and South America? Why should North America differ in products from those two regions? Why should Virginia?

But down below the purely business reasons for colonization, there was also a religious reason. The hope was expressed in the letters-patent for 1606 that the settlement of Virginia would tend to spread the Christian creed among the ignorant tribes occupying the country; and in the instructions for the government of the new dominion, the authorities at Jamestown were strictly enjoined to use "all good means to draw the savages and the heathen people of those territories to the true knowledge of God."

CHAPTER II

RESOURCES OF THE NEW COUNTRY

What kind of a country was it that the voyagers of 1607 saw in sailing up the reaches of the Powhatan in their search for an advantageous site for their projected settlement? It is not difficult for us to imagine the impression which it made on them from our own knowledge of that scene as it stands today, with its topographical features almost precisely as they were when the eyes of Englishmen first observed them. It should be remembered that the strangers had just finished a voyage which had, in turn, excited them with violent storms or deadened them with the monotony of the sea. The change to a land where nature had been lavish with trees and shrubs, and where Spring was then spreading over it all her verdant mantle, must have seemed to them enchanting.

As the three vessels slowly ploughed their way up the Powhatan, the people on board noted with delight all that was to be seen on the adjacent shores. First—and this was especially pleasing to the eye of the Englishmen, accustomed to the constant rain-clouds and the misty light of their native country— there was the brilliant sunshine which brought out so vividly every object of the landscape. Back into the land there melted away an interminable forest, filled with varieties of trees which they had never before known, and interspersed with great white and pink masses of blossoms of the dogwood and Judas trees. The ground too, as far as it was visible, was covered with flowers that reflected every color of the rainbow.

High overhead were passing flocks of land birds, while in the wake of the vessels wheeled and screamed many species of ma-

21

SIR THOMAS SMITH

rine fowl. The reaches of the stream ahead were constantly flashing into silver as the schools of small fish rose to the surface. Here and there, too, little groups of the swarthy inhabitants of the country could be descried gazing with silent curiosity at the white-winged ships as they slowly advanced up the river.

When the voyagers afterwards, in their letters home, came to describe the new country, they used expressions that were filled with a genuine enthusiasm. "Heaven and earth," said Captain Smith, who had seen the most beautiful regions of Europe, "never agreed better to frame a place for man's habitation." The author of *Virginia Richly Valued* spoke of it as "the garden of the world." "Virginia," he said, "gave the right hand to no province under Heaven." "I have traveled over eighteen several kingdoms," a member of the London Company declared, "and yet all of them, in my mind, come far short to Virginia." "Bring it under cultivation, and divide it among industrious people," remarked Dale, "and it will be equivalent to all the best parts of Europe taken together"; and Percy predicted that, in time, it would become as profitable to England as the West Indies had been to the kings of Spain.

How far was there substantial accuracy in all these delighted descriptions of the new country? Was there a good justification for the expectations which the natural display of its physical advantages raised in the minds of those who actually saw it in its original aspects?

What was the character of the soil? In the portion of it that formed the coastal plain—extending back to the falls, which, in all the great rivers, raised a barrier to the further inward flow of the tides—the ground was composed of alluvial sediment that had been left behind as the sea gradually receded eastward. Enormous beds of oysters and mussel shells, and the shells of other marine creatures, were to be found here and there below the surface of the earth. First came the terrace represented by the low lying shores of the modern counties of Accomac and Princess Anne. The upper soil of sands and clays here rested upon a substratum of marl. These lands in our own times have become the principal market gardens on the Atlantic Coast. The next terrace was composed of coarse gravel and sand, which lay upon a bed of marl and shells. The soil of both of these terraces, as well as of a third, which contained a combination of the soils of the first two, was thin and friable, and by careless tillage was quickly exhausted; but equally quickly it responded to the use of manures.

At the end of an hundred years, the historian Beverley divided the soil of the country under three heads. First, there were the alluvial bottoms situated along the banks of the lower sections of the principal streams. These were particularly adapted to the production of maize and tobacco in extraordinary abundance. When seen in the beginning, these low grounds were covered with a heavy growth of trees of different varieties. Second, there was the land lying along the banks of the upper sections of the same streams, which was not always as fertile as the bottoms situated nearer the Chesapeake Bay, but, nevertheless, was of good texture, and capable of bringing forth profuse crops of different kinds.

The ground between the rivers in this part of the country usually rose to a considerable height. These ridges were nearly always so poor in quality as to be only productive of thickets of scrub pines, small black oats, and stunted chinquapin bushes.

The lands situated at the heads of the great streams differed in the nature of their soil and in the character of the growth that covered them. Some parts were shaded by the boughs of the most magnificent woods; others lay bare to the sun in the form of beautiful meadows and savannahs, which gave nourishment to great masses of reeds and grasses; while others still had turned into bogs and swamps penetrable only by small and light-footed animals.

Several of the early writers thought that they could detect an aromatic taste in the earth when it was put in the mouth;

and they went so far as to assert that this fact gave a spicy flavor to the grasses, herbs, and trees which grew in it.

The most conspicuous object to be seen in Virginia when first explored was the forest, which covered the largest part of its surface. Wherever the eye turned, the woods rose in primeval majesty. The size, height, and variety of the trees deeply impressed the minds of the voyagers of 1607 and the colonists who followed them after the settlements had spread out over a wide area. One witness expressed the opinion of all when he said that no country on earth surpassed Virginia in the tallness and girth of its timbers; and these characteristics were made all the more notable by the fact that the woods were usually free from undergrowth, due chiefly to the Indian custom of burning up the leaves in the Autumn. This was done for the purpose of capturing the wild animals which haunted the forests by hemming them in by a gradual contraction of a belt of fire.

The impressiveness of the forests was further increased by the considerable space, which, as a rule, separated one tree from another. This roominess allowed the sunshine, in some measure, to reach them all, to the stimulation of their larger growth.

The tree which sprang up in the greatest abundance was the pine. It was the first to be seen as the little fleet of 1607 sighted the dunes in the vicinity of the modern Cape Henry. As far as the eye could reach, groves of pine, rising tall and straight from the sandy soil, loomed above the outer rim of land. It was said that the proximity of the coast was perceptible to the sense of smell even before it could be detected by the eye, owing largely to the resinous perfume which the heavy masses of pine tags diffused upon the wind blowing out to sea. This fact had been noticed by the sailors of Amadas and Barlow at an earlier date; and it was anticipated in the noble poem which Drayton addressed to the voyagers of 1607. This natural odor wafted across the waves was peculiarly strong in Spring, when the Indians had set fire to the undergrowth, which gave the odor a blended flavor.

How great was the size of the largest of these pines was indicated in the necessity imposed, in 1612, on the ship *Star*, sent to the colony for a cargo of masts, to reduce the length of forty of the eighty trunks which it was proposing to carry, before they could be stored in its hold.

It was said that, at least, one-fourth of the aboriginal forests was composed of walnut trees, and the proportion of oaks was still greater. Many of these trees afforded plank twenty yards in length, and two and a half feet square. Cypresses of extraordinary girth and height were found in all the swamps; and the mulberry trees, in many spots, grew so thickly together that they formed extensive groves. The presence of ash was noted with keen interest, as it held out the prospect of manufacturing soap-ashes in larger quantities. The cedar too was interspersed with other species of trees in all the woods, and its value as material for furniture was at once recognized. The sassafras covered the face of the abandoned Indian fields, and, owing to its medicinal qualities, was included among the earliest of the exports from the colony. A somewhat similar purpose was served by the balsam bush that grew in every brake.

Other trees were the laurel, the locust, the tulip, the poplar, the sugar maple, the chestnut, the chinquapin, the crab-apple, the cherry, the plum, and the persimmon. The nuts of the chestnut were found to be as pleasantly flavored as the nuts of the same species of tree which were so much esteemed in Spain, France, and Italy. The fruit of the crab-apple, on the other hand, was of inferior quality, but the fruit of the cherry tree was thought to be of extraordinary excellence. The clusters of fruit on the limbs of the persimmon tree reminded the first settlers of ropes of onions, and they commented with undisguised surprise on its sourness, unless in the last stage of ripeness. This fruit was afterwards freely used in the manufacture of domestic beer.

Many of the colonists preferred the Virginian black raspberry to the English red. The bushes of the wild whortleberry

grew in great abundance on the surface of the uplands as well
as in the fertile low lying lands along the smaller streams. The
cranberry was equally profuse in the bogs and swamps. Here
too sprang up and clung to the stunted trees the thick vines of
the wild grape. Its vines were also discovered encircling the
trunks and winding among the limbs of the largest trees, like
so many heavy cables. The principal varieties were the small
black grape, the thick-skinned sloe, and the musky fox. It was
said of the exuberance of the strawberries in Spring that one
could not wander about the old Indian fields without staining the
feet in the rich red dye of this fruit. In flavor, it was thought
to be superior to the English strawberry.

Other fruits as well as vegetables found in abundance were
muskmelons, squashes, gourds, may-apples, pumpkins, and
beans. The peach and watermelon were not indigenous to Virginia.

The products of the aboriginal soil which proved to be most
profitable were maize and tobacco. The value of maize was recognized from the start, but it was not until an interval had
passed that tobacco became a commodity of permanent importance. Other plants esteemed for domestic use were mattoum
—which resembled rye—the water flag and parsley, and the
kernels of the hickorynut. Everywhere fields of wild flax were
seen; and the surface of the open fields was covered with numerous varieties of grass and herbs.

Such was the quantity of flowers that Percy declared that
the ground above Jamestown was like an English garden in the
variety of its colors; and this aspect of the country was found
repeated wherever it was explored. Especially conspicuous in
Spring were the white clusters of the dogwood, and the purple
clusters of the Judas tree.

A charming characteristic of aboriginal Virginia was the
extraordinary network of streams that watered it. It was correctly said of it that there was a brook in every bottom. One
writer compared the country's surface to the human body inter-

SIR GEORGE SOMERS

From an engraving after the portrait by
Paul Vansomer.

sected with large and small veins. So great was the volume of fresh water delivered by the small rivers and creeks and brooks to the large streams that the latter remained almost untainted with salt from the inflowing tide within forty miles of the Chesapeake Bay. These natural highways proved to be of inestimable service to the planters in after years, for they formed a channel for the navigation of the vessels which carried off the crops of tobacco to the ports of England, and brought back to the front doors of the Virginian residences cargoes of English manufactured goods.

The coast line of Virginia was unbroken by dangerous head lands. It could be approached, it was said, as safely by night as by day. A noble harbor spread out behind the Capes Henry and Charles, and then as now, ships found a quiet refuge there when storms were making the sea outside perilous for mariners.

With such a great number of fresh-water streams and broad saline estuaries, it was natural that there should be found in Virginia an extraordinary variety of fish. So teeming with fish were the rivulets and brooks in the spawning season that the Indians were in the habit of killing them with sticks. Whereever Captain Smith and his companions, in their explorations of the Chesapeake, sailed, they saw schools of small fish flashing in the sunlight as they broke the surface of the water; and as many as were needed for food were easily scooped up with frying pans. The numbers of sheepshead, shad, sturgeon, herring, and rock, were beyond computation. The sturgeon was especially remarkable for its size. In places where it chiefly abounded, the first colonists were afraid to haul their seines in the apprehension that the nets would be torn to pieces by the weight and violent struggles of this huge fish. At Jamestown, sturgeons were often killed in the shallows with axes, as the only way of securing them at all.

Among other fish to be found in the same waters were porpoise, soles, mullet, salmon, roach, plaice, eels, cat, perch, tailor, bass, chub, flounder, whiting, carp, pike, and bream. How far the sea along the coast swarmed with fish was demonstrated by the fact that, in one haul of their seine off the beach of Smith's Isles, the men stationed there drew in enough to make up a cargo for an ordinary frigate.

So enormous was the accumulation of oyster shells in the rivers that they formed in places a menace to navigation, as if they were a solid rock. Mussels were as numerous as oysters. The crab—under which name the lobster was, perhaps, included —was occasionally large enough to furnish a meal for four men. The turtle too was often captured on the sands, and its flesh proved to be excellent in flavor.

As soon as September arrived, vast flocks of marine fowl of many species, migrating from the North, dropped upon the surface of the bay, and the entrances to the larger streams. In the upper waters of the Chesapeake, they were sometimes seen to be spread over a space a mile in width and seven miles in length. Here they fed on the wild oats and celery which grew in abundance wherever the water was shallow. The reports of the millions observed would seem incredible unless we recalled the fact that these swarms had been breeding for countless centuries without serious diminution by the feeble weapons of the Indians or the talons of predatory hawks and eagles.

The most conspicuous bird of all was the splendid white swan. Hardly less noticeable was the Canada goose as it floated upon the water or passed with his fellows in wedge-like formation in the sky overhead. There were many varieties of wild duck, such as the canvasback and the redhead, the mallard, widgeon, dotterell, and oxeye. The plover, snipe, and curlew were also to be found in the neighboring marshes, and along the sea and river shores, in incalculable numbers.

The finest inland bird was the wild turkey, which was sometimes seen in flocks of forty, and occasionally of several hundred. In weight, it often attained to thirty and even to seventy pounds. Other birds to be observed were black, gray, and bald eagles, fish, sparrow, and ringtail hawks, white, brown, and screech owls, crows, turkey-buzzards, herons, bitterns, bullbats, whip-poorwills—whose call was often imitated by the Indians at night as a signal—the jay, and the snowbird.

Two birds of extraordinary interest were the redbird and the mocking bird. The redbird was named by the English settlers the Virginian nightingale, owing to the clear and piercing harmony of its notes. Many of this species were sent to England to serve as ornaments for drawing-rooms, which they set off with the magnificent coloring of their plumage. The mockingbird was also a popular gift to English kinsmen, who were astonished at its ability to imitate the cries of other birds. Additional varieties were the meadowlark, the king-fisher, the martin—soon to become indispensable as a protector of farmyards from the incursions of hawks—the blackbird, and in beautiful contrast in color to it, the tanager and the blue bird. The partridge and pheasant were also seen.

But far exceeding most of the birds in number were the wild pigeons. So vast, indeed, were the aboriginal flocks that the sky, even at noonday, was darkened by their passage, and when they perched in the forests to feed on the acorns, their weight broke down many limbs of the trees. "In April, 1633," we are told by Devries, a sea captain "while we were lying in the Delaware Bay, there came on hundreds of thousands of wild pigeons flying from the land over the bay. Indeed, no light could hardly be discerned where they were." By persistent slaughter, carried on during several centuries, this noble bird, so typical of the teeming bird-life of aboriginal times, has been entirely destroyed.

Another bird which was seen in Virginia during that period, but which has disappeared from its old haunts, was the parakeet. Its wings were of a greenish color, and its head of a yellow, crimson, orange, and tawny tints. Its long tail was forked.

In spite of the greater ease with which animals could be captured by the Indian hunters, certain species were almost as numerous as the prolific birds. The most frequently observed of these animals was the deer, for the destruction of which the

savages had invented several methods—such as surrounding entire herds with belts of fire, or cornering them in narrow peninsulas and striking them down as they attempted to escape by
water. The fallow deer often dropped four fawns at a birth.
The buffalo was seen in the savannahs and reedy river bottoms
situated in the upper country. Nearer the settlements, packs of
wolves were constantly heard as they pursued their quarry after
night-fall; and they continued so numerous that the county
courts, throughout the seventeenth century, offered rewards for
their heads.

Gray and red foxes became a pest at an early date in consequence of their depredations on poultry, lambs, and young pigs.
The raccoon was taken by the first settlers to be a species of
monkey, but its flesh seems to have been highly esteemed from
the beginning. It was pronounced by some to be equal in excellence to a cut of mutton. Other animals were polecats, martins,
otters, minks, and wild cats. An occasional porcupine was also
seen.

But more interesting than even this rare animal was the
flying squirrel, which could cover a distance of thirty yards in
one flight in passing from tree to tree. It was in constant demand at first as an ornament for English parks; and even the
king was eager to obtain a specimen for his own preserves.
Another animal that aroused curiosity was the opossum. This
had a natural pouch on one side of its body, in which it carried
and suckled its young. There was a water rat, afterwards
known as the muskrat, from the strong odor which pervaded its
fur, that was remarkable for the size of its nest. This consisted
of a mass of reeds divided into two floors, with two rooms to
each floor. The structure, which had the bulk of a large hogshead, was always erected on the margin of a pond, which gave
its inhabitant access to water without first being seen. The cry
of the panther was frequently heard in the forests at night,
although this species of animal does not seem to have existed

in great numbers at the time of the earliest settlement. It was gradually driven back as the frontier of the colony receded.

In comparison with England, Virginia was found to be infested with an extraordinary abundance and variety of insects and reptiles. This fact was fostered by the presence of many marshes on the seashore and along the banks of the rivers, and also of bogs and swamps in the regions situated in the interior of the country. Especially notable, as might be inferred from the quantity of standing water, were the swarms of mosquitoes in many places; and in the light of modern medical research, there can be no doubt that they were one of the causes of the bad health which prevailed in the earliest plantations.

The presence of so much standing water also stimulated the propagation of frogs. The most imposing specimen of this creature was the bull-frog, which obtained its name from the deep bass sound of its far-reaching voice as it called to its mate from its perch on the bank of pond or ditch. Early attention was also drawn to the tree frog, by its ventriloquist cry, which was out of all proportion to the size of its body, and also by the color of its skin, which seemed to have some of the reflective properties of a chameleon's.

As late as 1700, rattlesnakes were seen in the neighborhood of Jamestown. Perhaps, they were not so numerous there, however, as they were discovered to be on the south side of the James when the second William Byrd was running the Carolina boundary line. Specimens bearing as many as thirteen joints were noted by the traveler Clayton at a somewhat earlier date. Among the other snakes remarked were species which still survive in Virginia, such as the moccasin, the puffadder, and the black, water, and corn snakes. During the first period of starvation at Jamestown, the unhappy settlers endeavored to ward off famine by eating every reptile that they could kill.

The characteristics of the Virginian climate were carefully noted from the beginning, and the progress of the years down to our own day reveals but little change in this natural feature.

The heat in summer and the cold in winter often reached extremes, but one rarely of long continuance. September was the most humid of all the months of the year. The last two of Autumn were remarkable for the beautiful coloring of the landscape and the briskness of the atmosphere. Winter brought snow, which, however, was rarely deep, and which soon, as a rule, melted away. In the second winter after the foundation of Jamestown, it is recorded that there were, on the average, about fourteen days of sunshine to every eight of overcast skies. Nevertheless, the river at this place was reported, during at least one frigid spell, to have frozen over from bank to bank.

In the course of the four months beginning with December, the winds coming from the north and northwest were peculiarly keen, but clear weather generally followed a blow from that quarter. The southeast wind was often attended by rain, while the wind from the south was tempered to a perceptible degree even at the height of winter. The wind from the southwest was almost always high, and sometimes swelled to dangerous storms, accompanied with brilliant lightning and violent thunder. These natural phenomena were thought to be on a more terrifying scale at their worst than they were in England, and they were said to have given rise to a distinct odor of brimstone in the atmosphere, while the tempest continued.

Hail stones, eight or ten inches in compass, were sometimes seen to fall when a storm was prevailing; and so great was the quantity discharged from the clouds that heavy damage was often done thereby to the growing crops and the vegetation in general, and even to men and animals exposed to its fury.

Every country when first opened up by the plough is apt to be unwholesome. Virginia, during its first years as a civilized community, was no exception to the rule. We have already pointed out the evil which resulted to health from the presence of marshes and swamps where millions of malarial mosquitoes were annually bred. Along the coast and the banks of the tidal rivers, the drinking water was often brackish to the taste, and this taint of salt undoubtedly intensified the malignancy of the bowel affections which carried off so many of the early settlers. These complaints were also produced and aggravated by the sudden changes of weather which were so characteristic of the climate during the greater part of the year.

But there were other causes for the epidemics of ill health that so frequently occurred, especially in the beginning. The substitution of corn meal for flour had something to do with it. The English colonists had also been accustomed to a very liberal use of liquors in their native land, where the coldness and dampness of the climate counteracted, to some degree, the bad effects even of intemperance. This habit of drinking steadily could not be kept up in the hot air of the Virginian summers without bringing on biliousness, which left the body open to the inroads of digestive diseases especially.

Much sickness was brought into the colony by the passengers after leaving the ships. In the indescribably foul and fetid cabins of the transporting fleets, the germ of this sickness was easily planted in the body, and one patient with a contagious trouble could soon transmit it to a dozen plantations after disembarking. In 1621, William Rowsley, his wife, and the ten persons who accompanied them, died, without a single survivor, only a short time subsequent to their landing. They must have scattered far and wide the seeds of the pestilence which struck them down.

Robert Evelyn asserted, in his *New Albion,* that, during the first thirty years, after colonization began, five of every six persons brought into Virginia perished miserably from the prevailing diseases. Another witness to actual conditions there, during that early period, estimated the number of deaths among the immigrants, during the first year of their residence, at one hundred and fifty to every three hundred persons arriving. Not less than one hundred thousand individuals are said to have lost their lives in the course of seasoning between the landing of the voyagers in 1607 and the year 1637. Among those who had been born in the country during the first half century, the mor-

tality was not as high as it was among the same number of persons born and living in England.

As the frontier gradually spread out, and more ground was
brought under cultivation, the health of the community steadily
improved. This condition prevailed even among the laborers
who had not been seated in the country long enough to have
passed the period of seasoning. Doubtless, the men and women
of this class had not, immediately after their arrival, been subjected to exposure in the fields under a debilitating sun. More
experienced attention was now paid to the best methods of warding off the diseases which had formerly decimated this branch
of the population.

CHAPTER III

INDIAN MANNER OF LIFE

How large was the Indian population at the time of the first English settlement? According to Capt. John Smith, who had personally explored those parts of Virginia in which the majority of the Indian villages were situated—such as the valleys of the Nansemond, Powhatan, Rappahannock, and Potomac—the number of individuals embraced in the different tribes residing within a day's journey of Jamestown did not rise above a total of five thousand. This enumeration did not include the Indians occupying the fertile area of Accomac, who were afterwards supposed to be about two thousand in all.

Strachey seems to have taken the number of warriors as the best basis on which to estimate the number of inhabitants. According to him, there were thirty-three hundred fighting men within a line running from the Pyankitank River to the falls in the James; thence along the banks of that stream to its mouth; and from that point back to the Pyankitank by way of the western margin of the bay. This would indicate a population of all ages and both sexes that fell little, if at all, short of ten thousand. The statement of Strachey was founded upon knowledge that had been acquired after Smith's departure from the country, and was, therefore, perhaps, more thorough, since it summed up the conclusions of many later explorers.

As a rule, the Indian village was built near a large stream. This fact was, perhaps, to be attributed to several motives. It assured, for instance, a wide area of fertile soil for the corn-fields, as this was always to be found in the low grounds adjacent to the rivers. It gave in addition an uninterrupted view in front

37

of the wigwams; and it also offered close at hand a place for fishing and killing wild fowl, as well as for bathing, to which the Indians were much inclined. The number of inhabitants to the village was not often large; it rarely rose above two hundred; and sometimes fell as low as thirty.

The settlements along the north shore of the modern Hampton Roads were the most popular of all. Taken together, they had the proportions of a considerable town; the wigwams numbered about three hundred, and the total population about one thousand. There is reason, however, to think that these houses were not massed together, but were really divided into villages, standing, perhaps, in sight of each other, yet not really forming a closely knit community. Such at least seems to have been the case when Smith visited that part of Virginia, for, at Kecoughton, the center of this open, well cultivated country, he found a village of only eighteen houses and forty warriors. The largest one which he mentions having seen elsewhere contained one hundred wigwams. Even this village was divided into several parts by the presence of groves.

A few trees were always allowed to remain near the village so as to afford shade from the fierce rays of the July and August suns. The mulberry was preferred, as offering not only a bower by its foliage, but also a palatable fruit. The locust too was frequently seen in the same proximity; and there was near at hand also a profusion of sunflowers. A perennial spring of fresh water was also considered by the Indian householders to be indispensable to their comfort and convenience.

The wigwam was constructed of saplings tied together with white oak strips, and covered over with mats and large pieces of bark. There were no windows, and only a hole at the top made possible the escape of the smoke. This evil was diminished by the constant use of dried pine for fuel. The beds, which were drawn up around the fire, were made of reeds resting on small poles supported by short posts. The cover consisted of a mat or skin. Sometimes, the Indian laid himself down flat on the floor, and drew a bearskin over his body. There was no regard to sex in the occupation of the wigwam; men, women, and children lived in it and slept in it promiscuously.

The village was occasionally surrounded by a strong palisade. This was always the case with the palace of the chief, which was higher, longer, and broader than the dwellings of the commonalty. The temples and their annexes were more imposing buildings. These were often sixty feet long. Powhatan's treasure house at Orapaks was on an even greater scale; it was sixty yards in length; and each of its corners was set off by a grotesque figure of a man or animal.

The productive fields of the Indians often spread over an area of a hundred acres. The crops were cultivated with remarkable care, and with such skill that the English settlers gladly adopted the methods of tillage employed by these primitive husbandmen. The principal crops were maize, tobacco, gourds, beans, peas, and pumpkins. The seed of the four vegetables were dropped between the stalks of the maize, while the tobacco was confined to separate plats.

There were considerable intervals of time between the planting of the maize, the object of which was to secure several harvests of roasting ears in succession. In the center of each maize field, a scaffold stood, on which there was a small cabin to shelter an Indian boy stationed there to frighten off the marauding birds. The fertility of the ground was revealed in the fact that the average yield to the acre was as much as two hundred bushels of grain, beans, peas, and pumpkins combined. When the maize was ripe enough to be harvested, the ears were pulled by the women and children, each of whom carried a small basket, which, when filled, was emptied into a larger one. When this too was full, it was taken to the place of storage and emptied on a mat, where the ears remained unshucked in the sun until they were thoroughly dry. These ears, stripped of their cover, were then carried to a crib which had been purposely built for their

An Indian Village

reception, and there they were preserved until the grain was consumed.

How enormous was the quantity of maize produced by the Indians was indicated by the number of bushels which they were able to sell the Englishmen at Jamestown, who, on several occasions, were saved from certain starvation by these purchases. Through one voyage to the Chickahominy alone, Smith succeeded in procuring seven hogshead of grain; and had he possessed adequate means of transportation could have increased the quantity to a load for a vessel of considerable size. Argall, at another time, brought back one thousand bushels from the villages situated on the Potomac.

Tobacco was cultivated in a plat entirely distinct from the cornfield. Then, as now, this plant required a high degree of intensive tillage. The ground had to be kept perfectly clear of weeds and grasses, and the suckers cut away. The stalk was allowed to run to seed, and when the leaves were pulled, they were dried in the sun or by fire. There can be no doubt that the earliest methods of producing this plant followed by the English at Jamestown, as in the case of maize, were learned from the aboriginal husbandmen.

Tobacco was much prized by the Indians, not only for the enjoyment of smoking, but also for the part which it played in their mystical ceremonies. It was sprinkled over fires lighted by the priests for their sacrifices, or scattered to the winds in order to propitiate the evil spirits that raised the storm, brought about the drought, and diminished the catches of the weirs. From the center of a circle made by the deposit of tobacco leaves on the ground, the priests offered up their invocations of gratitude to the life-giving sun.

Another curious property of the plant in the eyes of the Indians was its supposed power of increasing the virility of the married men. It was also used as a symbol of peace. As Newport and Smith were making their first voyage to the Falls in the Powhatan, an Indian warrior appeared at one point on the bank with a bow and arrow in one hand and a pipe filled with tobacco in the other. This was to warn the newcomers that peace or war was in their choice. This gesture was repeated on another occasion later on when Smith was, for the first time, exploring the reaches of the Rappahannock. A gift of tobacco was one of the most significant exhibitions of the spirit of the Indians' hospitality when parties of Englishmen from Jamestown visited their villages.

In plats as large as those which produced the tobacco, and in close proximity, the seed of gourds, muskmelons, and other vegetables, were planted in season. These vegetables when gathered gave variety to the meals of the Indian households; and this variety was further increased by the use for the table of the seeds of the sunflower—a beautiful object in every Indian village—and also of the mattoum, both of which were cooked along with the fat of the deer.

But the roots of the tuckahoe were still more popular when beaten into a flour and converted into bread by the heat of the fire. These roots were very strong in their juices, and without prolonged soaking in water were thought to be poisonous. The fruit of the persimmon tree was gathered in Autumn, dried, and eaten as a date. The kernels of the white oak acorn were ground into a flour, which was considered by the inmates of the wigwams to be palatable and nourishing. The nuts of the hickory, when pounded into a milky substance, gave out a liquor which was made to serve both as a potation and as a sauce for the stews concocted of the grain of maize mixed with several kinds of vegetables. This extract of the hickory kernel seems to have been the only spirits in use among the Indians.

Perhaps the most important food of the Indian household was obtained from the streams. Fish were caught in unfailing quantities by means of the line, spear, net, and weir. The spear was employed chiefly at night in canoes carrying a brilliant light. The sturgeon was often killed in this way, when its capture was impossible by other means. The weir was built in still water, while the traps were erected in streams where there was a strong descending current. The trap was in the form of a cone spreading into chambers. A less permanent choice was the portable hedge, which was thrown across a narrow creek after the tide had run in. When the tide ebbed, the fish which had entered were prevented by this barrier from swimming out again.

A weapon constantly used in company with the bow and arrow was the tomahawk. This could be made effective in case the victim, whether man or beast, had not succumbed to the arrow at once.

There were three other methods of killing game: the belt of fire; imprisonment in narrow peninsulas; and stalking in disguise. In the Spring, before the work in the fields of maize began, the Indians were in the habit of occupying the hunting lodges which they had built in the thickest parts of the forest. In these annual excursions, the men were always attended by the women and children. There, as if enjoying a long woodland picnic, the company remained during many weeks; and when they returned to their villages, they brought back with them a large quantity of dried flesh and raw furs for use in their wigwams.

The Indian way of cooking was simple yet effective. The meats were either placed directly on the live coals, or were laid on paralleled sticks, supported above the fire on little posts. The fish were prepared for consumption by suspending them to sticks that had been stuck in the ground in a circle around the hot flame. Both were sometimes boiled separately in a large pot. To the meat or fish, several vegetables, such as corn, beans, and peas, were often added to produce a mess that would be both satisfying and wholesome. Oysters were generally cooked to the consistency of a broth, or roasted on the coals. The grains of maize were beaten into a meal, which, after being mixed with water, was kneaded into balls and cakes, and then boiled; or they were allowed to dry and were then kept covered with hot ashes until thoroughly done. A popular way of using the grains of maize was to boil them without having first pounded them into meal. This was known in the Indian language as hominy, and by that name it is designated today.

The Indian way of serving food was as simple as their manner of cooking. The fish or pot with its contents, was placed on a mat, around which the consumers squatted closely together, while they only employed their fingers in helping themselves. Unlike the English, the Indians never ate bread and meat or fish at the same time. The roasting ears, however, which were always laid near the dish or pot, were apparently enjoyed along with its contents. When fish or meat had been cooked before or on the open fire, it was seized with the hand and devoured in successive mouthfuls. The only ceremony accompanying a meal was the casting of a fragment of the food into the flames as a propitiation to the evil spirit.

When the Englishmen were feasted in the Indian village, the abundance and variety of the victuals set before them made a deep impression on their minds, all the more remarkable, perhaps, because of the contrast with the narrow provender at Jamestown. The Indians, though sometimes sufferers from comparative famine, were not a really provident people. The maize was apparently the only form of domestic supplies which they husbanded and carried over into winter. But there was no reason why they should from year to year look much ahead. In the Spring, they could always rely upon their obtaining as large a quantity of fish as they would need, for it was at this season that the fish began to swarm into the streams to breed. In addition, there were deer, wild turkeys, pheasants, and squirrels to be shot in the woods with bow and arrow, and oysters to be scooped up from the bottoms of the estuaries.

During the whole of Summer, fish continued to make up the principal food of the Indians, and this was varied by the free use of the profusion of berries that grew in every brake. The roasting ear too was served at every meal. In Autumn, chestnuts, hickory nuts, maize, vegetables, berries, oysters, and the flesh of deer and fish, furnished the food; and these supplies were increased by the number of wild fowl shot or snared during this part of the year. In winter, the Indians turned for their chief sustenance to their stores of grain, which, as we have already mentioned, was converted by them into several kinds of nourishing dishes. Deer, and bear too, at this season, were devoured to satisfy the pangs of hunger. Fish were still caught in the weirs, but the supply had now sensibly fallen off.

The quantity of food on hand, whatever the time of the year, was never allowed to run so low that there were not sufficient materials in the larders of the wigwams for a liberal feast. When in Spring the annual migration to the hunting lodges began, the event was celebrated with a festival that was marked by an unrestrained enjoyment of the varied supplies which had been collected for the occasion. And a similar overflowing festival was held when the wild fowl returned from the north in November; and also during the same month when the harvest of the maize was completed.

We have so far given a general description of the Indians' dwelling houses, methods of tillage, and varieties of food. What was their manner of clothing themselves? In winter, the warrior protected his body from the cold with a loose robe of deer skin, but he so far dispensed with this in Summer that his only garment then, if garment it could be called, was a belt of leather drawn about his waist, from which was suspended, both in front and behind, a bunch of leaves or grass. Those individuals who were either more foppish or more opulent, were, in Winter, in the habit of wearing a mantle which had been made of the furs of otters, raccoons, and beavers. Both rich and poor were content with a shoe manufactured of undressed skin. This was known in the Indian language as the moccasin.

The Indian girl, until she reached her twelfth year, gave up in Summer all clothing, with the exception of a bunch of moss in front of her thighs, but after that age, a leather apron, falling from her waist to her knee, was worn. So soon as she arrived at a maturer period of life, she put on for special occasions a large mantle shagged at the skirts, and embroidered with beads and copper, or painted with the images of fruits and flowers, beasts, and birds. Still more beautiful was a garment worn at times by her which was made of the feathers of swans, geese, ducks, and turkeys, and dyed to whatever color her fancy happened to dictate.

Powhatan himself seemed to have been content with a mantle composed of raccoon skins, from which the tails hung down and almost swept the ground. On the other hand, the mantle of the priest was manufactured of the skins of the weasel, and on it too the pendent tails were retained. To give his appearance a touch of the terrifying, there were attached to this mantle the skins of numerous snakes. These skins, along with the weasel tails, were drawn together and tied in a knot at the top of his head, with the ends bobbing around it whenever the priest happened to move. It was a characteristic of his fellow mystic, the conjurer, that, but for a girdle and an apron in front, he went naked. The only addition to his scanty costume was a bag suspended to the girdle, and a red bird, with wings extended, tied to his ear.

It was the peculiarity of the conjurer, the priest, and the warrior that they shaved the right side of their heads; but the warrior did not, like the others, retain a lock, as the free use of his bow and arrow would have been impeded thereby. The hair of the women, whether married or unmarried, was tied in a long plait behind, while in front only the hair of the unmarried was closely clipped.

The warrior endeavored to exaggerate the impressiveness of his appearance by sticking in a knot on the side of his head the smaller antlers of the deer, plates of copper, and even the entire hand of an enemy whom he had succeeded in killing. For these ornaments, other objects were frequently substituted, which further emphasized the picturesqueness of his aspect, such as a hawk with his wings widely stretched out, or a duck, of beautiful coloring, in the same spirited attitude. The strangeness of his

appearance was further increased by the insertion in his ears
of strings, from which dangled bunches of hawklegs, claws of
squirrels, raccoons, and bears, spurs of turkeys, clusters of mussel pearls, or small plates of copper.

But what was far more singular were the live green snakes,
which, secured by the same string, were permitted to writhe and
twist in every direction around his already strangely decorated
head.

The women were more conservative in their ornaments. The
favorite wives of Powhatan wore around their necks triple cir-
clets of mussel pearls, while long ropes of the same beautiful
articles were drawn over their shoulders and under their right
arms. They also encircled their waists with highly decorative
bracelets made of copper and pearl.

The ingenuity of the savages in adorning their persons was
illustrated in their use of both oil and paint. These two materials
were obtained from natural objects, and formed a very important
part of their toilet. The paint, which was red, black or yellow
in color, was supposed, in times of war, to increase the fierceness
of the warrior's general aspect. It is not improbable, however,
that the oil was considered to be effective in balking the mos-
quito, which was one of the pests of the marshy and swampy
regions. But it too, like the red paint, fulfilled an ornamental
purpose. It was the custom of the members of both sexes to
smear the surface of the trunk of their bodies with oil, and then
attach to it the down of blue birds, red birds, and white herons,
which, thus combined, produced a general coloring that was at
once brilliant and varied. A village assemblage decorated in
this manner must have appeared to be at once wild and picturesque.

The women were not satisfied with adornments that could
be put on or dropped at will. The art of tattooing was not carried as far in aboriginal Virginia as in the South Seas, but it
was used with sufficient skill to excite the admiration of the first
voyagers. The portions of the female body selected for the dec-

oration were the shoulders, breasts, arms, and thighs; and the figures preferred for reproduction were those of birds, insects, serpents, fruits, and flowers; and they were so deeply and thoroughly burnt into the flesh that the passage of time did not serve to make them less conspicuous to the eye.

A life in the open air, constant exercise from childhood to old age, and an abundance of wholesome food, would naturally produce a race remarkable in its average members for large and vigorous bodies. This, however, was not always the case with the Indians of aboriginal Virginia. It is true that not a single instance of deformity was ever detected among them, but the absence of such was possibly explainable by their deliberate making away with all children afflicted with serious physical defects.

As a matter of fact, the size of individuals of the different tribes differed to a very perceptible degree. The Indians who were found in the valley of the Rappahannock were more imposing than those who lived along the banks of the Powhatan and Pamunkey, while the Indians whom Smith discovered in the vicinity of the Susquahannock River, were the most striking of all for the hugeness of their physical proportions. Powhatan's subjects were so small in frame and so low in height, as to leave the impression of diminutiveness in the minds of the Englishmen when first seen. On the other hand, the Susquahannock Indians appeared to them to possess the bulk and tallness of giants. Nor was this impression incorrect. Smith found the leg of the average warrior of the tribe to be three-quarters of a yard in circumference; and so deep was the tone of his voice that it sounded as if it were an echo from the walls of a cave.

Although the Indians varied in the size of their bodies, according to their separate tribes, yet the general physical aspect of all, as members of the same race, did not differ substantially. They were everywhere distinguished for full lips, wide mouths, flat noses, high cheekbones, and straight coarse black hair that fell in long locks from those portions of their heads which had not been shaved. Whenever a departure from the usual color of the hair was discovered, it was due, not to a vagary of nature, but to the effect of foreign paternity. Individuals with auburn or chestnut colored hair were seen by the first voyagers both at Roanoke Island and in the valley of the Powhatan. One Indian with a black, bushy beard was noticed by Smith in his voyage up the Rappahannock.

These abnormal specimens of the race were quite probably either themselves the offspring of European sailors, who had formerly visited the coast, or were sprung remotely from the Spanish settlers in the Southwest. It was reported that Powhatan and Opechancanough had originally made their way to Virginia from that quarter, and if this was true, they had probably been accompanied by Indians of the half blood, who were common enough in the Spanish colonial communities.

Black as was the Indian hair, it was not quite as black as the Indian eye. It was said by all the witnesses that not a blue or gray eye was noticed among the multitude of savages who were seen in the course of the early explorations.

Naturally, longevity was far from uncommon among them, and even up to old age, both men and women seemed to retain much of the activity, if not the agility, of their years of greatest strength. Powhatan is supposed to have passed his eightieth year when first beheld by the English; but there was small indication of that fact in his physical movements or in the reflections of his mental condition. He and his warriors stood firm and erect almost to their last hour, and yielded in the end to the infirmities of old age rather than to the inroads of any specific disease.

The Indians seemed to have but little need of medicines, and such as they used for passing disorders were unadulterated concoctions of bark and root, or had been gathered up in the form of plants and herbs along the banks of the watercourses or in the depths of the woods. In cases of wounds in battle or hurts through casualty, the remedy was sought in the application of the juices of these natural products. Where there had been a fracture of a bone, the case was far more difficult, and because of the use of crude methods of resetting, a perfect restoration was not often obtained. For fever, the sweating house was usually employed, followed by a plunge into the nearest stream.

CHAPTER IV

NUMBER OF INHABITANTS 1606-1700

Before we describe the industrial, educational, and other conditions which prevailed in Virginia between the years 1607 and 1700, it will be pertinent to give at least an approximate estimate of the size of the English population which, during that period, held possession of the land. We have already seen that the number of Indians who inhabited the tidewater region, when Jamestown was founded, was in very meagre proportion, not only to the extent of territory which they dominated, but also to the varied resources at their command for the support of their widely dispersed communities. It was one of the curious facts of this early history that the economic influence of the plantation system which the English established scattered the colonists almost as widely as the aboriginal manner of life had scattered the Indians.

What were the limits of the area of country which the white Virginian population occupied previous to 1700? On several occasions during that period an effort was made to explore the forests and thus indirectly widen the frontiers towards the southwest and the west. A small expedition had been sent to the Roanoke river at an early date, partly for the purpose of spying out the character of the intervening region. Walter Aston, in 1643, with a few companions, started for the mountains which were known to them to exist on the western horizon, but his expedition also was apparently balked of any real success. William Claiborne, also accompanied by a band of equal intrepidity, followed on the same general trail; but he too failed to reach the place of his intended destination. Berkeley, in 1668, after organizing a squad of volunteers, was prevented from taking up the exploration westward where Claiborne had left it. Abraham Wood accomplished practically nothing in clearing up the path. Loederer, in 1669-70, was moderately successful. He alone seems to have passed some distance beyond the line of the then existing frontier.

It will be thus perceived that the entire region now covered by what is known as Eastern Virginia was not only not occupied by English Colonists up to the foot of the Blue Ridge at any time before 1700, but it had not even been really explored as far as the edge of the long eastern shadow which the Range cast in the declining light of the setting sun. Previous to Spotswood's ascent of that Range, the frontier had advanced with extraordinary slowness up the main streams and their tributaries. In estimating, therefore, the size of the population of the country previous to 1700, we are compelled to confine our attention to the region east of the falls in all the principal rivers descending from the mountains. The region back of that line remained practically unknown to the colonists at large until the eighteenth century had made considerable progress in years. It was familiar only to trappers or the agents of the merchants who carried on a trade in furs with members of the Indian tribes dwelling chiefly towards the southwest.

The first instalment of population arrived in Virginia in the Spring of 1607. There were about 125 persons in this company, without counting the sailors who manned the transporting ships, the *Sarah Constant,* the *Goodspeed* and the *Discovery.* These seamen were not expected to disembark permanently with the band of regular colonists. The next complement of English settlers reached Jamestown in the vessels that brought over the Second Supply; and the next in the vessels in which the Third Supply was conveyed. After that date, the population was increased by steady additions to it landed from separate ships; and this continued until the end of the century.

RICHARD MARTIN

The vessels that bore the hogsheads of tobacco to the wharves of London and other maritime cities of England, brought back, not only cargoes of merchandise suitable for the uses of the people of the colony, but also men, women, and children, free or under indentures, who were eager to establish new homes on the soil of Virginia. It required a bold spirit in these immigrants to leave behind the safety, the comforts, and the conveniences of their native England, and embark on board of the ships trading with the planters. We have already mentioned incidentally the unwholesomeness of their cabins. The number of these immigrants was sensibly diminished by this unhealthiness long before they ever saw the looming shoreline of Cape Henry and Cape Charles. It was said that the passengers were packed under the hatches as closely as so many herrings in a box. Indeed, dysentery and typhus fever were so epidemic in these narrow spaces that, in the course of a certain voyage, one ship alone, when making for the American coast, is recorded to have lost 130 out of its roll of 180 passengers and crew. This was probably an exceptional case, but the rate of mortality on shipboard was always high.

We have seen that, until the area under tillage had greatly widened, the number of deaths on land after the gauntlet of the sea had been run, was appalling, and in two instances, at least, the massacres of 1622 and 1644, the tomahawks of the Indians, at two fell strokes, increased it enormously.

It would have been supposed that news of this dreadful loss of life on the sea, and after the arrival of the immigrants on the land, would have a dampening effect on the resolution of the English men and women who had decided to abandon their native shores and pass over the Atlantic. But there were few persons to report the violent diseases that prevailed on board of the ships or on the plantations. Rarely, in those early times, did the immigrant return to his native country. Such unpleasant or dangerous conditions as he had to face in Virginia, he was compelled either to make the most of, or to modify to the best

of his ability. The sailor alone could successfully spread abroad
the impression in England that the colony was not all that it
was represented to be; but this impression, so far as he had
created it, was to a large degree counteracted by the sight of
the heavy cargoes of tobacco and furs, which were landed from
the ships in the Virginia trade, on their reaching the ports of
Plymouth and Biddeford and London. As long as there was this
substantial evidence of profitableness in the sale of the products
of the colony, neither the would-be emigrant of means nor the
would-be emigrant who had only the labor of his hands to ensure
him employment oversea, was likely to give up in discouragement his original design.

As late as 1643-45, the population of Virginia was still so
small that no serious difficulty was encountered in drawing up
a full and accurate roll of the entire number of people to be
found within its bounds. The community for many years after
1619, when the first free simple title to land was granted by the
company, which allowed a subdivision of the soil into separate
holdings, consisted chiefly of small plantations, in addition to
the great tracts of land reserved for the support, by tenants, of
the principal public offices. These plantations, at the time of
the massacre of 1622, seemed to have stood off as separate settlements, which, in some cases at least, were as far apart from
each other as Kecoughtan and Henricopolis. The earliest formal
enumeration which we possess gives the names of the different
groups of plantations, with a list of the persons who resided
there. The principal citizen in each community, like Gookin or
Pace, for instance, was, of course able to report the name of
every member of his own family and the families of his servants.
The censustaker's only inconvenience was to pass through the
woods from settlement to settlement and receive the roll of the
inhabitants of each.

Apparently, the second formal enumeration was made after
the massacre of 1622. Its object was to find out who had survived that destructive event, and not to ascertain how many

people were residing in the colony. But the first census in the modern sense of the word seems to have been the one which was taken in 1625. The second occurred ten years later, and the third, twenty years. These regular intervals indicate that the present idea of a census was carried out precisely.

The census of 1644-45 apparently was the last which stuck strictly to the rule of making an actual count from house to house. After that year, a different method of finding out the size of the population was adopted. This new method was based only on the number of tithables. While the calculation was, no doubt, accurate, it could not have been completely so in every case. Very probably, this method was suggested by the spread of the population, since that fact had made an actual count both tedious and expensive, without any really proportionate advantage. The only reason which had led the authorities to make the count at all was the necessity of finding out how many persons in the colony were liable to payment of taxes. When it became difficult to enroll the people head by head for this general purpose, the plan of requiring each county to send to Jamestown a list of its tithables was substituted for the original census employed for the colony at large. Upon the basis of this list, the counties had already laid their respective levies for local expenses, and the House of Burgesses imitated their example in using the same lists to defray all public charges.

But from the point of view of the size of the population, the significance of these tax rolls consisted in the fact that the number of people in Virginia was computed to be at least three for every tithable returned. This would attribute to each tithable the possession of a wife and two children. On the whole, this method of enumeration must have been very conservative, and, perhaps, with few exceptions, fell under rather than ran over the number of persons belonging to the various communities, for it does not seem to have taken into account the existence of very old persons, or persons who were physically or mentally disabled.

Among the most interesting enumerations in the early history of the colony was the one preserved in the pages of the well known pamphlet entitled *New Description of Virginia*. The lists of persons, live stock, and other property which it gives, are apparently marked by the accuracy of an actual count. The date of this pamphlet is 1649, which would suggest that it was based on the tax returns of 1648. According to its author, there were 15,000 white people in Virginia at that time. These included the indentured servants as well as the owners of land, whether yeomen or planters on a large scale. There were only 300 negroes, which indicated that the importation of African slaves had as yet been restricted to very small proportions, since some of these bondsmen must have been born in the country after 1619, when the first black captive had been brought to Jamestown.

The number of livestock had increased more rapidly than the number of people, since, during the same year, there were in existence in the colony 20,000 bulls, cows, calves, and oxen, and 200 horses. The herds of hogs were either too numerous to be counted, or they ran so wild in the recesses of the far-reaching forests that only a vague conclusion as to their real number could be formed. The number of sheep was evidently too insignificant to be thought worthy to be recorded.

There was another reason for the requirement that a complete list of tithables should be annually sent to Jamestown by each county. It was only in this way that the military strength of the colony could be ascertained. The militia from one end of the county to the other was liable at any hour of public emergency to be called out by the House of Burgesses for the defense of the frontiers from Indian incursions, or of the shores on tidewater from foreign invasion. With the roll of tithables before them, the members of the General Assembly were able to decide at once the quota of troops which each county should furnish on summons.

We have stated that, in 1644, the size of the population was computed to be about fifteen thousand, three hundred persons in all. It will be pertinent to give also the figures for earlier years. In 1619, the population was ascertained to be approximately twenty-four hundred individuals of both sexes. The negroes had only just begun to swell the number of inhabitants. Immigrants from England were now arriving in considerable bands in every ship that dropped anchor in the James River. In the course of 1621, at least twelve vessels disembarked passengers in the colony.

The massacre during the following year seriously curtailed the number of people seated in the different communities. The population which had spread out and taken root in a dozen or more settlements, both on the north and south side of the Powhatan, was reduced almost in a night to twelve hundred and seventy-seven persons. Disease, resulting from famine, must have followed this great catastrophe, since three years later, we find that the population was smaller than it had been three years earlier. There were now only twelve hundred and two inhabitants. Between 1625 and 1628, however, immigration, which had been halted by news of the massacre of 1622, must have resumed its original flow, for the population rose to three thousand. By 1629, it had increased to four thousand, and at the end of an additional four years, to five thousand, one hundred and nineteen. This signified an annual expansion of about two hundred and fifty, which does not seem to have been imposing when it is recalled that the ships were bringing over each year a considerable number of emigrants from England.

After 1633, the volume of immigrants steadily grew larger. The explanation of this fact lay in the further improvement in the colony's general condition which marked each successive year.

There were, for instance, no longer, as there had been previous to 1624, when the great charter was revoked, any bickering between the factions of the old London Company to confuse the English people's impression of the advantages which Virginia had to offer to persons thinking of settling there. The community was now directly subject to the king, whose authority no one could dispute or balk. Moreover, title to land which, at one time, after the charter was recalled, seemed to be in jeopardy, was now confirmed in fee simple by royal letters patent; and everyone already in possession of a plantation felt that his tenure was secure; and everyone who was anxious to become a proprietor, perceived that it would be safe to buy. News of this happy condition had been carried to England, and it must have had a reassuring effect upon the minds of those who were considering removal to Virginia and the purchase of an estate there.

Another influence that tended to increase the stream of immigrants after 1633 was the clear recognition by this time that tobacco was so peculiarly adapted to the soil of Virginia that the cultivation of it was sure to be carried on there indefinitely. Here was a great staple which could be relied on to give a large return to capital and labor from year to year; and the assurance of this fact was further strengthened by the veto which the English government put upon the production of the plant in England, and by the practical exclusion of all importation of the leaf from the American colonies of Spain. The inference was perfectly allowable also that the English authorities, in order to retain the custom from the tobacco cargos brought from Virginia to the English ports, would endeavor, by every means in their power, to foster the prosperity of the plantations oversea.

There was other information arriving by this time from these communities that also tended to encourage an increased volume of emigration from the mother country. The colony was steadily assuming more and more the social aspects of the English shores. With the flight of the Indians to remote fastnesses in the woods, the plantations along the great rivers were becoming as safe from incursions as the homesteads of Sussex, Sur-

rey. or Devonshire.　A war cry in the night was as little likely
to arouse the sleeping Virginians residing far within the frontiers, as it was the sleeping Englishmen who were seated on the
banks of the Mole or the Dart.　In this quiet atmosphere, new
homes could be created without apprehension that lawlessness in
any form would interfere.　Steadily the number of these homes
was growing, and as far as the conditions of a new country
allowed, the essential manner of life that had prevailed in England for centuries was adopted by their inmates.　Knowledge of
this fact must have exerted a strong influence on the minds of
English women in reconciling them to accompany their husbands, sons, and fathers to Virginia.

But there was a more practical reason than this to swell the
stream of the best class of English immigrants which was pouring in even in these early years.　England at this time, as during
subsequent periods, was remarkable for the size of its families.
Children swarmed around the hearths of landowners, clergymen,
lawyers, physicians, and merchants.　How were these numerous
offsprings to be settled in life?　By the law of entail and primo-
geniture, the landed estate descended to the oldest son.　Rarely
was the owner of such an estate in the possession of sufficient
personal property to make provision for his other children.　Nor
was the clergyman often a man of means, nor was the physician.
The lawyer could hardly find room for more than one son in his
office, or the merchant for more than two behind his counter.

England, during those times, had no far-flung dominions
where the younger members of the family could find employment in civil positions; nor did its navy or army supply many
berths.　There was but one opening for these surplus sons—
apprenticeships to trade, either in London, and the other great
cities, or in a neighboring small town or village.　Accustomed
to the comfort and freedom of the parental home, not all these
sons were willing to sink to a secondary social station by adopting purely mechanical callings, as so many of them were forced
to do.　Rather, many must have decided, with their father's

encouragement and assistance to pass oversea to seek a different career in the plantation communities of Virginia.

Emigration to the colony, after the first mutterings of the Civil war were heard, showed a perceptible increase, which continued to the climax in 1649, when Charles was sent to the scaffold. It is not possible to calculate the precise number of cavaliers who came over to Virginia in those unhappy and tumultuous years, but with their families, servants, and followers of a lower rank, they must have made a large addition to the population of the colony.

In 1634, the number of immigrants disembarked from the English ships was shown by actual count to be twelve hundred. During the interval between this year and 1649, the population increased to fifteen thousand, three hundred persons. One part of this addition came from births in the colony; another very small part, as already mentioned, from the importation of slaves; but the much larger proportion from the introduction of settlers who had arrived from England. The mere fact that the number of men in Virginia, during this period, greatly exceeded the number of women tended to give the preponderance to newcomers from the Mother Country. At the same time, the fecundity of the women residing in the colony had been the cause of comment from an early date in its history. At least, there had been, on their part, no falling off in their reproductive power as compared with the reproductive power shown by their own sex in England, where families had always been notable for the number of children which they embraced.

It is quite possible that an impression prevailed in England at the beginning of colonization that the climate of Virginia, being, during certain months, highly enervating, would not be promotive of sexual fruitfulness because it was expected that this condition would lower health, and, thereby, diminish the strength of the women. Moreover, it was presumed that most of the members of that sex would be compelled to labor in the tobacco fields, a further tax on their vigor. Apparently, however, the extreme heat in summer, the sharp frigidity in winter, and the debilitating effect of work and exposure under the rays of the July and August suns, left no deteriorating stamp on the vitality of the Virginia wives; but possibly it did, by transmissive influence, make the children less capable of resisting the assaults of disease.

There are no statistics or observations made in those times available to show the comparative mortality of children in England and in Virginia during the first half of the seventeenth century. It is, however quite probable that the death rate among the young, during that period, was lower in the Mother Country: first, because the English houses were more protective, being solidly built; second, because the climate there was less subject to extremes; and third, because there the science of medicine was more efficacious on account of the greater experience of the physicians in actual practice, and the larger supply of useful drugs available.

We have seen that the growth of population at large had been suddenly checked in every part of Virginia in 1622, by the destructive blows of the tomahawk. Only a single event of that character took place afterwards. This was the massacre of 1644. But fortunately for the inhabitants, the strokes of the fatal Indian weapons during that year were confined to the widely dispersed settlements on the outer line of the frontier, and along one side of the colony alone. A long peace followed in consequence of the retaliation wreaked by Berkeley and his soldiers on the villages of the marauders. Apparently, the population of the different communities exposed in 1676 to the incursions of the Susquehannock and other hostile tribes were more or less remote from the sites of the vast majority of the plantations, and because of this fact, many families residing in the upper valleys of the Rappahannock and Powhatan were foully butchered before they could be rescued. From this period until the Revolution, war with the Indians did little to diminish the number of people who occupied homes east of the line of the Blue Ridge.

In 1675, the year before the insurrection under Nathaniel Bacon's leadership began, the size of the population was supposed to be about fifty thousand in all. Such was the number stated by the three commissioners who visited England in the course of that year to obtain a new charter for the colony to take the place of the old. No men in Virginia had had a better opportunity of informing themselves about all the resources of its communities than they. It is quite certain that their calculation was made by them on the basis of the number of tithables which had been returned during the preceding year by the commanders of the different counties. The accuracy of their enumeration was confirmed by the report which Culpeper, a few years later, made on the same subject to the English Government.

About twenty years afterwards, the number of tithables in the colony was computed to be twenty thousand approximately. Taking three persons as the proportion for each tithable, the population of Virginia at this time certainly did not fall short of sixty thousand, and quite probably it was equal to seventy-five thousand.

It must be admitted that this number hardly indicated a remarkable rate of growth during so considerable a period as two decades, especially if the fact is borne in mind that immigration by itself had been constantly enlarging the circle of inhabitants. At the most, the increase from births and immigration combined had not apparently run beyond one thousand in the course of each twelve months. By this time, the importation of slaves had come to assume a considerable volume, which was to grow larger and larger after the eighteenth century began.

CHAPTER V

UPPER PLANTER CLASS

Throughout the seventeenth century, there were to be observed in all the long settled parts of Virginia clearly defined gradations in social rank among the people who occupied the country. This seems natural enough when it is remembered that they were all either natives or descendants of natives, of England, where a rigid difference in social condition had been recognized and enforced for a thousand years. The existence of similar classes in the colony bore an important relation to its general history.

First, at the top were the planters who had arrived with their families with very considerable means in their possession, and also accompanied by servants, each of whom entitled his master, by the law relating to transportation charges, to fifty acres of land. There were also in the same rank the planters who had accumulated in Virginia large estates by their own energy and shrewdness, without the advantage of any English inheritance to start with. Into one or the other of these two conspicuous divisions of the upper class fell such famous families as the Armisteads, Banisters, Blands, Bollings, Burwells, Beverleys, Byrds, Carys, Corbins, Carters, Claibornes, Fauntleroys, Fitzhughs, Harrisons, Lees, Lightfoots, Ludwells, Masons, Pages, Peytons, Randolphs, Robinsons, Scarboroughs, Spencers, Washingtons, and Wormeleys. This list could be greatly lengthened. We have selected only names that were distinctly representative of the highest class in each community.

Below the social rank which these families occupied, there were numerous other families whose estates were on a moderate scale, and whose influence from the mere possession of fortune was small.

At the bottom of the roll of freeholders was found a vigorous class of yeomen, who made no pretension to either social or industrial importance individually, but who, in the mass, formed one of the most valuable constituents of the community at large. Many of these yeomen had been petty landowners in England before their emigration, and were not entirely lacking in means when they arrived in Virginia. Belonging to the same valuable class were the men, who, after serving under indenture, were able to save enough, by hiring themselves out, to purchase a small area of ground.

Below the divisions of upper planter, middle planter, and yeomen, were the white bondsmen and the African and Indian slaves. We will describe the condition of servant and slave respectively when we come hereafter to consider the subject of the general system of labor that prevailed in the colony. For the present, we will confine our attention to the upper and lower ranks of freeholders. It will be perfectly germane to a discussion of the economic aspects of the seventeenth century to inquire into the origin of these more fortunate classes, as only, in that way, can we learn the full secret of the personal influence that led to the conquest of the forests of Eastern Virginia, and the conversion of that fertile region from a primeval wilderness into a territory occupied by beautiful homes and reduced to a productive state of tillage, in spite of the more or less dispersed settlements of the inhabitants.

We will begin with the highest division of planters. With few exceptions, these belonged to the social caste that, in the Mother Country, were known as "gentlemen." This was a term, which, in that age had a recognized social meaning. It was used in both English and Virginia public documents with the precision which characterized a reference to a member of the peerage, although, in the case of the gentleman, there were, of course, no political privileges by themselves alone to raise him, as they

6—Vol. I.

had done the nobleman in England, to a distinctly separate social platform in the community.

From the beginning, even before the growth of the population and the extension of cultivation had created in the valleys of the James, York, and Rappahannock, a social system and a manner of life resembling those of England, there had been a highly favorable attitude towards Virginia on the part of the members of the higher social classes in the Mother Country. In the charter of 1612, the roll of incorporators included the names of twenty-five peers of the realm, one hundred and eleven knights, sixty-six esquires, and twenty "gentlemen." It had been calculated that not less than three-fourths of the men who petitioned the king in this document were members of the highest social circle in England; and that as many as one hundred and twenty had either been members of Parliament, or were still seated in that august assembly.

Merchants had predominated among those who obtained the charter of 1609, but while a large number of persons of that calling had signed the charter of 1612, they no longer possessed the degree of supremacy, after that charter was granted, which they had possessed a few years before.

The men of more aristocratic connections who overshadowed the merchants in 1612 were not all satisfied simply to lend their names as incorporators to the great enterprise overseas. Some of them either contributed to the establishment in Virginia of associations like Berkeley and Southampton Hundreds—small principalities in area and natural resources—but they went over to the colony themselves to reside there in the company of their families and servants. It was expressly asserted in the spirited defense of Sir Thomas Smythe's Government during the first twelve years of the settlement, that, among those who perished there in that interval were many persons sprung from "Ancyent Houses and born to estates of 1,000 pounds by the year, some more, some less." At this time, one thousand pounds sterling had the purchasing power of five thousand pounds in our age.

In examining the lists of adventurers who arrived in the Company's ships commanded by Captain Newport, who brought out the First, Second, and Third Supplies, the attention is immediately fixed by the distinction of the names of many of the passengers—Sandys, Percy, Throckmorton, Pennington, Wingfield, Waller, Wotton, Gower, Codington, Leigh, Norton, Hull, Yarington, and Russell, for instance. Wingfield was a descendant of the famous Veres, Earl of Oxford, and George Percy, of the Earls of Northumberland.

Not a vessel set out for Virginia after the first General Assembly convened that did not include among its passengers men of high social position in England. In one consignment made to Berkeley Plantation in 1619, thirteen persons in a list of fifty were entered as entitled to the designation of "gentlemen." In 1624, the Ship *Ann* brought over to the colony thirteen men in a band of thirty-two who were thus referred to in the certificate of conveyance. The remainder were artisans and farmers. Nor did the number fall off after the charter had been recalled by the King in the course of that year. On Governor Harvey's return to Virginia in 1636, twenty of the one hundred passengers who accompanied him—that is to say, one-fifth of the entire group—were stated in the license which they had obtained to sail, to be "gentlemen of quality."

In the ranks of the first Assembly, a body thoroughly representative of the highest class of planters, there were several members who traced their relationship to the principal county families in England, and thus had been connected with that proprietorship in land which had always exercised the most powerful influence of all bearing on the welfare of their native country. Yeardley, who was a member by virtue of his office of Governor, was one of the few present who had been associated with trade before his emigration. Francis West, through his father and brother, had been brought in the closest contact with the varied rural interests of his native land. John Pory had been a member of Parliament, and as such had used his vote to assure

SIR EDWIN SANDYS

the passage of different acts for the advancement of his country's rural welfare. Walter Shelley was supposed to be a cadet of an English family that had been seated in Sussex as owners of the soil during many generations. Thomas Pawlett was also identified with a similar proprietorship through his relationship to the Lord Winchester of that day. George Percy, who, at one time, served in the office of Governor, was a brother of one of the most conspicuous owners of land in England, the Earl of Northumberland.

There were other prominent men associated with the early history of Virginia who were sprung from English families which had been long identified with landed estates. Such was George Thorpe, who was related to the Throckmortons and Berkeleys, famous in the ranks of the titled class for their splendid seats in the English shires. Strachey, Secretary of State for the Colony, was a descendant of Sir John Strachey, the head of a family of conspicuous position among the landed gentry. John Rolfe had emigrated from Heacham, in the shire of Norfolk, where his family had dwelt from a remote period. Equally prominent in Cambridge shire were the Allingtons, to whom Giles Allington was closely related by ties of consanguinity.

Sir John Zouch, who did not remain permanently in Virginia, was a member of a celebrated land-owning family in Devonshire. William Claiborne, who filled many offices in the colony, such as the Secretaryship of State, a Commissionership of Parliament at the time of Virginia's surrender to the Commonwealth, and the Deputy Governorship, was a native of Westmorelandshire, where his family had owned a valuable landed estate from a remote date, and where it had intermarried with the Lowthers, the greatest proprietors of the soil in the north. Henry Woodhouse was sprung from Sir William Woodhouse, who had been seated at Waxham in the shire of Norfolk. Christopher Calthorpe also had emigrated from that shire, where his family had been immemorably identified with the soil. So had the Bacons, the ancestors of the famous rebel, Nathaniel Bacon, and the almost equally celebrated Virginian councillor of the same name.

Thomas Reede went back on the maternal side to the Windebanks of Hames Hill in Berkshire. Richard Kemp, who, at one time, was secretary of the colony, was a member of a family long associated with Gissing in the Shire of Suffolk. William Bernard was a brother of Sir Robert Bernard, of Brompton Hall, in Huntingdonshire. Colonel Nathaniel Littleton, of Accomac, a brother of Sir Edward Littleton, Chief Justice of England, had been born and reared at Henley in Shropshire.

It has never been clearly demonstrated whether Colonel Richard Lee belonged to the Lee family of Shropshire or Essex, but in either event he had been bound by intimate ties to the landed proprietorship of his native country. Christopher Wormeley was descended from the family of the same name which had been seated immediately at Hadfield in Yorkshire. Robert Throckmorton, the first of his name to settle in Virginia, was the grandson of Gabriel Throckmorton, lord of the Manor of Ellington in Huntingdonshire. Sir Henry Chichely, who served at one time as Governor of the Colony, had, before his emigration, been associated with Wimpole in Cambridgeshire. Henry Isham was descended from a family which had, during many generations, resided in Northamptonshire, where it had possessed valuable landed estates. The members of the Bland family, who settled in Virginia, were kinsmen of Sir Thomas Bland, who was the owner of Kippax Park situated in the neighborhood of the city of Leeds.

George Brent and John Clarke, both of distinguished social connections in England, had immigrated from the country districts of Worcestershire and Kent, respectively. George Luke was the grandson of Sir Samuel Luke of Woodend in Bedfordshire who took so patriotic a part in the defense of the kingdom Launcelot Bathhurst was sprung from a family which was in possession of a large landed estate in Gloucestershire. Hugh Yoe, who represented the county of Accomac in the House of

Burgesses, was a member of the family of that name in Devonshire who took so patriotic a part in the defense of the kingdom when the Armada bore down upon the Southern Coast. Long after Leonard Yoe immigrated to Virginia, he continued to hold property in his native shire. The Broadhursts, who came over to the colony in 1650, had been established before their departure at Lilleshall in Shropshire, while the Peachys had resided at Milden Hall in Suffolkshire.

But of all the families who settled in Virginia, the one most intimately associated with the rural life of England was the family of the Evelyns. Their residence at Wotton was among the noblest and most interesting homes in England, and still survives to show our modern age the splendid surroundings of the great English landed proprietors in the seventeenth century. Hardly less imposing was Hall's End in Warwickshire, from which the Corbins of Virginia came.

The ancestor of John Page, the immigrant, had possessed manorial rights in Bedfont Parish situated in the County of Middlesex. The Masons and Fowkes, who were supposed to have abandoned England in consequence of the defeat of the royal cause, were related to the Pudsey family, which filled a position of exceptional distinction in the ranks of the English landed gentry. Equally prominent as such were the Ashtons of Spalding in Lincolnshire, who were the ancestors of the Ashtons of the Northern Neck. Such, too, were the ancestors of the Burwells, who had immigrated from Bedfordshire, which had been their seat from an early period in English history. The Smiths of Abingdon Parish in Gloucester County were also connected with the rural gentry of England; and so were the Fitzhughs, who were supposed to have been related by blood to a family of the same name in Bedfordshire, which had inherited the barony of Ravensworth. William Fitzhugh, the founder of the Virginia branch, exhibited the versatility of his business capacity by accumulating a large fortune by means of tobacco culture on his own plantations, by the purchase of the leaf from his neighbors for shipment to England, and by the acquisition of a large body of virgin land and holding it for subdivision and sale to people arriving in the Colony.

Christopher Robinson, nephew of a Bishop of London of the same name, had left his old home, Hewick, in an English shire, and settled in Middlesex County, where he carried the fortunes of his family name to a still higher degree of prosperity. The father of the first William Byrd followed the calling of goldsmith or banker in London, but he was sprung from ancestry associated with English country life. The elder and younger Byrds were among the largest landowners who ever resided in the colony.

The Berkeleys also had been long identified with the ownership of landed property in England; and when, during the supremacy of Parliament, after the colony's surrender, Sir William Berkeley found a refuge at Green Spring, perhaps the most imposing estate in Virginia of that century, he eagerly followed the example of his English ancestors by interesting himself in the cultivation of the soil.

We have offered the names of only a few of the families in the colony who were sprung directly from the rural gentry of England, and who, long before they built new homes in the valleys of the great rivers that flowed into the Chesapeake Bay, had learned to love country life and the various occupations associated with it in their native land. When they settled on their own plantations oversea, they made but little alteration in those different pursuits which had previously engaged their thoughts and absorbed their energies under English skies. The list which we have given was selected simply because it was typical of the membership of the great class to which the colony turned throughout the seventeenth century, for social, political, and industrial leadership. To present a complete enumeration of the most important planters of the same English rural antecedents, would be to take up more pages than could be conveniently reserved for it.

Next to the influence exercised over the colony's welfare in these times by the principal landowners was the influence exercised by the English merchants who were interested in trade with the colony, or by their sons, who had been sent over to find a place among the proprietors already established there. With hardly an exception, the London guilds contributed large sums to the colonization of Virginia. Among the representatives of these powerful associations who signed the Charter of 1612 were ten mercers, twenty drapers, twelve goldsmiths, twenty tailors, seventy grocers, two salters, ten skinners, ten ironmongers, twelve haberdashers, sixteen clothworkers, and four vintners.

A very considerable proportion of the merchants who were shipping various supplies to Virginia from time to time, visited it in the course of these transactions. They went out to study the conditions of trade there in person, or to increase the number of the purchasers for their goods, or to collect debts that had been slow of payment. Doubtless, too, some of these merchants crossed the sea to take charge of certain ventures in tobacco speculation on a great scale. Either their interest or the inclination of the moment led many to buy plantations in Virginia, which they managed themselves, either for profit or for sake of the passing diversion. There not a few continued to reside during the rest of their lives without evincing any disposition to return to their native land. But apparently the majority occupied only at intervals these plantation homes, which, in some cases, had been purchased for the benefit of sons who proposed to live indefinitely in Virginia.

The presence of English merchants in the colony was especially notable during those civil commotions in the Mother Country, which preceded the death of the first Charles. Trade was too disturbed there at that time to have much room for profit, and this fact turned the thoughts of many persons who were engaged in business in London, and the other English cities, towards plantations overseas.

More numerous than the merchants themselves who went out to the colony, either for a time or permanently, were their sons or nephews who crossed the ocean without intention of returning in the future to their native scenes in England. Such was the founder of the Ferrar family, which is still represented in Virginia at the present time. He was descended from a member of the guild of skinners. It was his kinsmen in England who used every means in their power to increase the interest felt in the culture of the silkworm on the banks of the Powhatan. The Felgates were near relations of William Felgate, who followed the same trade as the Ferrars in London, while the Brooke family possessed a near English ancestor who was a clothier. John Brewer, whose sons had all removed oversea, was a member of the English guild of grocers. Isaac Allerton, ancestor of the distinguished family of that name in the Colony, was a merchant tailor. The original Corbin and Ashton, who were connected, as we have already mentioned, with English landed proprietors before their immigration, were also connected, like so many well known families of England of that day, with trade. There were leather sellers and haberdashers among their English kin. This was also the case with the families of Richard Bennett, Henry Batte, and Philip Ludwell; and it was also the case with the families of Thomas Vaulx, William Munford, Hugh Stanford, and Thomas Griffith, all men of high personal and social standing in Virginia.

Miles Cary, who founded a family of particular distinction, was the son of a woolen draper, who was a citizen of Bristol, while the Lees of York County were near kinsmen of George Lee, a merchant of London.

The Bolling family, which occupied a high position in the social history of Virginia, through intermarriage with the granddaughter of the Princess Pocahontas, was sprung from a member of the Saddlers Guild, although it went back still further to the original owners of Bolling Hall. John Pleasants, founder of a family that was long identified with the sect of Quakers, descended from an English worsted weaver. One of the ancestors of Christopher Branch was Richard Branch, a woolen draper of Abington. The Fabians of York County were sprung from Edward Fabian, a merchant tailor of London. Edward Lockey, of the same county, was a brother of John Lockey, a member of the London guild of grocers. John Mercer, also of London, where he pursued the calling of haberdasher, was represented by a brother in Virginia; so was Micajah Perry, of the most celebrated firm engaged in the tobacco trade of the Colony. Perry had been, at one time, Lord Mayor of London.

Sarah Offley, who married Adam Thoroughgood, of Lower Norfolk County, the most influential citizen seated south of the James River in those times, was the daughter of one Lord Mayor of that great town, and the granddaughter of another. So was the wife of Samuel Matthews, who accumulated a large estate by planting and trading. She was the daughter of Sir Thomas Hinton, Lord Mayor of London, and the granddaughter of Sir Sebastian Harvey, who had also filled that lofty office. All these Lord Mayors had risen to eminence through their success in various branches of English trade.

The Baskerville family were descendants of a member of the Fishmongers guild in London. John Starke inherited the entire estate in Virginia of his father, a merchant of that city; and this was also the case with the children of John Juxon, a London salter. One of the nearer relations of the Filmer family was a wealthy grocer of Kent. Rev. Thomas Teakle, a clergyman of distinction in the Colony, had married the daughter of a London merchant. The Peytons traced their descent back to Sir Edward Osbourne, who was a member of the Guild of Clothworkers.

Henry Freeman, a landowner of York County, was sprung from a family of mercers residing at Chipping Norton in Oxfordshire, while Isaac Clopton, of the same county, belonged to a family of haberdashers. Henry Sewell, from whom Sewell's Point on Elizabeth River derives its name, also belonged to a family engaged in trade in his native country. William Collin,

whose father apparently was a member of the Weavers Guild
in London had also immigrated to Virginia. And so had William
Beacham, whose immediate ancestry had the like association
with English trade. The forebears of John Ralph were merchants of Lynn. The Buckners, Sandfords, and Booths were all
descendants of merchant families in England. So were the
Timsons, the Crews, and numerous others who occupied a position of prominence in the social and industrial life of Virginia
in the course of the seventeenth century.

There were many families who were sprung from English
seacaptains engaged in transporting tobacco to England, and in
bringing back cargos of merchandise and bands of agricultural
servants for the use of the planters in Virginia. Navigation of
the sailing vessels of those days called for a high degree of technical knowledge and skill. Those sea-captains were also men of
coolness and firmness, qualities imperatively required for the
proper control of their ships in the midst of the perils of the
ocean passage. Sudden danger faced them from the moment
they set out to the moment they had made their port.

Possessing a wide acquaintance among the planters residing
along the banks of the Virginian rivers, whose practical experience was of special value as relating to investments in land,
these sea-captains, as the county records disclose, were often led
to purchase plantations for themselves. To these plantations,
when this last voyage had ended, many of them retired to pass
in quiet the closing years of their lives. Some became the founders of distinguished families in those parts of the Colony where
they settled. Such was the Doodes family, who took the name
of Minor, from the use of that term by their Dutch ancestor to
distinguish him from his father, the senior Doodes. Such was
the Ball family, sprung from Thomas Ball of Lancaster County,
who was described in deeds as "mariner." So was Thomas Wil-
loughby, the founder of the well known family of the name
which was seated in Lower Norfolk. So too were both William
Gainge and Isaac Foxcroft.

Robert Ranson and Samuel Milburn, of Elizabeth City County, had also been sea-captains; and so had Cornelius Calvert of Lower Norfolk. It was said that Calvert brought up each of his numerous sons to the calling which he had followed so long and with so much success.

The great majority of the Virginian families of that day whose names we have mentioned as originally connected with the landed interests, the trading interests, or the shipping interests of England, had come directly to the Colony from the Mother Country; but there were some who had first passed an interval of time in the communities of New England or of the West Indies. The Sturgis, Smalley, Dewey, and Washburn families had removed to Virginia after a sojourn in Massachusetts. Colonel Isaac Allerton was the son of the Pilgrim Father of the same name, and the grandson of William Brewster, the leader of the Plymouth Company. Among other families arriving from the same quarter were the Broughtons, Lords, Shermans, and Storys. Members of these families served in the House of Burgesses and were owners of large estates.

From the Barbadoes came the Walkes of Lower Norfolk, and the Perrins and Marshalls of Elizabeth City.

With the exception of the Doodes or Minor family, all the families that have been named, traced their ancestry back to the British Islands. The number of planters of continental origin was unimportant until the arrival of the Huguenots, who established themselves in the country above the site of the present city of Richmond, and kept their racial characteristics by holding firmly together during a considerable period after their first settlement in Virginia. A majority of the Frenchmen who landed in the Colony in the seventeenth century hailed from England, where they had been domiciled, perhaps, during many years before deciding to pass overseas. After their arrival there, they had become gradually anglicized by marriage and exclusive association with English speaking and English thinking people. Their descendants of the first and second generations were not to be distinguished from the colonists of pure English blood. This was also true of the immediate posterity of the comparatively small number of Dutchmen, Germans, and Italians who found a home in Virginia in those times. Of general French origin were the Martians, Slatiers, Roziers, Sebrells, Pettits, Le Grands, Fontaines, De La Brieres, Constanceaus, De Contees, Pettigrus, Cralles, and Lempriers. Among the clerical French families were the Fouaces, Boisseaus and Latanes. Others of the same stock were the Servants, Du Puys, Pardoes, Thelaballs and De Barrys.

The Dutch and German families were not so conspicuous, but, in Dr. George Hacke, they possessed a representative of high accomplishments. Among other persons of the same general foreign blood were Hugh Cornelinson, Hendrick Wagaman, Thomas Harmanson, Daniel Derrickson, Abram Jansen, and Abram Van Slot. Some of the Dutch immigrants belonged to families of English origin, like the Moseleys and Custises.

There were a few families who traced back to Portugal or Italy. Among these were the Lupo, Rodregues, Debello, Mazingo, and Iago. Amaso de Torris was probably a Spanish Jew. The most important immigrant from Ireland was Daniel Gookin, but he was only nominally of that country, as his family had long been domiciled in England.

There is no room to doubt that a large area of land in the aggregate was held by the members of the social and industrial class known as Yoemen. This class was entirely distinct from the two divisions of landowners to which the families enumerated in the preceding pages belonged. But like most of the persons of the latter rank residing in the community, they too could correctly assert that the majority of their number were natives of the Mother Country. It was also as true of them as it was of the large planters, that they included in their circle individuals who had held property in England before their immigration. The means thus obtained enabled many of them to purchase land so soon as they arrived in Virginia. The position of these yeomen was, of course, not as fortunate as that of the upper classes in the point of estates, but they were always in the enjoyment of the suffrage, and showed on all proper occasions a firm and independent spirit.

Equal to them in industrial importance, although not in social perhaps, were the men who, after passing through a period of indentured service, had accumulated funds sufficient to buy plantations of a few hundred acres.

At the end of the century, three of every four landowners living in Virginia owned estates that ranged from a few acres at one extreme to five hundred at the other. There were seven hundred and fifty families that owned from five hundred acres to one thousand; and four hundred and fifty who owned from one thousand to ten thousand or more. This was exclusive of the counties in the Northern Neck.

II

THE COLONIAL PERIOD 1607-1700

CHAPTER I

THE PATENT

When the immigrant arrived in Virginia, with the intention of becoming a permanent resident of that community, what step did he take to acquire an interest in the soil? It was the prospect of owning land that had induced the great majority of these immigrants to abandon their homes in England. Landed proprietorship had always made a seductive appeal to Englishmen of means, large or small, and in the seventeenth century, where could this aspiration be realized so fully and so easily as in the colony oversea?

Almost immediately on the newcomer's arrival there, he either bought a plantation of some resident landowner, who had gone over before him, or what was far more frequently done, he sued out a patent to ground that had not yet been appropriated. This gave him a fee simple title to his new estate provided that he fulfilled certain conditions, to which we shall refer at length hereafter. Before we do this, it will be illuminating to dwell to some extent on the source from which it was supposed the original title proceeded.

In the beginning, with the ruthlessness that then characterized the English dealings with the unfortunate savages, the whole country—which had been occupied by them during uncountable ages—was claimed by the English sovereign. They were not considered to be even the subjects of the king, for that would have given them certain rights and privileges which even he could not disregard.

There was a feeble attempt by some to prevent this complete dispossession of the Indian proprietors. The interceders were

Ætatis suæ 21. Aᵒ. 1616.

POCAHONTAS

certain members of the London Company, which succeeded to the supreme right of the king in the soil. They urged that all land actually in use by the Indians should remain permanently in their hands, without interference. But this attitude was not shared by the great majority of the company. In reality, the recommendation was impracticable, as it failed to take into account the fact that the Indians depended for their livelihood principally on hunting and fishing and not on planting, and these means of procuring food could only be enjoyed with any degree of ease if the face of the entire country was open to their excursions. So soon as their right to roam wherever they thought best in pursuit of game, was restricted, either by English guns or by English plantations, the progress towards actual starvation had begun, unless they abandoned their old haunts and retired towards the mountains.

The fierce disposition shown by Powhatan's subjects on nearly every occasion before Pocahontas's marriage to John Rolfe—which brought about a certain degree of comity between the two races—caused the English to make some effort at fair dealing about the soil, which, however, was a mere feint on their part at first for a temporary purpose. Doubtless in their hearts, in these early years of the settlement, the very men who took title to land from Powhatan or his vassals, were aware of the futility of that act. Thus, in 1609, Smith persuaded the Indian chief at the falls to convey to Captain West and his garrison stationed there a large section of the surrounding country. As Smith was now in disfavor, it is quite probable that this grant would not have been recognized by the company even if West himself had not refused to accept it.

A gift of land to Sir George Yeardley by Opechancanough, in 1617, was approved by the council of that body, not because they admitted the Indian chief's title to the ground, but because the present was a proper reward for Sir George's services to the colony. It was only a few years afterwards that the company was conveying the soil in fee simple to hundreds of patentees;

and when Yeardley, then governor, informed the council in London, in 1621, that he had made one transfer conditional upon Opechancanough's consent to it, his act raised an outcry because he practically acknowledged that the possession of the original title was in that "heathen infidel."

After the revocation of the charter in 1624, a wiser policy was adopted, not because of the Indians' inherent right to the soil, but because it was now clearly perceived that it was essential to the colony's peace that the Indian title to vast unoccupied bodies of land should be recognized in a general way. The dispossession of the Peninsula by the exertion of force during the first years of settlement was even put on a fairer basis by negotiations with Nicotowance, the Indian ruler, nearly forty years after the foundation of Jamestown. This chief, however, was required to acknowledge that his title to the territory which he retained was derived from the King of England.

From this time, the Indians in several parts of the colony were permitted to convey their lands, but, in every case, the transaction was required to receive the approval of the government at Jamestown. In 1658, we find that government stepping in still more determinedly to protect the race from the consequences of the fraudulent devices employed by unscrupulous colonists to deprive them of their interest. No further fault could be found with the policy which, from this date forward, was pursued toward the Indian proprietors. The General Assembly even went so far as to take away their right to convey title to the ground, in the hope that this would put an end to the abuses which were reducing them rapidly to the state of a landless people. In the end, the Indian population fell off to such a degree that some of their reservations were no longer occupied, and it was only when this condition arose that the colonists were permitted to enter and acquire title to the soil.

During the existence of the London Company there were several requirements on which a grant of land by that body was based. The first was the purchase of a bill of adventure for the sum of twelve pounds and ten shillings. It was announced in the beginning that the soil was to be subdivided, in 1616, in fee simple holdings, and every person who had purchased such a bill, which was really a share in the Company, was then to receive such a portion of the soil as would amount to two hundred acres when the land had been seated.

It was not until 1619, the year of the First Assembly, that this division began to the degree originally planned. Associations were formed in England for the purchase of thousands of acres in Virginia. For instance, a subscription to two hundred shares of stock gave title to twenty thousand acres, and so soon as these were seated, another twenty thousand became their property. These patents were known as subpatents, and their purchase carried well defined special rights. In 1620, five subpatents were sued out, the largest number in the history of these grants. The patentees of Southampton Hundred are said to have expended 6,000 sterling in the improvement of their property, which embraced an area of 200,000 acres. Martin's Hundred covered an area of 80,000. Ultimately, these vast tracts of land were broken up into small holdings.

In addition to the acquisition of the patent by purchase in the time of the company, it would be obtained by the performance of meritorious services of different kinds. Patents were granted for that reason to Captain Newport, Lord Delaware, and Sir Thomas Dale, and also to persons of inferior rank who had advanced, in one way or another, the fortunes of the colony. This provision remained in force after the charter was recalled in 1624, but the reward in this form for important services was generally reserved after that year for men who had organized bands of rangers for the protection of the frontiers.

Another kind of service in the company's time which was similarly compensated, was manual work done for the public welfare. Such was the labor of the tenants who cultivated the lands of the company, and who, afterwards, established homes of their own.

THOMAS WEST
Third Baron Delaware

But the normal basis for the grant of a patent was what was known as the headright. This came into existence in 1618, and remained in operation throughout the rest of the seventeenth century. The headright was by far the commonest of all the grounds for the conveyance of land in that way. Every shareholder in the original company received a patent to fifty acres of land for every person he had transported to the colony, provided that this person continued to stay there during a period of three years. This privilege was not restricted to individuals who had purchased stock of that corporation. Any one who had immigrated to Virginia at his own expense, or had brought in an immigrant at his own cost, was entitled to the same number of acres.

In March, 1625, the law of headright was expressly approved by the act of the king, and there was never afterwards any serious attempt made to curtail or revoke it. On the contrary, the right was again and again confirmed, and wisely so. What the colony needed most, was an increase of population. How otherwise could the forests be cut down and the soil cultivated in a just proportion to the vastness of the territory suitable for tillage? The headright was the best method of stimulating immigration, because it carried its immediate reward in a patent to land. At the same time, there was a definite outlay attending it. To transport one's self to Virginia from England, or to send over an agricultural servant or other person, in order to acquire the patent, imposed an expense of six pounds sterling, or, in the purchasing value of our modern currency, about $150. This would indicate that each acre in the fifty which had been received had cost the patentee about $2.85.

Moreover, the patentee, if the land acquired was in forest, as it was almost certain to be, had to defray the heavy charge of clearing away the trees, unless he was able to undertake this task with his own hands. If the work was shared by a servant, it was necessary, not only to feed him, but also to clothe him, and this latter by itself could be done at an outlay of three pounds and seven shillings. In many cases, the patentee had purchased his servant or servants from an English importing merchant, and in that case, he was compelled to pay the additional charge of the merchant's profit.

The headright was subject to numerous perversions of the theory on which it was based. No matter how often a patentee had crossed the ocean, he was allowed fifty acres for each passage, although, in reality, only one immigrant, himself, had come in. There is an instance on record in which the patentee acquired by this subterfuge 400 acres. Lapse of time, however great, since the voyage ended, did not serve to bar the right. Occasionally a sea-captain obtained a patent on the basis of his passengers, and even of his seamen, and this fraud was not infrequently repeated in other parts of the colony by the same man many times. More frequently still, he sold the certificate of these headrights to some person who, as a permanent resident of Virginia, was planning to increase the number of the acres in his possession.

The captain's example was constantly imitated by the members of his crew, who would swear that they had paid the charges of their own transportation, and were, therefore, entitled to the headright. It was said by one familiar with the conditions in Virginia during this century that, for every individual brought in, not less than 200 acres was often allotted. The shipmaster obtained fifty acres for conveying him oversea; the merchant, fifty acres for purchasing his time of service after his arrival; the buyer from the merchant, a third fifty acres; and a purchaser of a half interest in the servant from this last buyer, a fourth fifty acres.

Even worse perversions of the headright than this were to be found in still other devices. The patent, for instance, was sometimes granted on the basis of a long list of names copied by the patentee from the county record books. A further fraudulent step was taken when the clerks in the office of the Secretary of State, imitating this example, sold lists of their own selection for the sum of five shillings for each name that was included. Towards the end of the century, the custom had crept in of purchasing a patent by simply paying a general fee in the Secretary of State's office. There was no legal warrant for this disregard of the law of headright, but it seems to have been permitted without any criticism.

As a matter of fact, excellent as the law of headright was, when fairly enforced, it was, under some circumstances, an impediment. It happened very often that a planter in possession of a considerable estate, was in need of a wider area for the use of his cattle, which, as a rule, found their own subsistence during the winter and summer months alike. To be compelled to purchase twenty indentured servants, for instance, in order to acquire an additional 1,000 acres, would be no hardship if these servants were bought to till the land, since their work in the ground would make an ample return for what they had cost; but to purchase these twenty servants when the only object was to enlarge the bounds of the plantation's forest land, which would, thereby, produce no more income than it had done before, would necessarily impose the burden of a considerable outlay, without any proportionate advantage to occur from it. It was in such a case as this, no doubt, that the violation of the law of headright was most frequently connived at.

When a certificate of such right had been obtained from the secretary's office, the next step was to carry it to the surveyor who had been chosen to run the lines for the tract selected by the owner of the document. This surveyor had been commissioned by the surveyor-general or by the College of William and Mary. Many of these men were of the first consequence for rank and integrity in the life of the colony, but others were either ignorant of their profession, or unscrupulous in their performance of its duties. This was the real reason for the confusion so often occasioned by overlapping patents.

In order to cure some of the defects of the original surveys, the General Assembly passed a law requiring every person resid-

ing in each neighborhood to assemble at least once in the course of every four years to march in a body to inspect the boundary landmarks of each plantation situated in that precinct; and should these landmarks have been removed, or fallen in decay, their replacement or renewal was to be undertaken at once. If a dispute arose between two owners of adjacent plantations about some apparent conflict of lines, then these lines were to be run a second time by the surveyor who always accompanied the processioners.

When the original survey of the boundaries of a patent had been completed, it was formally platted and the document returned to the office of the secretary of the colony, where it was recorded. With the plat in hand giving him the boundaries of the new plantation, the clerk, for a stated fee, drafted the patent and delivered it to the governor to be signed. This having been done, the seal was attached to it. At one time, no fee was required for this act, but, during Howard's administration, one of some importance was imposed. This was afterwards dropped, owing to the indignant opposition which it excited.

Having obtained a patent to his new plantation, the owner was required to perform two conditions in order to assure the permanency of his title—first, he had to "seat" his land, to use the technical phrase of the time; and secondly, he must pay an annual quit-rent to the king, or to any consignee whom the king should name.

A legal seating was effected without any serious sacrifice of money. It was deemed sufficient should the owner of the land have erected a frail cabin of small dimensions on its surface; have allowed a few cattle to browse for a year about its woods; or have cleared a small extent of forest and planted it in maize or tobacco. As a rule, however, the new plantation was occupied at once; a substantial house was constructed on it, with the necessary outbuildings; fences were put up to restrain the wanderings of the cattle; and a large area was brought under the hoe and plough for the production of the usual crops. If the patentee failed to take any step to fulfill the conditions indispensable for a permanent holding, he was considered to have forfeited the estate.

The quit-rent was payable to the treasurer of the colony, who had been designated by the king to receive it. It amounted to one shilling for every fifty acres; and, annually, became due at Michaelmas.

There was a feeling of strong popular opposition to this tax as it seemed to be a curtailment of full ownership of the land. During long periods, it was evaded to a very grave degree, in spite of the complaint and interference of the royal governors. At first, an effort was made to collect it in coin, but owing to the scarcity of metallic money in Virginia, this resulted in gradual failure, and tobacco came to take its place at the time set for payment. On more than one occasion, however, the old law was revived, but even in face of the fact that the English government was behind it, its enforcement was generally admitted to be almost impracticable. After 1688, the quit-rents were paid in tobacco alone, at a valuation of the leaf that did not exceed one penny a pound.

The tobacco for the quit-rents was gathered up by the sheriff of each county and delivered to the auditor of the Colony. This official sold it chiefly to the members of the council, who paid for it in the form of coin or bills of exchange on England. This money remained in the auditor's hands, and was disbursed ultimately on warrants from the governor, drawn in obedience to instructions received from the English authorities over sea. Sometimes the quit-rents were used for the support of the colonial government; sometimes for the restoration of the local defenses; and sometimes for the assistance of the new College of William and Mary.

When the entire Colony was granted by the second Charles to his favorites, Culpeper and Arlington, the quit-rents were included in the gift, but after the revocation of that gift, they were turned over again to their original purpose.

It is in harmony with what was to be expected to find that the area of land which had fallen back to the king, after it had been patented, was very extensive. The reversion occurred in every case in which the same land had, for this reason, been forfeited as often as two, and even three times. A plantation once seated—even though the cabin erected had rotted down, even though, too, the acre once cleared had grown up in wood again and the cattle that once roamed about it had been dispersed—could not be brought into the category of deserted ground. In the cases in which the patentee failed to prove that he had really complied with the law as to seating, he was not deprived of the ability, through his headrights, to obtain another proportionate grant of land. This could be patented elsewhere.

No doubt, many patentees, after acquiring title to a definite extent of the soil, found, in further inspection, before seating it, that it was devoid of fertility or such other advantages as it had been supposed to possess. Under these circumstances, he was perfectly willing to allow the title to lapse to the king. Had the same grant been obtained by purchase, as in later times, there would have been no conditions to fulfill, and he could not have escaped the consequences of his original defective judgment.

There was one temptation that influenced many persons to patent land, seat it as the law required, and then desert it. This temptation lay in the fact that a custom had sprung up which relieved the holder of such a grant of the payment of quit-rents, should there be no personal property on the land to become an object of distraint. The only impediment to the repetition of this subterfuge was, that, in time, it might grow difficult to prove that such a plantation had ever really been seated. Such a question might easily have arisen should some other person —thinking naturally enough, after the inspection of the deserted land, that it had never before been patented—have taken steps under the influence of this impression, to acquire title to it in the usual way. The original owner was then expected to come forward to show his superior right, and if he was able to do this, the petitioner for the second patent was compelled to withdraw his application.

In the aggregate, a large body of land reverted to the king from the failure of heirs, when the last heir had left no will. It was the rule at one time to give the preference to the person who established himself first upon any tract which had thus escheated. A different regulation was afterwards adopted—so soon as a tract fell in, the escheator of the county in which it was situated, summoned a jury of twelve men to take an inquest, and a certificate of the inquest thus taken was returned to the office of the secretary of state. Here the document was held for a period of nine months. In the meanwhile, the governor had selected from among the petitioners the person to whom the new patent was to be issued, in case no one appeared with proof that he was the lawful heir of the original owner, who had died intestate, and supposedly without any one who could rightly claim by blood possession of his estate.

It was one of the numerous perversions connected with land titles during the seventeenth century, that, in time, the mere certificate of inquest served the purpose of giving title as fully as if a second patent had been granted. The patent fee was thus evaded, but, as formerly, it was still necessary to pay a fine of composition of two pounds of tobacco an acre.

Another perversion still more commonly in use was for the administrator of an intestate estate to convey title in case of its sale as a whole or any part of it by him, just as absolutely as if he owned the property in his own right. In this way, the law applicable to an escheated estate was rendered nugatory so far as that law related to the principal charges imposed on such estates. So numerous in time grew instances of this kind, that an act was passed by the General Assembly requiring the enumeration of all such estates then in existence, and compelling the persons in possession of them to pay two hundred pounds of tobacco for every forty acres thus held illegally by them. If the petition for a clear title was not entered in the office of the secretary of state, within two years—afterwards reduced to eight months—then the right of tenure ceased altogether.

In 1661, that part of Virginia known as the Northern Neck was bestowed by the king on Lord Culpeper and six other English noblemen. In 1669, their patent was revoked, and another grant was made in its stead. By 1688, the whole of the Northern Neck had become the property of the second Lord Culpeper.

In the sales of the land situated within these boundaries, the representative of the absentee proprietary was impowered to give title just as fully as the governor and council of Virginia were empowered, as representatives of the king, to give title by patent to grantees in the rest of Virginia.

In the deeds to the soil of the Northern Neck, a quit-rent of two shillings was reserved upon every two hundred acres conveyed. If these two shillings remained unpaid for a period of three years, the proprietary possessed the right to reenter the forfeited tract. There was no provision in the law applicable to grants by him or his agent which allowed every one who brought in an immigrant an area of fifty acres.

The system of acquiring title to land in the Northern Neck was based upon purchase alone. No interest seems to have been felt by the proprietary in the increase of the population residing within those boundaries. His rule of selling the soil for money, regardless of whether it was to be seated or not, led to great abuses of engrossment. Enormous tracts of land in that part of Virginia fell into the hands either of small associations of purchasers or single individuals. William Fitzhugh acquired possession of nearly twenty thousand acres in one tract; and he negotiated on one occasion for the purchase of one hundred thousand acres more, on condition of making himself liable for the payment of their quit-rents for a period of ten years. A natural consequence of this system of purchase without any provision for seating, was that a larger area of land in the

Northern Neck remained unoccupied after it was patented than was to be observed in any other part of the colony.

Originally, all deeds of secondary conveyance in Virginia at large were required to be recorded at Jamestown. After 1623, they could be entered with the clerks of Charles City and Elizabeth City. Subsequently, when the shires were erected, provision was made for recordation of all deeds to lands belonging to a county in the clerk's office of that county. This rule was an advance on the system which prevailed in England at this time, where all documents relating to title were subject to many distinctive vicissitudes because kept in the hands of the families to whom they belonged.

CHAPTER II

INDENTURED SERVANTS

Having obtained a clear title to the land which he had patented, how did the new owner bring its soil under tillage? This was effected by means of the persons who had been the basis of the headrights which had assured his grant. In these headrights, the entire membership of his own family had been included—his wife and children, if he had had any, and also such laborers as he had already imported. If he was a man of humble rank, he would quite certainly look to himself chiefly for the performance of the principal work to be done in his fields, but, if he was a man of considerable pecuniary resources, the regular laborers in the list of his headrights would be sufficient in number to afford him all the aid which he would need in producing his crops of maize and tobacco, and caring for his livestock.

We have already described, at some length, the influences which impelled persons belonging to the English higher classes to immigrate to Virginia. What were the influences that moved the members of the English lowest class to imitate their example? There were two governing their action. The one was in operation in England; the other was in operation in Virginia; and the two were equally powerful, though essentially different in character.

After the reign of Elizabeth, the situation of the persons in England who obtained their livelihood by the use of their hands had not been one of advantage for all. By an act passed in the time of that sovereign, the individuals who wished to engage in

99

Princess Elizabeth

some one of the arts or trades had first to pass through a regulated apprenticeship; but as there was room only for a few in these special provinces, the great majority of the people were constrained to turn to digging and ploughing in the fields in order to earn a subsistence. For this labor, they were paid a definite sum, which had been fixed by the justices of the local magistrate's court. There were many years in which these wages were insufficient to purchase all the food which they really required, owing to the rise in the price of wheat. It followed that, in these years, a great number of people were forced to turn to public alms for a support.

Under an Elizabethan statute, provision had been made for regular assessments for the benefit of the indigent, but this law was not strictly enforced, in consequence of the burden which it laid on the taxpayers. By 1622, there had arisen such a multitude of impoverished people wandering about the country in search of the employment which could not be found, that the different English parishes, acting each in its own defense, adopted regulations which prevented the intrusion of the poor from the other parishes, should these poor be unable to give security against their becoming a burden on the public. As a direct result of this rule, the mass of the agricultural laborers and artisans of England, during the seventeenth century, were confined to their respective native parishes, however limited may have been their opportunities there of securing employment by which to live.

Only in prosperous years were the wages considerable enough to assure a support without a general public tax to make good a deficiency. It has been estimated that, in the interval between 1600 and 1700, while the wages of the agricultural laborer increased only three shillings by the week, the price of a quarter of wheat advanced from nineteen shillings to about forty-one shillings. Fortunate, but rare, indeed, was the laborer who was able, by extreme frugality, to lay up a small competence against the arrival of old age.

Was it strange, in the light of these conditions, which prevailed universally in England among the members of this class, that so many of them were eager to enter into indentures that would authorize their employers to carry them oversea to till the fields in Virginia? Was it at all singular that the authorities of the English parishes should have been equally eager to diminish their eleemosynary taxes by promoting the emigration of at least a part of their agricultural population to that colony?

This condition of impoverishment was not limited to the common people who dwelt in the country. The number of the indigent was even larger within the precincts of London. In 1622 it was stated by Rev. Mr. Copeland, a distinguished clergyman of that day, "that he had often to listen to the tearful complaints of industrious laborers in that town, who declared that, although they, their wives, and children, rose at an early hour and wore away their flesh throughout the day in the performance of the most exacting tasks, went to bed late, and fed upon brown bread and cheese, yet it was with difficulty that they could secure food enough to appease their hunger or clothing sufficient to hide their nakedness."

A similar state of want was observed in all the towns of England. In 1615, Sheffield, which was a typical English community in this respect, was forced to provide, by private and public charity, for the support in part or altogether, of seven hundred and twenty-five persons in its population of two thousand two hundred and seven. It was stated in an official survey of this city, made in the course of that year, that so narrow was the margin of livelihood that a week's sickness suffered by the head of the household would bring his family to the edge of absolute beggary.

Not only did the separate parishes encourage the emigration of those of their inhabitants who were without permanent means of subsistence, but the statesmen of that age also gave the same movement their earnest backing. It was thought by them that there was no immediate prospect of England's wealth increasing to such a degree that ample occupation would be created for the idle and the indigent. In reaching this conclusion, they were proved by time to be right, for it was not until the rise of the factory system in the nineteenth century, in consequence of the use of steam, that the hands of thousands, who, during the previous periods, had failed to find work, became so busy that the lower population grew in numbers to a degree never before either actually known or imagined.

One of the most important reasons for the colonization of Virginia, as we mentioned in our first chapter, was the expectation that it would offer a certain solution for this alarming problem of a surplus population in both town and county. It was not members of the criminal class whom parish and statesmen alike were anxious to remove, so much as the members of the class who were willing enough to work, but lacking the opportunity, had become a burden on the community, with a tendency —the result of their situation alone—to merge into the criminal class themselves.

But there was an additional reason, in the eyes of the English authorities, why the emigration of the surplus English inhabitant should be stimulated; and this reason, we may point out, was strongest during the early years of the settlement of Virginia. If the colony was to supply the mother country with all those commodities which the latter was importing at heavy expense and with irksome inconvenience from the continent of Europe, the volume in which these commodities would be sent to England would be in proportion to the number of workingmen in the Virginian fields and forests. Increase that number by depleting the English parishes, and so much the greater would be the size of the shipments from the Virginian plantations.

Just as there were powerful influences operating in England to promote the emigration of English workingmen, so there were equally powerful inducements existing in Virginia to draw them to its different communities. All the persons who knew the conditions that prevailed in the colony were unanimous in thinking that labor alone was dear there. This was as true of the last years of the seventeenth century as it was of the first years. As late as 1680, Governor Culpeper gave this fact as his reason for dispairing of the production of silk in Virginia.

While it was certainly true that there were thousands of families whose own members supplied all the persons needed by them in working their small plantations, there were also other thousands who were eager to obtain the aid of indentured servants. The peculiarities of tobacco culture chiefly explains this fact. In that age, there were no artificial manures which could be used to restore the richness of soil that had been exhausted by prolonged tillage. The only way of securing the fertility required for the profitable production of tobacco was to open up new grounds, either on the original plantation, or on a supplementary one recently patented in order to attain this very purpose. This new surface was certain to be fine in quality, and for that reason to be covered with a large growth of timber. The destruction of the woods went on interminably, and this was the most exacting task which had to be carried out by the owner of every plantation. How could it be hastened? By the acquisition of additional hands to assist him. But how could these additional hands be secured? By the purchase of indentured servants from the merchants, who had brought them in for sale like so many bundles or packages of goods.

The larger the area of a plantation, whether it had been just acquired by patent or had been in the owner's possession during many years, the more acute was the need of laborers to open it up to cultivation at the start, or afterwards to extend the ground fitted for tillage. The most fertile soil was what every prospective patentee sought. Where was this to be found? Along the banks of the important streams; but it was the very land thus situated which brought forth the most enormous growth of trees, necessarily the most difficult and expensive of all to remove. Probably no virgin country outside of the tropics was ever clothed in such magnificent timber as that which lay, at the time of the first exploration, on either side of the Powhatan, Nansemond, Pamunkey, Pyankitank, and Rappahannock rivers and their principal tributaries. All this had to be removed before a hoe or a plough could be used to prepare the ground for maize or tobacco.

Another reason also for the patenting of these river lands, in spite of the greater labor required to clear them of their original growth, was the fact that the streams watering them, being navigable for ocean going vessels, furnished a channel at the planter's front door for the transportation of his crops directly to England, and in turn for the transportation of goods from England to his private wharf.

It has been correctly said that, had no indentured servants been procurable from the mother country in the seventeenth century, Virginia would have remained indefinitely a community made up of peasant proprietors alone. It is true that the necessity of opening up new fields would have continued from decade to decade, but this necessity could have been met by these peasant proprietors restricting their clearings to such small areas as they, by their own hands, would have been perfectly able to prepare for crops. But instead of there being a dearth of workingmen ready to bind themselves for a term, England offered, in the members of her lowest class, a supply of laborers which, not only the laborers themselves, but also the English parish authorities and responsible statesmen, were anxious to furnish the colony to the fullest extent of its need. And there were ample means of transportation for this class of emigrants. Indeed, every condition then in existence, whether involving the interests of England at large, or the emigrants themselves, or of the colony, encouraged the departure of that class from their native shores and their settlement on the plantations oversea.

In the beginning, all the agricultural servants who came in belonged to the London Company. From the time of the First Supply, every ship that crossed the Atlantic to Jamestown carried over a considerable number of laborers for the fields; and none of these were freed without restrictions until Dale, leaving for England, had turned the government over to his chosen successor, Captain Yeardley. The only benefits conferred on these laborers by the company, during their service, were food, clothes, and lodging; but after the termination of their articles of indenture, a certain interest in the soil was bestowed on them on condition of their continued performance of definite manual tasks.

By 1617-1619, the great associations known as Hundreds had begun to import agricultural servants in large numbers for the purpose of cultivating some part of their extensive tracts of

AUTOGRAPH OF SIR GEORGE YEARDLEY

land. This was also done by persons of means, who could defray all the charges for transportation.

To what extent did the servants brought over in the time of the company belong to the more or less vicious class which were then to be found in every English parish? This class, it should be recalled, was made up chiefly, not of hardened felons, but of the idle and dispairing elements of the community. Was the London Company willing to accept persons utterly depraved? The authors of the early pamphlets relating to colonization were unanimous in urging that only persons of good character should be dispatched to Virginia to till the land. The wisdom of such a policy was obvious, and it was only with extraordinary precautions that the company admitted for this purpose men, women, and youths whom the English local authorities were anxious to get rid of, not only because they were a burden on the financial resources of their respective communities through their helplessness, but what was, perhaps, still more objectionable, because they were supposed to be, by their poverty, the principal originators of the epidemics of disease which so often swept through the English towns and rural neighborhoods of that early date, decimating all classes of people as they passed.

The extreme care exercised by the company in picking out the best individuals of such antecedents when offered was shown by the advantages which that body promised to give them after they had settled in Virginia and passed through a term of service; namely "a house, orchard, and garden for the meanest family, and a possession of lands to them and their posterity." It is not probable that such benefits as these would have been bestowed on a set of people who were notoriously depraved. Indeed, the company later on went so far as to announce that it would accept "only those who were trained in the useful callings" such as it had already specified. "Nothing but damage to the welfare of the colony," it was declared, "would result from granting permission to parents to send their licentious sons to Virginia, or to wives, their shameless husbands, or to masters, their ungovernable servants."

It was not inconsistent with this attitude of discriminating prudence for the company to consent to receive men and women, who, without any avoidable fault of their own, had become dependent on the poor rates of their respective parishes. Nor did that body consider that there was any insurmountable objection to accepting children who had been offered by the mayors of London and other cities for transportation, after providing five pounds sterling—equal to at least one hundred dollars in our modern values—for the equipment and conveyance charges of each one. The company itself, on its part, agreed to educate them all in trades or professions. At first, each of these youths was to remain in service for a definite term, and after its expiration, he was to be granted a patent to fifty acres of land, and provided with a cow, seedcorn, implements, utensils, and a gun and ammunition.

The company's determination to keep out of Virginia all persons who could be truthfully described as criminals was unbroken from the beginning to the end of its existence. Its rigid supervision was extended even to the passenger lists of private vessels. If a genuine felon did enter the gate of the colony, there were mitigating circumstances surrounding his case, or powerful family influences had been at work in his favor, in the hope that a transfer oversea would lead to his reform; or he was a skilful mechanic, who would be useful to the plantations, either with his own hands, or by training apprentices.

How bitter was the feeling of opposition in Virginia in 1619 to the introduction of criminals, was shown there by the impediments thrown in the way of receiving certain "dissolute" persons from Bridewell in London, whom the king had recommended to be transported. And that the like impediments were raised, and successfully, too, in all similar cases at a later day is to be inferred from the fact that, of three hundred and ninety-two servants in Virginia whose ages are stated in the census of 1624-1625, the average age was only twenty-three. One hundred and fifty-four had not reached their twenty-first birthday. There were only thirteen whose respective ages equalled or exceeded forty. It is not at all probable that, in this body of indentured or apprenticed servants of such youthful years, there were any individuals who could have been justly taken as belonging to the category of real criminals.

The hostility to the introduction of felons was as vigorous and resolute after the revocation of the charter in 1624 as it had been before that event. It was symptomatic of this inimical attitude, that, in 1632, two pregnant maids, who had recently arrived in the colony, were sent back on the first ship returning to England. It should be remembered that, in these times, there were three hundred offenses, which, on conviction, were punishable by death. Some of these offenses were so trivial that even the more or less indurated consciences of the judges of that period shrank from inflicting the capital penalty. These men compromised with their merciless and distorted sense of justice by passing a sentence of transportation instead.

It is doubtful whether, during the long interval, between 1625 and 1650, a single convict was imported into Virginia whose crime would not, in our age, be considered to be a mere misdemeanor, or at least softened by circumstances. But the people of the colony were not disposed to make any allowance for this fact. As late as 1667, when eighteen felons were sent out from English prisons, a loud protest was raised; and under the influence of the like feeling, the General Court in 1671 expressly prohibited the further introduction of English criminals into the colony. This was in obedience to the royal order of the previous spring, which forbade the further importation to any of the colonies of the inmates of English jails.

Apart from the objection to such an element in the population from social and political points of view, there was the objection based on the apprehension that such felons might combine—as certain old soldiers of Cromwell had done in Gloucester County in 1663—and start out on a bloody excursion. This was one of the reasons back of the General Court's action when it was found, in 1671, that a prominent merchant had violated the requirements of that court's order by bringing in ten jail birds. He was placed under bond to carry them away before the end of two months; and to make certain his doing so, his bondsmen were enjoined to give security in the enormous sum of one million pounds of tobacco.

A very large proportion, if not the largest proportion, of the servants brought into Virginia, during the seventeenth century, as a punishment for offenses committed in England, were men who had been implicated in rebellious movements there. They were Irishmen who had been conquered by Cromwell while defending their country and firesides from ruthless invasion. They were Scotchmen or Englishmen, who had only too much reason to resist the cruel measures of the Stuart kings after the Restoration. When Droghada fell in 1649, every officer among the defenders was shot, every tenth soldier in the rank and file executed, and the remainder shipped away to the American plantations. It is said that not less than sixteen hundred of the followers of Charles II in the Battle of Worcester were transported oversea after their sale to merchants engaged in the Virginia trade.

In 1678, when the insurrection in Scotland had been finally quelled, a large number of the offenders were consigned to the same remote destination; and this was also done after Monmouth's defeat at Sedgemoor. There was no really criminal element in these large batches of immigrants. On the contrary, they numbered among themselves hundreds, if not thousands, of men of good education, patriotic fervor, and high and resolute character.

Not all the servants who were landed in Virginia had been sent out in accord with the strict regulations of England relating to that class. In the principal towns from which the vessels transporting them sailed, there were numerous miscreants of both sexes who earned a revolting subsistence by slyly drawing idle boys and girls from the streets into the nets of their houses, where they altered their appearance, and, perhaps, even drugged them into half consciousness, and afterwards took them to the cookshops, where bands of servants were collected for sale to more or less unscrupulous merchants or sea-captains, who were supplying labor to the plantations in Virginia. What a large proportion of the passengers on the outgoing vessels belonged to the list of kidnapped was revealed in the number of persons in that category who were found on board of a vessel sailing from London in 1657. There were nineteen servants in all; and of these, twelve had been obtained by illegal means. One had been enticed into the ship by the pretense that it was a lodging house; another, by a promise of employment in Virginia, which was represented to be as near to London as Gravesend; while a third had accompanied on board a soldier, who had sold her to the ship captain in the teeth of her protests. The rest appear to have been youths who had been caught up and disposed of against their will.

There were many instances of parents seeking to recover their children either from the cookshops or from the vessels that were going to bear them away forever from the scenes of their early lives.

In spite of the vigorous and persistent efforts that were put forth to suppress the so-called "spirits," who were engaged in this atrocious business of abduction, they continued to flourish in a subterranean way. Among the most notorious persons residing near the wharves of London, Bristol, and other ports, were women who had been often arrested for committing or attempting to commit, this crime. No witch in those superstitious times was the object of more deadly fear, or was regarded with deeper loathing, than these female "spirits" of mature years, who lurked about, with the shadow of their evil intentions only half veiled in the expression of their faces.

But it was not always necessary for them to have recourse to force, half hidden or not, to secure their victims. There were in the English ports so many impoverished and despairing people of a suitable age that they were only too ready to listen to the seductive picture which a "spirit" drew of the advantages of Virginia, and follow her on board of the first ship known to be starting for the colony. And, no doubt, too, the mere prospect of adventure made many young men who led a precarious life on the streets, turn a consenting ear to the same alluring voice. The temptation to go was still stronger in the hearts of those who were afraid of falling into the clutches of the law on account of some dark crime or small misdemeanor which they had committed.

However heinous the act of the "spirit" in carrying off to the cookshops or the sailing ships children who had been gathered up from the streets against their will, or however venal their motives in persuading indigent young men and women to emigrate, there is reason to think the ultimate effect on the fortunes of these persons, who were so unhappy in their native situation, was most beneficial on the whole for the great majority of them. It is true that all, after arriving in Virginia, would have to run the gauntlet of the period of "seasoning," which was certain to prove fatal to a considerable number. But after this period had terminated, the survivors would find themselves in the atmosphere of the open field, instead of being confined to the foul precincts of English alleys. They would be sheltered by well built cabins, instead of having to sleep in cellars and rookeries; and they would receive daily an ample amount of wholesome food in place of the precarious crusts of bread and wormy scraps of meat which they had been accustomed to in their native haunts.

After the service of their terms was ended, it was in their power either to hire themselves again to some planter or to acquire a patent to fifty acres of their own.

There were numerous offices, legitimately established and legally administered, where any one who wished to go out to Virginia under articles of indenture was sure of an encouraging reception and a scrupulous regard for all his rights. It was with these offices that the merchants principally dealt. Naturally, the great majority of those engaged in the tobacco trade with Virginia were disposed to be cautious in choosing servants for transportation, and especially opposed to obtaining them from the "spirits." This was not only because the character of the persons coming to them from that source were open to censure, but also because they were likely, at any time, to demand their release, on the ground that they had been inveigled into the promise to sign their articles of indenture against their will.

It was through the merchants' influence that the office of register was created. It was the register's duty to keep a record of the names, ages, and places of birth and residence of every person who had announced his intention of going out to the

American colonies to do the work of an indentured servant; and a certificate signed by such person to the effect that his emigration was entirely voluntary was also required and preserved. This new agency did not prove to be very successful in suppressing the "spirits," and this fact led to a law of Parliament which provided that death should be inflicted upon every one of this class who should be found guilty of carrying on that nefarious business.   And yet so ineffective was this law, that, not many years after its passage, it was calculated that not less than ten thousand individuals of different ages were "spirited" away annually to the colonies through the instrumentality of the kidnappers.

CHAPTER III

INDENTURED SERVANTS—Continued

What were the mutual obligations assumed by the master and his servant in signing the ordinary indenture? The only difference between the indenture drafted in England and the one drafted in Virginia was, that the master in England became responsible for all the charges for the servant's transportation to the colony. As a rule, the first master was an English merchant, who was either sending laborers to the plantations for sale, or was going over himself, in the company of men and women bound to him whom he intended to put to work on lands owned by himself there. If his object was to sell in the colony the servants whom he had purchased in England, then, when the time came to dispose of them, all that he was called on to do was to transfer their indentures to the new purchaser, and in the bargain recoup himself for the transportation charges. The other provisions, which had laid down the extent of his obligations to these servants, then became a part of the new master's liability. There was no alteration whatever in the responsibilities of the servants themselves.

Independently of the expense of transportation, which only arose if the indenture had been drafted in England, the master agreed to furnish the servant with food, clothing, and drink while his term lasted; to shelter him fully from the weather; to take proper care of him in case of sickness; and to treat him kindly and humanely under all circumstances. In many cases, the master bound himself to teach the servant the art of tobacco culture.

114

Sometimes, the servant was able, before signing the indenture, to obtain better terms than these, but this depended on his possessing a special influence with the master. It was of advantage to him, for instance, to be granted the right to pick out with care the new master to whom he expected to be sold after his arrival in Virginia. This privilege was frequently allowed him in case he had shown himself to be superior in character or skill to the average laborer. He might also prescribe, with his master's consent, of course, the exact amount of tobacco which he should be required to produce in the span of a single year. On the other hand, his master might demand that a sentence of several additional years of work should be imposed on him for failure to be present in the harvest fields in August and September, unless the cause of his absence was unavoidable.

What was the average length of the servant's term? If he had entered into service without a written contract with his master, he was required to continue in it for a period of four years, should his age exceed twenty-one; but, on the other hand, should his age fall below twenty, he was to continue in it for five years; and if below twelve, seven. The length of the time in all these cases was later on considerably increased.

In every instance in which the servant was under twenty-one and without indenture, he had to be brought into court to have his age inquired into, and finally decided. The rule that was adopted in the end was to the following effect: if the servant without indenture was still under nineteen years of age, his connection with his master was to terminate when he had arrived at his twenty-fourth year. If he was over nineteen, he was to remain a servant for a period of five years. This was called indenture by the custom of the country, and it was pertinent to all who could not show that they had originally bound themselves by formal written covenants.

All the evidences pointed to the humane treatment of the servants by their masters. This was not only the natural course to pursue, but also the politic course. It was especially observable in the time of the Company, which organization kept up a close supervision over every branch of the Colony's interests, whether private or public. During that period,—when, owing to the small size of the population, and its greater concentration than later on, his oversight could be more easily exercised, —strict regulations were in force to assure the good quality and the sufficiency of the food which was supplied to the servants. It was expected that he should receive for his daily meals an ample quantity of hominy, fish, and beef; in most cases, boiled in a single mess. Doubtless, vegetables of the common varieties were also furnished, for these were raised in the soil of the Colony in extraordinary abundance.

There was also a full supply of bread made of the meal of maize. Fifteen cans of this meal were allowed for each period of seven days. This allowance seems liberal enough in comparison with that wretched scantiness of victuals from which even the most industrious working people in London and other England cities suffered at this time. The most generous repast ever enjoyed by members of this class consisted of milk, cheese, eggs and bacon. That the substantial character of the servant's food in the Company's time did not fall off after the recall of the charter was indicated by the custom which prevailed, apparently everywhere, under which a supply of wholesome meat was allowed every servant by the week. The provision for clothing was equally substantial.

If, in any case, a servant had just reason to think that he had not been provided by his master with the food, clothing, and lodging, to which he was entitled, it was only necessary for him to make complaint to the nearest magistrate's court. And this was his right also should he have been the victim of harsh treatment. In every case of these several kinds, the master was summoned to defend his conduct; and if neglect of his obligations to his servant should be proved, he was ordered to correct it, under severe penalty for a failure to comply. It sometimes happened, that, should the master disclose by his acts the possession of a rough and cruel disposition, he was commanded to release the servant from his indenture; and was even enjoined from employing another to take his place.

At the beginning of the next century, there was in force a statute which expressly forbade a master from whipping his servant on his naked back. As there was an inclination on the part of some of the masters to delay calling in a physician when their servants were taken sick, because the medical charges at this time were so excessive, the General Assembly passed a law that imposed a heavy penalty on every practitioner who should formally demand a greater fee than the circumstances of the case really justified. Nor did that body stop at the mere physical protection of the servant,—as far as possible, it saw to his moral improvement by requiring his master to take steps to assure him religious instruction. If he had never received such instruction, he had to be sent away every Sunday to the parish church to be familiarized with the Lord's Prayer, the Catechism and the Ten Commandments by the clergyman occupying that pulpit.

It can be clearly perceived that the severest labor expected of the agricultural servant was not such as could be performed by a woman under indentures. The heaviest task was the removal of the original forest from the surface of the most fertile soil, which was usually situated in the low grounds along the rivers. Here, as already mentioned, the timber was always enormous in height and girth. The work of its destruction by the ax often looked so insuperable that the Indian method of clearing was adopted instead. This consisted of tearing away the bark of a tree near its foot in the fashion of a belt, by which means the annual flow of sap to the branches overhead was entirely cut off, and thus, in time, the vitality of both trunk and limb was completely extinguished. Throughout the Colony, even in these early years, fields of considerable area were seen with the ground planted in tobacco or maize, but interspersed with the gaunt forms of mighty oaks and poplars no longer able to cast a shadow, and thus impede the growth of the crops waving beneath them.

This manner of clearing new land could only be followed where the original growth was not massed to a noticeable extent. If the wood was somewhat of a jungle of trees, of a height and girth moderate in some and great in others, the belting was only possible for the large boles. The rest had to be cut away to prevent the intervention of two much shade. In nearly every case, therefore, the removal of the average forest was a task for men of the most stalwart type. Fortunately, its recurring performance was restricted to one part of the year.

When women had a share in agricultural work, it was in the planting of the tobacco in hill after hill; in the extraction of worms from the spreading leaf; and perhaps, in the gathering up of the cut stalks and in their carting to the barns for the process of curing by fire. They, doubtless, also took part in the dropping and covering up of the maize, and also in the grubbing of the weeds that sprang up between the rows. No doubt, too, they assisted in pulling off and shucking the ears in season, and also in harvesting the wheat. In a press of farm work, women of the best character were also put to the hoe, but, as a rule, the members of the sex who toiled in the fields were persons of the most ordinary kind, and not infrequently, of low sexual instincts in addition. Thrown there intimately as they were with the lowest class of male servants, their continence was often open to suspicion.

The most respectable division of the female servants were retained under their masters' roofs for the performance of domestic tasks. Before the introduction of negro slaves in large numbers, which did not occur until the end of the seventeenth century was nearly reached, the household service was chiefly thrown on these white women under indentures.

The hours of labor in the fields for both men and women were not excessive. It is true that in summer this period apparently extended over the long interval between the hour of sunrise and the hour of sunset, but during that interval, a suspension of work for five hours was permitted for rest and refreshment. The master was perfectly aware that exposure to the midday sun in August and September would almost certainly bring on an attack of malaria, which was the worst phase of the distemper to which so many old comers as well as new succumbed. Common prudence suggested to him to be considerate of his servant's health, rather than to press them too hard, under the mistaken impression that, in this way, the most was to be got out of them individually, and in the mass.

As the plantation grew in size, with a proportionate increase in the number of servants engaged in cultivating them, the need of overseers to assist the owners in the work of general superintendence became so imperative that a important set of men of that calling sprang up in the different communities. Ordinarily, a servant was chosen to act as headman, but the relation between the servants on the same plantation were so close, as a rule, and their interests so identical, that no one of them could always be trusted to constrain their fellows to put forth their full strength. This was best assured by the employment for this office of a person from the outside.

The position was one which required a variety of strong qualities to fill with success. In the first place, it was necessary that the occupant should be well versed in the art of cultivating tobacco. A mere smattering of knowledge about the process was soon detected by master and servant alike, and led only to contempt for his usefulness or his authority. In the next place, it was necessary that he should be both watchful and energetic. A lazy overseer was soon surrounded by an indolent band of workers, who, when he lounged away, were quite certain either to drop their hoes or to rest on them. Should he go to sleep under the nearest tree, they too were likely to seek a similar repose. But what was, perhaps, the most important of all the qualities with which he should be endowed was vigor, if not fierceness, of temper. Unless he was able thus to win the respect of his promiscuous gang from the start, he was not apt to do so before the end. He could only impress them by firmness and courage in his general bearing.

Among the persons under his supervision, there was always one or more who were desperate in character, or incorrigible in their worthlessness. Some of them were villains from the slums of England, whose influence on their fellow-servants was altogether bad; some were men of a naturally uncontrollable temper, when aroused, even by some slight cause of offense; some were congenitally callous and indifferent to the performance of every duty. These particular persons were representatives of different types of the England lowest class of that day, and here in the Virginian tobacco and maize fields, they were brought under the direction of a single overseer, who was expected and required to possess and to show from day to day the very qualities required for their control and management to the best advantage. Possibly, only a few of the overseers, unless young, were remarkable for so many valuable characteristics, since those in the possession of such traits were apt to have made independent headway by acquisition of plantations, however small, of their own.

It was not altogether the overseer's fault that absconding servants were so numerous. There were many influences at the bottom of this fact. As we have already mentioned, the great majority of the class were under twenty-five years of age; indeed a large proportion even of these had not yet reached their nineteenth birthday. This youthfulness was naturally promotive of a spirit of restlessness, thoughtlessness, and recklessness. An instinct of mere wantonness, apart from oppressive or irritating environment, alone prompted many to run away. In England, before they emigrated, they had, in many instances, been in the habit of leading idle and wandering lives, and to be tied down in the Colony, practically by force, to a fixed and exacting employment, was, in itself, a cause of discontent, which only grew more irksome the longer it had to be endured. In such cases as these, the disposition and conduct of the overseer played no part at all. Whether he was too lenient or too cruel, was not chiefly involved in the motives that shaped their action. Young men of this character and antecedents would, perhaps, have ultimately run away, even if they had not been subject to any restraint and discipline at all.

But there was a class of servants who were not influenced by mere restlessness to desert their plantations. These were the servants who found it impossible to stand a course of rough treatment by the overseer, especially if the master connived at it. It is true that this set of persons had, in the Mother Country, been accustomed to a hard condition of life, but, nevertheless they had there enjoyed a certain degree of independence of movement. To live in the Colony under the watchful eye of a merciless and ill-tempered taskmaster from the hour of twelve o'clock one day to the hour of twelve the next, was a harsh experience that made even the wild forests around them appear inviting in comparison; and the temptation, in consequence, to steal away under cover of night was, in the case of many of them, irresistible. Even encounters with wild beasts and the shadow of starvation were preferable to the burning sun and the falling lash.

But the disposition to abscond was not always due to either restlessness or the spirit of revolt against bad treatment. It was attributable somewhat to the fact that labor was so much in demand in the Colony, that unprincipled planters were led to entice away the servants of others to work in their fields, or to give them other employment, should they find them wandering along the public roads. As there was little passing to and fro between the remoter neighborhoods of the Colony, there was always a good chance that the presence of a servant who had accepted a new master before his original indentures had expired, would not be discovered. And whatever risk there was

of detection, both he and this new master were always ready
to take.

The General Assembly, alive to the complaints about such
conduct on the part of so many planters, endeavored to remove
the evil by statute. It was enacted that no one should be permitted to engage a servant apparently idling aimlessly about,
unless he could show a certificate of discharge from his last
master, countersigned by the chief military officer of the district in which he had formerly lived. If the planter gave him
employment in spite of the fact that the necessary certificate
had not been offered, he made himself liable to a penalty of
twenty pounds of tobacco for every night the servant was har-
bored under his roof.

So great was the pecuniary loss caused by the runaway that
the General Assembly thought itself justified in adopting a still
stricter law in order to put an end to it. Not only must every
vagrant of that character carry a legal discharge from his former master, but every person who had never been under indentures, must, when he sought employment, present a certificate
that he was an absolutely freeman. To forge such a certificate
under any circumstances, was taken to be a heinous violation of
law, and was punished with unusual severity.

The value of the servant's labor in both house and field was
so great that the masters of those who had run away were always
eager to recover them, and numerous as were the obstacles that
stood in the way of a successful pursuit, it was always pressed
with energy. The country was bisected by broad rivers, which,
when once crossed, raised in favor of the absconding servant a
barrier that at least delayed the advance of the master in his
track, and increased the runaway's chance of getting away entirely to some remote plantation near the frontier. In later
years, Maryland was the most popular asylum for these runaways, since once they landed on the north shore of the Potomac,
they were quickly swallowed up in the labyrinth of the widely
dispersed plantations.

The master had more than one reason for eagerly seeking to capture his runaway, and to bring him back to his former home. He not only thereby returned the man to his work in the field, but he also acquired the right to increase materially his length of service. If the servant had fled at a season of the year when the crops were not yet planted, the punishment inflicted on him for his flight was the doubling of his term. If, on the other hand, the crops had sprung up and were in need of daily attention, the punishment was raised to the point of almost trebling the term called for by the original indentures. And to make his predicament still worse, he was often compelled to recoup the master for all the expenses incurred in his pursuit. As it was rarely possible for him to pay such a sum, he was forced to substitute for it a further lengthening of his term of service.

It will be perceived, from the foregoing paragraphs, that the servant assumed the risk of heavy penalties when he ventured to run away from his master. It might mean virtual imprisonment for a long series of years, accompanied by hard and continuous labor. And to cause the sting to be sharper, it was not infrequently preceded by a sound lashing on the back at the whipping post set up within the precincts of every county courthouse to be found in the Colony.

It was perfectly consistent with the character of the servant's situation that he was not allowed to exercise any of the higher privileges of citizenship. It is true, as we have seen, that he had certain clearly defined rights, in the employment of which he was fully protected by the Courts; and he was also under just as much obligation to obey the law as if he were free of his indenture. Not even his master, as has been stated, could impinge upon what was due him as an individual. To murder, to rob, or to mistreat him in any way, was as great a crime or misdemeanor as if it were his master, and not himself, who was involved. But he could not vote; he could not hold office; he could not make any protest against harsh or unwise civic measures. In short, he had no existence from a political point of view.

It was only in a great emergency, which threatened the lives and the property of the whole community, that he was permitted to take a weapon in his hand; and even then, there was always a fear lest he should use it to cut the bonds of his own servitude. This attitude of distrust appears strange in the light of the fact that the servant himself knew that his term was not to be indefinite in its length, but, on the contrary, that it was to end on a day already fixed, when he was to leave the plantation of his former master as free as that master himself.

While his indenture continued, the servant was as much a piece of property as a bale of merchandise. He could be sold; he could be exchanged. If his master was in debt, he was as subject to the sheriff's distraint warrant as a horse in the stable or a cow in the pasture.

The servant's importance in the economic life of the community in which he lived was not restricted to his work in the tobacco lot or in the maize field. He constituted not only the headright which was accepted as the chief basis of the patent to land, but also the principal basis of taxation in the all important annual general and local levies. The question was: how many tithables were there in the parish, in the county, in the Colony? When this was ascertained by each of these divisions, each adopted a rate of its own that would assure the funds needed to pay their respective public expenses. It was the servants who appeared most conspicuously in these annual enumerations, and it was their strong arms that chiefly enabled the government of each of those separate civic entities to continue to operate.

Every female servant required to labor in the fields had to be returned by her master as a tithable; and also every youth who had passed his sixteenth year. If the servant was in the hand of the merchant who had bought him, but who had not yet put him to work, he was allowed to remain untaxed for a period of twelve months.

At the end of the servant's term, his freedom was assured by a formal ceremony. Accompanied by his master, or bearing the master's written testimonial that he was now free, he went to the courthouse of the county in which he had been living, and obtained from the county clerk a certificate that his indenture had expired, and that he was now at liberty to follow any employment which he preferred. It is quite possible that, in most instances, the former servant returned to the plantation from which he had just come, and entered the service of his old master as a laborer for hire. This was especially likely to have occurred if he had been kindly treated and all his rights strictly respected.

But whether the discharged servant went back to his former master, or not, there is little probability that he failed to claim the privilege to which, as a newly released servant, he was entitled by the provisions of the existing laws. What were these provisions? In the time of the Company, a grant of one hundred acres of land was made to him; and should he carry out the requirements as to seating, he was to be allowed a second grant of the same extent. After the Company was abolished, the servant apparently, at first, could make no claim to the customary fifty acres for a headright, and it was not until the middle, if not the latter, half of the century that there was adopted a definite regulation which assured him a personal interest to that degree in the soil.

It is easy to perceive that it was not to the advantage of the existing landowners that such a rule should have been in force, for if the former servant could not retire to his own small plantation thus acquired, he would be compelled to return to the employment of his old or a new master.

But there were certain benefits of which the released servant could not be deprived either before or after the adoption of the provision for granting him fifty acres. His former master was required to supply him with grain sufficient to afford him a subsistance for the period of one year. Ten bushels were considered necessary for this purpose. He had also to be supplied with two suits, a pair of trousers, two shirts and one felt hat. It was calculated that these different articles of clothing, would, in their purchase, call for an outlay of about ten pounds sterling.

No large proportion of the men who had worked at first under indentures in the Colony rose there afterwards to a position of wealth and importance, as indicated by the possession of land and a seat in the House of Burgesses. In some of the Assemblies, however, there were not infrequently several members of such antecedents, as in the Assembly for the year 1629, in which there were three; and for the year 1654, in which there were two. Many of the agricultural servants were young Englishmen of good social position, great energy, and some private means. They had signed indentures in order to obtain a knowledge of tobacco culture. There were others without pecuniary resources who had signed in order to earn a livelihood, but being shrewd and willing to work after their terms had expired, found no insuperable obstacle to stand in the way of their rising to financial independence, if not to actual wealth.

Some attained this desirable condition by accepting invitations to become overseers; some by renting plantations for their own tillage; some by earning a share of the crop as the reward for their labor; some by receiving high wages in compensation, for same, to be afterwards invested to advantage in lands and servants of their own. Those among the discharged servants, —and they made up the large majority,—who were lacking in intelligence, ambition, and energy, remained throughout the rest of their lives in the position of dependence and subordination in which they had begun.

CHAPTER IV

THE SLAVE

The fundamental reason that drew the English indentured servant to the tobacco fields of Virginia was equally at work in drawing the African slave. Only in the case of the servant was the introduction voluntary and the employment limited in time. In every instance, the negro arrived against his will, and could not look forward to a single day of freedom, however long he might survive. The same economic influence which had operated to bring him, a helpless bondsman, to the Colony, namely, the constant need of labor there, was even more inexorable in his case than in the case of the white man who wielded the hoe, or ran the plough, in the same field of tobacco or maize as himself. This was because there were certain advantages to his master which went along with his enslavement that did not accompany the servitude of the white man at his side.

These advantages can be summed up in the preliminary statement of two facts. First, he was a slave for life, unlike his white companion, who was simply a servant for a term of years of no extraordinary length. Second, having been born and reared in the hot climate of the Guinea Coast or the West Indies, he was not liable to pass through the period of "seasoning," which rendered the white servant useless for several months after his arrival, and exposed him, by the ill effects which it left behind, to a recurrence of sickness, though in a more moderate degree, so soon as each summer returned.

First, in the enlargement of the previous paragraph, what were the advantages of ownership in the negro for life? In the

127

first place, it relieved the planter of the necessity of looking forward to the day when the man or woman had to be replaced unless he or she was in such a state of health as threatened an early decease. One of the serious drawbacks to indentured servants was the recurring need of a substitute for each servant so soon as his term should expire. Another had to be purchased to take his place, and this signified a second outlay of money. During the time that the planter was reaping the benefit of the labor of one stalwart slave, it might have been imperative for him to buy not less than five, or even more, white servants in succession, to fill the vacated position of the last in the descending list. Here was an expenditure of funds large enough to make up a sum sufficient for the acquisition of several slaves.

Besides this expenditure, the planter was certain to lose at the end of each of these successive servants' terms a man who had reached the height of his skilfulness in planting, tending, and harvesting the crops. The person taking his place had to be trained in his turn, and in his turn, he was lost when most experienced. On the other hand, each year found the slave more expert, without any danger of this wider knowledge being withdrawn from the planter's use. Only the encroachments of old age would reduce his value, and even in his decrepitude he could act the part of a watchman.

There was another advantage which the average slave offered. As we have pointed out, the most exacting task which the plantation hands had to perform was the removal of the heavy growth of timber in the new grounds, in order to provide area for the opening up of new lots for tobacco culture. The negro was more robust than the white man. He was more capable of enduring severe labor, and for a longer time. Under supervision, he would cut away the enormous trees at a more lively rate; and in the tobacco lot, if not superior to an indentured servant in activity, he was apt to be superior to him in skill, because his experience in handling the plant had probably been more prolonged.

Another advantage which the slave offered lay in the fact that he was more cheerful in disposition, and more tractable in temper, than the average white servant. This seems the more remarkable when it is remembered that he had probably grown up in an African community where there was neither law nor order observed, and where the life of a human being was of no more importance than the life of a vagrant dog. In his new situation, on the other hand, he was at least protected from the spears of his enemies, and could sleep at night without fear of being carried off to be dished up for a cannibal feast. The contrast may have increased his contentment. Doubtless, in his native country he had been compelled to do part of the communal labor, and work was not, therefore, an irksome task because it daily recurred in his new environment.

The slave was a child of the sun, resigned to his lot, and trusting to sensual pleasures for happiness in the intervals of his absence from the field. There were, of course, individual slaves who were sullen in temper and truculent in spirit, and conspiracies led by one of this nature were not unknown; but, in the mass, the members of the race were easily controlled, and their cheerfulness was spontaneous and instinctive, in spite of the apparent cruelty of their general situation. Thrown together—in many cases, for the length of a life time—the relation between master and slave was more sympathetic than the relation between master and indentured servant.

Among the other advantages arising from the possession of slaves was the fact that it was not difficult to supply them with acceptable food. They did not need the quality or the variety which alone would satisfy the indentured servant, whether it was allowed him or not. They were content with a simpler and coarser fare. It is doubtful whether the average indentured servant ever became fully reconciled to the use of maize bread in

10—Vol. I.

the place of the wheat bread to which he had been accustomed in the mother country, before he immigrated to the colony.

There was still another advantage and one equal in value even to the greater cheapness of providing food for the slave. This was the absence of any obligation to furnish him with the outfit required in every indentured servant's case on the expiration of his term. It is true that the slaves had to be supported in old age when incapable even of serving as an infirm guardian or watchman about the plantation quarters and outbuildings; but the expense of the provision for his sustenance and clothes during his advanced years could never have been a serious item in the pages of the plantation ledger.

There was no sentiment in any corner of the world in that age which looked upon the enslavement of the negro as a crime. On the contrary, there was a feeling even among the benevolent, that he was such a raw savage that any means of raising him to a plane which approached that of civilized man was perfectly justifiable, however harsh in operation. As a matter of fact, most of the persons who were seeking to use his strength and docility for their own erichment, never gave a thought to the moral aspect of the act of seizing him and forcing him to labor for their benefit; or if such a thought ever really occurred to them, they defended themselves in their own consciences by asserting that he was more of an animal than of a man. Indeed, they honestly believed with the lady of Barbadoes, as reported by Rev. Mr. Godwyn, in his *Negro's and Indian's Advocate,* that "it was just as well to baptize little puppies" as little pickanninnies for any spiritual good that it would do them.

In the eyes of many slaveholders, the Christian religion was not intended for these uncouth creatures out of the wild jungles of Africa. This was the view held universally in the West Indies. It was far less generally entertained in Virginia even about the bestial newcomers, and not at all about their descendants born in the country and reared under civilizing influences. The only objection to baptizing the young negro ever heard in

the colony arose from an impression that he was really entitled
to his freedom, should this rite be granted to him.

There was, however, no more reluctance in Virginia than in
the Spanish colonies to hold the negro in slavery, and compel him
to work in the tobacco and corn fields. The eagerness to acquire
him in that capacity rapidly increased as his superiority to the
indentured English servant—for the various reasons already
mentioned—became more perceptible with the progress of the
seventeenth century. Had the facilities during that century for
obtaining him been as great as they were for obtaining the white
agricultural laborer, the introduction of the latter would have
slackened far sooner than it did. Indeed, the history of the
eighteenth century would have been repeated from an early period in the seventeenth, and the white laborers, instead of con-
stituting the majority of the tillers of the soil down to 1700,
would have formed a very small minority.

The first negroes brought into Virginia had been the victims
of a double crime. They had been torn away from their native
country, and afterwards had been snatched from their captors
by a hostile man-of-war. They were nineteen in all—the most
fateful cargo from some points of view ever landed upon the
shores of North America. They were disembarked in 1619 from
a Dutch privateer at Jamestown, and were subsequently consigned to the lands belonging to the office of governor. Apparently, none of these slaves perished in the terrible massacre of
1622, by which time the original band had been increased by a
few additions through birth or separate introduction in later
ships. During the following year, as the census disclosed, they
were widely scattered among the plantations that survived that
awful blow.

Five years afterwards, the number of negroes in Virginia was
increased by the arrival of a vessel that had captured a large
cargo of slaves off the coast of Angola. Down to 1650, the slaves
added to the colony's population were brought in by ship-cap-
tains who were either sailing under letters of marque, or on

their own private enterprises. It is true that a charter had been
issued as early as 1619 to Lord Warwick and his associates to
authorize them to carry on traffic in African negroes, but apparently this company was not instrumental in introducing many
of that race into Virginia.

In 1631, twelve years later on, another company was organized on a large scale, and chartered by the king, to utilize the
trade of the Guinea Coast, including the purchase of slaves from
the native tribes; but this company's transportation oversea of
negroes so acquired, must, during many years, have continued
small, for as late as 1649, as we have mentioned, the black population of the colony did not exceed three hundred in all. A portion of this population must have been the first of the natural
increase.

Nevertheless, the land patents for each year, beginning with
1635, reveal the introduction of a few slaves in the course of
every twelve months. In 1635 itself, there were twenty-six; in
1636, seven; in 1637, twenty-eight; in 1638, thirty; in 1639,
forty-six; in 1642, seven; in 1642, eighteen; and in 1649, seventeen. During the interval of ten years between 1649 and 1659,
there was one instance in which thirty were brought in in one
band. By this time, Dutch shipmasters had begun to land negroes in the colony for sale; and in doing this, they were respond-
ing to the special encouragement which had been held out to them
by the General Assembly. This encouragement consisted of relieving them of the heavy duty placed on all tobacco exported in
foreign bottoms, provided that it had been obtained by exchanging slaves for it. This trade was stopped so soon as the new
Act of Navigation, passed after the restoration of the Stuarts,
had come to be strictly enforced.

In 1662, in order to reserve for the profit of English merchants alone, the increasing trade in African products, the Royal
African Company, in which even the members of the king's family were interested, was chartered, with the exclusive right to
import negroes into the different colonies of England. This

right, however, could be subgranted by the company to other associations, and even to individuals, on the payment by them of three pounds sterling for every ton included in the weight of their ships carrying over these human cargoes. Sometimes, as in the case of the West Indies, the tax was fixed by the head; but this was not done as yet in the case of Virginia.

By 1671, the slave population had grown to two thousand—not a remarkable rate of increase. This fact is explained by a statement made by Berkeley during that year, namely that the number of cargoes had, for a long period, not exceeded two or three. The colony, from this time to 1680, was in a state of civil commotion, and the planters were probably too impoverished to patronize the slave ships that entered the rivers. By 1682, however, the trade was resumed, and from this time, one of the most successful agents in the introduction of the negro was the New England shipmaster, who obtained the supply which he brought to Virginia from the West Indies. The trade between the New England Colonies and the plantations in the Carribbean Islands had, by this time, expanded to a large volume. Before the return northward of these colonies' ships, it was easy enough to add numerous slaves to the hogsheads of sugar and casks of rum already on board; and both could be landed along the James or York with hardly a break in the voyage.

Apparently these thrifty skippers, engaged in importing negroes along with ordinary merchandise, into Virginia, were compelled, like the masters of English bottoms, to show that they had secured a license from the Royal African Company; and their possession of this license had to be made clear to the captain of the guard ship so soon as they passed into the Chesapeake. The force of this requirement was occasionally avoided by disembarking a human cargo in some quiet harbor along the coast of Accomac. As many as 120 slaves were thus smuggled in on a single voyage that took place in 1687. The ship in this case had come directly from Africa. The object which the master had in view was to evade the tax on the negroes as well as to escape the regular fort duties.

The increase in the number of slaves imported became very perceptible during the last ten years of the century. At this time, an entire cargo would be made up of Africans. Patents were obtained on such headrights alone, and in some cases, they swelled to as many as sixty-four, seventy-nine, and eighty-five. Even in the small grants, the proportion of slaves to white indentured servants was as high as one-third of the whole. As a rule, the negro headrights either equalled or surpassed the white.

By this time, there were so many Africans in the colony, independently of the recently arrived cargo from the coasts of Guinea and Angora, that the planters were often able to supply themselves with hands for their crops by the purchase of negroes from their neighbors; and among these were included many individuals who had been born in the country, or had lived there so many years that they had become civilized in their manners. These latter were considered to be particularly desirable because they offered a good example in spirit and bearing to the entirely raw Africans who had been bought to work beside them in the tobacco and corn fields.

The price set upon the slave steadily rose as time advanced. There was, of course, a difference in value between a man and a woman, and between a child and an adult; but in each case, an augmentation from decade to decade was to be noticed. Nor was the difference between the price of a man and the price of a woman as great as might have been anticipated. The reason back of this fact was that the woman, if of robust body, was as enduring and productive a worker in the field as a man in the possession of equally vigorous health.

In 1640, the price of an adult male slave was eighteen pounds sterling; and a negro woman was held at precisely the same figure. Twenty years later, a young negress brought as large an amount as thirty pounds sterling. Twelve years later still, a negress of the same age sold for thirty-two pounds sterling. Sub-

sequently, negro women of more mature years could be purchased for twenty-five, and negro men, for thirty. A mere child
could be acquired for fifty-three shillings. By 1694, a boy of
twelve was valued at twenty pounds sterling; a girl of ten at
fifteen; and one of six, at ten. In some of the outlying countries,
the price of slaves of different ages ranged at a still higher figure. In 1697, for instance, the African men and women belonging to the estate of a prominent citizen of Middlesex were appraised, as the average for both sexes, at thirty-one pounds sterling. In the case of a second planter, four of his slaves were
inventoried at forty pounds apiece. In Rappahannock County,
the average appraisement was apparently even greater. There a
boy was listed at twenty-six pounds, and a girl at twenty-four.

The price of slaves was increased by the import tax placed on
their heads when landed. At the end of the century, this tax
amounted to twenty shillings for each negro. The indentured
white servant was also subject to a similar imposition.

As the mulatto appeared within a few years after the introduction of negroes into the colony, the question arose: should
his status follow the condition of his free white father, or the
servile condition of his African mother? Every influence of the
English law at that time, as well as of the planter's interests,
dictated that the child should be born a slave, and remain a slave
throughout his life; and a child sprung from this child, in her
mature years, as the result of cohabitation with a white man,
was also to continue a slave, in spite of the fact that her negro
blood had been so greatly diluted.

The age at which the African bondsman became tithable
seems to have been sixteen, although, at one time, twelve had
been formally adopted as the lowest limit. If a negro child
had been brought in by a slave-ship, he had to be carried before
the nearest court for the number of his years to be ascertained
and recorded.

There was a remarkable difference between the status of the
white indentured woman and the status of the female slave in

the point of their liability to be taxed. The negress was listed as a tithable whether she worked under her master's roof or in his tobacco lot and corn field. On the other hand, no female servant was ever entered as a tithable, if her tasks were confined to the domestic hearth. A possible explanation of his difference lay in the fact that, with few exceptions, the negresses were fully prepared at any time to leave their master's kitchen or dining room and to take up the hoe. They were under all circumstances potentially agricultural servants as long as their physical strength held out. This was the case with only a few of the white women, since they were more delicately organized in body and, therefore, less adapted to hard labor under the burning sun. Probably, too, as the demand for an increase in the number of white women in the colony as possible wives was always great, public policy suggested that their immigration should be encouraged by exempting their masters from paying a head tax for their possession.

In the progress of time, female slaves took the place of most of the white women in the households. Trained from childhood to serve under the master's roof, they gradually came to form a band of thoroughly capable domestics, who could not claim, like the white woman, the right to leave on the expiration of a contract.

There are numerous proofs that the treatment of the negro bondsmen was marked as much by kindness as by firmness. Among the wills of the seventeenth century, there are to be found many which make a special provision for the proper care of the testator's slaves in their old age. This care was to be as vigilant and liberal as if the superannuated men and women who were to be the objects of it were still capable of prolonged and profitable labor in the fields or the barns. The food, clothing, and the other necessaries, which they were to receive, were to be regularly and promptly distributed among them.

The daily rations of the slaves, whether they were robust or too decrepit to work, consisted of hominy, cornbread, pork, fish, potatoes, and other vegetables. Some of these vegetables came from the garden patches which had been laid off for them at the side of their cabins, and which they were permitted to cultivate on their Saturday half-holidays. The clothes furnished for young and old were, of course, as simple and inexpensive as was to be expected when the fact that they were intended for persons who were, or had been, laborers in the muck of the fields was remembered. For the men, these garments consisted of a full suit, a doublet, a pair of drawers, a pair of shoes, and a cap. Quite certainly another suit was reserved for Sunday. In the tobacco lot, there was no need of a coat.

The contents of the cabin were few and rough in character. An inventory recorded in 1697 shows that, at that time, the usual furniture embraced a bed and several chairs; and the utensils, an iron kettle, a brass kettle, an iron pot, a pot hook and pot racks, and a frying pan.

Improper sexual relations began between white men and negresses at an early period. This was encouraged by the fact that persons of the two races and two sexes handled the hoe side by side in the tobacco lot and corn field. Only a small proportion of the white indentured servants were married; and not many of the rest could, in their poverty have had any sense of personal responsibility to restrain them. But the general sentiment of the community at large had no toleration for such illicit intercourse. The penalty, when it was detected, was always severe. The guilty white person was compelled to confess his fault in the face of the congregation of the parish church, and in addition, was soundly thrashed at the nearest whipping post. The woman in her turn was also sternly punished.

In those cases in which the father was a negro and the mother a white woman, the penalty was even more drastic. If she was not an indentured servant, but a free woman, she was, in case she was unable to pay a fine of fifteen pounds sterling, bound out by the church wardens to serve a period of five years. The child remained in the custody of the parish officers until he or she had reached his or her thirteenth birthday. The mother was sometimes banished to the West Indies.

With this sharp disapproval of sexual commerce between whites and blacks in vigorous existence, it followed very naturally that a legal marriage between persons of the two races was rigidly prohibited; and the clergyman who defied this regulation of joining a couple of this double origin, was fined to the extent of ten thousand pounds of tobacco.

The misdemeanor of running away from their masters was not as common among the slaves as among the indentured servants. In many cases, the disposition to abscond would not have arisen at all had they not been corrupted and enticed away through the influence of their white companions in the fields, who were dissatisfied with their tasks and restricted prospects. It is quite probable that the large majority of the negro runaways were men who had not long been living in the colony and who, for that reason, were inclined to chafe under the confinement to which they were continually subjected. Slaves who had been born in Virginia, and had passed all their years on one plantation, must have felt the restraining force of the affection which that fact had created in their hearts.

There was brought to light during the seventeenth century the existence of several settlements in remote fastnesses founded by runaway slaves, and there were instances of detected conspiracies under the very noses of the planters themselves. Some of the fugitives, hiding themselves in the nearest swamp, became notorious depredators at night in the farm yards of the contiguous neighborhoods. No negro was permitted to carry a club, gun, sword, or staff, in his hand; and if he was found with either far from home, and without his master's passport, he was arrested and whipped by the constable of the county where he was taken up, and then escorted to the next county, where he was again whipped, and so on, county after county, until he had reached the plantation to which he belonged.

There were many negroes in the colony who had been either born free or had been liberated by will. In the latter case, provision was always made for their support for a year at the expense of their late master's heirs. Sometimes, an emancipated slave was devised a considerable area of land. Livestock, in the form of cows and hogs, were also often added. Not infrequently, the provision was extended beyond the first year. Under the terms of one well known will recorded in the seventeenth century, an emancipated negro was to receive annually fifteen bushels of maize, and fifty pounds of dried beef. Besides this continuous benefaction, a gift from year to year of a coat, a pair of trousers, hat, a pair of shirts, and two pairs of shoes and stockings, respectively, were to be made him on a fixed date. He was also to be furnished with a hoe and ax, and his levies were to be paid regularly.

There were numerous instances of free negroes who had acquired independent estates of some importance. These were not permitted to employ white indentured servants, but no interdiction was placed on their securing the assistance of Indian servants and servants of their own race. Apparently, these black freeholders were in the full enjoyment of the suffrage. There is no reason to doubt that they lived in a manner comparable with that which was led by the small white planters of the same quality of fortune.

The Indians captured in the wars that occurred in the later years of the seventeenth century were held as slaves for life. Previous to Bacon's Rebellion, that condition was not to be observed among them, owing to the desire then to conciliate the various tribes that prowled along the frontiers.

CHAPTER V

PLANTATION PRODUCTS—1607-1650

The island on which Jamestown was founded in 1607 was chosen as the site for the first English settlement in Virginia, not because it offered peculiar advantages as a scene for the future agricultural operations on which the Colonists expected to depend chiefly for a subsistance, but because it met all the conditions which the Council of the London Company had, in their instructions, emphasized as necessary for the protection of the community, in case it should be compelled to defend itself from a Spanish assault on the side of the river. It is true that the country contiguous had a wide area of fertile soil, which could, by the use of the axe, be made fit for the application of the hoe, but had the Colony been established at Kecoughtan, several thousand acres of open land cultivated there by the Indians would at once have been at the newcomer's disposal, without their having to raise their hands to clear it of its natural growth. To have seized such ground without regard to the Indian right to it, would have been flagitious in itself, and repugnant to the desired policy of production, since peace with the aborigines would have been jeopardized at the very start, and appeasement of their fierce warriors' anger thereafter made impossible.

Moreover, Kecoughtan was very much exposed to an invasion by sea. Had the voyagers set down there, so soon as they arrived in Virginia, they would have been kept in a perpetual state of apprehension of attack by the enemy's ships sailing in between the Capes. The wholesomeness of the spot, owing to the absence of extensive marshes, and the presence of cleared

140

fields, would not have been any compensation for this extreme disadvantage.

The English had not been seated on Jamestown Island more than a fortnight when they began to sow wheat in the ground which they had been able, during that interval, to prepare for seeding. It is possible that the area chosen for the first field of

JAMESTOWN ISLAND

grain was the one that had been stripped of trees in the course of obtaining the timber required for the construction of the fort. That this virgin soil was extremely fertile was demonstrated by the fact, that, by the middle of the month of June, the stalks had sprung up to the height of a man after only seven weeks' growth. The products of this first year were not restricted to wheat. The seeds of melons and pine-apples were also planted. The potato too was placed in the ground. But the most interesting experiment was made with the seed of cotton and oranges.

The adaptability of the soil to tobacco was taken for granted, as the leaf was in common use among the Indians, and it was known that no part of their abundant supply of it could have been imported from a distance. The Colonists recognized the profitable possibilities of this plant from the beginning; and even during their first Spring in the country, ventured to predict that it would ultimately become a saleable commodity. The fact that it did not do so at once was due to the diversion of the settlers' attention from all agriculture for a time by the necessity of defending themselves against the assaults of the savages. John Rolfe was the first of the Colonists to raise a crop of tobacco for sale in London.

In the Spring following the arrival of the English, they attempted again to produce a crop of wheat, but the grain could not have been satisfactory in quality, or in abundance either, for we find the Colonists preferred to rely chiefly on the supplies of maize which were purchased at the numerous villages situated in the valleys of the Powhatan, Nansemond, Pamonkey, and Chickahominy.

Smith, so soon as he became Governor of the Colony through his incumbency of the office of President of the Council, endeavored to provide at least a part of the food needed by the community by planting grain of maize, instead of the grain of wheat. For this purpose, he made use of the knowledge of two Indian captives, who were directed by him to show his men the method of pulverizing the soil, and afterwards of planting it, followed by the native cultivators. There is no doubt that the experiment proved successful as far as it went, but it required a wider area of ground than was at his disposal at this time to assure the entire quantity of corn meal which was called for by the mouths which had to be fed.

There was one serious drawback to the production of maize near the town in the course of these first years. The long rows of tall corn stalks, with the undergrowth of pea and pumpkin vines, created a dense hiding place for the sly Indians, who crept under the covert during the night, in order to assault the workers so soon as they should enter the corn field in the morning. This happened on more than one occasion; and so great was the damage inflicted on them that they naturally shrank from recreating another year such a fastness for their secretive foes.

The original area planted in maize was forty acres in extent, but it is doubtful whether much of its grain was harvested. It is known that the ears growing upon the stalks of seven acres were pulled and devoured by the persons who had come over in the Third Supply, and this too while the grain was still in an immature state.

No plough was used in preparing the ground embraced in these forty acres. Apparently, the hoe and spade were the only implements employed by the cultivators.

There was but one species of domestic animal which throve in the struggling Colony during these first years. This was the hog. The hog was turned loose to run at large in the marshes, swamps, and forests. Here he and his fellows rapidly increased, owing to the quantity of roots, acorns, and seed, to be found there. The climate, during winter, was so mild that the hog did not need any warmer shelter than he was fully able to make for himself by gathering together the dry grasses and leaves for a bed. The Indians, at that time, not being in possession of guns, had to rely upon bows and arrows to bring down the hogs that crossed their path while hunting, and the destruction, by this imperfect means, was too small to check the numerical growth of these hardy animals.

Sheep, oxen, cows, and horses, wandering in the woods around Jamestown, did not thrive so readily, nor were they able to escape so easily the primitive weapons of the savages. Moreover, unlike the hog, which was both more wary and more pugnacious, they were not so capable of resisting successfully the attacks of the wolf and the panther. During the first years of the Jamestown settlement, the concerted cry of packs of wolves, in pursuit of their prey, was constantly heard at night in the woods adjacent to the island. No sheep, no ox, could have escaped being pulled down, had it met one of those fierce and ravenous packs in the coverts of the forests. The panther too, haunted these fastnesses; and so did the bear; and both were ready on the instant to make an attempt to seize and devour the colt, the calf, and the lamb, had those helpless animals come within their reach.

One of the principal objects which Dale had in view in founding Henricopolis was, by running a palisade from the line of the Powhatan to the line of the Appomattox, to create a broad yet protected area for the browsing of the livestock. There were twenty square miles embraced within these boundaries, and this land, which was composed of champaign and forest, was, by its fertility, particularly well adapted to serve as a permanent pasture. In order to shelter the watchman who kept the hogs and cattle ranging this pasture always under their eye, block houses were erected at intervals on the line of the paling.

How had these animals been first obtained? No doubt there were already considerable herds of either kind in the Colony when Dale arrived, but, from his own caraval, he added sixty cows to their number, while Gates, a short time afterwards, added one hundred kine and two hundred hogs.

The cultivation of tobacco as a commodity for sale began in 1612. Previously, there had been no crop which the people of the Colony could rely upon with perfect confidence to supply all those articles,—like clothing, for instance,—which could not be dispensed with, and yet could not be manufactured so far in Virginia. It is said that Rolfe was led to turn his attention to the production of saleable tobacco, on an important individual scale, by the fact that he was an habitual user of the cured leaf. As the Colonists were now so constantly at war with the Indians, a steady acquisition of that leaf could not be looked for from that quarter.

Apparently, tobacco was not simply a weed that sprang up wherever the soil was fertile and open to the sunlight. Planting the seed was imperative if the people were to produce leaf of the best quality.

So eagerly was the new crop seized upon, as promising great profit, that a special regulation had to be adopted by Dale that no one should be permitted to cultivate it unless he had already sowed two acres in grain. And to prevent the newcomers from undertaking its production too soon after their arrival, while still entirely ignorant of the proper method of planting, tending, and curing it, they were forbidden, during their first year, from using their ground for any crops but wheat, maize, roots, and herbs, all of which could be converted into food. As compensation for this interdiction, a rule was adopted that every immigrant who had brought over a family with him was to receive, after settling in his own homestead, a definite number of hogs, goats, and cows. So important were all these domestic animals, as well as the horse, dog, turkey, and chicken, considered to be, during the rule of Dale, that any person killing them, whether they were his own property or not, without the Governor's permission, was liable to be sentenced to death, or a brand in the center of the palm of his hand.

During the same administration, an attempt was made to encourage the planting of vineyards. There was an impression among the Colonists at first that the native grape, if carefully and skilfully tended, would be as profitable as the finest species of Europe. This impression proved in time to be too sanguine. The first Assembly, which met in 1619, passed laws to encourage the use of the grape as likely to furnish an excellent wine for export. On one occasion, twenty gallons were expressed, and it was thought to resemble French wine in flavor. Another chronicler, who was of Spanish blood, was reminded by its taste of the celebrated Alicante.

But the high value put on the local grape did not deter the importation of foreign wines. In 1619, French vignaroons arrived, with many slips from the most celebrated vineyards of Languedoe. At this time, every householder was compelled by law to plant at least ten cultings; and furthermore, he must have himself thoroughly trained in the art of dressing the vines. The

11—Vol. I.

planters were so infatuated with the culture of tobacco that they were not disposed to observe this regulation strictly, since it interfered with the continuous pursuit of their main occupation. Possibly it was due to design on their part that the wine which was manufactured in Virginia during this period reached England generally in so sour a state that it was thought to be discreditable to the Colony. It is also probable that the destruction of the vineyards by neglect after the great Massacre of 1622 was not seriously regretted by the householders who survived; but the General Assembly, under the spur of the Council in London, promptly adopted measures to restore the extent of ground that had previously been covered with vineyards.

Among the laws of the General Assembly of 1619 was one that aimed to encourage the production of silk. Dale had already introduced the best foreign silk-worms. This had been done under the special auspices of the King himself. Numerous Continental weavers and throwsters had established themselves in London about 1607, but their trade was hampered by the import tax on the raw material, which they could only procure abroad. The effort to increase the cultivation of the mulberry tree in England for the creation of silk-worm nurseries had not proved to be really successful, in spite of the royal patronage, and there was a hope that the indigenous mulberry groves in Virginia would soon be making good the deficiency.

To complement the number of these trees already growing in the Colony, the Assembly required that, during a period of seven years, every householder, great or small, should plant half a dozen slips. It was estimated that each tree, when matured, would produce silk to the value of five pounds sterling. Many copies of Bonoel's famous treatise on the *Culture of Silk Worms* were, about this time, bought in England and dispatched to Virginia, accompanied by cocoons obtained from the royal collection. An expert, trained at the Royal Silk Establishment, was also sent out to demonstrate the proper method of handling the

JAMESTOWN IN 1622
VIRGINIA

[Enlarged from a cut in the *Scheeps-Togt van Anthony Chester Na Virginia, gedaan in het jaar 1620.* Printed at Leyden by Peter Vander, 1707. A pamphlet. 12mo.]

worms, and also of producing the silk. Silk-worm seed too were imported from St. Valencia and forwarded oversea.

The massacre of 1622 had a chilling effect on the production of silk in the Colony. George Sandys, who had been ordered by the London Company to renew the attention that had formerly been paid to silk culture, drew all the silk men into Elizabeth City, which was carefully defended against Indian assault. He endeavored, at the same time, to procure two silk experts from the Royal Silk Establishment in England; but his encouragement was small, since the planters were more absorbed than ever in the production of tobacco, because it alone assured them a perfectly reliable income from year to year.

In 1619, there was an attempt to increase the production of merchantable flax by enacting a law which required every family in the Colony to tend at least one hundred plants. A few years afterwards, linen manufactured out of this indigenous flax was sent to England to have its quality tested, and the verdict passed on it was, that, in texture, it was quite equal to the linen which was obained from Cambaya, the most celebrated in the world, at that time.

At the end of Governor Yeardley's administration, the number of people residing in the different communities of Virginia was supposed to be in the neighborhood of two thousand; and they were so prosperous, from the returns from their lands, that it was said that each householder "gave free entertainment to his friends and to strangers." The planters of this period were not satisfied to limit the use of their soil to the production of tobacco and maize, and the familiar English vegetables. They tried its capacity for bringing forth those fruits which had hitherto flourished only in the rich mould, and under the warm suns, of the West Indian Islands. The seeds or slips of figs, lemons, olives, ginger, almonds, plantains, cassala and pomegranates were inserted in the most fertile grounds to be discovered; and some of them proved to be generous in their yield, while others turned out to be barren; doubtless in consequence of the blight of harsh winters.

Tobacco and corn were still the principal crops. Maize, like the vegetables and fruits, was cultivated for domestic consumption, while the tobacco remained the product relied upon for the purchase of all the merchandise needed by the households. At this time, it was estimated that two robust and experienced men could plant, tend, and harvest a crop of this commodity that would sell for fifty pounds sterling when unloaded on the wharves of London. It was at this time that an improvement in the method of curing the leaves was effected by stringing them on a long line. This line was the forerunner of the modern stick on which the tobacco is now hung in the barn. That building was already in use, but apaprently not yet for the purpose of drying the suspended leaves by means of fire. These were shipped at first, not in hogsheads, but in rolls that sometimes weighed as much as one hundred and five pounds. Almost from the beginning, the tobacco was inspected with care, appraised, and separated into two groups according to quality. All the inferior leaf was destroyed.

The cultivation of wheat made little progress, although not entirely neglected. The reason for this fact was that maize offered a more abundant and also a more nourishing form of bread; and it was also more easily converted into meal than wheat could be converted into flour. Wheat could not be expected to find a profitable market in England, because the expense of shipping ate up all the margin of gain.

The richer the new ground in the river bottoms planted in tobacco, the greater the financial return, while the same land sowed in wheat brought forth such a heavy growth of stalk that the grain was lost in straw. The only soil really adapted to wheat was that which had previously borne a crop of tobacco, but the planter preferred to allow this soil to spring up in a secondary growth of trees as a means of recuperation, or to let it lie open as a pasture for cattle, rather than to try to obtain from it a moderate crop of wheat, which would be useless in feeding his live-stock and of no real service as food for his own household.

Among the elements of advantages which tobacco offered in comparison with wheat was that it did not require so large an area for its tillage. The forest, as a rule, had to be cleared off only over a few acres when new grounds were to be created for tobacco. On the other hand, had the cultivation of wheat been in view, it would have been necessary to denude many acres of their heavy growth. It was impossible for wheat,—even if sold in Virginia in order to escape the ocean charges for freight,— to meet the heavy cost of labor imposed by the need of constantly cutting down the woods. An intensive crop like tobacco, which was enormously productive to the single acre, was the only one that could have borne up profitably under the expense of the system of labor which prevailed in the Colony during that period of its history.

The ease with which tobacco could be packed in bulk in a ship was another advantage which it possessed over every other agricultural product of Virginia.

Under the operation of all these practical influences, the cultivation of tobacco rapidly increased. Indeed, there was but one limit to its production, and that was the size of the population. As the bounds of the plantations spread out, the volume of the crops in the aggregate proportionately swelled. In 1619, shipments to England amounted to twenty thousand pounds in weight. During the following year, 1620, the Company is said to have exported by itself not less than twenty thousand pounds. This quantity was probably doubled by the quantity produced by the numerous householders. Two years afterwards, the quantity had risen to sixty thousand pounds, in spite of the rupture of so many plantations by the Massacre which occurred during that year.

The King, at this time, was very apprehensive lest the shipments of tobacco from Virginia, by curtailing the market in

England for Spanish leaf should arouse the hostility of the
Spanish Government. Under the influence of this fear, he endeavored to restrict the exportation of tobacco from the Colony
by increasing the custom charges. He went even further than
this, for he issued a proclamation which limited the combined
shipments from Virginia and the Somers Isles to fifty-five thousand pounds. In order to escape the burden which this regulation created, Virginia, leaving this whole amount to be sent
over by the Somers Isles alone, endeavored to find a market for
its own product in the cities of Flushing and Middleburg in Holland. In this the Colony was successful, and, in consequence, in
a short time a complaint was made by the commissioners of the
customs that the revenues from tobacco had been seriously lowered. A compromise followed: the King agreed to permit all the
Virginian tobacco to come into the English ports, and to shut
out all Spanish, after an interval of two years. In return for
granting this exclusive market, he was to receive one-third of the
Virginian tobacco for himself, and, in addition, was to possess
the right to levy a duty of six pence on the remaining two-thirds.

Another clause in this important contract declared that the
cultivation of tobacco in England and Ireland should be strictly
prohibited.

As late as 1627, so much tobacco was cultivated in England
that a royal proclamation was issued to prohibit it; and when an
effort was made to destroy the growing plants in obedience to
that order, the public officers entrusted with this duty were, in
many places assaulted by the persons who were trying to evade
the measure. Three years later, the proclamation, having proved
to be ineffective, the Virginians, through the agency of their
Governor, petitioned Parliament to pass a law that would, by the
severity of its terms, put an end to the production of the plant in
English soil. It was complained that so large was the quantity
of tobacco reaped in the English shires that the Colony's prosperity was seriously impaired by the contraction of its market in
London owing to the influx of the English leaf.

Why should the soil of the English landowners have been turned to such a purpose when the raising of this crop on it was admitted to be hampered by the lack of hot sunshine at the season when the leaf most needed it?   It would have been supposed that the almost constant rains of the English climate throughout that season would not only have diminished the weight of the leaf, by washing away its gummy substance, but also have prevented the whole plant from acquiring the flavor which made both the Spanish and the Virginian product so valuable.   All this really happened, and yet the quantity of English tobacco marketed reveals that it remained profitable to do so in spite of that fact.   Indeed, the demand for all tobacco was so great that even inferior brands found purchasers.

The King's sympathy was naturally on the side of the Virginians.   Not only did he recognize that the Colony was dependent upon the production of tobacco for its people's subsistence, but he also found no difficulty in perceiving that, should the importation of the leaf from Virginia fall off, the volume of his customs would proportionately decline.   Charles, who deprecated Parliament's interference, even in a loyal spirit, with the sources of the independent crown revenues,—and such the tobacco duties were considered to be,—issued a vigorous proclamation forbidding the further cultivation of tobacco in England, and threatening cumulative penalties should it continue.   But the prospect thus created of a greater and more assured market in England did not influence the planters to stop the shipment of much of their tobacco to Holland.   There appears to have been no objection to this course by the English Government, provided that the vessels halted by the way in an English port, and paid the required customs.   It is quite possible that this was done by a few of the English vessels engaged in transporting cargoes of tobacco to the Low Countries, but by none of the Dutch bottoms taking part in the same traffic.

In 1631, the number of cattle in Virginia was supposed to approximate five thousand.   An ox, at this time, was valued at

fifteen pounds sterling. This was because it was used as a
draft animal in the fields. As beef, its price was, perhaps, very
much lower, as it was only killed when it had grown old or had
been injured. A cow was valued quite as high as a robust ox,
since it was held in particular esteem, not only for breeding
purposes, but for its milk.

Few horses were to be found in Virginia during this period.
There were several reasons in explanation of this fact. Although
by 1631, the separate plantations had spread out to a considerable extent, there could not have been in operation any real
system of public roads. Little room existed, therefore, for the
use of this animal for the mere pleasure of riding, or even of
getting about from place to place outside of the boundary lines
of the plantation to which it belonged. The principal highway,
at this time, was the river. The plantations then laid off fronted
either on the Powhatan or on its tidewater tributaries, like the
Appomattox, the Nansemond, and the Chickahominy. The boat
was the most convenient means, and the water the most unobstructed path, by which visits were paid from neighborhood
to neighborhood. The horse, however, must have served a purpose of some value in dragging the plough, but if so, there is
little indication of that fact by the few appraised in the contemporary inventories.

Sheep were small in number, owing, perhaps to the narrowness of the pasturage, the scarcity of forage in winter, and the
depredations of wolves. They were only serviceable for the
table, but there was no difficulty in obtaining food from many
other sources that gave far less trouble, and could be more confidently relied on. Goats were far more numerous, no doubt,
because their milk was highly valued, and the kids were looked
upon as offering a very palatable delicacy. One planter alone,
Adam Thoroughgood, was, at the time of his death, in possession of one hundred and seven goats. Another mentioned in the
records owned fifty-one of both sexes and different ages.

Now that the Indians' hunting grounds had been curtailed by the spreading out of the plantations, there was a disposition on their part to turn for food to the domestic animals found browsing in the forests. Through these huntsmen, the large herds of hogs were gradually decimated, and the number of cows, calves, sheep, and goats were steadily diminished. As early as 1623, it was proposed to create a protected area that would bar the further intrusion of the savages, and also provide abundant pasturage for livestock of all kinds. This was to be done by running a palisade from a spot on James River, within the bounds of Martin's Hundred, to Cheskiack on the Charles River, the modern York. The space thus to be enclosed was equal in extent to the English shire of Kent.

But it was not until Harvey became Governor that this great fence was erected, and it proved to be entirely successful in accomplishing this purpose for which it was built. Between it and the two wide rivers, as far as the Bay, and the modern Hampton Roads, a country spread out composed of marshes, open fields, and forest, that offered provender for livestock throughout the year, without any addition through cultivation. Remnants of this barrier were to be observed scattered along its old site as late as the middle of the century, a reminder of a day when prowling Indians were still feared, even near Jamestown, as a constant menace to human lives as well as to the lives of the valuable herds of cows, oxen, goats, sheep, and horses then in the planters' possession, as far as the country had been settled.

CHAPTER VI

PLANTATION PRODUCTS, 1650-1700

In previous chapters, we have referred incidentally to the famous Navigation Acts passed by the English Parliament about the middle of the Seventeenth Century. The first Act, which became law during the Protectorate, was never rigidly enforced; but the second, which was entered in the English statute book after the Restoration, was carried out with all the legal and physical power that the English Government was able to bring to bear in its support. There can be no reason to doubt that the operation of the Second Act caused serious damage to the only profitable agricultural interest then existing in the Colony, —the production of tobacco.

The great philosopher Bacon, in his essay on *Plantations,* laid down a principle which was peculiarly applicable to the conditions prevailing in Virginia at this time. Every Colony, he said, should be permitted to exercise the privilege of selling its crops in the open markets of the world. No barrier whatever should be raised to keep its loaded, outgoing ships from seeking the wharves of any port however alien to the Mother Country. We have seen that the English authorities, before the passage of the Navigation Acts, did not offer any strong objections to such a disposition of colonial tobacco, provided that the vessels had stopped in the progress of their voyage to the Continent and paid the English custom duties for which their cargoes were liable. But this was not satisfactory to Virginia, for it really signified that two sets of customs would have to be paid,—one in England, the other in Holland, if that was the final destination.

155

What the planters wanted was the right to export directly to Flushing and Middleburg, because this course would enable them to save, as so much additional profit, the amount of the English duties on their tobacco; and in hundreds of cases, they accomplished this by giving no attention to the injunction of the English commissioners of the revenue to put into port when passing with a cargo eastward or northward along the English coast.

The Virginians asserted that the profit of tobacco culture was too narrow in margin to permit of the payment of the two sets of customs. Moreover, they said that, should they have access to Continental markets free of the English duties, they would never have any surplus crops to rot in their barns, for all that could not find purchasers in London would find them in the ports of the Low Countries. This was a perfectly sound position to take from an economic point of view. With the markets of the whole of Europe open to them, there would, perhaps, never have been a surplus stored away in their barns for want of buyers. All the tobacco produced would have been sold, and the addition to the wealth of the planters would have been in proportion. The frontier would have spread out more rapidly, and the community on a whole would have enjoyed more substantial advantages of all kinds.

The argument advanced by England in support of her right to monopolize the trade and transportation of the Virginians was a specious one. How could the English Government protect the Colony from foreign invasion and internal disorder, without having at its disposal the customs received from the cargoes imported into England? Was not that Government entitled to some compensation for the loss in revenue incurred when the cultivation of tobacco in English soil was prohibited?

So far as the question of protection was involved, the planters might ruefully point to the small aid afforded them, when, on at least two occasions, Dutch fleets bore down in Virginia waters and carried havoc among the merchantmen then riding in the York and the James Rivers. So far as the quick suppression of internal dissension was concerned, was there any encouragement in the history of Bacon's Rebellion? The whole country was thrown into disorder, and continued in that condition many months after the news of the insurrection had been received in England. When English troops did arrive at Jamestown, the commotion had died out entirely.

By the terms of the First Act of Navigation, passed in 1651, all foreign articles brought into English ports were to be transported without a single break in the voyage from the place where they were produced or manufactured. The Second Act of Navigation was much more voluminous and drastic in its provisions. It not only sought to protect English shipping by restricting exportation from the Colonies, and, in turn, importation into them, to vessels owned or built by Englishmen and commanded by English masters, with two-thirds of their crew English in allegiance, but it also required the planters to ship their tobacco only to England and the English Colonies, and to confine their purchases of European goods to articles which had been conveyed from England in English bottoms.

For a period of many years, various devices were used to evade this Act, and the English treasury suffered severely by their success. In 1663, the annual loss was estimated at a figure as high as ten thousand pounds sterling. As time advanced, the Act was more strictly enforced; but this only increased, its unpopularity with the Virginian planters. Indeed, the Act exercised a distinct influence towards increasing the discontent that ultimately led up to the Insurrection of 1676.

One effect of the two Acts was to augment the zeal and energy of the English authorities in suppressing all attempts to cultivate tobacco on the soil of England. Another,—and this was the result of the constriction of the market for the sale of the tobacco,—was to encourage further experiments with the silkworm. Several planters were now conspicuously interested in this industry, and they seemed to have persuaded the General Assembly to require every man in the Colony who owned considerable land to plant ten mulberry trees for every one hundred acres in his possession. An Armenian was employed at public expense to teach the art of handling the worm with the most productive skill. So excellent was the texture of the silk produced that Charles the Second pronounced specimens which had been sent to him to be as fine as any that he had ever worn on his own person.

How numerous the cattle in the Colony had become by 1673 was indicated by the estimate made by those destroyed in the phenomenally harsh winter of that year. It was said that the loss during that season amounted to fifty thousand head. This diminution in the existing herds was increased by the violent civic commotions of 1676, when little scruple was shown by either side in carrying off every animal that could be converted into food. There were throughout this period a large number of cows, oxen, and horses running wild in the woods. They seem to have escaped the fangs of the wolves, owing very probably to the destruction of the large packs of those ravenous animals. A reward of considerable value was now offered by each County Court for every wolf's head that should be delivered to the magistrate.

Tobacco being the most vital crop of the Colony, the supervision to which it was subjected was unremitting. No means was left unnoticed and untried in the effort to preserve the excellence of quality. Planting of slips, for instance, had to cease on the tenth of July. This prevented the production of a large quantity of leaf that would certainly have been caught by frost, and thus damaged irretrievably. This consummation would have lowered the average quality of the whole crop of the Colony for that year. The preservation of shoots of the second growth on the stalk, known as seconds, were also prohibited by law. These, like the leaves touched by frost, were usually of a mean texture, because pulled before maturity in order to hasten the expansion of the large remaining leaves. They too would serve to reduce the average value of the Colony's general crop, and tend to injure the desirability of that crop in the London market, with a consequent decline in price even of the finest grades.

Another regulation called for the burning of all ground leaves so soon as they had dried, after being stripped from the stalk. The planter who ventured to pull these leaves, cure them, and ship them in hogsheads to England, was penalized by the imposition of a fine of ten hogsheads of merchantable tobacco. So far did the General Assembly go that it enacted a law that, if five pounds of ground leaves should be found in a hogshead, the owner of that hogshead should be compelled to pay, as a penalty for his delinquency, the sum of five thousand pounds of tobacco.

So low had the price of a pound of that commodity fallen by 1662, that a movement began in the Colony in favor of petitioning the English Government to order a total cessation of the cultivation of the plant in both Virginia and Maryland. This application, reasonable as it was, met, when made, with a cold reception in London, since it would mean, if complied with, the complete destruction of all revenue to the customs from that source so long as the interdiction lasted. Later on, the Privy Council, under continued pressure, yielded to the appeal that it should authorize commissioners of the two Colonies to convene and pass upon the practicability of the proposed scheme. In the end, that scheme fell through, even in the modified form suggested, because the commissioners of Maryland could find no crop to substitute for tobacco that would assure even a small part of the income which the plant brought in, even when very low prices prevailed.

In the course of the following year, the two Colonies produced at least fifty thousand hogsheads. This represented a rate of one hogshead and a half for every individual to be found in the two communities north and south of the Potomac. It was estimated that the people of Virginia and Maryland incurred in that year through their joint crops a debt of fifty thousand pounds sterling. Another effort to obtain a cession of culture of the plant which followed this disastrous experience also ended in failure.　Production continued, and on such a scale, that it was said, at the time, that Virginia exported to England every two years such a quantity of tobacco that the people of that country were not able to consume it all in three.

One result of the very low prices for that commodity was the partial diversion of the planters' attention to other crops.　It was again hoped that silk could be produced in the Colony with profit.　Laws were now passed to encourage the development of this industry.　Every landowner was again required to plant ten mulberry slips for every one hundred acres in his possession. A subsidy of fifty pounds of tobacco was offered by the Assembly for every pound of silk of local manufacture.　The result of these measures must have been very promising, for Governor Berkeley reported to the English authorities that so many mulberry trees were then rapidly maturing in Virginia, that, by the end of a few years, the quantity of silk produced would be only limited by the capacity of forty thousand people to tend the worms.　He admitted that the prospect of success in flax culture was unfavorable, owing to the expense of cultivating the plant.　He had undertaken that culture himself, and has already lost one thousand pounds sterling in the course of his experiments.　It seems that he had been compelled to turn to French experts, which greatly increased the cost without the compensation of proportionate success in the quantity or value of the harvest.

It was so easy to obtain virgin lands by patent, or previously occupied lands by purchase, that there was no general disposition in the Colony to lease any part of the soil from the owners. Men of little or no means served either as overseers or as hired laborers, who were always in great demand.　Nevertheless, there were, in the various districts of the different communities, a considerable number of persons who leased small plantations on terms previously agreed upon.　It is possible that a landowner was often willing to lease a certain area of ground on condition that the tenant should clear away the heavy growth

of timber, provided that his use of the new soil should be limited
to two years at the most.   There were instances, however, of a
planter definitely prohibiting his tenant from removing the trees
growing on a part of the area leased.   This provision, perhaps,
was only likely in the cases of landlords who wished to keep
their woods untouched so as to serve the purpose of a run for
their cattle and horses.

It was a subject of comment in those times that a very large
proportion of the land rented was the property of men who
either resided in England or lived on an estate in Virginia so
remotely situated that they were unable to give their personal
attention to the plantations under lease.   Occasionally, the period of time covered by the terms of a lease extended over as
many as twenty years.   Sixteen, thirteen, and eight were far
from uncommon periods.   But seven seem to have constituted
the average term.   Unless the lease called for a tenure of considerable length, the lessee was, quite naturally, unwilling to
make any improvements.

The rent agreed upon was paid in different forms.   Now it
was in tobacco, the usual medium; now in wheat, maize, and
other grain; and sometimes even in cider.   This latter probably
only occurred in a case in which the amount of the rent was
small.   When paid in coin, the rate adopted in the thinly settled regions was apparently about twenty shillings for each
area of one hundred acres.

With a vast space even in the older parts of the Colony still
open to clearance and cultivation as late as 1645, it was to be
expected that little attention would be paid to the use of domestic manures.   As long as there were axes with which to belt
or cut away to the root the large bodies of standing trees in
order to secure a new lot, there could be no profit to the planter
in renewing the fertility of exhausted ground by the laborious
application of such fertilizing material as was produced in the
cow pens. This was the only source from which such an artificial stimulant to the soil was to be obtained.   The intensive

system of cultivation had not as yet been carried very far even in England, which really owed to Holland such modern improvements in agriculture as it had adopted. In the Mother Country the rule prevailed that a field was to be sown in wheat for a period of two years, and, thereafter, during one year was to lie fallow. The Virginians with unlimited virgin land, at their disposal, not unwisely preferred to turn to fresh soil for a substitute for their impoverished fields rather than to that contracted method of restoration through the cow-pen which was left to them as the alternative.

At a very early date, the possibilities of marl as a fertilizer had been considered as soon as it was found that vast deposits of it underlay the surface of the country adjacent to the tidewater rivers. Apparently, the virtue of this material was never tested to an important extent, although both Rolfe and Governor Yeardley had set the example in its use. The settlers preferred to abandon an old plantation devoid of room for new grounds rather than try the experiment of restoring fertility to their exhausted tobacco lots and corn fields by sprinkling pulverized marl over the attenuated surface. A plan to emigrate was submitted to the Governor, in 1649, by a large body of planters residing on the south side of the York, who wished to obtain his permission to establish themselves on the north side. "Our situation," they said, "is one of great and clamorous necessity. Our land will only produce mean tobacco, and our cattle have fallen into decay because their range is restricted."

It is probable that the usual manner of remunerating the overseers exerted a decided influence in discouraging the use of barnyard manures. The most common way of paying for their services was to allow them a share in the annual crops. It was to their interest, therefore, that these crops should be as large in volume as was practicable, and there was no reason to doubt that a lot, newly cleared of its primeval growth, was more productive than a lot, the fertility of which had been restored in some degree by the use of cow and horse droppings, mixed with corn-stalks or leaves.

There were in many communities broad spaces still given over to forest, swamp, and tidal marsh. In these remaining woods, the bottom lands had lain unaltered for centuries, with only the slope of the ground to carry off the water after a rain or flood. Stagnant pools had in some places here widened into small ponds, but everywhere else trees and bushes had sprung up to form a tangled mass which it was hard to clear away. The salt marshes were at least open to the sunshine, and they were covered with thick weeds and grasses. Some of the swamps along the streams were turned into solid ground for planting by careful drainage; but most of them, like the marshes, were only fit for affording the cattle a coarse forage of leaves or grass.

As in France there have always been certain districts famous for a special variety of wine, so in Virginia, during the Seventeenth Century, some regions enjoyed, from the beginning, a higher reputation for the quality of its tobacco than others. This was particularly the case with a tract in York County which bore the name of Digges Neck. It was thought that the odor and taste of the leaf produced in its soil were superior to the odor and taste of any leaf raised elsewhere in the Colony. Apparently, no difference in these two qualities was observed between the tobacco harvested in the valley of the James and the same commodity harvested in the valley of the Rappahannock. The principal brands were known as the Oronoco and the Sweet Scented. The latter enjoyed over the former a great advantage in its ability to be packed into a closer degree of compression, which, by diminishing the proportionate space that it occupied, reduced the relative amount of the charge for its freight.

How was a tobacco crop disposed of towards the end of the century? If the owner was in debt to a Virginian or English merchant, its possession so soon as cured passed to him. He, in his turn, shipped it to his agent in London. In many cases, the

merchant obtained the crop by purchase.   If the planter was
not in debt, he either sold his tobacco to a local trader, or to the
representative of a firm that carried on business in England.
In most cases, perhaps, the planter dispatched his tobacco from
his own wharf to some English port like Bristol or London,
where it was received by his English factor.   If the stream near
his house was too shallow to furnish room for a seagoing vessel, the tobacco, by means of sloops or shallops, was transported
to the place where the ship was anchored, and there the hogsheads were taken on board by the crew.

One of these vessels was capable of affording space for casks
ranging in number from two hundred to six hundred, and
weighing from one hundred and twenty thousand pounds to
three hundred thousand. It was apparently the rule with the
planters to divide their shipments between several vessels in
order to minimize the risk of a total loss of the whole by the
possible wreck of the single vessel to which it might have been
consigned. Moreover, the founding of merchantmen at sea not
infrequently occurred in these times; and during a war they
were also often captured.

The amount of the freight charge varied but little in different decades. For many years, it remained at the rate of
six pounds sterling a ton. Subsequently, it rose to seven pounds,
and finally to fifteen. In the meanwhile, there were instances
of the payment of even seventeen and eighteen pounds. This
charge was made possible by the scarcity of shipping occasioned
chiefly by hostilities between England and Holland. It was
claimed by the sea-captains that the freight rates would have
been reduced materially had they been able to pick up these
cargoes without the loss of time caused by the necessity of passing from river to river and wharf to wharf.

A large quantity of tobacco was transported to England, not
in hogsheads, but in bulk. That method of shipment offered
some substantial advantages. First, there was no delay in for-
warding it, after it was cured, because it was not necessary to

assort and pack it. The removal of this impediment enabled it
to be shipped much earlier than the leaf stored in hogsheads,
and, as a result of this fact, it was sold at a higher rate, since
the competition was not so great at the beginning of the season as it was when the market afterwards was flooded. The
smaller freight charge which was made for a shipment in bulk,
because it could be packed on board with more compactness,
also warranted a reduction in the figures at which it was offered
for sale. The planters were convinced that shipment in bulk
was detrimental to their interests, and they showed vigorous
opposition to its continuation.

An official statement, published in 1689, discloses the fact
that, during that year alone, which was, doubtless, an average
one, 11,646,600 pounds of tobacco were exported from Virginia
to London, and 3,882,200 pounds to other English cities on the
seaboard, a total of over fifteen million pounds.

The progress of time only confirmed and strengthened the
planters' disposition to increase the quantity of tobacco which
they were producing. This course had its justification in two
facts: first, this crop was the most profitable of all those to
which the soil was adapted; and second, which was almost as
important, it was the only medium in which the quit rents,
tithes, and parish, county, and public levies were paid. Nevertheless, the landowners' attention was not entirely withdrawn
from the cultivation of other commodities. It was indispensable that they should annually harvest and store up a certain
quantity of grain. How was bread to be procured unless either
wheat or maize was produced to serve that vital purpose? It
was impossible, even at the end of the century, to impart any
kind of grain in such volume as to make good any real deficiency
in the local supply. Wheat or maize had to be cultivated from
year to year or the people would have starved, whether the
price of tobacco was high or low.

Although wheat, oats, and barley did not yield in great
abundance on most of the lands given over to them after sev-

eral crops of tobacco had been harvested, still there were few
plantations of the average size which did not contain a considerable number of acres sown, in season, in these grains;
and this too in spite of the fact that every wheat, oat and barley field had to be fenced to keep out the vagrant hogs, horses,
cows, and oxen. Without such a barrier, the owner of these
animals could not be held liable for any damage which they
caused. Some of the planters produced a sufficient surplus of
wheat to justify them in exporting it to markets situated outside of the Colony. These markets were found chiefly in New
England, Barbadoes, and Madeira. In the West Indies, the
cargo was bartered for slaves, rum, and sugar. If the voyage
had terminated at Madeira, the famous wine of that island,
which was in common use in Virginia, was taken in exchange
for the wheat. The grain had been separated from the chaff
in the Virginia barn either by treading it out with the feet of
oxen, or beating it out with the flail. The sieve was also used.

The bread made of the meal of Indian corn continued to be
the chief form of that kind of food to be found on all the tables,
whatever the class in the community to which the owners belonged. There was no restriction upon the cultivation of this
grain. The soil of the fertile lowgrounds was exactly adapted
to its growth. The finest agricultural scene on the plantation
was a field of maize as its long blades, green as an emerald,
waved and rustled in the faint breeze of a September day. The
stalks grew to an imposing height, and at the top, burst out
in beautiful tassels. In the late autumn, when the heavy ears in
their dry shucks hung down, this grain was more representative of abundance than any other crop produced in the Colony.

A rarer crop, though far from being unknown, was cotton.
The soil of the counties along the Carolina boundary was highly
favorable to the production of this plant, but, apparently, the
only use made of the soil of the Colony as a whole for this
purpose was to provide enough of the material to satisfy the
demand for the local household manufacture of cloth. Every

planter's residence, and many cabins for the slaves or indentured servants, contained a rude loom or spinning wheel; and both were instrumental in supplying a very large proportion of the garments which the people wore. Seemingly, there was no attempt made,—certainly not to a conspicuous extent,—to produce raw cotton in such volume as to encourage its export.

Silk culture by the end of the century had been practically abandoned.

A large quantity of fruit was produced in the Colony at this time. Some of the orchards contained as many as three hundred peach and three hundred apple trees. There were others in which not less than twenty-five hundred apple trees alone could be counted, and on examination in season, they were found to be bearing all the then well-known varieties of that fruit. It was said that the hogs throve so well on the droppings from the peach trees that separate orchards of that species were planted in order to afford in summer an abundance of this nourishing food. The apple and peach orchards alike were sources of another kind of return,—they were used to furnish the material for the manufacture of cider, which was either consumed in the owner's home, or sold to any one who wished to buy it. So large was the sum obtained by some planters from the sale of their cider that it amounted in some years to fifteen thousand pounds of tobacco.

William Fitzhugh, who was remarkable for his enterprising spirit in his agricultural operations, experimented with the olive on one of his plantations, but, apparently, his hope of success with it was frustrated; doubtless, by the cold spells occurring during the midwinter season. The orange, by this time, had disclosed unmistakably its inability to take permanent root in the soil of the Colony; so had rice; and so had other commodities really suitable only to a climate continuously mild.

The foreign vine seems also to have proved itself to be an unprofitable shrub in Virginia. This, perhaps, was chiefly due to the negligence which the planters exhibited towards their vineyards. They neither pruned nor grafted the vines, but left them to grow up in the way which nature dictated, just as if they were so many wild vines dangling to the trees in the forests, or overspreading the bushes springing up along the banks of the lonely brooks.

During the closing decades of the Seventeenth Century, so many horses wandered at large in the woods at all seasons of the year that they were hunted down by the planters as if they were really deer or bison. So regular was this sport in its annual recurrence that domestic horses were trained for the special purpose of enabling the riders the more easily to capture them. So completely were these vagrants considered to be beyond the protection of law that they could be shot without offense if discovered trespassing on the corn fields. Untamed cows and bulls were equally numerous in the forests; and they too were pursued with ardor and destroyed without mercy, unless they bore the marks of some individual owner. Sheep were now to be counted in large flocks, and the hogs belonging to the greater estates were so numerous that they were no longer appraised in the inventories.

CHAPTER VII

ECONOMY OF THE HOUSEHOLD

In previous chapters, we have given a description of the agricultural growth of Virginia during the seventeenth century and the condition of the indentured servant and the slave, who were so productively associated with this side of Colonial life. We have now come to the subject of the domestic economic aspects of that life. What were the contents of the plantation residence at its best? What were the size and appearance of the house itself? What was the character of the household dress, food, and drink? How did the family travel from place to place?

In a general way, it may be stated that the contents of the home in those times, as in these, were, as a rule, in proportion to the owner's wealth. Practically, these contents were the same as were to be seen in a house of the same pretension in England at that date. With a few unimportant exceptions, the furniture in the sitting and bed rooms had been imported from the Mother Country. This was equally true of the furniture used in the dining room. It was also true of the utensils in the kitchen. Bedsteads, chairs, and chests had been brought from across the ocean; so had the tables, the pewter dishes and cups; so had the ladles, pots, kettles, churns, and pails. These various articles had once rested in the very stores to which the English householder had also gone when he wished to furnish his own dwelling house. They had traveled far, but this fact had not changed their appearance or diminished their usefulness at all. It had only made them more valuable. No doubt, many pieces

169

of rough furniture of local manufacturers were found even in
the wealthy planter's home, but these were confined to the
domestics' apartments, where the principal work of the household was done. The rude chairs, beds, and stools in the cabins
of the slaves and indentured servants were all made in the local
carpenter's shop; but even in the case of these cabins, the
knives and plates had been imported from England, since none,
unless of wood, could be fashioned in the Colony.

To enter more into particulars: the furniture in the planter's mansion was often of a luxurious character. The large
feather bed was surrounded by heavy curtains supported by
rods resting on it from high posts. The valances were frequently made of serge, a scarlet stuff, or kidderminster, also
of a bright color. Thrown over the blankets and linen sheets
of the best quality were coverlets of green and white cloth or
quilts of mixed patterns to give additional distinction to the
bed. In the chamber, a spreading couch or two were placed to
serve as a support in sleeping or resting. The frames of these
couches were often upholstered in Russian leather or Turkey-
worked cloth.

The great chest was the main receptacle for the most valuable garments, and always descended from one generation to
another. Many of them were adorned with brass nails and
bands. They ranged in size from a large trunk to a little box
that could be easily carried by hand. The small chest was a
place of storage for coin, jewels, and other precious articles.
The chairs, like the couches, were, in many cases, highly ornamented with Russian leather or Turkey-worked cloth. In the
houses of planters of means, two dozen of these chairs were
sometimes seen.

The wood in the fire places of the residences rested on andirons made of shining brass and iron, and often fashioned in
the shape of dogs; or, perhaps, the front upright section had
been cast in the shape of a pigmy man; sometimes in uniform.
The fire burning on the hearth was not the only means em-

ployed in heating. The warming pan was in as common use in Virginia as in England. The floor was covered with a carpet manufactured of leather, or of some thick cloth decorated with flowers or picturesque figures. Tapestry for the adornment of the walls was sometimes observed; and additional color was lent to the rooms by screens similarly decorated, or by tall clocks built of darkly seasoned wood.

The most conspicuous feature of the diningroom was the table, which, in some cases, was made of black walnut, and in others, of cedar. There were several kinds of this furniture, —the folding, the falling, the Spanish, and the Dutch oval table. The mistresses of many of the plantation mansions took an excusable pride in displaying the several specimens of table-cloths which they possessed. The finest was of damask. One well known hostess in those times, Mrs. Elizabeth Digges, owned nine table-cloths made of this material; and there were to go with them thirty-six damask napkins.

The cupboard erected against the wall presented to view not infrequently a very striking array of highly polished pewter plate, composed of cups, dishes, and spoons. There were many varieties of drinking utensils, some of which were very artistic in shape and valuable in quality. They included the mug, the flagon, the tankard, and the beaker. There were also sugar-pots, custard cups, bottle cruits, and porringers. The material of which this ware was made was very frequently silver. The silver utensils had, in some cases, been inherited from English relations, but, in most, had been bought in England through the agency of the tobacco merchants with whom the planters traded. The purchase of this form of household property was encouraged by more than one influence. It was not acquired simply for display. It was acquired chiefly because it was considered to be a safe permanent investment, which could be transmitted to heirs without any prospect of a decline in value. William Fitzhugh, on the occasion of his giving one order alone, instructed his factor to send him four silver dishes, ranging in weight from fifty to seventy-two ounces; a set of castors, that were twenty-six ounces in weight; a salver and a pair of candle sticks, thirty ounces in weight a piece; a ladle, ten ounces; and a case to contain a dozen silver hafted knives and forks respectively. The inventories of other wealthy planters indicated their possession of a large quantity of silver plate that compared favorably in value with the list of the same precious articles owned by Fitzhugh.

There is no conspicuous evidence that the walls of the principal residences were adorned with many pictures, although their presence in the rooms of some of these mansions is recorded. Among other objects observed, there were certain musical instruments which had been immemorially associated with the English home, such as the handlyre, the cornet, virginal, fiddle, violin, recorder, hautboy, and flute.

It will not be necessary to dwell, except briefly, on the contents of the kitchen. The utensils to be found there were made of wood, pewter, brass, tin, and clay. The variety of these utensils was extraordinary. One of the largest of them all was the boiler made of copper or brass. Its use was not confined to the preparation of food, for it was also important in the process of brewing. Indeed, it was as much valued for this purpose as for the purpose of ordinary cooking. The iron pot was hung from iron racks riveted to the chimney, but it could be moved out of doors; and this was, doubtless, always done in summer. Suspended to two posts in the shade of a tree, with a fire kindled under it, it was the receptacle for the vegetables and pieces of meat which were thrown into it to be converted into a nourishing mess for the appeasement of the hunger of the plantation workers, whether slave or servant. Some of the kettles weighed as much as fifteen pounds.

In every kitchen, there was a spit swung directly in front of the live coals for roasting mutton, venison, or fowl. The gravy was caught in a large pan and thrown back on the simmering flesh with ladles of a proportionate size. Near at hand were gridirons used in broiling, iron skillets used in baking, and pans in frying. Chafing dishes were grouped on the shelves. Saucepans, mortars, sifters, knives of various sorts, flesh forks, powdering tubs, meal barrels, galley pots, pepper boxes, rolling pins, steelyards, and other utensils necessary to the kitchen, were to be counted, each ready nearby to serve the purpose for which it was designed. The great oven stood on ground in the immediate vicinity of the residence. Here too was situated the small house used as a dairy, which contained a large collection of churns, piggins, tubs, strainers, cheese presses, and earthen butter-pots.

Such were the principal contents of the dwelling houses of the planters who were in possession of comfortable fortunes.

What was the character of these houses in their outer aspect? The great majority were simple and plain to the eye, with no real claim to architectural beauty. This was just what was to be expected in a country as recently settled as Virginia, and having as yet only limited supplies of building materials of the best grain and finish. Bricks were made in the Colony in the seventeenth century in large quantities, but probably they were not as substantial as the English brick, owing to the makers' ignorance of some of the latest appliances in their manufacture. At Henricopolis, the first story of each house was constructed of this solid material, but elsewhere the building above a narrow brick foundation was of frame obtained from the adjacent forests.

After the dissolution of the Company, an effort was made by law to compel the erection of houses composed entirely of brick, and their size was directed to be in proportion to the extent of the plantations on which they stood. The local impediments to the construction of brick houses in great numbers discouraged the enforcement of this act, except so far as it related to chimneys.

The use of wood in building residences was promoted by the existence in Virginia of so many varieties of trees suitable for the production of lumber. There were oak, pine, cypress, cedar, hickory, and chestnut on every plantation. It was only necessary to cut and saw these trees in the proper length, and dry out the fiber. Some of the planters employed their laborers at times to make plank with a view to its sale to persons wishing to build. Large quantities were often left to heirs by will. This plank entered into the composition of the houses of the most affluent planters.

The important residences were not erected as it were at one stroke. It was noticed in the case of nearly every one of them that they steadily expanded by the addition of new rooms, as the family increased in size. Houses were to be seen in the oldest and wealthiest parts of the Colony which represented the various stages in the growth of the community. First, there was a log cabin, in which the father of the owner,—perhaps a pioneer,—or the owner himself in his early years, had lived, Next, as the fortunes of the household prospered, a frame, sometimes large, sometimes small, was joined on to the log structure; and as the final stage in the evolution, a brick room or two were afterwards attached.

How many rooms were to be found in these domestic buildings? The average house, which was of frame, with a brick chimney at either end, and a wide hall running through it, had generally two rooms on each floor, with a room in the ceiled garret. Most often a house of this kind had on the ground floor one large apartment for a withdrawing room on one side of the hall, and two small apartments on the other side. Every house of this size, doubtless, possessed a capacious cellar, where many articles of food, like potatoes and apples, were stored during the winter.

Governor Berkeley's residence at Greenspring near Jamestown contained six rooms of commodious dimensions. This structure was built entirely of brick. Owing to the heat of the climate, it is probable that the upper rooms in this house were sacrificed in height to the lower. Most of the superior residences in the Colony at this time could boast of more or less lofty ceilings in their lower rooms, which gave the heated air the space to circulate high above the floor.

The dwelling house of Fitzhugh contained under its roof as many as thirteen apartments, but so great a number was exceptional, even among the wealthiest planters. The home of Nathaniel Bacon, the elder, which contained an old and new hall, apparently had four large chambers within its partitions, one of which was occupied by the head of the house and his wife. There was also another chamber of a smaller size. In the house in which Mrs. Digges lived, there was a hall together with a withdrawing room on the ground level, and on the level above, there were two apartments, known as the yellow room and the red room. There was a small room in addition, and also a kitchen, dairy, and storeroom. These were duplicated also in the home of Bacon, already referred to. These two mansions were typical of those belonging to the most prominent persons in the Colony.

There was a wide yard situated in front of each house. This was generally bordered by shrubbery, chiefly box, and overshadowed by tall oaks and elms. Behind the house, the garden was usually placed, and it was laid off, as a rule, in the form of terraces. Here every variety of English flowers flourished. In one part of the garden, vegetables were cultivated; and on the outskirts, orchards of peach, apple, plum, and cherry trees had been planted. At some distance in the background the servant quarters, stables, cowpens, and poultry houses, were to be seen; and not far away rose the roof of the spring house, in which all the perishable table supplies were preserved from day to day.

Rarely have there existed a people who enjoyed as great a variety and abundance of food as the Virginians in the seventeenth century. Every medium of supply contributed to this good fortune. For the garnishment of their tables, they could count on animals, both wild and domestic, birds of the air, fish of river and sea, and fruits of the soil. The cattle afforded not only veal and beef in large quantities, but also, from day to day, all the milk, butter, and cheese which each family needed for its own use. It was only in a dry and salted state that the beef could be kept for long, since, apparently, there were no ice-houses attached to the residences. The only means employed for the preservation of fresh meat was the cold water passing through the spring house which caught the flow of some natural fountain near at hand. This was only of temporary service; and to avoid a loss, most parts of a slaughtered ox were distributed at once among the nearest neighbors. The beef in use was of inferior quality unless the animal had been long stalled and carefully fed in the interval.

No real attention was paid to the welfare of the cattle in general by their owners. The stock running at large in the woods, and obtaining only the food to be picked up there, steadily declined in physical size and robustness, and in their natural state were little fit to be converted into food. During the time of the Company, many cows, bulls, and oxen were imported from England, but after the recall of the Charter, few, if any, were brought into the Colony. Thereafter, the degeneration made rapid progress. The want of nourishing food, except in the spring and summer, and continued exposure to the harsh temperature in winter, reduced the breed to a point of physical impoverishment that took away much of their value for the table as well as for the cultivated fields.

The hog was also subjected to the same depleting conditions, but its flesh was improved, not damaged, in taste, by the provender on which it fed in the woods. There it devoured the acorns, which, in autumn and winter, bestrewed the ground, and at other seasons, the roots of the grasses which grew in the swamps and marshes or carpeted the wide savannahs. This succulent food imparted such a fine flavor to the meat of this animal that a Virginian ham was pronounced by discriminating judges of that day to be as excellent as the famous hams of Westphalia. This reputation it has maintained down to the present age. The Smithfield ham is now, perhaps, the most popular of its kind in the western world.

In the seventeenth century, pork, with beans, peas, or greens, formed the principal food of a large proportion of the people. To this must be added the flesh of chickens, which were raised in large flocks by the humblest householder, and even by the slaves and indentured servants. As mutton was rarer than beef and pork, it was eaten with the keenest relish. Indeed, it was thought to have been more esteemed than venison. Deer, being killed more frequently than the domestic animals used as food, was, for that reason, regarded with less favor when dished up for a meal. The people are said to have grown tired of its flavor.

This was not true of the wild fowl which were brought down by the hunter. One of the largest of these was the turkey, which ran in numerous flocks in the depths of the woods. There it was captured by various artifices as well as shot with the gun. One of the devices employed was a low square trap made of parallel sticks. The bird entered by a narrow, dug-out passage in the ground under one side of the trap, and was too stupid to find its way outside again. It was allured to the hole by a string of grains of maize that had been laid so as to run straight to the place of entrance. Sometimes as many as a dozen turkeys were captured in this manner at one time.

The wild geese from the North were as much esteemed as food by the Colonists as the wild turkeys. They appeared only in autumn and winter. Along with them arrived great flocks of wild duck belonging to several varieties, all remarkable for the delicious flavor of their flesh,—such as the canvas-back, the mallard, and the redhead. Plovers and snipes also haunted the seashore and the marshes in numbers beyond calculation. Among the birds shot in the upland fields or swamps were the partridge, robin, and woodcock. The hunter's bag was further swelled by hare and squirrel in the day time, and by raccoon and opossum at night.

The water was equally generous and liberal in supplying fish for the Colonial tables. Among the most esteemed varieties were shad and sheepshead caught in the salty estuaries, and perch, bass, and chub, in the fresh untainted streams. The oyster was equally as much enjoyed; and so was the crab in its early stage of growth.

We have seen that such an unlimited quantity of apples and peaches was produced that the mere droppings from the branches furnished ample provender in season for the planter's herd of pigs. In all the gardens there were to be found the grape vine and groups of fig bushes, which brought forth with the same abundance as the principal fruit trees. Besides these two varieties, the same plat furnished large quantities of straw-berries, raspberries, and every species of English vegetables. Early in the history of the Colony, it was said by a woman householder who had come from England, that she could pro-vide out of the few acres which she had enclosed as much nour-ishing food in one year as she could produce in London by an expenditure of four hundred pounds sterling. Joined on to the terraces set aside for the vegetables was an equal area reserved for flowers, and these furnished the material needed by the bees, which occupied the planter's numerous hives, and supplied him with honey through the twelve months. From the neighboring woods, he obtained the nuts of the hickory, walnut, and hazel.

An abundance of spices, sweetmeats, oranges, lemons, rais-ins, and prunes were imported from England, the West Indies, and the Island of Madeira and the Azores. Salt was obtained either abroad or by local manufacture.

As Englishmen themselves by birth, or descended from Englishmen in the first or second generation, the Virginians were not disinclined to enjoy the pleasures of the cup. This was true of them without any implication that drunkenness was a common vice in their communities. The evidence is to the contrary; but in their general society, the taste for liquor was not restrained by any lurking regard for the superior wholesomeness of entire abstinence.

As early as 1609, when the Colony had been in existence for two years only, the Company advertized for brewers who would be willing to emigrate to Virginia for the purpose of providing its communities with spirits, to be manufactured after their arrival. The call for men experienced in that art was repeated a short time afterwards, when Gates was about to set out from London on his long voyage to Jamestown. The reason for the demand for brewers lay largely in the impression that one cause of the high mortality among the persons going through the seasoning on the plantations was the fact that they were compelled to drink water, since they no longer had at hand the supplies of beer which they had used regularly before leaving the Mother Country.

In 1625, it was noted that the two brew houses then in Virginia, could, with difficulty, furnish the quantity of malt liquor desired by the inhabitants. The grains of the Indian corn were soon discovered to be rich in alcohol; and the spirits distilled from them became popular with the immigrants. Malt, however, continued to be imported by the hogshead; especially during the existence of the Protectorate in England. Local substitutes for it were found in the fruit of the persimmon tree; in potatoes and pumpkins; and also in the Jerusalem artichoke. There were, by the middle of the century, numerous brew houses in the Colony. Those planters who did not own private distilleries were satisfied to possess worms and limbecks. Cider, as we have already mentioned, was produced in copious quantities, and butts of it very often formed a part of a testator's estate. Perry, brewed from pears, and brandy from peaches and apples, were also manufactured to meet a continuous demand.

Owing to the ease with which madeira and other island wines could be imported, these beverages were consumed very liberally in the Colony, not only at all the private tables, but also at all the public. Claret and Rhenish too were in constant demand; and so was Mathegelin, which was concocted of honey and water, and was very freely used by the common people for refreshment.

Governor Harvey, in 1638, became impatient with the popular indulgence in spirits of all sorts, which he asserted swallowed up the proceeds from one half of the Colony's annual crop of tobacco. The progress of time brought about no decline in this thirst for strong waters. Liquor had to be provided for officials on every public occasion, beginning with the magistrate of the County Courts and the members of the Council and running down to the supervisors of the highways. Not even an ordinary contract was signed without a draught. It was as easily procured in the inns as so much water, and in order to prevent extortion at these public bars, the law required that the charges for each liquor and each dram should be set by the Court. Any disregard of the figures adopted was punished by heavy fines, which were strictly enforced.

We have dwelt at some length on the general background of the planter's life; the character of the house in which he lived; its contents; the food which he ate; and the spirits which he drank. How did he and the members of his household dress?

There was the same taste for fine apparel among the people of the remote Virginian Colony as prevailed in all the communities of England in the same age. "Our Cowkeeper in Jamestown, on Sunday." records Pory, Speaker of the Assembly in 1619, "goes accoutered in fresh flaming silks." A contemporary, who was the wife of a man who had been a collier at Croydon, but afterwards emigrated to Virginia, "wore," we are told, "her rough beaver hat with a fair pearl hat-band and a silken suit." A few years later, one of the merchants of the Colony bequeathed to friends a remarkable collection of showy garments, such as a cross cloth of wrought gold, numerous pairs of silk stockings and red slippers, sea-green scarfs edged with gold laces, felt hats, black beavers, fur caps, camlet doublets, swords, and gold belts. So far was this eager taste for ornamented garments carried about the middle of the century that a law had to be passed to repress it. It was then ordered that no silk should be imported, except for the adornment of hoods and scarfs; no silver, gold or bone lace; and no ribbons decorated with gold or silver. This regulation apparently did not remain in force during any considerable length of time.

The people of Virginia, always keenly conscious of their social connection with England, were as averse to separating themselves from it in their style of dress as they were in their general manner of living. On all public occasions when members of both sexes came together, there was no real difference in quality or aspect between the garments worn by them and those worn by Englishmen of the same social position who had met for a similar purpose. Bright colors were equally conspicuous among both peoples in the like surroundings, whether it was a congregation gathered for church services, or a company assembled under a plantation roof for the enjoyment of a dinner party or a dance.

Large quantities of various fabrics were purchased in England by the Virginians to supply themselves with the material for the making of various garments, both for common use and for distinguished occasions. These were converted into clothes of all sorts by the hands of the mistresses of the several households or by those of their female servants. But, perhaps, the largest proportion of the most showy suits for men, and the most elegant dresses for women, in a completed form, were purchased in London or Bristol, where the tailors were more skilful in making such costly articles of wear. The ladies' wardrobes were especially attractive for their contents, which included petticoats of Indian silk, silk-gowns, scarlet waistcoats with silver lace, prunella mantles, blue satin bodices, holland sleeves with ruffles, silk and cambric handkerchiefs, and silk stockings. Among the ornaments worn by the owners of these beautiful garments were pearl necklaces, gold pendants, gold handrings, and silver earrings.

One of the most interesting souvenirs of these times was the mourning ring. A testator often reserved as much as twenty-five pounds sterling to provide rings of this significance for distribution among his friends after his death.

The carriage was not unknown to the planters' families. Governor Berkeley owned a coach, which was driven by a servant in livery. Fitzhugh possessed a calash, which he had imported from London. But the most popular means of conveyance on land was the horse, as it could move so easily over the rough public highways. It seems to have been used as much by women as by men. Pillions and side saddles were frequently mentioned in the inventories. The men's saddles were, in some instances, very handsome, covered as they were with purple leather or crimson velvet, and with fine saddle cloths attached. As most of the residences were situated on the rivers or salt water creeks, the passenger boat was in constant use, and the members of the planter's household were as accomplished with the oar and the sail in handling it as they were with the riding nag.

CHAPTER VIII

ARTICLES OF LOCAL MANUFACTURE

We have seen that the perishable supplies of all sorts used in the Colony's households were produced in the soil of the plantations. Before considering the extent to which the needs of the inhabitants were met by the importation of articles of foreign manufacture,—we have referred to this incidentally already,—we will give some account of the development of local manufactures as far as it had gone in Virginia in the seventeenth century.

Powerful influences were in operation to discourage the establishment of such manufactures on a scale of real importance. One of the reasons for Virginia's colonization, as we have shown, was to create a market for articles that had been made in England. It was expected that the Colony, as it grew in population, would absorb an ever increasing quantity of English merchandise; and the actual upshot proved that this anticipation was well grounded. In ordinary times, the planters were fully satisfied to rely upon the English manufactures for all the artificial goods which they required from season to season, but there rolled around harsh years when the expense of purchasing these imported articles became greater than the shrunken means of the people could stand; and in such years as these, there was a natural disposition on their part to make at home with their own hands whatever would serve as a substitute.

There was no inherited dislike among the Virginians to manufacturing as an employment. Many of the persons who came out to the Colony in these early years had been engaged in work of that character before they passed oversea, where local circumstances, and not mere personal preference, had directed their energies to the cultivation of corn and tobacco. Perhaps, when, in lean years, the planters' pecuniary resources were so shortened as to destroy their ability to purchase the cargoes of manufactured goods brought in by the arriving ships, they sometimes found relief by the discovery among their indentured servants in the field of a man or woman who was capable of making clothes at least, because they had learned to do so in the English cottages of the country sides where they had formerly lived. Apparently, there was not often any real difficulty in finding under the home roof domestics who were skilful in the use of the needle and the spinning-wheel, and possibly of the loom. Such persons were apt to have been present and available both in impoverished and flourishing periods.

But this was not necessarily so in the case of individuals who were versed in the higher mechanical trades in general. There were, roughly speaking, two different sets of persons who were continuously employed in these trades. One set was composed of men who had been imported under indentures because of their previous mechanical training. The other was drawn from the mass of freemen of moderate means.

As a rule, the planter of fortune, recognizing the constant need of the presence of experienced mechanics on his land, such as the carpenter, cabinetmaker, saddler, blacksmith, brickmaker, bricklayer, and shoemaker and the like, took advantage of the first chance open to him of acquiring artisans of this type to satisfy all the mechanical demands that arose from time to time on his estate. The indentured mechanic was not, however, as easily procurable from England as the raw agricultural servant. As a class, the artisans were in a more advantageous position in their native land than any other particular division of the lower population in the different English communities. It followed that not so many of them, in proportion to their number, emigrated oversea. At the same time, it was

well known to them as a class that the Colony offered very
·unusual opportunities for obtaining steady work, and, perhaps,
of acquiring small estates. Those who decided to take advantage of these opportunities, but were lacking in the means to
pay their own transportation charges, had recourse to indentures, and under the provisions of these documents came out
to Virginia, where they soon found themselves, on account of
their special training, in constant demand.

In all the importations of laborers in the time of the Company, mechanics were included in very considerable batches.
There were brick makers, bricklayers, founders, shipwrights,
carpenters, calkers, coopers, tanners, smiths, and shoemakers.
These men were reserved for the Company's use, and were
granted privileges of great value in its employment.

After the Company passed out of existence, mechanics for
a time grew scarce in the Colony, and when a public building,
like the State House at Jamestown, had to be erected, it became
necessary to send an agent to England to procure the workmen
required for its construction. Gradually their number increased,
in consequence of the tempting offers held out by individual
planters to induce emigration to the Colony. The period of their
indentures was limited to a few years, as a rule. The planter
bound himself to pay the charges for the mechanic's transportation, and also to provide him, after his arrival, with the tools
needed in the pursuit of his trade; to shelter, feed, and clothe
him properly during his term; and to refrain from assigning
him to another employer while the contract lasted. It often
happened that his master agreed to convey to him at the end
of his service a tract of fifty acres of land, and also to support
him until his first crop of tobacco had been garnered. The lib-
erality of these provisions indicates how far the planter was
often willing to go to secure the exclusive right to a mechanic's
labor even during a brief interval of time.

The exacting character of such concessions must, as the
years passed, have had an important influence in causing every

owner of a large plantation to train an intelligent slave to take the place of a white mechanic under indentures when these expired. The negro remained with his master continuously throughout his life. He might always be more careless and less skilful in his methods than a white servant mechanic, but, at least, he could not be drawn away by other offers of employment at any hour. He was practically an indentured workman for the same person, his owner, until the infirmities of old age had crept on him and weakened his grip on saw, hammer, trowel, and shuttle.

The number of mechanics in the Colony under bond was increased by the accession of orphans without estates, who were bound out to free artisans in order to learn a trade which, throughout life, would afford them a permanent means of subsistence. These orphans were apprenticed under strict provisions for the preservation of their health, and for their acquisition of expert knowledge in their respective pursuits. They were not to be withdrawn from the shop to labor in the tobacco fields, but they could be used in gathering in the maize, if there was, at the time, a shortage in the number of servants or slaves needed to complete the task.

It was an interesting feature of an orphan's bond that the master was required to teach him the arts of writing and reading, and also to ground him in the rudiments of arithmetic. After the expiration of his term, he was to receive, as an assistance to him in starting his independent life, a full set of tools adapted to his special calling, and also a considerable quantity of clothing. He then became a member of the Company of free mechanics who were following their trades in the different communities of the Colony. These men, by a law passed in 1633, were forbidden to drop their business even temporarily, in order to cultivate tobacco; and the military commander of each district was held responsible, should this injunction be violated.

A few years afterward, the mechanics were required to leave their plantation stands and open shops in the places which had been chosen by the General Assembly as sites for towns. How great was the anxiety of that body to increase the prosperity of this class, and thus make them more loyal to their trades, is revealed in the law of 1661-62, which exempted all handicraftsmen from the payment of levies, provided that they abstained from the production of tobacco either for their own or for another's benefit. There could not be a more impressive evidence of the importance attached to the trades than this, for the General Assembly was always extremely reluctant to grant such a privilege, since it augmented the burden of the rest of the taxpayers. In 1680 that body went so far as to relieve all handicraftsmen settled in the towns from personal arrest for failure to pay their debts.

Notwithstanding the advantages which tradesmen enjoyed there was a strong disposition on the part of a large number to break away from their calling entirely, and give themselves up to the pursuit of planting. It was not simply the prospect of the higher profit which this course held out to them that .influenced their action. Owing to the dispersion of the plantations, and the paucity of passable roads, an extraordinary degree of time was lost by mechanics in tramping from neighborhood to neighborhood in search of jobs. This was both fatiguing and unremunerative.

In spite of this drawback to the prosperity of tradesmen in Virginia during this century, there were many persons belonging to that class who had succeeded in acquiring estates of considerable value; but there is reason to think that these men had accumulated these estates as much by the cultivation of tobacco as by the pursuit of mechanical crafts. Nevertheless, those crafts had been sufficiently profitable to induce the masters of them to continue in their practice in the face of the larger returns to be reaped from the devotion of all their time to the tillage of the soil. Blacksmiths, coopers, and carpenters could always rely upon a steady custom. The blacksmith had iron instruments or horseshoes for the planters to fashion; the cooper, hogsheads to construct; and the carpenter, cabins and barns to erect. There was never any cessation in the demand for the work of these tradesmen.

The boatwright followed the calling that enjoyed the highest distinction in the mechanical province, for it merged in that of the shipwright from time to time. One of the most popular means, as we have seen, of passing from plantation to plantation situated on the navigable streams,—as all the most important were,—was by sail or oar. These boats ranged all the way from a cockle-shell to a shallop and a sloop. They were required to be strongly constructed, and also to be thoroughly staunch in riding the waves, since the waters in the large streams were often rough, and gusts of wind arose with great suddenness, requiring knowledge, especially of the handling of sails, to avoid a catastrophe.

Boatwrights were sent out to Virginia during the time of the Company, and they continued to be found in every community down to the end of the century. Ample lumber was furnished for the building of barks, pinnaces, and other small vessels, by the numerous sawmills in the Colony. But as late as 1655, no sea-going ship had been laid down in Virginia. The nearest approval to such a ship was the vessel which ventured only to skirt the coast. A few years afterwards, there was built in the Colony a vessel that was able to carry forty guns and to make the voyage to England. Its appearance and action were so fine that it was confidently expected that ship construction would some day become an industry of importance in Virginia, but this anticipation was never realized during this century, in spite of the rewards in different forms which were held out by the General Assembly to encourage it.

Perhaps, the most repressive influence brought to bear upon it was by the English Government. The authorities in London looked upon the building of sea-going vessels in Virginia with an eye of zealous disapproval, and, in consequence, Culpeper, in 1680, was ordered by them to withdraw all the inducements which had been offered by the General Assembly to promote it. It was claimed by the English Government that the spirit of the Navigation Act would be violated by the pursuit of such an industry in the Colony, for had not one of the main reasons for the passage of that Act been the expansion of England's shipping? How could the interests of this shipping be advanced if Virginia should be permitted to build entire fleets of merchantmen to displace oversea those which hailed from London, Bristol, and the other English ports?

How unnecessarily anxious were the English authorities in their view of ship-building in Virginia at this time is revealed by a petition of the principal planters, which mentioned incidentally that there were only two sea-going vessels in its waters that had been constructed in a colonial shipyard.

The earliest object to be manufactured in the Colony was glass. This was undertaken apparently, not to supply material for window panes or for drinking cups, but to provide an abundance of beads to facilitate trade with the savages. These beads had an extraordinary fascination for the Indian eye, and in return for their acquisition, these untutored bargainers were eager to exchange maize, furs, and, indeed, whatever else they possessed, considered to be of value by the English settlers.

The persons employed in making glass were four Italians, who, quite probably, had been obtained from Venice, the city then the most famous in Europe for this branch of manufacture. They were assisted by two men under indentures, who, doubtless, were expected to do all the rough work in turning out the articles. The exclusive right to produce glass by means of these six men, four of whom were experts, was granted to Captain William Norton, who was required to give his personal supervision to the manufacture, and also to train apprentices to skilfulness in carrying out the process. Accompanied by the members of his family, and the experts, he set sail for Vir-

GEORGE SANDYS

ginia, and on his arrival there, began at once to construct the
necessary furnace; but apparently, he died before it was completed.

George Sandys took his place, and finished the structure;
but he soon found that the sand both at Jamestown and at Cape
Henry lacked the quality called for by his purpose. The curious
fact then occurred that he was compelled to send to England
for the right sort of material for the production of glass. In
the meanwhile, the Italian artificers, homesick and half fam-
ished, had grown dissatisfied with life in the Colony, and, in
consequence, endeavored to raise an excuse for their return to
Italy. They first pursued their work so slowly and so capri-
ciously that Sandys, in his impatience, denounced them as the
most "damnable crew that Hell ever vomited." But he soon had
more serious cause for disgust. In their determination to put
an end to the industry, they deliberately cracked the furnace
beyond all hope of its repair.

The earliest attempt to manufacture iron in the Colony,
seemed at first to be highly promising, but, in the end, col-
lapsed in a terrible disaster. At this time, iron was made in
large quantities in the English shire of Sussex, but the draft
on the forests, of the kingdom for this purpose was so heavy
that apprehension was felt that, outside of the parks, the woods
would be completely destroyed. In the meanwhile, a large
amount of iron was also annually imported from the continent,
but this supply was subject to numerous vicissitudes which
were likely at any hour to interrupt its flow.

These two circumstances,—the gradual shrinkage in the
existing English forests, and the constant liabliity to extreme
fluctuation in the importation from abroad,—made the English
authorities eager to develop the production of iron in Virginia so
soon as the presence of ore was discovered there. Stress was
laid upon the necessity of doing this in an early communication
to the London Company; and that body, always warmly respon-
sive to every suggestion that might increase the amount of the

exports from the Colony, took steps at an early date to test the practical value of the ores which had been seen cropping up in various places. Captain Smith had already sent out to England two barrels of stones showing superficial traces of iron. Captain Newport had followed Smith's example. These specimens, when smelted, produced about seventeen tons of metal, which was purchased by the East Indian Company, and found to be excellent in quality.

As early as 1610, machinery had been imported for the manufacture of pig iron. It was already known that a mine existed on the banks of the modern Falling Creek; but advantage apparently was not taken of this fact until some years had passed. In 1619, the adventurers of Southhampton Hundred decided to increase a donation made by an English philanthropist for Indian education by investing it in an iron furnace in Virginia. Captain Blewit, accompanied by eighty men trained in mining iron ore and in converting it into metal, went out to the Colony at the Company's expense, but before the work could even be begun, Blewit died. This caused the project to drag until John Berkeley, some time afterwards, arrived with a reinforcement of twenty experts.

According to the original plan, three furnaces were to be erected, but one alone apparently was built. This was situated at Falling Creek. The other two mines were, perhaps, neglected so soon as it was found that the one at Falling Creek was richer and more voluminous in its deposits. That the furnace at this place was erected on a scale of importance is proven by the fact that five thousand pounds sterling were expended in its construction and in the support of the workingmen attached to it. This sum had, in those times, the purchasing power of at least one hundred thousand dollars at present.

The fate of the settlement at Falling Creek is one of the most tragic in Colonial history. With the exception of a boy and girl, every person connected with the iron works perished by the blow of the tomahawk in 1622, on the occasion of the terrible

massacre that occurred in the course of that year.   The tools of
the workingmen were thrown into the river.   Seemingly, the
works had not expanded far enough to be very productive of
finished articles for sale.   The enemies of the Sandys Administration, which had encouraged the erection of the furnace, sneer-
ingly averred that one iron shovel, a pair of tongs, and a bar of
iron, formed its entire completed output.

There were several spasmodic efforts to revive the production
of iron in the Colony during this century, but nothing of substantial value resulted from this renewal of practical interest
in the subject.   Both Fitzhugh and Byrd endeavored, but in vain
to enlist the aid of English friends by shipping to them specimens of ores which they had found on their estates.

One of the early expectations for Virginia, as we have mentioned, was that, through the abundance of the flax which grew
wild in its soil, it would become a seat of linen manufacture on
a large scale, but it was not until 1646 that this manufacture was
even attempted.   The General Assembly, during that year, gave
orders that two houses should be built for this purpose at Jamestown; and that each county should furnish two children of impoverished parents to be instructed there in the arts of carding,
spinning, and knitting.   These children were to be supported
by their native communities.   Whether this ambitious scheme
was carried out to the extent projected or not, there were certainly numerous planters residing in the Colony at this time who
were successful in producing linen under their own roofs.

In 1682, a specific reward was offered for every pound of
flax suitable for the manufacture of this stuff, which was carried to the County Courts for appraisement; but this enactment
failed to obtain the approval of the English Government, and
was, therefore, revoked.   Nevertheless, the production of linen,
without the subsidy, continued.   This is disclosed by the number of linen wheels listed in the inventories.   The subsidy was
revived in 1693 in favor of every person who could bring in at
least three pieces of linen of different grades in texture which

had been made by himself or by his servants and slaves.   In
the vicinity of every cabin, there was planted a small cotton
patch, the product of which, when harvested, was used in a small-
way locally to manufacture a rough cloth.   These patches were
to be noticed throughout the Colonial period; and similar ones
are still to be seen in the Southern divisions of Virginia, a survival of an agricultural custom which began almost with the
plantation system.

The English Government, apparently, never endeavored to
interfere with this form of domestic manufacture, but the stand
which it took against the manufacture of woolen cloth in the
Colony was even more determined than its stand against the
manufacture of linen cloth.   This fact was the more remarkable
as sheep husbandry had never been pursued to an important
degree by the landowners.   Still, in the aggregate, the quantity
of wool sheared must have reached respectable proportions in
many of the communities; and the supply was made the more
reliable by laws passed from time to time prohibiting its exportation.   To increase the facilities for converting this wool into
cloth, every county was required, in 1659, to erect a public loom,
for which a public weaver was to be provided at the county's
expense.   Children were ordered to be picked out of indigent
households and trained as they grew up to be skillful in handling
both looms and spinning wheels.

The planters took the same advantage of the laws in encouragement of woolen manufacturers as they had done of the laws
in promotion of linen.   On one occasion alone, five landowners
in the County of Middlesex delivered to Court for the award, two
hundred and fifty-nine yards of woolen cloth woven on their
respective estates.   This action on their part was duplicated in
all the wealthiest communities of the Colony.   The industry
had reached proportions of importance, with promise of still
greater, when the English Government, alarmed by the report
of the Commissioners of Customs, positively vetoed the existing
statute which had granted the subsidy.   The reasons which it

gave for this act of inhibition were those which that government was to offer in opposition to local manufacturers throughout the Colonial period, and it will be pertinent to restate them briefly. Such manufacturers, it was said, weakened the tie between Virginia and the Mother Country by decreasing the occasions for correspondence between the two; it fostered a spirit of independence in the Colony; it diminished the number of British sailors by lessening the quantity of freight to be carried; it curtailed the market for English manufactures; and it increased the rate for transporting tobacco to the English ports by cutting down the cargoes of English goods sent oversea in return.

These were weighty considerations if regarded only from the point of view of the interests of the Mother Country. Fortunately for the Colony, the English Government, however able to suppress the subsidies granted by the General Assembly, could not put an end to the manufacture of woolen cloth which went on under every important planter's roof. Not even that Government, bent as it was on restricting the extent of Virginian production in this province, was bold enough to enter the doors of the people's homes and cut to pieces the different families' spinning wheels, spindles, and looms. The nearest step which it could take towards such extreme action was to forbid the exportation of the output of local manufacture from one Colony to another, or from county to county.

This law at least would be able to confine the sale of such articles to a very narrow sphere. As long as it should remain on the statute book, Virginia could not hope to supply any more than its own households with such goods; and this too only within the boundaries of a county so far as that county's own manufactures would go. Each county was thus made dependent on itself for satisfying its needs in this quarter. These needs, if not fully met within the county, had to be supplied from England. Such a handicap as this put an end to the smallest prospect of Virginia ever becoming a seat of manufactures for the English Colonies in the west, a possibility which the English Government held in constant dread, although the peculiarities of tobacco culture, with its tendency to large plantations and the suppression of urban growth, made the development of manufactures in Virginia on as highly organized a scale as was to be observed in the Mother Country, practically impossible. Among the most prosperous tradesmen in the Colony during this century were the tailors, who converted the domestic cloths into the garments that were required by the people at large. They owned an extensive area of land, and like all the other artificers in the community, evidently combined the pursuit of tobacco culture with the art of the needle and the scissors.

The shoemaker and the tanner occupied a position of equal usefulness. Many of them were freemen, whose homes were situated on their own properties. A large number still were indentured servants. Governor Samuel Matthews had under his direction in this character eight shoemakers, who were, no doubt, employed also in the work of his tannery. Colonel Edmund Scarborough too owned an establishment of this kind and had listed in his service nine men, who had been trained to the use of the last. Many planters of equal wealth devised by will large quantities of sole leather and hides, which had been accumulated either for sale or for conversion into shoes. At one time, the law forbade the exportation of these materials.

With Chesapeake Bay and the ocean beyond accessible to makers of salt by evaporation, there was, perhaps, only a small amount of this material brought into the Colony by English ships. The quantity produced was evidently ample to supply the people with all that they needed. Mills for grinding grain into meal or flour were to be found in many places; and mills for sawing lumber were equally numerous. Pitch and tar were produced with little inconvenience or expense, owing to the enormous forests of pine that grew all along the sea coast.

CHAPTER IX

ARTICLES OF FOREIGN MANUFACTURE

The importation of merchandise into the Colony from England, that began with the arrival of the First Supply under Captain Newport's supervision, was the inauguration of British commerce with America, which was destined to increase enormously in volume with the progress of the years. Even as early as 1664, the value of the articles of all sorts unloaded from English vessels at the wharves in the streams of Virginia and Maryland amounted, in the course of every twelve months, to about five million dollars in our modern currency.

Towards the end of the London Company's existence, the expense of carrying across the ocean the various supplies needed by the planters, which were now chiefly in a manufactured form, was borne by the persons who had subscribed a definite sum for the purchase of the goods that were required. The cargo of each ship designed to meet these wants represented a separate mercantile venture, not on the part of the Company as a whole, but on the part of a special band of buyers belonging to the membership of that body, who were ready to risk their money in the hope of a profit.

During an interval of some years, all goods imported into Virginia, whatever, might be their special nature, were exempted from every kind of custom or subsidy. At first, these goods, known as the magazine, were stored under the roof of a building which had been specially reserved for them, and here they remained in the custody of an officer who bore the title of cape merchant. This officer was assisted by two clerks. His function at first was to act as a supercargo, but afterwards he came to superintend the exchange of the contents of the magazine for plantation products, and saw that these products were safely shipped to England. After 1609, when the second charter was issued, which was signed by most of the London trading guilds, a great volume of supplies, the larger proportion of which was food and clothes, was sent to Virginia. Such supplies, for instance, accompanied the fleet which Gates commanded; and the like quantity was conveyed over-sea by Delaware. These had been purchased with the money that numerous corporations, and many noblemen and gentlemen, had subscribed. Subsequently, a large quantity of goods for the Colony had been obtained by means of lotteries, which, in that age, was a popular way of raising funds. The issuance of a third charter, with an addition of new members, had also swelled the London Company's resources.

By the year 1612, when this charter was granted, it was calculated that forty-six thousand pounds sterling had been subscribed by individuals and associations, or obtained through lotteries, for the purchase of merchandise in the Colonists' behalf. This represented approximately one million dollars for a period of five years.

During the administrations of Yeardley and his successor, Wyatt, a certain degree of free trade prevailed in the Colony's relations with England. Private adventurers, who, apparently, had no connection with the Company, were now transporting goods to Virginia to exchange for tobacco. These independent traders supplied a great quantity of liquors and sweetmeats. The majority of them were Dutch merchants, who seemed to have engaged in this commerce regardless of the hostility of the English Government, which was anxious that it should be confined to English merchants; first, because it would increase the business of the latter by the sale of their goods, and second, because it would swell the contents of the English treasury by the receipt of additional customs from the tobacco now diverted to Holland.

It is quite possible that the Company did not look upon this intercourse with the Dutch with keen aversion, since it tended to the Colonists' advantage by enlarging the quantity of the supplies placed at their disposal. The Company was confronted at this time with a condition of almost complete financial depletion, after an expenditure, in different ways, of at least one hundred thousand pounds sterling without having derived any profit in the course of this outlay. And to make the shareholder's condition still worse, the Massacre of 1622, which so nearly destroyed all the settlements and plunged the entire community remaining into poverty, threw upon the Company, as a whole, the obligation of rescuing the Colonists from starvation by sending supplies to Virginia at once. This obligation could not be escaped, for each shareholder was compelled by an order of the Privy Council to contribute at least ten shillings to the purchase of food, clothing and like, for the preservation of the lives of the surviving people.

A magazine of the articles needed was soon accumulated and dispatched to the plantations, under the charge of a specially appointed cape merchant. Flour seems to have formed a large proportion of this cargo. Other magazines followed in quick succession. Some of these cargoes had been brought from Flushing, where the Company had set up a factory for the sale of the tobacco which it had been transporting to Holland. A large supply of fish had also been obtained from New Foundland.

Some of the planters, who possessed kinspeople of wealth in England, received private consignments from them in these disastrous times. A brother of George Harrison, for instance, sent to him, for the benefit of his suffering family, a large quantity of flour, oatmeal, peas, and cheese.

The revocation of the charter in 1624 broke down what remnant survived of the Company's monopoly in connection with the Colony. Free trade, in the sense of the right of any Eng-

lishman or association to despatch merchandise of all kinds to
Virginia to exchange for tobacco was destined from this time on
steadily to expand.　There was no longer the London Company
to encourage individuals or corporations to make such ventures;
but the English Government took its place in this respect, under
the influence, not only of a proper regard for the Colonists'
urgent needs, but also of a determination to put a stop to the sale
of tobacco to Dutch traders.　Orders were dispatched to the
municipal authorities of several seaports to send out ships
loaded with the supplies which were so much required in Virginia.　This example was quickly followed by private specula-
tors, who repeated the experiment more than once when they
found that it was attended with profit.　The people of the Colony at this time testified gratefully to the fact that their wants
had never been so fully satisfied.

We have referred incidentally to the supplies that were obtained from the Dutch while the London Company was in existence.　After the revocation of its charter, down to the successful enforcement of the Second Navigation Act, Holland continued
to furnish, in return for tobacco, a great store of all those articles which were needed by the planters.　The English Government again and again repeated its disapproval of this commercial intercourse, and sought by every means in its reach to put a
stop to it.　In most instances, the authorities in Virginia either
tacitly refused to second these efforts, or they offered some
excuse that was, after all, a mere evasive subterfuge.　Thus, in
1626, when England made a protest against the purchase of the
cargo of the *Flying Hart,* after its arrival at Jamestown from
Flushing, the Governor and Council defended this purchase by
the statement that the vessel was really owned by Englishmen,
although sailing under the Dutch flag.

How serious was the effect of this interference by Dutch
bottoms on the volume of trade with England was shown in the
case of two cargoes from Zealand, which were sold in Virginia
in 1633.　It was calculated that the indirect loss of profit to

English merchants through these two transactions alone amounted to one hundred thousand dollars in our modern values. Nor did it give those merchants any comfort to know that the owners of many of the Dutch cargoes sent out to Virginia at this time were English traders who had established themselves in the pursuit of business in the cities of the Low Countries.

How bold and open the captains of these ships sailing under the Dutch colors were in their movements was revealed in a case recorded in 1634. The master of a vessel, which, during that year, brought in a large quantity of supplies from Holland, not only made the voyage straight to the Virginia Capes, but, in passing the Bermudas, took on board one hundred and forty English immigrants, and landed them safely on the banks of the James.

One of the most famous seamen engaged in the transportation of merchandise to the Colony was Captain Devries, a Dutchman. He distributed each of his cargoes among the planters in the Spring on credit, and returned in the Autumn to collect the debts due him in the form of tobacco. He was authorized to carry on this trade by a special license from the Governor. He himself acknowledged that these transactions were attended with extreme risk, because, as he had no representative in the country to receive the tobacco to be paid so soon as it was cut and cured, the English factors got ahead of him by approaching the planters and bargaining for their crops, and also carrying these crops off, before Devries himself could arrive on the ground to assert his prior rights.

The English authorities, having endeavored in vain to stop this commerce with the Dutch, finally, as a kind of compromise, consented to such intercourse during periods when the Colony was suffering from shortened production. There is reason to think that the Governor and Council put a very liberal interpretation on this permission, and found it easy in most years to decide that the people's condition was one of great distress on account of the small returns to their labor. There were, dur-

ing the civil wars, times when the resources of England were so
seriously curtailed, even for its own inhabitants, that, but for
the cargoes of the Dutch vessels, the Colonists would have been
brought almost to a state of complete depletion in the point of
those articles which they had always depended on importation
from Europe to furnish them with. . Governor Berkeley, in
1651, referred with warm gratitude to the relief which the
Dutch merchants had afforded the members of the planters'
families, their servants, and their slaves, by timely shipments
of just such supplies as were needed in the absence of English
assistance.

Some attempt had been made, a few years before, to legalize
this trade by requiring the captains of the vessels from Holland
to give a bond on their departure from Virginia that they would
stop in an English port and pay the amount that would have
been payable had the tobacco on board been really designed for
that port.   But to the English authorities even this rule, which,
perhaps, was not always observed, was open to objection because
it acknowledged indirectly the right of the Dutch to import supplies into Virginia, which signified, as we have pointed out
already, a heavy loss to the English merchants by reducing the
volume of their trade.   In the course of one year alone, 1649, as
many vessels from Holland as from England arrived at Jamestown, and with equal ease, as a matter of course, obtained the
necessary licenses to exchange their cargoes for tobacco.

So large was the quantity of Dutch goods stored away in the
Colony at the time of the surrender to Parliament that a special clause had to be inserted in the treaty signed on that occasion to protect them from the reprisal that would have been
entirely legal otherwise, owing to the fact that England and
Holland were then plunged into hostilities with each other.
The character of these goods is disclosed by a petition of Dutch
merchants submitted to the States-General about this time, in
which they mentioned incidentally that they had been trading
with Virginia during a period of twenty years.   The goods in

question consisted principally of coarse cloth, linen, brandy, beer, and other varieties of liquor.

The passage of the Navigation Act of 1660 did not at once put an end to the trade with the Low Countries. For a time, it was evaded with success, but gradually the English Government was able to enforce it. At the close of 1670, Secretary Ludwell reported that few alien vessels now entered the waters of the Colony; and that the captains of those which did enter were promptly arrested, tried, convicted, and seriously punished. This statement was not strictly accurate as relating to the Eastern Shore. Illicit trading went on there throughout the rest of the century, but owing to the narrow area embraced in that part of the Colony with a proportionately small population, the volume of foreign supplies brought in for exchange for tobacco could never have been on a large scale.

The commerce between Virginia and New Amsterdam was always important, and it seems to have continued so even when England and Holland were at war. After that city became a possession of England, under the name of New York, the volume of trade expanded rapidly, until, by 1700, it had grown to be of great value. A large quantity of supplies were also imported from Maryland, New England, and the West Indies. The articles brought in from these islands consisted principally of sugar, rum, and molasses, while horses were imported from Maryland and flour from New England.

As the bulk of the supplies arriving in Virginia came directly from England, it will be pertinent to give some description of the methods pursued in the course of this trade.

There seems to have been little casual business done by the English merchants with the planters. By this statement it is meant that it was only rarely that a ship set out from the Mother Country with a cargo, suited to the needs of the Colonists, which was intended to be hawked about without a factor from river to river after its arrival in Virginian waters. Slaves seem to

Colonel Philip Ludwell

have been sold sometimes in this casual way, but not so often articles for personal use.

The custom that was followed from year to year was to send the goods to an agent, who, either temporarily or permanently, resided in the Colony, and who had been instructed to receive the various articles on their arrival and to take care of them until sold. It is quite certain that some of the English merchants had built warehouses at convenient places, and here the packages were safely stored until disposed of by the factors. But, in most cases, it was probable that this agent went on board the ship at the first wharf where it stopped, and afterwards accompanied it from river to river until the cargo had been all dispersed among reliable purchasers. This, as we have seen in the case of the Dutch seaman, Captain Devries, generally took place in the Spring.

When Autumn arrived, it was the factor's duty to collect, in the form of the newly harvested tobacco crop, the exact quantity that was due the merchant who had imported the goods. No doubt, the agent was often called upon to sell a cargo in Autumn also, and take possession, at the same hour, of the tobacco for which it had been exchanged. There was less risk in such a course as this, should purchasers be found, since no goods would be delivered unless payment followed immediately; but there was always a likelihood of a limitation to trade because the great majority of the planters had, during the previous Spring, bound themselves definitely to certain factors by accepting articles from them, with the promise to pay at the close of the tobacco harvest in the following September or October.

Apparently, there were numerous merchants in Virginia who owned stores of their own, and who annually replaced their shrunken stocks with newly purchased goods, delivered to them either by the factors of English traders or by the captains of English vessels despatched to the Colony with cargoes for special consignments. In addition to these local merchants, who invariably combined tobacco culture and trading in tobacco with the management of their shops, there were many persons who had come over from England and established themselves for a time in the Colony, in the hope that they would be able to accumulate estates by their commercial transactions. These men also served as excellent customers for the merchants of London and Bristol and other English cities on the seaboard.

What was the margin of profit in these importations of English merchandise? It might be said in a general way that the Virginia trade enjoyed no high reputation for lucrativeness. One of the most impressive evidences of the prosperity of a line of business in London in that age was the number of Lord Mayors whom it had furnished the city. These officials were always men of great wealth, which had been accumulated in their particular commercial province. The only Lord Mayor of high distinction whose company had been associated with the Virginia trade on a large scale was Matthew Perry. There is no proof that this trade had been the means of founding families of eminence in English social history. Nevertheless, good estates must have been built up through its returns.

But whatever the profit, it is to be inferred that it was subject to serious fluctuations. In 1623, when all prices were high, owing to the disastrous effects of the recent massacre, it was estimated that a cargo of wine, butter, cheese, sugar, and other provisions, would assure a margin of at least fifty per cent, with a possibility of still larger gain. In 1626, when normal conditions had been restored,—which really signified that the price of tobacco had fallen to its former value,—the English merchants were reluctant to make any shipments to the Colony, because, they said, the margin of profit had become too narrow to justify the risk.

About twelve years afterwards, the profit on each pound of tobacco accepted in payment of goods was calculated to range between six and ten pennies. Near the middle of the century, the gain does not appear to have been large. Indeed, it seems to have been only moderate. It is true that, if an article cost twenty shillings in England, it was saleable in Virginia at thirty; but this difference did not really represent a clear profit, since the freight charges, which were always heavy, had to be deducted, and if the cargo consisted of liquors, the Virginia import duties also.

As late as 1690, the margin had contracted to such an extent that very many of the English merchants refused to take the trouble and assume the expense of transporting their goods to the Colony. So far, indeed, was this stubborn attitude of opposition carried during that year that wealthy planters like Fitzhugh anticipated an entire failure of shipping in the course of the next year; and this fact, he asserted, unless the English Government should interfere, would mean a shrinkage in the importation of all domestic supplies. It was a situation like this, which might occur during any year, that made the planters keenly regret the destruction of the trade with the Dutch, and which also turned their energies to the manufacture of clothing under their own roofs.

The disadvantages of a slackening in the supplies from England were remedied to some extent in the case of the large planters by their own factors; but even their ability to do this was, as we have seen, dependent upon their means of transportation. This was limited in a measure by the degree to which the English merchants exported their goods to Virginia in any single year.

The bill of lading which accompanied the shipment of tobacco by the individual planter was addressed to an English merchant, with whom, perhaps, he had had similar dealings through a long course of years. This merchant was authorized by that document to sell the hogsheads embraced in its list for the highest price obtainable in the market at that time. The fund which was thus acquired was either placed to the credit of the planter in London, or, what was far more frequent, used, after the deduction of the commission and custom, in the purchase of various articles designated in a letter which was dispatched along with the tobacco when it left Virginia. Should the cost of the article exceed the amount of the proceeds from the sale, an abatement was to be made, or the overdraught was to be debited, with the understanding that it was to be wiped out by the shipment of the succeeding year. Many disputes arose between planter and merchant on account of the poor quality of the tobacco, or because of the low price at which it was disposed of in the English market. In some cases, the merchant advanced the planter sums that ran into hundreds of pounds.

The orders for goods covered all the manufactured articles in common domestic or plantation use. They ranged from objects of small value to objects of great. The instance of a certain special order given by William Fitzhugh, a planter of large fortune, may be mentioned as characteristic of his contemporaries of the same wealth,—we find him instructing his merchant in London to send him, on some one occasion, such merchandize as a feather bed, quilt, table, looking glass, carpet, a pair of shoes, oil, and glass. In another order, he directed the purchase of a variety of cloths, such as holland, kenting, dimity, kerseys, cottons, coarse canvas, and shoes. A third order embraced a more miscellaneous set of objects, such as a large quantity of iron ware, a hundred weight of cheese, and numerous hoes and axes. In the most notable order of all, he invested a very considerable sum, in the form of tobacco, in several very handsome examples of silver ware. William Byrd, the elder, who was equally liberal in making purchases through his agent in London, showed the same taste for variety in his selections, which ranged all the way from a hat to a dozen Russian leather chairs; from letter paper to neckcloths and linen stocks; and from iron ware to the rarest continental wines.

In the course of the voyage to Virginia, many of these articles,— especially the liquors and sweetmeats,—were exposed to the depredations of the seamen; and in addition, the rough

weather experienced during many voyages caused, not infrequently, severe injury to the cargo. If a war was going on between England and Holland, as so often happened in the course
of the seventeenth century, the destruction of goods designed
for the Colony was very great. This occurred in 1665, when
a fleet of merchantmen was either sunk by gunfire, or burnt
with the torch, or carried off to sea, after a victorious raid upon
the vessels as they lay in the James or the Chesapeake Bay.

So much damage too was to be constantly expected from the
presence of pirates in those waters that every ship engaged
in the Virginia trade was armed with heavy guns, numbering,
in some cases, as many as twenty-four; and it was also required
that there should be men on board who had been trained to
load and set them off with accuracy.

In transporting merchandise to Virginia, the heaviest burden that had to be borne was the outlay for wages and freight.
The amount which the captain received for his services was
nine pounds sterling for the period of one month; and the remuneration of the sailor was thirty shillings for the same
length of time. The charge for freight by the ton did not fluc-
tuate very much during this century,—it maintained, indeed,
an average of three pounds sterling. The seamen were often
the cause of inconvenience and loss. Unsettled by the reports
of profitable tobacco culture, which came so frequently to their
ears while they were moving up and down the rivers in Virginia, seeking purchasers for their ships' cargoes, they were
disposed to shirk their contracts and run away to the heart of
the country. So often was this done that every ferryman in
the Colony had received instructions from the General Assembly to refuse to set these fugitives across the streams, unless
they could show letters of permission from the captains of their
vessels.

Every ship arriving in Virginia with a cargo on board was
required by law to pay an import duty. In the beginning, this
consisted of one barrel of powder and ten iron shot for the use

15—Vol. I.

of the fort at Point Comfort. Later on, the duty was changed to another form,—a tax of twelve pence a ton was placed on every pound of the cargo which the incoming vessel contained. Subsequently, the tax was raised to one shilling and three pence.

Another expense, after arrival in the waters of Virginia, was the charge for pilotage.

During the early years of the Colony, no vessel was permitted to land any part of its contents before anchor had been dropped at Jamestown; nor could any person go on board, before that port was reached, in order to make a private purchase of merchandise. The principal object of the regulation was to prevent any one from buying a portion of the crop, with the view of selling at a high price, the articles which he had thus obtained. This was known as engrossing, which was punished with unusual severity. In spite of this fact, the law was so often evaded, that, finally, an officer was placed on board of every vessel arriving at Point Comfort, with orders to accompany it until its entire cargo had been disposed of in a circuit of the river.

The ability of the people to purchase English goods was not restricted to dealings with London merchants, local factors, or ship captains. Stores were found in every populous neighborhood along the large navigable streams. It was a subject of complaint at one time that these stores were so far social centres, as well as trading, that they discouraged the growth of towns. They either took the form of a separate building, or they were large rooms on the ground floor of a planter's dwelling house. Among the contents of these stores was every article which was called for in the economy of the domestic hearth or the plantation at large. Quantity, quality, and variety were all represented.

Their custom was not restricted to the planters and agricultural servants. There was enjoyed by many of them a lucrative trade with the Indians, for whose benefit there was always kept on hand,—to be bargained for furs—guns, ammunition, rum, blankets, knives, hatchets, and beads. Commerce with the tribes also went on beyond the frontiers. Annually, traders made their way in caravans into the forest to barter for Indian goods.

CHAPTER X

THE MILITARY ARM

In taking up the consideration of the various institutions that existed in Virginia during the seventeenth century,—such as the military system, the system of law, the system of religion, the system of education, and the political system,—we have come to those aspects of our general subject which are most directly associated with the immemorial community organization of the Mother Country. This organization was inherited by the Colonists in England; and it was subsequently brought with them to Virginia. It was simply a transfer to the valleys of the Powhatan, the Pamunkey, and the Rappahannock, of that framework of society in all its ramifications which had been crystallizing in England in the course of centuries.

The military system was the same,—only modified to some degree to suit the necessities of Indian warfare; the religious system was the same,—without substantial alteration beyond the abolition of an incumbent's vested interest in his pulpit; the system of law was the same,—except that a greater diversification of the power of the courts was demanded by a smaller and more dispersed population; the political system was the same,—only the sphere of operation was more contracted and less dignified; the system of education was the same,—only it was not possible, from the lack of the necessary wealth, to reproduce on the same scale the English means of imparting knowledge.

The transferred community was poor, thin, and unimposing in comparison with England, but the spirit was the same throughout, in spite of imperative divergences caused by a difference in conditions springing from an alien climate, an alien soil, and alien products.

It was the colonists' earnest aspiration to preserve amongst themselves all the characteristics, economic as well as social, which belonged to the country oversea from which they had emigrated. This fact will come out clearly in the description of the general framework of the community which we are now about to give.

First, let us consider the military organization. This was the supreme force which held the community together, either potentially or actually, if disorder had broken out. Who were the persons liable to serve? The military organization was based on a militia. No attempt was made to set up the smallest approximation to a regular army, unless a troop of rangers could be looked upon as falling in that category. In 1626, only freemen apparently were subject to military duty, and the age limit in one direction was fixed at sixteen, and in the other, at sixty. In 1639, on the other hand, the indentured servant, but not the slave, was included in the list of the eligible for enrolment. There were sound reasons, however, which at later periods excluded him. In the first place, military exercises would interfere with his labor in the field at the height of the season in planting; and in the second, so many members of this class were lawless or discontented that a military training might raise a spirit of insurrection. These objections were still more formidable in the case of the slave.

In 1672, the only white servants who were permitted to be drilled were those whose terms were about to expire. It was felt that these could be trusted, now that they were so near to the enjoyment of all the rights of citizenship. The claim of the Quakers to exemption from military service was not allowed until after the passage of the Act of Toleration, when it was foregone in the payment of a fine.

In 1681, it was estimated that there were at least fifteen thousand fighting men living in the colony, but this list probably included the male agricultural servants. Eight thousand, perhaps, was the figure closest to the mark, if immediate availability was the test. At the end of the century, the number of persons of military age was calculated by Beverley, the historian, to be eighteen thousand. Every county at this time kept ready a body of troops, both horse and foot, which could be summoned into service in the course of a few hours. These soldiers were entitled to a definite sum as wage while employed on military duty at large.

The colony, from an early date, was divided into roughly outlined districts, which were subject to the supervision of military commanders, assisted by lieutenant-commanders. During the first years, these military officers, whenever they had reason to anticipate an Indian attack, were authorized to raise as large a body of men as the threatened danger called for. They were expected to be always on their guard. After the county system was established, each commander and his lieutenant were restricted to the military oversight of that particular area, but at the same time, their duties were extended to other details. They became, for instance, superintendents of the regulations for the preservation of the public health, and they were also expected to enforce the law for church attendance.

Subsequently, the Colony was divided into four military districts, each of which was placed under the control of a major-general, assisted by two adjutants. The office of deputy commander seems to have been created in each county subject to the supervision of a commander whose jurisdiction extended over a group of counties. The grade of the officers ranged from that of a colonel down to that of a lieutenant. These officers numbered amongst themselves the foremost citizens of Virginia. Every person of military rank in the Colony was under the orders of his immediate superior ascending to the governor, who was the commander-in-chief of all the military force of all the counties as the representative of the King.

During some years following the foundation of Jamestown, armor continued to be used because it was impervious to the impact of the Indian arrows. Quilted coats and buff coats were equally effective for the same purpose. There was at this time a constant importation of powder from England, at the Company's expense, and this was accompanied by shot and raw lead. After the Charter was revoked, ammunition was obtained by a county assessment, and all the court fines were also expended in swelling the quantity. Fire-arms were produced by the same means. These weapons, about the middle of the century, consisted of cutlers, with waist belts, carbines, muskets, pistols and holsters, swords, and sword belts. They were imported annually from England under the supervision of the officers of militia. In order to ensure their preservation when no war was in progress, they were generally stored away in the respective courthouses by order of the county magistrates. The powder, on the other hand, was left in the custody of the military commanders of the counties, owing to the danger which might arise from accumulating it in one place.

The powder and fire-arms in the possession of private citizens were impressed without scruple whenever the country was threatened with a foreign invasion or Indian incursion. There was a large quantity of both hoarded in the dwelling-houses on the lonely plantations, both for protection to person, and for the hunting of wild game.

The life to which the young Virginian was accustomed almost from childhood prepared him for the physical exposure and the military discipline which he had to undergo at intervals, from the time he was enrolled in the body of the militia. He had passed the greater part of his previous existence out of doors, regardless of the cold of winter, the heat of summer, or the rains of spring. The snow storm, the icy wind, the driving hail, the roaring thunder, the flashing lightning, the tropic rays of August, the miasmatic breath of September,—he had known them all in turn, and he faced them with equal indifference. Having been a hunter from the time he was able to shoulder a gun, his aim, from long practice, was unerring. He could pursue his quarry on foot all day and all night without fatigue, though the way led him over the pathless hill and through the tangled forest. His seat on horseback was as secure as if he had been a Bedouin of the desert. All these manly experiences had given vigor and steadiness to his nerves and muscles and clearness to his eye, and confirmed his native intrepidity.

During the early years of Colonial history, the time selected for the drill was the holidays; and a muster general was appointed to compel the attendance, on those occasions, of all liable to military service. Afterwards, it became the duty of the commander of each district to enforce this rule, and he was also probably the principal drill sergeant at first. Later on, he was succeeded by the captain. In 1642, the drill took place once a month in each district. Thirty years subsequently, a general muster of the Colony was held thrice in the course of a year; but the local drill was no doubt repeated in each county as often as the several commanders decided it be judicious. The details of the military training were strictly in harmony with the English regulations; but allowance was made for the imperative requirements of warfare with Indians. This was a stealthy warfare under cover, and not warfare in the open field, as in Europe. But while the movements in these forest campaigns were remarkably free, they were, nevertheless, governed by rigid discipline because it was essential to guard against surprises.

There were three forms of warfare which had to be kept in mind and promptly confronted when they arose; namely, an Indian attack, foreign invasion, and internal rebellion.

The Indian attack was the one which occurred most frequently. There was always a frontier, and the frontier was always open to an Indian incursion, either, by local tribes, or by tribes from a distance. When a band of warriors passed this barrier and began to commit every sort of atrocity, the inhabitants of a wide region of country were at once aroused; and the first step taken by the local military organizations was to start upon what was known as a "march" to drive back the marauders and punish them for their murders and depredations.

The most remarkable instances of the march during the time of the Company occurred after the Massacre of 1622, when several detachments of troops pursued the foe to their remotest villages, killed their warriors, burnt their wigwams, and cut down their maize. Food, spirits, and ammunition were provided for the soldiers in these arduous expeditions of destruction. The funds to cover the expense of later marches were obtained by a levy, which embraced every tithable in Virginia.

In the course of time, the entire Colony was divided into separate groups of counties, and each group established its own military association, which promptly furnished the troops for special expeditions designed to protect its own area from Indian intrusion. The whole expense of an expedition was borne by the association sending it out; and the necessary fund for this purpose was raised by an assessment upon all the tithables belonging to that group of counties. The plan of the campaign, and the general charge of the actual movements, were subject to the direction of a council of war.

The rule prevailed previous to 1680 that no military step, however urgent the demand for immediate action, could be taken without first obtaining the Governor's consent. Afterwards, the authority to strike at once was granted to a small group of military officers residing in each of the five divisions of the Colony.

In the first years of the original plantations, every residence was surrounded by a stockade, and this protection was only abandoned when the Indians had been driven from the region of Jamestown. The next method adopted was to erect a pali-

MASSACRE IN 1622

sade across the Peninsula from the Powhatan to the modern York River. The third was to build a few forts back of the line of the outer settlements situated east of the falls in the great rivers. These forts were used as places from which to observe the Indian's movements, and also as starting points for expeditions against the savage marauders. They were always occupied by a small garrison.

In 1675-76, a chain of forts extended from the Potomac River in the north to the Nansemond in the south. The men who composed each garrison were provided liberally with food, guns, ammunition, and implements. The militia of the nearest community were ordered to come to their aid so soon as they received the command to fly to arms; and if the task of driving off the enemy proved to be formidable, the military force of the entire Colony was to be summoned to assist.

In 1680-81, the number of occupied forts seems to have been reduced to four. These were situated at the head of navigation in the four largest streams, and by means of sloops they were easily supplied with all that their garrisons needed. It is probable that they were substantially built. Some of those which had been erected earlier were merely temporary block houses that rapidly decayed when abandoned.

Some years before the end of the century, the garrisons were withdrawn from the forts still standing, which were then allowed to go to ruin, and a body of forest rangers substituted in their place as a means of defense. As long as war with the Indians continued, these rangers served as scouts, but the daily beat which they followed was probably confined to such short distances that they doubtless returned nightly to the nearest settlement. But after 1682, when no war was in progress, the bands of rangers were in the habit of advancing far and wide through the forest during the day and bivouacing in the woods at night. Their duty was to keep a strict outlook for wandering companies of Indian warriors or hunters, and to report their presence at once to the nearest military commander.

The rangers were accomplished riders. They belonged to the most enterprising and adventurous section of the young men of the Colony. Even when the main body was finally disbanded, a certain number of light horsemen were retained for duty as scouts in time of peace.

The prospect of foreign invasion was less frequent, but not less serious than the prospect of Indian incursions, but, on many occasions, from the beginning to the end of the seventeenth century, it caused the people of the Colony acute concern. It was only from the sea that such an attack was looked for; and the principal means of protection relied upon was the maritime and river-side forts. These forts, having more formidable forces to resist, were more elaborate in design and more solid in fabric than those erected at the heads of the rivers to hold back the savages.

The first to be built was the fort at Jamestown, which was shaped like a triangle, with a base of four hundred and twenty feet resting on the Powhatan. It was defended by heavy ordnance. A second fort was afterwards erected by Captain Smith on the southern side of that stream, on a hill rising some distance back in the country and commanding a wide outlook. A block house was subsequently built to protect the approach to the town from the mainland. A very important fortification was also raised at Point Comfort, which created a barrier to the passage of the narrow channel in the Roads off the shore at that place. In the beginning, it was simply an earthwork armed with cannon. A stockade was soon added to protect the garrison of forty men which was permanently stationed there.

Delaware, in the course of his first voyage up the Powhatan, ordered a fort to be constructed on either side of the mouth of Southampton River near Kikatan. The object of these two strongholds seems to have been to afford military protection for the bands of newly arrived immigrants while they were recuperating from the fatigues of their long ocean voyage. They were defended by ordnance of the heaviest calibre.

It seems to have been Delaware's intention to build a fort of some kind below the falls in the Powhatan, but if it was ever erected at all by him, it must have been of material too flimsy to endure the vicissitudes of the climate successfully. Henrico-polis was so placed by Dale within the great coil of the Powhatan at the modern Farrar's Island, that it formed a natural fortifica-tion, with no need of an artificial protection beyond a stockade.

But a short time had passed when it was found that the only two forts that had resisted decay were those at Jamestown and Point Comfort; and these, in 1619, were said to be so poorly armed and garrisoned as to be incapable of resisting an attack from the sea. A few years subsequently, Captain Each asked the Company's permission to build a fort on the foundation of the great mass of oyster shells which had accumulated off shore at Blunt Point on the Powhatan. An examination proved that it was impossible to penetrate this mass to the extent required for support, and another site for the projected fort had to be chosen on the mainland, but before the structure could be fin-ished, it had to be abandoned for lack of supplies and materials.

While no fortifications in the strict sense of the word existed in 1623, there were at six places a larger number of heavy ord-nance, which lay exposed to the weather, it is true, but were still capable of effective use if the occasion arose for it. These can-non consisted of culverins and demiculverins. The same condi-tion existed in 1629-30. In the meanwhile, the number of these outlying great guns had been increased by the ten which had been mounted at a commanding spot in Pierce's Hundred. It is probable that more than these had been added to the original number.

By this time, it was generally recognized that the only site in the Colony that offered a combination of advantages for a really useful fortification was Point Comfort. If such a fortification could be maintained there, all the plantations lying along the James, Elizabeth, and Nansemond Rivers, could be successfully protected, because the passage of the channel which led to them all would be barred. It is true that the Pamunkey and the Rappahannock Rivers would be open to invasion, but the valleys of these streams were as yet but sparsely, if at all, settled.

By the end of February, 1631-32, the new fort at Point Comfort had been completed, chiefly through the energy and at the expense of Samuel Matthews. For its upkeep, every ship dropping anchor under its guns was ordered to pay one barrel of powder and ten shot for each one hundred tons of the vessel's total weight, while every passenger was subject to a tax of sixty-four pounds of tobacco for each tithable included in his family. Additional charges were imposed from time to time on the merchantmen arriving.

In 1639-40, a levy was laid by the General Assembly to raise the fund that was necessary for the repair of the fortification at Point Comfort, as it had fallen by neglect into a state of decay. In 1642, the garrison consisted of a captain and ten men. Special privileges were granted to the members of this small force in order to keep them contented in their somewhat isolated and insalubrious situation. A large sum was annually raised for their benefit by public assessment; and they were especially exempted from the legal process of distress. During many years, the castle duties, which were payable on all exports and imports, were considered to be the property of the commander of the fort, although in theory at least supposed to be levied for the maintenance of the fort itself alone.

As the plantations spread along the banks of the other great streams, the importance of the fort at Point Comfort diminished, and the necessity for erecting fortifications elsewhere increased. Nevertheless, the General Assembly, owing to the cost of such defenses, was reluctant to build them. It was not until 1665 that steps were taken to erect a fort in the immediate vicinity of Jamestown, but before any progress had been made, the Privy Council in England instructed Governor Berkeley to abandon the project and to concentrate all the labor and money at his disposal on the restoration of the old fortification at the Point, which was again in a state of disrepair. Apparently, that fortification long remained in this condition, since, owing to the difficulty of obtaining a solid foundation there, stone could not be used, and it was not possible to convey to so remote a situation all the lumber which would be required for a really substantial structure.

In 1667, the General Assembly decided to build five forts in those parts of the Colony where it was thought they would be most effective in preventing an invasion of the rivers by foreign men-of-war. The construction of each fort was undertaken by an association of the surrounding counties, but the manner of their building was so impermanent that they, in a short time, began to fall into a state of dilapidation. An attempt was made to substitute brick for wood, but not even this material was able to preserve these forts against the effect of continuous neglect. The fortification at Point Comfort had, by this time, been practically abandoned.

Just after Culpeper reached Virginia in 1681, he visited all the forts, and he stated in his report to the English Government that there was not one that was in a condition to protect a ship from capture even should the ship be lying directly under the guns of the fortification. He asserted that the only forts that could prove effective would be such as had been erected so high up the streams that large men-of-war could not reach them, on account of the shallowness of the water.

Howard undertook to restore the maritime and riverside forts. When he arrived in the Colony, there was not a cannon to be found in their dilapidated confines that rested upon a sound carriage. He repaired the platforms at Jamestown and Rappahannock, supplied them with new supports for their ordnance, and a large quantity of ball and powder. The forts at Nansemond and Tyndall's Point were also restored, but all the other fortifications were left in decay, and without any protection whatever for the cannon which they still contained. At Corotoman, there were twenty-four great guns lying in the sand near the shore, and there were six at Yeocomico, on the Potomac, in the same abandoned condition.

Nicholson, in 1691, personally inspected all the fortifications then in existence in Virginia, and declared that not one was in such a state of repair as to serve the purpose of defense for which it was designed. Even in the Jamestown fort, there was not sufficient shelter for the preservation of the stores belonging to it, and they had to be transferred to the protection of a private residence. This was also the case at Tyndall's Point. A few years afterwards, an attempt was made to restore these two fortifications to their original good condition, but there was no element of permanency in the repairs.

The public indifference towards the maintenance of the fortifications at the end of the century was justifiable on the following four grounds: however strong a fort might be, it would be always feasible for the enemy to land on a plantation in the vicinity and assault the structure in the rear; secondly, the people were too impoverished to indure the burden of taxation which the constant need of expensive repairs entailed; thirdly, the presence of ammunition in a fort would be a temptation to seditious persons to seize it, and carry out their treacherous designs; and finally, the rivers were so broad that trading vessels, taken by surprise by the enemy, would not have the time in every case to gain shelter under the guns even of the nearest fort. In the popular view, it was better that the merchants should, at long intervals, incur a great loss than that the Colony should be compelled indefinitely to go on building or restoring a number of ineffective and unserviceable fortifications.

It was the general opinion, during the last years of the century, that the guardships which the English Government maintained in the waters of Virginia could be relied upon to defend the plantations from attack when a war was in progress. Such a vessel could pass quickly from point to point as its services were needed. Numerous guardships in succession were stationed in the Chesapeake and the estuaries of the James and

York Rivers, and the part which they performed was eminently useful, not only in checking the illegal trader in time of peace, but in hampering, in time of war, the efforts of enemies like the Dutch, should they send armed vessels to Virginia to capture the fleets of English merchantmen.

The guardships were especially successful in protecting the coast from the incursions of pirates, who swarmed up and down in the neighboring seas on the look-out for prey in the form of incoming vessels from England loaded with cargoes of European merchandise. These marauders gave no warning of their approach. They rose, as it were, out of the waters of the ocean; disembarked, if not opposed, and committed ruthless depredations, and then disappeared below the horizon. The shores of Virginia were infested with these buccaneers to such a degree in 1683-84 that a special code of signals had to be adopted in the maritime counties of the Colony to put the people on their guard. Watchmen were appointed to give these signals and also to send word to the nearest military officer whenever a suspicious vessel had been seen off shore; and he, in his turn, was ordered to call out the militia to drive away the outlaws if they attempted to land.

Bands of pirates were frequently captured in consequence of these energetic measures to intercept them on land, or to seize them as their vessel lay at anchor. It was in the latter case that the guardship was most successful. Occasionally, the pirate vessel was too formidable to be boldly boarded, but the presence of the man-of-war restrained the lawless crew from making an incursion on shore or trying to overhaul merchantmen entering the Capes. In most instances, however, the guardship did not hesitate to join battle with the buccaneers. The most celebrated encounter of this kind in the waters of Virginia during the Seventeenth Century, was the sea fight in Lynnhaven Bay in 1700, between the *Shoreham* and the *La Paix*. It was a conflict which lasted from dawn until late in the afternoon of the same day, and ended in the capture of the pirate ship after

it had been completely disabled by the bombardment of the
Shoreham's cannon and musketry. One hundred and ten buccaneers surrendered to the master of the guardship on this occasion. Three of them were tried in Virginia and hung. The
rest were sent to England for the judgment of the Crown.

During the Seventeenth Century, there was only one internal
conflict of importance, namely, Bacon's Rebellion. It is true
that Governor Harvey was expelled by the members of his
Council, with the approval of the people at large, but there was
no military movement accompanying their action. Furthermore, some of the old soldiers of Cromwell, who had, after the
Restoration, been transported to Virginia, entered into a con-
spiracy to take possession of the local government; but their
plot was frustrated before it matured. In short, no previous
event of its kind in the Colony's history compared in magnitude
with the Insurrection of 1676. Indeed, for so remote and thinly
settled a community as Virginia was at that time, it was an
uprising on an imposing scale. Not only did Bacon, the youthful leader, organize a strong military force for the conquest of
the Susquehannocks; not only did he fight a pitched battle on
the Roanoke River with the warriors of the Occaneechees, and
afterwards carry out a bloody march against the Pamunkeys;
but in the later battle at Jamestown, in which he was engaged
with the followers of Berkeley, he threw up strong entrenchments, resisted an assault with firmness, and then made a
vigorous sally, that drove the enemy back to the town in confusion and closed with its capture and destruction.

The energy and skill in command which Bacon exhibited, and
the ability which he displayed in winning the devotion of his
men, indicated that he possessed military talents of such a high
order that he would have won a wide reputation as a soldier had
he been playing the same part on the broad theatre of Europe,
with far greater forces behind him than those which were sup-
porting him in his campaign in the thinly inhabited communities of Virginia.

CHAPTER XI

LAW

In establishing their new community oversea, the immigrants of 1606-1607, laid its foundation, as we have already stated, on the solid rock of the institutions of their Mother Country. In no province was their determination to carry out this inherited policy so conspicuous as in the legal organization of the Colony. The English legal system was put fully under way just so soon as the size of the population had made it possible. It was not simply the spirit, but also the letter, of the English law which was introduced. On more than one occasion, the English Government, in its instructions to the early Governors of Virginia enjoined upon them the necessity of adhering as closely as practicable to the common law of England. It was only under the stern rule of Gates and Dale, when a rigid military discipline was indispensable, that the application of the requirements of this common law was suspended.

Every judge on his appointment to office, was expected to take an oath that he would "do justice as near as may be to the English laws." "We are sworn," said the General Assembly in the noble Declaration of 1651, "to govern and be governed, (as far as possible the place was capable of) by the lawes of England," and that body, very truly asserted that they had "inviolably and sacredly kept these laws so far as their abilitys to execute and their capacitys to judge, would permit."

Trial by jury, Magna Charta, the Petition of Right, and the writ of Habeas Corpus formed a part of the fundamental ordinances of Virginia even in this early colonial age.

227

As all the General Assembly's Acts only became permanent laws after the King had approved them, his assent made valid any statute, however, repugnant to English jurisprudence, but it was only rarely that a regulation of this kind passed the royal signet, and only then because the circumstances of colonial life applicable to that particular Act justified a course different from what would have been followed in England. For instance, in Virginia, all mortgages, first or second, were required to be put on record within three months after they were drafted. The reason for this regulation was that the same estate might otherwise be transferred to a second mortgagee as if he was really the first. The first mortgagee might be an English merchant, who, not being on the ground, would be unaware even by hearsay of this fraudulent transaction. The entire system of credit on which the Colonists chiefly depended in their relation with the English traders would thus be shaken.

During the Company's existence, the body of laws in force consisted, in addition to the common law, of the royal instructions; the ordinances of the President or Governor and Council; the Acts of the General Assembly subsequent to 1619; and the ordinances and constitutions promulgated by the Company's quarter courts sitting in England. After the revocation of the Charter in 1624, the laws in force in the Colony, in addition to the common law, were the royal instructions given to the successive governors, the terms of the commissions of oyer and terminer, the terms of the commissions of the justices of the county courts, and the numerous Acts of the General Assembly which had not been annulled by the veto of the King.

Justice was administered in the Colony through the agency of six courts, namely, the Magistrate's Court, the Parish Court, the County Court, the General Court, the General Assembly, and the Court of Admiralty.

The lowest of these Courts was the Magistrate's which was established in 1642, and limited in its jurisdiction to amounts not exceeding at first two hundred pounds of tobacco and after-

KING CHARLES THE 1st

wards, three hundred. Its object was to relieve the County Court of a multitude of civil cases, the settlement of which would have taken up too much of the time of the county justices, already pressed with cases of greater importance. The Magistrate's Court was also impowered to arrest and bind over any person rightly complained of as a law breaker, or as an utterer of violent threats against life or limb. It could release servants who were held illegally by their masters after the expiration of their terms, or issue a warrant for absconding laborers who had been working under indentures.

Apparently, the only parish court in Virginia during this century was situated in Bristol parish, which embraced an area belonging in part to Henrico County and in part to Charles City County. Its jurisdiction covered the same grounds as the jurisdiction claimed by the County Court. The reason for the creation of this Court is not clearly known. It was, however, important enough to be a Court of record. Its membership was restricted to the justices residing within its bounds.

The court that executed the largest amount of legal business was what was known at first as the Monthly Court, and, afterwards, as the County Court. At the start, this Court was held in what was termed a precinct, which consisted of a cluster of plantations. It was designed to relieve the General Court of a great mass of litigation, which, by diverting too much of their attention, prevented them from administering justice in general with even reasonable promptness. The General Court at first was required to pass upon every case that arose, whether criminal or civil, and as the population of the Colony increased, the burden of delivering so many decisions became intolerable. The establishment of new monthly courts kept step with the spread of this population.

When a system of shires was erected in 1634, the Monthly Court came to be called the Court of Shire or County Court, and one was assigned to each shire, certainly as early as 1642. During that year, the Governor of the Colony, as required by an

Act recently passed, selected a site in every County for a local court building; and he was also authorized by the same Act to name the justices who were to sit on the County Court bench. This latter power he had undoubtly possessed in the time of the first monthly courts; and he also enjoyed the right to fill all vacancies on these benches as they occurred.

The incumbents were known in the beginning as commissioners, and afterwards as justices of the peace. They were chosen from the ranks of the foremost citizens in their respective counties. In many cases, their names seem to have been suggested to the Governor for his acceptance, for it was impossible for him to have known personally all the men in the Colony who were fitted for this honorable office. The membership of each County bench varied at different periods, but the number that usually sat ranged from eight to ten.

In 1634, when the system of shires was first erected, one of the Governor's Council attended the sessions of each of the eight shire Courts; and this custom was continued in a modified form many years after the County Courts had grown very much in number. As late as 1662, councillors are found participating in the proceedings of County Courts; not, however, with the approval of the people, as their presence on the bench increased the charges which every session of these courts entailed.

A quorum, by the terms of every commission, consisted of the four members of the County Court whose names were specifically mentioned as such in that document. Any one individual among these four could form a valid court by associating himself with three other members of the body. The presiding justice was sometimes spoken of as "Chief Justice," but more often was referred to simply as the President of the Court. The office carried no salary, and in the strict sense of the word, it was accompanied by no perquisites. It was only during the existence of the Long Assembly, which did not convene until after the Restoration, that the justices of some of the County Courts ordered a levy to defray their own expenses while actually sitting

PHILIP LUDWELL'S THREE HOUSES

Country House

PHILIP LUDWELL'S THREE HOUSES

THIRD STATE HOUSE 1665-1676
FOURTH STATE HOUSE 1685-1698

STATE HOUSE BLOCK RESTORED
(FIRST of CHURCH)
1656-1657

BUILDINGS ON THE THIRD RIDGE RESTORED

upon the bench.   All seem to have held their positions, as a rule, as long as they desired to do so, provided that they remained citizens of the same counties as formerly.

A strict course of upright conduct was required of them continuously, not simply as justices, but as private citizens.   Even social improprieties on their part were punished by either temporary or permanent suspension from office.   In their judicial proceedings, they were distinguished for extraordinary scrupulousness as well as for the fine decorum which they rigidly enforced.   The story is told of William Randolph, that, when, on one occasion, he was as a justice, called upon to join in passing judgment on a planter who had been sued on a tobacco contract involving a claim to cask also, he asked to be excused, on the ground that he "was himself a considerable dealer in the tobacco trade," and that he was unwilling to expose himself to the risk of being charged "with partiality."

Any act that smacked in the least of contempt for the dignity of the Court was instantly and sternly rebuked and punished. Committal to the stocks was one of the most frequent penalties which the culprit had to pay for his temerity.   If, on the other hand, it was not an act of contumely, but a word of insult, the same retribution followed immediately.   It was only when the affront was committed in their presence as a court of justice that their resentment was so emphatic and summary.   If that affront had come to their ears by hearsay alone, they seem to have contented themselves with sending a complaint to the Governor and Council sitting as the General Court, who were always quick to punish any offense of this kind, because it was calculated to lower the court in the respect of the people at large.   The county court did not assume jurisdiction even when the insult was directed at one of its members in person, provided that he was not seated at the time on the bench.   In an instance of this kind also, the General Court's intervention was always invoked.

The justices were strict in repressing even the smallest misbehavior in the court room.   They fined, not only one of their number guilty of smoking on the bench while the tribunal was in session, but also any person among the spectators who dared to violate the regulation; and if either party persisted in continuing the offense, he was placed in the sheriff's custody and led away to jail or thrust into the stocks. The retention of the hat on the head after an order had been given to remove it, was liable to the same punishment; nor was it taken to be any condonation that the culprit was a Quaker.

The County Court convened at least once in the course of every two months. It was in the justice's power to meet more frequently, should it be necessary for the transaction of special and urgent business. Whether this was so or not, seems to have been decided by the quorum, and at their request, the summons was delivered by the sheriff. An extra session was very often occasioned by a dispute between a sea-captain and his crew, whose stay in the Colony was rarely protracted, and who, therefore, desired a quick decision. The records of the different counties for the Seventeenth Century disclose the fact that the number of the sittings of the respective County Courts ranged on the average from seven to ten. It was not often that a County Court, in the course of a single year, convened once a month. There was no common date for the meetings of them all. Each court came together on the day which its members considered to be most convenient for their particular body. In fact, the selection made by the different courts ranged all the way from the first to the last day of the month.

The hour of meeting varied from seven to ten o'clock in the morning, and a session was frequently held at night to hasten the transaction of business. The average attendance did not exceed two-thirds of the membership, owing to the distance to the courthouse to be traversed, the vicissitudes of weather, the badness of the roads, and the advanced age of many of the justices. Each one, however, was liable to the payment of a fine if he absented himself without the leave of his associates, and he was similarly mulcted if he returned home before the Court adjourned without having secured for a good reason their formal consent.

In the course of the early years of the Colony's history, the justices of the County Courts met under the roof either of a tavern or of a private residence. There were, probably, not a separate courthouse in Virginia previous to 1642, and there were only a few in use as late as 1660. Such buildings of this kind as did exist after that date, were, perhaps, modeled on the architecture of the average private residence of those times, namely, a structure of frame resting on a brick foundation, and having a chimney of brick at either end. Where a great stream, like the Rappahannock, divided a county into two parts, the legal business of the people required the erection of a courthouse on either side. Under the roofs of these two the Court convened alternately.

Whether the courthouse was constructed entirely of timber, or partly of brick, the courtroom was always an apartment of spacious dimensions, with ample light entering through its windows at all seasons of the year, and with sufficient heat arising in winter from its great fire places at either end. There was on one side of the room a long platform for the seats of the justices, and on the other, a wide space for the spectators. A balustrade that ran the length of the apartment, separated the public from the section of the floor which was occupied by the jury, the lawyers, and the clerk, whose chairs and tables were placed next to the platform of the justices.

What was the jurisdiction of the County Court? In 1623-24, it was provided by law that this Court should determine finally all suits which involved an amount or subject not greater in value, actual or estimated, than one hundred pounds of tobacco. That commodity, at this time, was sold at a far higher price than was recorded during later periods. The Court had not yet been granted jurisdiction in criminal cases. In 1631-32, it was empowered to decide finally suits in which as much as five pounds sterling in value was in dispute, and also to give judgment in cases in which life or limb had been in jeopardy. By the Act of 1634, this criminal jurisdiction was retained, but the exclusive jurisdiction in civil cases was extended to a valuation of ten pounds sterling. Apparently, if the case involved more than ten pounds sterling, there lay a right of appeal to the General Court.

In 1641, the sole jurisdiction was possessed by the County Courts of remote counties, like Accomac and Henrico, in all cases in which the valuation rose as high as twenty pounds sterling. In other parts of the Colony, ten pounds seem to have still been the limit.

The County Court's jurisdiction embraced the entire ground covered by the decisions of the combined English Courts, whether Chancery, King's Bench, Common Pleas, Exchequer, or Ecclesiastical. Until the Court of Admiralty was established, the County Court included the jurisdiction of that Court in addition. The justices too executed the functions of a separate Orphans Court, a separate Court of Claims, and a separate Court of Probate. It was also a court of record. By the provisions of an Act passed in the year 1642, all mortgages were taken as fraudulent unless copied into the books of either the General or the County Courts. Sixteen years before this Act was adopted, all deeds of conveyance had been copied into the books of the General Court at Jamestown, but, at a subsequent period, they too were entered, along with mortgages, in the books of the County Court.

What were the forms of trial followed by the County Court? By the ordinances of 1621, the tribunals then in existence in the Colony were directed to imitate the English tribunals in their manner of settling controversies. This was interpreted as requiring all cases to be decided by the judgment of a court or by the verdict of a jury, if one of the parties to the suit demanded it. Trial by jury was in use in all criminal cases apparently from the beginning. In both civil and criminal cases, an appeal to the Court's chancery jurisdiction was often made to prevent

the jury's verdict being put in effect before there had been further investigation.   No one was permitted to serve on a jury
who was unable to show that he possessed an estate of at least
moderate value.

The majority of the cases entered on the docket of the County
Court were settled by a decision of the justices without the intervention of a jury.   What were their qualifications for such
an important duty?   Most of them made no pretension to an
exact knowledge of the principles of law; but as many of them
had been educated in England before their immigration to Virginia, and some of them had served there on the magistrate's
bench, there was not a total lack of information among them,
either of the forms of law or of its substance.   The rules of English pleading, both on the common law and the chancery side,
were always strictly followed in their proceedings, and common
sense was relied upon as a guide wherever ignorance of the science in minute detail confronted them.   Beverley, the historian,
who was familiar, both as an observer and as a practitioner, with
the character of the County Courts, complimented their members
as a body by saying that they never admitted unnecessary "im-
pertinences of form and nicety"; and that they avoided the
"trickery and foppery of the law."

It should be borne in mind that the justices were the first
men in wealth and talent in their several communities, and as
they, as a rule, had sat on the bench during a long period of
years, it was to be expected that they would show at least practical efficiency in the performance of their functions on the
bench.   Moreover, there was not only a collection of law books
available in every courthouse, but there were also present, during every session of Court, an experienced clerk and a group of
competent attorneys.   Indeed, the attorneys were so plentiful,
as early as 1642, that an Act of Assembly was passed reducing
their number within more reasonable bounds; and a schedule of
fees was also then adopted.   Subsequently, this regulation was
made so severe that the professional lawyer was completely

thrown out of court. His place was taken by the clerks or such persons as the justices might select among the people at large to conduct a case.

But it is as inconvenient to abolish the professional lawyer as it is to abolish the members of the female sex, and in a brief time, the regular licensed practitioner reappeared in the Courts of the Colony, and was never again banished from those precincts. The community was now growing in population and in wealth, and men of this calling, in spite of the gibes at their expense, became as indispensable as physicians or clergymen. That their services were considered to be highly valuable was revealed in the liberty that was allowed them down to 1680 to fix their own fees. But, during that year, it was enacted that their remuneration should not, in any single case, exceed one hundred and fifty pounds of tobacco.

The lucrativeness of the practice, in the latter part of the century, drew to its membership numerous men of high standing, decided talent, and no inconsiderable learning. Attorneys like William Sherwood, William Fitzhugh, Edmund Scarborough, Robert Beverley, Denis McCarty, and Arthur Spicer, could have held their own with distinction in the courts of the Mother Country.

Subordinate to the justices of the County Court, but almost as important in their own sphere, were the clerk and sheriff. Both were essential instruments in the administration of the law. The duties of the clerk differed hardly at all from his functions at the present day, except that he sometimes, as already mentioned, performed the part of a practicing lawyer. In the beginning, he received his appointment from the Governor, but afterwards, for a time at least, from the Secretary of State. The clerkship, like all the offices of importance, were filled by men of influence in their several communities. The fees were sufficiently high to attract to the position incumbents of superior qualifications and indisputable social distinction.

In the early history of the Colony, the duties of the sheriff were executed by the provost marshal. After the creation of the counties, a sheriff was appointed by the Governor to serve in each, and the number of these officers increased as the counties grew in number. A custom seems to have prevailed during the Commonwealth that their selection by the Governor was to be made from lists to be handed to him by the justices of the different County benches; but after the Restoration, when there was a return to the original rule, the Governor was at liberty to follow the dictates of his own discretion in choosing an incumbent for a vacancy. At one time, the sheriff was required to be a member of the bench. At that period, every member of that body was expected to serve in turn, if the Governors approval of each nomination in rotation had been granted.

The sheriff's duties were multifarious. He collected the quit-rents and also the public and county taxes. He served all subpoenas; made all arrests; sued out all attachments; executed all writs; and carried out the successive orders of the justices of the County Court . He also summoned the people to cast their votes for the candidates for the House of Burgesses, and he announced the annulment of every Act of Assembly which the King had vetoed. The office was attended with profit; and it was also invested with the high dignity which had always marked its character in England.

What were the punishments adjudged by the County Court? Every case involving the possible loss of life or limb was tried by a special court known as the Court of Oyer and Terminer. The County Court had no part in such a trial, but the sentences passed by the Superior Court was carried into effect by the officers of the County in which the crime had been committed.

The criminal jurisdiction of the County Court was limited to the less serious offenses. Its simplest form of punishment was the fine, which was most commonly imposed in the case of convictions for pilfering,—especially in connection with articles of food. Because such articles were produced in the Colony in great abundance, it was doubtless thought that payment of a definite quantity of tobacco would be sufficient compensation to the owner for a loss of this kind. The lash was much in use in the case of misdemeanors that involved a certain degree of social turpitude,—such as illicit commerce between the sexes. One of the parties to a depraved act of this particular kind was generally sent to the public whipping post, while the other,—the woman, as a rule,—was required to appear in church at the hour of morning service enveloped in a white sheet. On that occasion, she was ordered to face the whole congregation and formally acknowledge her guilt.

Insolence to superiors too was punished with the official whip. The number of strokes in a case of this kind was usually limited to twenty. A woman who had given a loose rein to a slanderous tongue was also compelled to submit her naked back to the thong in the vigorous hands of the constable. If, after the first beating, she refused to admit that she was at fault, she was taken to a plantation at some distance off and there scourged a second time; and so the punishment continued from place to place, until she denied that she had any ground for uttering the libel with which she was charged.

Abduction of a servant belonging to another exposed the guilty person to the lash; so did the unauthorized removal and appropriation of a neighbor's boat; and so too did a wrongful abstraction of powder and shot. Servant, boat, and ammunition, were considered to be indispensable to their possessors, and it was not looked upon as a sufficient damnification to receive a sum of tobacco for their respective losses. This was also the case with clothes, which were expensive to procure. Sometimes, the culprit, instead of being flogged, was punished by simply tying him to the whipping post. Every courthouse green was flanked by a conspicuous pair of stocks. To this instrument were committed those persons whose offenses were not thought to be so heinous as to justify a whipping. The pillory nearby was equally ignominious, and was always employed if the stocks were occupied.

These three instruments of punishment,—whipping post, pillory, and stocks,—offered at every meeting of the County Court a silent warning to the assembled people of the penalty that would overtake all who violated the simpler requirements of the law. The use of the three possessed the practical advantage of reducing very substantially the cost of inflicting punishment for misdemeanors.

The old English penalty of ducking, which was usually the fate of all witches and scolds, was a still cheaper form of imposing retributive justice on the guilty.

Imprisonment was another manner of punishment. Every county was in possession of a public jail, which was usually constructed after the model of the typical Virginian farm-house, with brick underpinning and framed walls. It was said throughout the century that they were easily broken through by the prisoners, unless the custodians were constantly on their guard. In some instances, a tavern served,—at least temporarily,—as a jail. The structures for confinement of the accused were very rarely in excess of fifteen by ten feet in dimensions.

The General Court was the most important judicial body in the Colony, unless the right of appeal to the General Assembly, which existed at one time, converted the latter into the Supreme Court. The General Court was composed of the Governor and his Council, and, the date of its establishment went back to the foundation of Jamestown. At first, the administration of justice was entirely restricted to its control, with the exception of the period covered by the rule of Gates and Dale, when the Divine and Martial Laws were in force. It possessed both civil and criminal jurisdiction in the time of the Company, and also after the revocation of the Charter in 1624. The usual place of meeting during these early years was Jamestown, but the court sometimes convened at Elizabeth City, or some other important cluster of plantations. After the erection of the first State

House, a room was assigned in that building to its exclusive use. During the not infrequent intervals when the State House was a ruin, through the action of fire, accommodations for the Court were obtained in private residences.   There were four terms of the court,—the March, June, October, and November terms. For this reason, it was often referred to as the quarter court.

The membership of the General Court was composed of the foremost citizens of the Colony.   Its practical competency was precisely the same as that which has already been noted in the case of the county court.   The judges were not lawyers by profession; but through their general experience of life, and by long incumbency of the office, they had acquired efficiency in the performance of their judicial duties; and, apparently, they gave from session to session no serious cause for dissatisfaction.

The General Court's jurisdiction was both original and appellate, and it only arose, in either instance, whenever, the amount in litigation did not fall below sixteen pounds sterling or sixteen hundred pounds of tobacco.   This Court's criminal jurisdiction at first extended to all indictment for murder, arson, treason, mutiny, piracy, and rape, but the actual trial in the case of each of these felonies seem, after 1624, to have been conducted by the ancient Court of Oyer and Terminer, which was commissioned by the Governor.   Apparently this court was composed of certain members of the General Court, who had been specially selected by him for the purpose.   The Court of Oyer and Terminer was practically a substitute for the General Court, and exercised what was virtually a delegated power.

The chief officers of the General Court were its clerk and the Attorney-General of the Colony.   Both were men of distinction and influence in the community at large.   The Attorney-General was assisted by a solicitor general at the end of the century.

During a long period, there was a right of appeal from the General Court to the General Assembly.   The ground for the appeal was first considered by the Burgesses' Committee on Private Causes, and then reported to the House as a whole, who, after a rehearal, determined the case finally by a majority vote. This right of appeal was withdrawn during the administration of Culpeper.

It was not until 1697-98 that a Court of Admiralty was formally established in the Colony. Previous to that year, all maritime cases were decided by the County Court, or by the General Court, if they had come up on appeal.

CHAPTER XII

THE CHURCH

The parish was the local unit for the administration of the community's ecclesiastical affairs, and for the protection of its moral health. It was established in Virginia during the time of the London Company, and it remained as a local division throughout the colonial age.

The creation of a separate parish was in the General Assembly's discretion, and as soon as the spread of population made it advisable to erect one, that body authorized the justices of the county in which the new parish was to be laid off to have the boundary lines surveyed and platted for the Assembly's approval and adoption. Some of the parishes in existence in 1643 embraced such a wide area that it was often inconvenient for all their inhabitants to attend the services in the parish church. The disposition was to subdivide such parishes as these so soon as their population justified it. Sometimes, however, the drawbacks of a single place of worship were overcome by erecting a chapel of ease in the remoter region. This was especially necessary whenever a large stream split a parish into two local sections.

Whenever the expense of maintaining two parishes of moderate size became unduly heavy, an Act was obtained to merge them into one; but this did not often occur. Still rarer was the abandonment of a parish. This only happened when the soil was found to be too poor to support the required population, or the atmosphere had proved to be unhealthy on account of the presence of swamps, or the neighborhood was rendered unsafe by its proximity to hostile Indian tribes on the frontier. When these tribes were driven away permanently, the former practical status of the parish was restored.

Each parish was laid off into precincts by the action of the vestry.

It was found by actual count in 1661 that the number of parishes at that time did not exceed fifty. Each of these divisions was under the oversight of a body known in Virginia, as in England, as the Vestry. This body was composed of the foremost citizens of the community. Their public services were not confined to its duties, but extended in addition to the duties of the House of Burgesses, the Governor's Council, and the County Court, to which they also belonged. The social example which these men set left a deep permanent impression on the social character of the Colony. They represented all that birth, education, and fortune had to offer, and it was largely attributable to their influence that the social life in those thinly dispersed communities was so attractive, even during the early years of Colonial history.

At first, the members of the vestry were appointed by the monthly court, but, by 1641, the people of the parish seem to have chosen them by ballot; and this continued to be the method as late as 1670. One of the causes of Bacon's Insurrection some years afterwards was the vestry's unwarranted assumption of the power to fill permanently all vacancies in their board without regard to the public preference. A law of Bacon's reforming assembly required the popular election of each vestry at least once in the course of three years. After the close of that movement, this right of election was retained by the voters of the parish. Their choice, however, had to be confined by the justices of the County Court.

Between two popular elections, the vestry possessed the right to fill all vacancies temporarily. The number of its members seem to have been limited to twelve. They were required to convene at least twice in the course of a year.

The first duty of the vestry was to appoint the clergyman of the parish. The second was to inquire into such gross delinquences as drunkenness, adultery, and the like moral offenses; and if the accusations proved to be well grounded, to submit them to the County Court as a basis for formal indictment. The third duty was to lay the parish levy, which was used for the payment of the clergyman's salary, for the repair of the church edifice, and for the settlement of every form of the current parochial indebtedness.

The agents employed by the vestry to carry these duties into practical effect were the church wardens, who seem to have been limited in number to two. They were named once a year, and the entire vestry were expected to serve in rotation. It was the church wardens who represented that body in presenting the names of offenders to the county justices; and it was also they who received all collections made by the sheriff under the provisions of the parish levy; and it was they too, who, subject to the vestry's direction, disbursed these amounts. They were also responsible to the vestry for repairing the church edifice, for purchasing whatever was necessary for the equipment of its interior, and for registering births and deaths. Furthermore, it was incumbent on them to protect the resources of the parish from the drain that would have been caused by the support of youthful bastards. This was done by selling the mother for a term of service, or compelling the father to contribute to the maintenance of the woman and her offspring. They also bound out all bastards who had passed their childhood. In the performance of all these general duties, they were assisted by two officers known as sidesmen.

The funds needed for constructing a church building were, by the Act of 1631-32, ordered to be paid by the people of the parish. The assessment was made in the form of a regular tax, which was collected in the same manner as the county and public levies. It was often supplemented by liberal gifts of money from persons of pious inclinations.

As a rule, the edifice itself did not extend beyond forty feet in length, and twenty-five in width. It was usually built of wood, but, beside these churches of frame, there were a number constructed of brick. This was most often the case when the edifice was situated in the midst of a well-settled community, where there had been time for wealth to accumulate. Such communities were those of Jamestown and Smithfield. As the structure was generally of wood, the cost of annual repairs was always heavy, owing to the variable characters of the climate, which ranged all the way, with great suddenness, from dry to wet and from hot to cold. The principal seat in the parish church of the Colony, as in the English churches, was held by the most prominent families; and permanent possession of a particularly convenient pew was sometimes obtained by a special contribution to the erection of the building with that understanding; or it may be the pew had been put together at the cost of the occupant.

The plate and ornaments to be seen in the chancels were often of very handsome designs. Gifts of communion plate or bequests of large sums, to be invested in that form, frequently occurred, both during the time of the London Company, and after it was abolished. These were, as a rule, presented as memorials to persons who had worshipped under the particular roof which was associated with these acts of benevolence. In case there had been no gift, the church wardens were required to procure the necessary vessels and articles by purchase.

A plat for burial was laid off in the immediate vicinity of every parish church, but it was not used to the extent long customary in England. Perhaps, the principal reason in explanation of this fact was to be found in the more or less flimsy construction of the average building for religious purposes, which naturally created an impression of impermanency. Nothing would be lost by the desertion for another site in the case of most of these edifices; and should such removal occur, the plat set apart for interments would soon lapse into the jungle of the original forest. The people in the mass, therefore, preferred to reserve a burial ground, in the neighborhood of each home, for the deceased member of the family as offering more assurance for the proper preservation of so sacred a spot.

How was the vacant pulpit filled? So far as known, not a single clergyman in Virginia during the seventeenth century was a native of the Colony. They had all been drawn either from Scotland or England, with the numerical preponderance in favor of the latter. Those who came over had been induced to accept an invitation to do so by the superior advantages which most of the Virginian parishes had to offer as compared with the average parish in the Mother Country. At this time, it was said that ten of every eleven clergymen residing in the English rural districts occupied a position but little above that of a higher domestic servant in the way of income, comfort, and independence; and that many of them were compelled to till their glebes with their own hands, aided by those of their sons who were under age, while their daughters earned a precarious livelihood as seamstresses and ladies' maids.

In spite of the straightened condition of their families, the supply of English clergymen who were willing to immigrate to the Colony was never quite equal to the demand there for their services, except during the period of the Puritan Supremacy, when so many of the English divines lost their benefices and were only too eager to seek a refuge in Virginia, where they, after their arrival oversea, continued to find the Anglican service in use. These clergymen were not raw applicants for pulpits, but trained and experienced ministers of the Gospel remarkable for their learning and their talents.

It was proposed in 1660-61, to establish in Virginia a college, largely for the purpose of educating young men for the church. It is true that its graduates, should it be founded, would have to visit London to be ordained; but this was thought to be of small importance in comparison with the expectation that, by means of the college, the Colony would no longer have any reason to complain of vacancies. In addition, these young men, having been born and reared in Virginia, would, on taking possession of their rectories, be found to be more in sympathy with their congregations than any native Englishman just arrived in the country would be likely to be. How great was the need for ministers of the Gospel as late as 1697 was shown by the statement of the Commissary, in making his report to the Bishop of London, in the course of that year, that only twenty-two of the fifty parishes in Virginia were in possession of incumbents. And yet in spite of these vacancies, no parish was willing to accept any candidate for its pulpit unless he should submit a testimonial to prove that he had received ordination from an English prelate. A deacon was preferred to an unordained minister and many men of that ecclesiastical grade, in consequence, were accepted as substitutes.

The rule followed in Virginia of filling a benefice differed from the one which prevailed in England. In England, the power to name an incumbent belonged to the patron of the living, who might be either a person or a seat of learning. When once a nominee had been inducted there, he held his pulpit by a vested right, of which only the grossest misconduct could deprive him. In Virginia, on the other hand, the vestry alone chose the clergyman, and bound him by the terms of a definite contract that left them at liberty, at its termination, to refuse its renewal. He was prevented from acquiring a permanent tenure by their studied failure to offer him to the Governor for induction. In short, he was the creature of the vestry, to be retained or discarded in their discretion. This power seized by them without authority was one of the few radical departures from English law, but it arose, like the others, from the peculiar conditions which prevailed in Virginia. Necessarily, there could be no large number of patrons of livings in so new and so poor a community as the Colony was during most of the seventeenth century. The vestry was the only possible substitute for a patron as known to English ecclesiastical law.

It was this divergence from the rule at home that discouraged many English clergymen from emigrating, as they were naturally reluctant to abandon their native land for a position of such uncertain tenure. On the other hand, the vestries, by this regulation, protected their congregations from the permanent imposition of ministers of the Gospel whom they could know nothing of, in the beginning, and who might reveal themselves to be entirely lacking in talents and learning, and even in character. This plan of employing clergymen by contract, apparently had the advantage of influencing them to be more energetic, more circumspect and more faithful in their conduct, in order to strengthen their hold on the good will of their vestry and congregation alike.

There does not seem to have been any public sentiment in opposition to the clergyman's production of tobacco in as large quantities as his glebe allowed. In this way, he was able to supplement the sum granted him as his regular salary. In 1623-24, his remuneration was fixed at ten pounds of tobacco and a bushel of corn for each tithable listed in his parish, and these amounts in kind could be increased in the levy, should there be some special reason for doing so. In 1656, the clergyman's pecuniary resources were indirectly improved by the exemption of himself and six of his servants from the annual assessments, whether parish, county, or general; but the reforming assembly which convened in the time of Bacon's government restricted this privilege to himself alone. His servants were then again entered on the roll of ordinary tithables.

It was estimated, in 1666, that the total amount which the clergyman received did not fall below one hundred pounds sterling, which was equal in purchasing power to the modern twenty-five hundred dollars. In 1690, his salary was worth about eighty pounds in coin, a smaller figure. Five years afterwards, an Act of Assembly allowed each minister of the Gospel then in active service the sum of sixteen thousand pounds of tobacco,—subject, however, to a charge for the value of the cask, and also to an increased fee for collection. In the opinion of Beverley, the historian, the clergyman's income at the end of the century was as large as that of a planter who possessed a working force of twelve slaves. In addition to this remuneration in tobacco, he obtained fees of importance for performing wedding and funeral services.

Every rectory had a glebe attached to it, which embraced at least one hundred acres of field and woodland which had originally been selected with unusual care; and these small plantations were stocked with hogs, cows, and oxen, and not infrequently with several slaves also. The parsonage itself did not differ in size, or in comfort and convenience, from the average plantation home of that day. The libraries under some of these clerical roofs were remarkable for the number as well as for the choiceness of their volumes. These included works in the Latin, Greek, and English languages alike.

Many of the occupants of the pulpits, independently of their salaries and glebes, owned estates of considerable value. Patents were obtained in 1635 by two clergymen alone, which entitled them to one thousand eight hundred acres respectively. In each of these typical instances, the property had been acquired on the basis of headrights. Their example was followed by others, who, however, did not limit their purchases to land; many were in possession of numerous heads of livestock; and many also were owners of slaves. The inventory of Rev. Robert Powis, in 1652, showed the valuation of his personality alone to be as high as twelve thousand pounds of tobacco, while Rev. Thomas Teakle bequeathed an estate estimated in modern values at fifty thousand dollars. In numerous cases the clergymen were in the possession of property situated in England.

As early as 1619, the incumbents of the different pulpits were required to report all christenings, burials, and marriages that had occurred in their respective parishes during the preceding twelve months. They were also required to teach the young people belonging to their several congregations the Ten Commandments, the Lord's Prayer, the Catechism, and the Articles of Belief; and in addition to these duties, they were expected to visit all persons among their parishioners who were afflicted with sickness. Annually, a convention of the clergymen of the Colony was held at Jamestown, and on the occasion of this assembly, the affairs of the church in general and the parishes in particular were fully discussed.

Every clergyman who was in charge of two parishes was compelled to travel far to occupy both pulpits, one at the morning, and the other at the afternoon services. There must have been many stormy Sundays when a clergyman so situated was unable to arrive in time for the first or the second; but when he was thus unavoidably prevented from being present, his place was taken by the clerk, who had been impowered to act as his substitute in part under these circumstances. Not infrequently, however, someone had been especially named to read, like the clerk, the lessons. In 1680, the law required that such a person should be appointed for every parish in which there was no reader. His duty extended to the reading of a selected sermon also.

There is no reason to think that the character of the Virginian clergyman of the seventeenth century fell below that of the average English clergyman of that day. The divines who ministered to the spiritual needs of the people of the Colony in the time of the London Company were among the noblest men of their calling recorded in modern history. Rev. Robert Hunt and Rev. Richard Buck were faithful exemplars of all the loftiest characteristics that have adorned the Christian religion in its highest manifestations from age to age. Those who immediately followed them were equally deserving of honor and veneration. Throughout the century, the largest number of the clergymen in Virginia were graduates of English universities, and were also persons of prominent social connections in the

Mother Country. All the records of that century prove that the great body of these divines were men who performed the duties of their sacred calling in a manner that fully entitled them to the respect and reverence, as well as to the gratitude, of their respective parishioners. There were undoubtedly offenders in some of the numerous pulpits, but there is reason to think that their conduct was not condoned, and that they were punished by the sharp disapproval of public opinion, if not by actual expulsion. Each vestry had, as we have mentioned, reserved the right to terminate their contract with the incumbent of their parish pulpit at the end of each year, and this fact must, in itself, have been sufficient to check any disposition on his part, —should he have felt any,—to show disregard of the ordinary proprieties and decencies of life.

From the beginning, down to the Act of Toleration, there was a resolute effort on the part of the local authorities to enforce absolute conformity with the doctrines and ceremonies of the Anglican worship. Dissent and schism were abhorred by the people of the colony at large, and were treated without moderation or leniency by the governor, the General Court, and the General Assembly, whenever a question involving disloyalty to the established church came before them. Among the harshest provisions of the Divine and Martial Laws of Gates and Dale were those directed against the rejection of the canons or neglect of the religious observances of that church. Again and again, the successive governors were enjoyed by the Privy Council to regulate the religious affairs of the Colony by the English ecclesiastical laws and statutes. The effect of these instructions were seen in the passage of the long series of acts that were designed to carry them out in full.

In 1642, the General Assembly not only required that all the canons and constitutions of the Anglican Church should be rigidly obeyed in Virginia, but that all persons who refused to do so should be expelled from the Colony. No pastor was to be permitted to hold a living who declined to be governed by the Anglican regulations; and no applicant for a pulpit was to be accepted unless he could submit a certificate from the Bishop of London that the bearer conformed to all the doctrines of the Anglican Faith.

The principal dissenters were the Quakers. The opposition to them was not entirely to be attributed to their religious belief. Their conduct, under certain circumstances, was naturally calculated to arouse prejudice and suspicion against them. They assembled always in the profoundest secrecy; by refusing to pay their share of the parish taxes, they increased the burden of the levy for the rest of the community; they declined to join in taking up arms when there was a threat of civil commotion or invasion; and finally they were disrespectful in their bearing towards persons in authority, which seemed to indicate that they were disloyal to the Government both in Virginia and in England.

In 1658, the General Assembly ordered that every Quaker residing in the Colony should be compelled to leave it. The sect, through the influence of active missionary work, and also by the force of persecution, had recently been increasing with great rapidity. It was even apprehended by the authorities that the Colony's government would be overturned, and its different communities thrown into a state of confusion, by the aggressive action of these religious dissenters and political delinquents. "Their lies, miracles, false visions, prophecies, and doctrines," said the General Assembly in 1659-60, "tended to destroy religion, laws, communities, and all bonds of civil society." Whichever sea-captain brought in a member of this detested sect was subjected to a fine of one hundred pounds sterling; and every person who entertained an exhorter in his house was liable to the same penalty.

An additional blow at the Quakers, although they were not mentioned by name, was the revival of an old law which prescribed that any one who failed, without an acceptable excuse, to attend the services at the parish church every Sunday during

the whole of a month was to be mulcted to the extent of twenty
pounds sterling; and should he continue to absent himself during another eleven months, he was to be forced to pay two hundred and forty pounds sterling. These penalties were actually
imposed in recorded cases, whether the delinquents were able to
defray them or not.

But the Quakers were not to be constrained even by such a
law as this to modify their principles or change their course of
conduct. Indeed, as a religious body, they grew in size and
waxed in spirit the more relentlessly they were persecuted. How
outrageously extreme was the hostility towards them was revealed in the case of John Pleasants and his wife. Because they
had been married according to the Quaker manner alone, they
were indicted for illicit cohabitation, and each was fined twenty
pounds sterling a month for the time they had refrained from
attending Anglican religious services. As one of the tenets of
their faith forbade them to baptize their children, they were
punished for obeying this doctrine by being required to pay
two thousand pounds of tobacco; and an additional five hundred were imposed for their permitting a conventicle to be held
in their house. Absolute ruin would have fallen on this noble
couple, in consequence of these fines, had they not been saved
by the announcement of the passage of the first Act of Toleration by the British Parliament, under the influence of a Catholic monarch.

The Revolution of 1688 confirmed the freedom of religious
worship granted by this Act, and, thereafter, the Quakers were
not seriously molested, in spite, of the prejudice against them
as a sect, which continued to exist. This was the natural result
of their still vigorous refusal to perform various important
civil duties which were thought by the people at large to be
common to every person in the community, whatever his religious connections. It was noted in the Colony that so soon as
the Quakers were at liberty to make converts to their faith without a legalized and organized opposition to overcome, the pros-

perity of their sect began to fall away; and by the end of ten years, they had shrunk to a few small congregations, composed of members who were lacking in public and private influence.

During the civil wars in England, a truculent antagonism sprang up between the Puritan and the Churchman, but it was not until the passage of the great English Act of Uniformity in 1662 that the Puritan assumed the distinct status of dissenter, such as the Quaker and Separatest had occupied from the beginning. Some of the noblest of the early clergymen of Virginia belonged to the Puritan wing of the Church of England. A large congregation of this leaning within the folds of the church settled, under the leadership of Edward Bennett, on the south bank of the Powhatan. They were practically nonconformists in some of their doctrines.

An act of the General Assembly was passed in 1643 to require all ministers of the Gospel residing in the Colony to conform to all the canons of the established church. Should any refuse, they were not to be permitted to preach or teach at all, and if they persisted in doing either, they were to be compelled to withdraw from Virginia.

During the existence of the Protectorate, the Puritans in Virginia were not exposed to any form of interference with the utterances of their religious doctrines in private or in the pulpit. They were, however, too small in number to retaliate upon their recent persecutors by persecuting them in turn. But this interval of peace and liberty only made the upheaval which followed the Restoration the more destructive in its effect on the prosperity of their religious sect. The Act of Uniformity deprived them of all their advantages by placing them squarely on the footing of dissenters. A large body of Virginian Puritans immigrated to Maryland, in the just expectation of enjoying a degree of religious freedom there which had been denied them south of the Potomac. The remainder seem to have gradually lost their religious identity in the fold of the Established Church in the Colony.

Presbyterians and Roman Catholics never rose to any real importance in the religious life of the community. Indeed, the former did not appear at all in that life until towards the close of the century, when they obtained some foothold in Norfolk County. In 1702, the Presbyterian congregations, which were confined to the county and Accomac, were limited to four in number.

No hostility seems to have been felt towards this sect of dissenters, but the animosity shown to the Catholics never lost its bitterness. The Quaker, the Puritan, and the Presbyterian never denied the political supremacy of the English King, although they refused to consider him as the head of their different denominations. But they did not attempt to put any one in his place in that respect. The Catholics did attempt to do so; and this was taken by Protestants as signifying disloyalty also in affairs purely temporal. The Pope was supposed to be plotting for the overthrow of the civil as well as of the spiritual power of the English throne. How could he hope to undermine that throne without the sympathy and cooperation of the entire English membership of his ecclesiastical fold?

No papist at first was permitted to occupy an office in the Colony, and every priest of the Roman Catholic Church who was found in it was liable to immediate expulsion. It was not until the passage of the Act of Toleration that such a priest dared to claim the right to celebrate the mass in Virginia, or to observe the other rites of his particular form of worship. This suspicion against the Catholics continued deep seated down to the end of the century. In 1688, a report spread through the Colony that the papists of Virginia and Maryland were conspiring with the Indian tribes on the frontier to butcher the Protestants. A general panic quickly flamed up, and the men in every community seized their guns to repel the expected invasion. This was not an atmosphere in which Catholicism could thrive, and it was natural enough that it acquired no real foothold in the Colony.

18—Vol. I.

The atheist was looked upon with the same unceasing distrust as dogged the feet of the Romanist. He was forbidden to aspire to public office; he was not permitted to serve as a guardian or executor or to accept a legacy; and if he remained contumacious, he was liable to imprisonment for a period of three years.

A witch aroused more personal hostility than even a Catholic or an atheist, for a strange emotion of the supernatural entered into the sinister impression which the mere sight of her caused. The belief in witchcraft prevailed universally in that age, and while many cases involving the supposed exercise of sorcery came before the courts of Virginia, during the seventeenth century, there is not a single instance of a sentence of death being passed on a witch recorded in its history as a Colony. A dip from a ducking stool seems to have been the most serious punishment inflicted on the most uncanny of these victims of popular delusion and of their own self-deception.

CHAPTER XIII

SCHOOL AND COLLEGE

The system of plantations that prevailed in the Colony, during the seventeenth century, was not in itself favorable to the spread of popular education. Popular education flourishes best in communities which approach nearest to the village form. This was the explanation of the prosperity of the public school in New England from the start. That region in general had been first settled by large congregations of people, who, for mutual protection or helpfulness, had thought it to be wisest to join in groups in appropriating the soil.

In Virginia, on the other hand, the disposition had been to avoid such grouping. The frontier was enlarged gradually by the issuance of patent after patent to the land, each, as a rule, dovetailed into the next, with only gaps here and there, where the ground happened to be naturally thin and poor. Most of these patents gave titles to very considerable areas of soil. Taken as a whole, they indicated a population dispersed over broad reaches of country, each family residing on its own estate, and, to a marked degree, independent of the families occupying the adjacent estates. There were not only no towns, unless Jamestown, by a stretch of the real meaning of the word, could be taken as such, but there were no villages. The people came together at the courthouse, at the church, and on the musterfield, at stated times, but they were never associated in the daily intimacy of a village community.

What did this signify? That the Colony's inhabitants dwelt so widely apart that it was not practicable for them to establish

259

a schoolhouse which could conveniently and within a reasonable time be reached by the great majority of the children belonging even to one country side. The distance to a site which might have been chosen, would, under the most favorable circumstances, have been considerable; and this fact was rendered more formidable by the bad condition of the public roads which existed. Moreover, not every family was in possession of a horse to serve as a means of transportation. To accommodate the children of any one plantation district, it would have been necessary to erect more than one schoolhouse, and to employ more than one school-master. The people, as a whole, were unable to provide the money for such an expensive system of popular instruction.

But it did not follow that the planters, as a body, were indifferent to education. A very large proportion of them, throughout the century, had been born, reared, and taught in England. The sentiment among them in favor of a training in letters was almost as strong as the sentiment in favor of a religious training. How did this fact exhibit itself? In the establishment of old field schools here and there, and in the employment of tutors under the several planters' roofs. Towards the end of the century, the sentiment in favor of education took the more decided form of a demand for a college; and this sentiment was not, as we shall see, satisfied until that college had been built and put in actual operation. In the meanwhile, several free schools, which had been established, had been successful in meeting the need for instruction in more than one community in the Colony.

There are numerous indications in different ways of the value attached by the people of Virginia, at this time, to education. One of the most impressive proofs of that fact are the provisions embodied in numerous wills for the instruction of children. Special funds were assigned in these last testaments for carrying out the purpose of this nature which the maker of the will had in view. The most common means adopted to assure these funds was the accumulation of the proceeds from the sale or the use of livestock. Sometimes, a round sum in pounds sterling was reserved for the accomplishment of the same end; sometimes, it was the tobacco to be received for the labor of a slave who had been hired out to a neighbor, or to an older member of the family. In many instances, the whole estate of the testator was made liable for the proper education of his offspring. Not infrequently, his prescription did not extend beyond the rudiments, but as the instruction was, in many cases, to be continued until the child had reached his nineteenth year, the paternal requirement called for the acquisition of a more or less advanced education, as it was understood in those times.

The same sentiment in favor of education in general, was reflected in the series of orders adopted from year to year by the justices of the County Courts. These officials had supervisory charge of the affairs of many orphan children of good estates. At least once in the course of every twelve months, a session of each bench was held to pass upon all questions that concerned the welfare of these children; and one of those which elicited the court's special attention was the question of their being provided with teachers. The guardian of each child was required to submit his accounts on that occasion, and the items which were examined with the most scrutiny were the ones that related to the child's instruction. If the proper provision for this had not been made, the delinquent was certain to receive the justice's censure, along with an order to make good the deficiency.

It was distinctly provided by statute that the cost of the orphan's education was to "be in proportion to his estate." Another expression in more popular use was, that his education must be "according to his quality."

The number of orphans who had inherited no property was greater than the number who had inherited some. It was the duty of the County Court to bind these indigent children to an apprenticeship, through which they might learn a trade for their own support. Whether the child was a boy or a girl, the court was equally specific in requiring that he or she should be instructed in the rudiments, at least, by a competent teacher. Such a provision was included in the terms of every apprenticeship. Nor was this a dead letter or a mere formality. Indeed, the court was so scrupulous in enforcing these terms that it was not possible for a negligent master to evade them.

It was natural that a planter of wealth should have preferred to have his son instructed in England, but there were serious drawbacks to his carrying out his wish. The long and dangerous voyage was one obstacle. The separation by a wide ocean was another. Nevertheless, many of the young Virginians were sent oversea to be educated in English private schools and colleges. Among these were members of the Lee, Wormeley, Byrd, and Parke families, perhaps the most distinguished and influential in the Colony.

But a far larger proportion of the young men of high social position were educated by tutors under the paternal roof in Virginia. Frequently, the sons of the neighboring planters of the same position gathered daily in a single home and received instruction from the same teacher. Many of the teachers had come to the Colony from England in order to serve in this capacity, while others were natives of Virginia. The position was not unprofitable. In more than one instance, its reward, at the end of an engagement, was a deed to a very respectable area of land. Occasionally, the tutor was serving his employer under the terms of a regular indenture. Some of the agricultural laborers were adventurous young men who had received a fair degree of education in the grammar or public schools of the Mother Country, and were, in consequence, sufficiently equipped to teach the ordinary lessons of the average pedagogue.

There were in Virginia, during this century, numerous schools of the kind known, at a later date, as the Old Field School. These were usually situated at some spot which had been abandoned for tillage, and yet had not had time to be covered with a secondary growth of trees, although, here and there, perhaps, the young straggling pines had begun to show their green tufts above the surface of the earth. Such a spot was always within convenient distance of the homes of numerous planters of moderate wealth, and their children were able to walk to the school house, if they were not in possession of quicker means of traversing the intervening space. Not infrequently this schoolhouse was a part of the residence of the teacher himself.

The head of the school was quite often a clergyman, who thus eked out his salary and what income he obtained from the sale of the products of his glebe. Those of his parishioners who lived not far from his rectory constantly employed him to instruct their children; and in most instances, they found in him a very capable preceptor, as the majority of the clergymen had been educated in the best colleges of England.

The other persons whose services were engaged for the work of these parish schools were often men of excellent equipment for their important office.

To make certain the acquisition of teachers of the proper degree of learning, it was expressly provided in the instructions given to the governors towards the end of the century that no one recently arrived from England should be permitted to offer himself for the position of pedagogue without first satisfying the authorities that he had received a license to do so from the Bishop of London. In 1686, the teachers then employed in the Colony were required to prove their competency in their profession by passing a special examination to test their knowledge. It was essential also that they should demonstrate their fidelity to the doctrines and forms of the Church of England.

The only influence that operated to encourage the building of towns in the different counties was the desire of the people to possess good schools, which were thought to stand a better chance of erection in a community of that size than in the sparsely settled countrysides then in existence.

The anxiety of the county justices to obtain teachers was illustrated in their willingness to offer one high inducement which was rarely accorded to any other members of the community. The court, as we have seen, was always especially reluctant to exempt from taxation, even temporarily, anyone liable to the levy, and yet pedagogues were often granted this great privilege in order to influence them to open schools in neighborhoods which were entirely lacking in such facilities. The fee that they were called upon to pay in order to obtain a license was reduced to an almost nominal figure. Indeed, it was designed as a compensation for the clerk's trouble in drafting the document rather than as a contribution to the county treasury.

The charge for a pupil's instruction extending over the scholastic year did not exceed twenty-five dollars in the purchasing power of modern coin. Each teacher was allowed by law a free hand in making the most advantageous contract with a patron whom he was able to secure. That some of the school masters, like some of the tutors, found their calling quite profitable was disclosed by the fact that they were able to accumulate estates of considerable value. Many more of them held plantations of a few hundred acres, which they also had probably acquired by their fidelity and industry as pedagogues.

On a famous occasion, Berkeley boasted that there were no free schools in existence in Virginia. In uttering these words, he must have consciously deceived himself, since there were two respectable schools of this character in a day's journey of Jamestown at that time.

During the period of the London Company, the East India free school was projected, and its site chosen, but the Massacre of 1622 brought the scheme to a premature end. It was the knowledge of this prior school which, perhaps, influenced Benjamin Symmes, in drafting his will in February, 1634-35, to

provide for the foundation of the earliest free school which was
ever established in reality in America. This school was modeled
on the grammar schools of his native country, England. It was
supported by a devise of two hundred acres of land, supplemented by a bequest of eight cows. Its educational benefits were
granted only to the children to be found in the parishes of
Elizabeth City and Kikotan. This school has remained in a
prosperous condition down to the present day, after being
merged with the Eaton Free School, which had its origin in
the same century.

The endowment fund of the Eaton Free School was more
valuable than that of its predecessor, for this endowment consisted not only of a large tract of land, but also of slaves and
livestock. The land was occupied by a comfortable residence,
which was, doubtless, expected to serve as a school house. The
Eaton Free School was under the control of a board of trustees
composed of the vestry of the parish in which it was situated,
and also of the justices of the County Court.

There were a few other free schools in the Colony at this
time. One of these was established by Hugh Lee in Northumberland; another by John Moon, in Isle of Wight; and a third,
by Richard Russell, in Lower Norfolk. More important than
any of these three was the school founded by Henry Peasley
of Gloucester County. The endowment which this school received through his will consisted of six hundred acres, ten cows,
and a breeding mare.

What attempts were made in Virginia, during the seventeenth century, to establish seats of higher learning? The first
related to what was known as the Indian College. The means
necessary for carrying out this scheme were raised in large
part by the direct encouragement of the King; valuable gifts
for its support were afterwards added by private individuals;
and a great tract of land was laid off by the London Company
for maintaining it through the labor of imported tenants.
Mechanics were sent out to construct the required number of

buildings, and there is reason to think that the proposed institution would have been set up and put in scholastic operation had not the Massacre of 1622 confused the plan beyond all hope of immediate revival.

A university had been involved in this plan, and many thousand acres had been reserved for its use. Had the Company retained its charter, it is quite probable that work on both the college and the university would have been resumed in time, and carried out to the full consummation of all the purposes which its projectors originally had had in mind. When, in 1624, the charter was revoked, the only organization that was interested in the revival of the plan for higher education in Virginia was extinguished. No single body of men remained after that event who possessed either the inclination or the means to rehabilitate the original scheme, even in a modified form. None arose.

But as time moved on, the sentiment among the higher class of planters in the Colony grew stronger and stronger in favor of creating the means of obtaining a more or less advanced education without having to cross a wide ocean to secure it in the colleges of Oxford and Cambridge. Apart from all other considerations, the cost of the voyage, added to that of matriculation at those seats of learning, without mentioning the expense of a residence there, made even wealthy fathers of sons shrink from such a venture. They were forced, as we have already pointed out, to fall back on the local tutor and the private school; but neither pretended to carry their pupils beyond a limited field of imparted knowledge.

Thirty-six years were to pass before a really practical step was taken to found such an institution of learning as would satisfy, even to a moderate extent, the higher educational needs of the younger men of the Colony. It was clearly recognized, during this long interval, that the planters must look almost exclusively to their own pecuniary resources if they were determined to realize their purpose. Their only hope of securing any aid in England lay in their demonstrating their willingness and ability to collect by subscription amongst themselves the far larger share of the fund required. In 1660, the impression spread that the hour was now opportune for carrying out the scheme for the erection of a college which had been long brewing. It is calculated that the Colony at this time did not contain more than twenty-five thousand inhabitants. Necessarily, such a limited population could not have been in possession of a large amount of wealth. Such wealth as existed was almost entirely in the form of land and livestock, which it was almost impossible to convert into actual money.

But the citizens at the head of the movement for the acquisition of a seat of higher learning were not to be deterred by narrow financial resources from pushing their project. During the session of the General Assembly in the winter of 1660-61, three acts were passed, which described in detail the benefits to be expected from the college, which was now specifically authorized to be built and put under way. These were first, instruction in the higher branches of knowledge; and secondly, the education and the special preparation of candidates for the ministry. The aim of the projected institution was, in a general way, to encourage learning and nourish religion.

No sooner had the college been incorporated, when the subscription list was opened in all the counties. The governor headed the list; the names of the members of the Council followed; next came those of the County Courts; and at the close were written the names of many of the planters at large. It was provided in the subscription roll that no sum was to be paid until a site for the college had been bought, and the erection of the necessary structures had been begun.

If any step was taken to solicit the aid of the people of England in carrying out this scheme, no evidence of it has survived. It is most probable that no such supplementary effort was ever made because the attempt to collect in the Colony the amount expected of it proved to be abortive, owing, not to the

indifference of the people most interested, but the comparative
poverty of the members of every class represented in the several
communities.

It is cause for surprise that the plan adopted in the time
of the Company was not imitated by the promoters of the College, in 1660-61, when they found that the subscription list
could not be relied upon to produce the sum that was required.
It will be recalled that an enormous tract of public land was
reserved by that body for the erection and support of the projected college and university. There was in 1660-61, an equal
extent of fertile unoccupied land situated along the frontiers
which could have been held back for residential and agricultural
uses, subject to rental returns indefinitely, for the building and
support of the institution then under consideration.

The long series of years that followed before the College of
William and Mary was incorporated, which event occurred
towards the close of the century, was so filled with disturbing
influences, like, for instance, the opposition to the Navigation
Act, the low price of tobacco, the outrages by marauding Indians, and the Insurrection of 1676, that the thoughts of men
were entirely diverted from the old scheme for the erection of
a seat of higher learning. Indeed, it was not until 1690 that
Nicholson, then serving in Howard's place as Lieutenant-Governor, revived the plan of 1660-61 by issuing a proclamation
that called upon all with the means to subscribe to contribute
to the building of the college, now once more brought to public
attention.

The first site suggested for the new seat of learning lay on
the north side of York River; the second proposed lay on the
south side. Middle Plantation, which was situated on the ridge
between the York and James rivers, was finally chosen as combining the most advantages in the points of both health and
convenience. A board of distinguished trustees was appointed,
on which both the church and the land-owners were represented.
An address to the King and Queen was drafted, and the Rev.

James Blair was nominated to deliver it in person. A large sum was appropriated to cover the expenses of his journey.

As commissary, Blair was favorably known in England; and he was for other reasons, in addition, particularly well fitted to make an excellent impression on the minds of those persons in the Mother Country whose good-will was essential to the success of the purpose that he had in view, which was to obtain, not only a charter, but also the pecuniary aid of the throne, the church, and the nobility. Permission was to be asked to confer on the proposed seat of learning the name of the Royal College of King William and Queen Mary in honor of their majesties. The subjects which were to be taught, if the authority to do so were granted by the charter, were the Latin and Greek languages, divinity, philosophy, and mathematics. Blair was instructed to engage a schoolmaster, usher, and writing master, while he was in England, with assistance of persons connected with the universities.

By 1691, about two thousand pounds sterling had been guaranteed by the people of Virginia, and probably most of it delivered in the form of tobacco; and they also bound themselves to make up any deficiency which might exist after Blair's report of his collections in England had, on his return, been delivered to the General Assembly. Different plans for swelling the resources of the college so soon as completed were adopted by that body; and most of these were subsequently allowed by the English authorities when submitted to them for approval.

In September, 1693, a copy of the charter which had been obtained by Blair was delivered by him in person to the General Assembly. His ability, energy, and devotion to the purposes of his mission had been the chief influences in winning success, but he had also enjoyed the advantage of a sympathetic King, Queen, and church from the moment of his arrival in England. This fact only increased the warm satisfaction which was aroused in the Assembly by the reception, through him, of a document which had been so long desired, and which was ex-

pected to confer such lasting benefits on the people of the
Colony. Two warrants were drawn at once. One was directed
to the auditor of Virginia, the senior William Byrd, for the sum
of eleven hundred and thirty-five pounds sterling, while the
other was directed to the executors of the lately deceased auditor, the elder Nathaniel Bacon, for the sum of eight hundred
and fifty pounds sterling. These warrants were made payable
to Governor Nicholson and the other members of the Board of
Trustees. Thus was obtained the first fund for use in the building of the royal college in Virginia.

The foundation stone was laid in August, 1695. By the middle
of the ensuing October, the structure had begun to rise from
the ground. Eighteen months afterwards, the walls had reached
the roof. Two years from the date of turning the first spadeful
of earth, the college was in a condition far advanced enough
to receive pupils. The expenditures for completing the building,
—which was composed of stone, brick, and wood,—amounted
to the round sum of thirty-eight hundred and thirty-four pounds
sterling. Owing to the reduced price of tobacco, there had been
some difficulty in collecting the subscriptions still unpaid by
many of the planters, and suits had to be brought against these
delinquents.

By the end of the century, the college was in full operation,
with a substantial promise already of the successful career
which it was destined to run throughout the rest of the colonial
age. Several gifts of value were soon bestowed on it, with the
view of increasing its usefulness. One of these, which amounted
to one hundred and fifty pounds sterling, was made by the distinguished lawyer, Henry Hartwell; the other by Robert Boyle.
The latter donation consisted of the manor of Brafferton, which
brought in an income of two hundred and fifty pounds sterling.
One fifth of this income was reserved for the improvement of
the new England Indians, while the remainder was paid annually to the trustees of the college in Virginia, to defray the
cost of board, lodging, literary education, and religious instruc-

HON. ROBERT BOYLE

tion, of nine or ten young Indians, who were to be furnished periodically by the tribes seated along the neighboring frontiers.

Although many years were to pass before the institution would rise above the level of a grammar school of the contemporary English model, it was from the beginning dignified with the right to return a burgess to the General Assembly. Its constituency apparently consisted of two electors only: the President, who was Commissary Blair, and the schoolmaster.

The celebration of the final exercises held at the College in April, 1699, was long remembered for its unusual interest. The governor and burgesses attended in a body. A multitude of people gathered from many parts of the Colony, some coming by horseback, some by boat. There was a general feeling of mutual congratulation over the fact that the citizens of the various communities were now in possession of an institution on their side of the ocean which offered the fairest opportunity for the acquisition of a really satisfactory education.

However deficient the Colony was in advantages for higher instruction previous to the completion of the College, there is no reason to think that the homes of the substantial planters were at any period lacking in books. It should not be forgotten that the great majority of these men had been born and educated in the most cultivated and enlightened communities of England; and that they had brought oversea with them the intellectual tastes which they had both inherited and acquired. Apparently, but one printing press was to be found in Virginia during the seventeenth century, but the Mother Country supplied as readily volumes for the planter's library as she did furniture for the chambers of his mansion, or garments for the bodies of his family. One was as easily procurable as the other.

The inventories disclose the number and character of the books which had been accumulated under his roof year to year. The far greater proportion of these had been printed in England, but there were many which had come from the presses of the Dutch and French. Among them all were numerous masterpieces, not only of modern times, but also of ancient. The collections included volumes belonging to every province of human thought, with works on religion leading, followed closely by works on belle-lettres. History was also a popular subject. Naturally, the libraries of men who followed the professions of law and medicine were especially rich in the standard treatises relating to their respective callings. Some of the collections were made up of a small number of volumes only. Some, on the other hand, contained such a number and variety of titles that they would be justly considered, even in our own day, to constitute libraries of indisputable importance.

Apart from the possession of these libraries, the surviving letters and papers of the Virginians of the seventeenth century prove that they were far from lacking in literary culture. Scattered through the county records of that century are numerous private epistles of one kind or another, which are not only correctly expressed, from our modern point of view, but are also clear, vigorous, and pertinent in substance. Such letters are those which passed between Mrs. Mosely and Capt. Francis Yeardley in 1652, and between Benjamin Harrison and Col. Daniel Parke, in 1698. Such are the letters of Samuel Matthews, Charles Scarborough, and Hugh Yeo preserved in the same pages.

The *History of Virginia,* written by Robert Beverley, and the *History of the Boundary Line* written by the younger William Byrd, both of whom were representatives of the best colonial culture during the latter part of the seventeenth century, reflect great distinction on the talent for composition which existed at that time. Equally remarkable in a different way was the noble Declaration of 1651, in which the General Assembly protested against the Act of Parliament prohibiting all commercial intercourse between Virginia and other countries.

19—Vol. I.

An examination of the county records for the seventeenth century reveal the following facts: fifty percentage of the persons who served on juries were capable of signing their names; about sixty-five percentage of those conveying land or giving written testimony possessed the same accomplishment. Of every thirteen thousand persons whose names appear in the records in these connections, whether men or women, over seven thousand understood the art of writing. If the women are considered apart from the men, about one in three alone is found to be literate.

CHAPTER XIV

FRAMEWORK OF GOVERNMENT

The government of Virginia as a Colony was first organized under the letters-patent or charter of 1606. That charter embraced two great principles which have had a deep and permanent influence on the history of the British Empire: first, the projected community was to be put under the direct control of the Crown, and not of the Crown and Parliament combined; second, its inhabitants, whether natives of Virginia or England, were to enjoy all the liberties, franchises, and immunities possessed by the King's subjects in the Mother Country itself. The King retained the right to exercise the supreme authority in person or to delegate it to a company.

Down to 1609, the new community remained under the exclusive control of the monarch acting through a council appointed by him and sitting in London. This council was empowered to name a second council, which was to reside in Virginia, but this in its turn was to be guided by the ordinances and instructions which it was to receive from the first council in England, the agent and voice of the King.

Unfortunately for the success of the first charter, the enterprise called for a larger sum than the signers or the King were willing to furnish. This was soon perceived, and, in consequence, steps were taken in 1609 to organize a joint stock company resembling several of the same kind already in profitable operation. A second charter was obtained in the course of that year for the expressed purpose of providing the funds that would be needed to assure the proper utilization of all the

275

material resources of the new country, and to promote its early occupation by English immigrants. To encourage liberal subscriptions under the new charter, the King granted a number of important privileges to the signatories. It was to his advantage to do this, for while he would not be able to obtain a direct share in the profits of the joint stock ventures, he would secure indirectly a handsome return through the addition to his treasury from the collection of customs on all the imports from Virginia.

By the terms of the second charter, the Colony was to be governed by the ordinances and instructions of the Company's Council in London. To this body was now fully delegated all that supervisory and controlling power which the king had exercised under the letter-patent of 1616. There was a subordinate council seated at Jamestown, whose duty it was to carry out the instructions of the Council in England, and only to act on the dictates of their own judgments when there was no law in existence on that particular point to guide them to a decision.

The head of the administration both in England and Virginia was known as the treasurer.

It was under the third charter, granted in 1612, that the most productive work of the London Company was done. That body now assumed a new political significance through the influence of Sir Edwin Sandys, and his principal supporter, Lord Southampton. There seems to have been a deliberate purpose by them to set up a more liberal form of government in Virginia than prevailed at that time in England. One of the finest evidences of this enlightened determination was the authorization of the first General Assembly to meet at Jamestown. This body was destined, in spite of royal oppression at intervals, to continue to be the principal conservator of political freedom in the Western Hemisphere.

This great event was followed in 1620 by the drafting of a code which bore a close resemblance to a formal constitution. By the provisions of this memorable document, the Company still reserved the right to appoint the Governor and Council of Virginia, while the existing General Assembly was empowered to convene in the course of every year. Each town or settlement was to be entitled to the representation of two burgesses. The governor was to possess a negative voice in the framing of legislative acts; but no act was to become a law until it had received the approval of the King. Under the operation of this wise code, Virginia offered a spectacle which contrasted very favorably with the conditions that prevailed in contemporaneous England. At a time when the Mother Country was practically governed by the arbitrary decisions of an obstinate and foolish King, Virginia was subject to the laws of an assembly and the clauses of a written code which kept always in view the permanent welfare of a free people, and not the temporary interests of a monarch at once shortsighted, selfish, and intolerant.

Under the influence of a faction in the Company, encouraged by the open favor of the throne, dissension broke out among the members of that body, which, in the end, gave the King an excuse for cancelling the charter, and restoring the Colony to his own direct control. Such was the fate of the London Company. Had it been permitted to continue its work of advancing the Colony's welfare by promoting immigration, by erecting schools and colleges, by diversifying agricultural products, by encouraging manufactures, and by fostering every form of popular rights, there can be no doubt whatever that there would have arisen in Virginia a community which would have anticipated, at an early date, the possession of all that political liberty, and all that material prosperity, which it did not acquire in full until, at the end of one hundred and fifty years, it had thrown off the yoke of the British Government.

Under the new form of administration that followed the revocation of the letters-patent in 1624, the King appointed the governor of the Colony and the members of his council, the treasurer, and the secretary of state. The General Assembly, on the other hand, was composed of burgesses elected by the people at large.

The communications of these officials with the English authorities were made at first to a commission in London composed of the foremost servants of the Crown, known as the "Council of Foreign Plantations." About 1676 this body was designated the "Lords Commissioners of Plantations." It was chosen entirely from among the members of the Privy Council. Apparently, it was not until 1696 that the Commission in charge of all the Colonies assumed its permanent form and name, "The Board of Trade and Plantations." Its membership seems not to have been limited to the Privy Council. The powers engaged by all the commissions after 1624 was practically the same, although different names were borne by the body at different times in the course of the century. In theory, the King supervised its general work, but it is not at all probable that he interested himself in its duties, except on special occasions, and then only in a general way.

The most important officer in the government of Virginia during the seventeenth century was the governor. How was he appointed? Under the charter of 1606, the president of the council in Virginia served as governor of the Colony. He was chosen by his fellow members of that body. Under the provisions of the letters-patent of 1609 and 1612, the governor, as he then came to be known, was selected by the Company's Council sitting in London. After the recall of the charter in 1624, he was appointed directly by the King.

There were three ways in which a vacancy in the governorship could be created: by voluntary resignation; by forcible removal; and by death. Only a single instance of the first occurred during the seventeenth century; there were several instances of the second; but none of the third.

During the whole of that long period, provision was made for the election of a governor in case the office became empty for any of these reasons. In the time of the Company, the council in Virginia was required to fill it within fourteen days, but this election was only to confer authority upon the person chosen until the council in England had had an opportunity to make a permanent appointment.

In 1679, half a century after the recall of the charter, the following rule was adopted to meet the contingency: the first in succession was to be the lieutenant or deputy governor; the next, in case the lieutenant-governor also had died in office or was absent from Virginia, was to be the secretary of state; and the next, the major general in command of all the military forces. The commissions of several of the governors, however, altered the normal regulation by granting the succession either permanently or temporarily to some person selected by the Governor himself, or what was more common, to the president of the council.

Most of the governors of the Colony during the seventeenth century had been appointed to office with the expectation of their serving in person throughout their terms unless disabled by sickness or compelled to be absent from Virginia. Beginning with Nicholson, however, the actual duties of the office were performed by the lieutenant-governor. The governor himself remained in England, and without making any return, was satisfied to draw the largest share of the salary of the position.

What was the period of time prescribed for the governor's tenure? At the beginning, when the charter of 1606 was in force the length of the term was limited to one year. On the other hand, the term of Lord Delaware, who was appointed by the Company under the provisions of the charter of 1609, was to last during his life. By the ordinances of 1619-1620, the Governor's term was restricted at the most to six years. Three, however, seems to have been usually adopted in actual practice. After the recall of the charter in 1624, the rule was established by royal order that the Governor's tenure was to continue until his commission had been cancelled by the King, or his successor had been appointed under a new commission. This rule was suspended in the time of the protectorate, but was readopted after the restoration. It was again suspended during Culpeper's administration. He had been appointed for the period of his life, but owing to his neglect of his duties, the old rule was for the second time restored.

Under the charter of 1606, the president of the council in Virginia, the name then borne by the governor of the Colony, was to carry out all the orders which he should receive from the King, the Privy Council and the Virginia Council resident in England. He was to act as the commander in chief of the military forces to be raised from time to time in the Colony, and in case of a tie in the balloting of the local council, was to cast the deciding vote.

Delaware, under the charter of 1609, had received powers of a large scope. He was not only governor, commander, and captain-general of Virginia by land and sea, but he was also authorized to put martial law in force whenever he deemed it to be imperative; and he could also exercise his own judgment in reaching a decision, should his instructions be inapplicable to the circumstances of any case which he was called on to consider. He was further authorized to join with the council in Virginia, in adopting such regulations as were not out of harmony with the privileges acquired by the Company under the charter of 1609.

After Delaware's death, the governor's duties were prescribed by the terms of his commission and his formal instructions; and this continued to be the rule throughout the rest of the century. In a general way, it may be stated that the governor's power entitled him to suspend or appoint temporarily the members of his council; to summon, prorogue or dissolve the General Assembly; to approve or veto its acts; to sit as the head of the General Court; to commission judges and to sign all warrants on the public treasury; to pardon petty offenders, grant reprieves, remit fines, and collate to the benefices; to levy, arm, muster, and command the militia; to execute martial law;

to serve as vice-admiral; to administer oaths of allegiance and supremacy to all immigrants; to grant patents, with his Council's consent; to establish markets, custom and ware houses; to issue proclamations, and, at one time, to naturalize foreigners.

Where did the governor reside? The first incumbent of the position who took steps to build an adequate home for himself in his official character was Ratcliffe. This house was so imposing even in its foundations that it was known from the start as "Ratcliffe's Palace"; but it never reached completion because Smith halted the work, on the ground that it would serve no practical purpose. Gates erected a mansion for the Governor's occupation; but this was probably of small dimensions, as it was subsequently enlarged by Argall. One of the first orders which Yeardley gave on his arrival in 1619 had in view the complete restoration of this building. He was not, however, content with its possession alone. Under his directions, a residence for the governors in turn was constructed on land which belonged to the Company, and which was cultivated by its tenants.

Berkeley, during his administration, made his home at Greenspring, which was situated not far from Jamestown. There was a brick mansion on the famous plantation where he lived until his departure from Virginia after the collapse of the Rebellion of 1676. None of his successors seem to have favored the erection of an official residence either in Jamestown or in the country, as such a possession would have seriously increased the expenses of the tenure. They preferred the allowance of one hundred and fifty pounds sterling which was paid them for house rent.

During the company's existence, the office of governor was supported by the income from a large tract of land specifically assigned to it. This income in time fell off so much that Harvey complained that it was entirely inadequate to defray the charges which the office imposed. In 1637, the regular salary that the governor received amounted to one thousand pounds sterling annually. In Berkeley's case this sum was supplemented with gifts from the General Assembly, and it was also increased by special assessments in kind in proportion to the number of tithables enrolled in the Colony. During the protectorate, the governor was paid a salary of twenty-five thousand pounds of tobacco, which was collected as a part of the public levy. This amount was augmented after the restoration to fifty thousand. Subsequently, the original salary of one thousand pounds sterling annually was again allowed, but the sum was really calculated in pounds of tobacco and not in coin. Culpeper persuaded the English Government to increase the amount of his benefit to two thousand pounds sterling, which was equivalent in purchasing power to fifty thousand dollars in modern currency.

The most influential body of men in the local administration was the Governor's Council. Wealth and ability were its tests of membership, and of the two, the possession of fortune was the most important; not because of any desire to make the office socially imposing, but because each councillor, in the performance of some of his duties, handled large funds, and unless he was the owner of a fine estate would not be in a pecuniary position to make good a deficit in his accounts.

We have already mentioned the fact that, during the absence of the governor and the lieutenant-governor, the president of the council was usually called upon to take their place.

The council, as a single body, served as the Upper House of the General Assembly, but what was, perhaps, more important still, it made up the General Court, which exercised the combined functions of all the higher courts of England. The duties of the councillors considered separately were as follows: they acted as the military commanders of their respective groups of counties; they enforced, as naval officers, the navigation laws, and cleared all vessels sailing from their several districts; they received as collectors of customs all the import and export fees; they were allowed the lucrative privilege of form-

ing the quit-rents, which they obtained from the auditor on very
low bids; and finally, they acted as escheators, which offered
unusual opportunities for profitable investments.

Under a system that concentrated so much power and so
much profit in the hands of such a small body of men,—already
the foremost in the Colony in social influence and accumulated

BACON'S CASTLE

wealth,—grave abuses, as might have been predicted, arose from
time to time. Bacon denounced the councillors as "sponges to
suck up the public treasury," and "as wicked and pernicious
aiders and assistants against the community;" and the like
bitter criticism was leveled at them at a later date by the
Benjamin Harrison of that day. Naturally, as they owed their
appointment to the governor's good will, subject to the King's
approval, they were inclined to be subservient to his wishes. It
was a sordid and grasping age, and the reflections on their
probity were not always due to envy and jealousy; but taking

the whole body from period to period, they were not entitled to such sweeping condemnation. The length of time during which most of them filled the office was attributable, not so much to suppleness of spirit, as to the increased competence for the performance of their duties which experience gave.

It was not considered necessary to provide a large salary for each councillor, since his office was very profitable in itself; but he was apparently paid enough in actual money to reimburse him for his incidental expenses. During Bacon's supremacy, the sum of one hundred pounds sterling was distributed among all the members of the body for this purpose. This was increased afterwards to two hundred and fifty pounds sterling. In 1687, each of the councillors received about forty pounds. Their number at this time was limited to seven individuals. It was estimated that this amount would be just sufficient to embrace all the charges incurred by each councillor for himself, his servants, and his horses, while he was performing the duties of his office. Apart from this sum, and the various large profits accruing from his position, he was at one time granted certain exemptions from taxation; these formed an extraordinary advantage in themselves; but at a later date they were withdrawn and were never again allowed.

The member of the council who had held his seat longest was usually accorded the honor of the presidency of the body. His name always stood at the head of the list.

The councillors, as a rule, convened in the governor's mansion, whether it was his official or his private home. During Berkeley's administration, the sessions were generally held under his roof at Greenspring. On one occasion, however, the council assembled as far away as Nomini. In 1685, its meetings were held in the Sherwood house at Jamestown.

The secretary of state, like the councillor, was appointed to his office by the King on the special recommendation of the governor. The incumbent of this position was always a man of great importance both social and political. William Strachey,

Christopher Davison, William Claiborne, Richard Kemp, Richard Lee, Daniel Parke, Ralph Wormeley, Philip Ludwell, and Nicholas Spencer, were some of the distinguished figures who occupied it in succession. They were all men of large estates, of superior talents and accomplishments, and of ripe experience.

In the beginning, the principal function of the secretary seems to have been to transcribe all the letters dispatched in the name of the governor and council. He was also the custodian of the Colony's great seal. At a later period, in addition to these duties, he drew up and registered all public documents, prepared all passports, made copies of all licenses, drafted probates of wills, recorded wills, inventories, accounts, orders of court, marriage bonds, and similar legal documents, and also made a written report of the Assembly's proceedings. Down to the end of the century, the office continued to be, in the main, one of registration; and most of its tasks were still altogether clerical. Theoretically, the secretary was the principal clerk of the General Court, but instead of occupying that position in practice, he really sat on the bench as one of the judges.

The first law-making body to act in the Colony was the original president and council, appointed under the charter of 1606; but their power in this province was contracted by the supreme ordinances and instructions of the Company in England. It was not until 1619 that a legislative assembly in the modern sense of the word convened in Virginia. This assembly met at Jamestown. The earliest as well as the latest one of the seventeenth century was composed of the governor and council, sitting as the senate or the upper chamber, and of a certain number of elected delegates, sitting as a House of Burgesses or Lower Chamber. Of the two branches, the House of Burgesses was the most powerful and the most distinctive.

What was the basis of suffrage in the election of the Burgesses? It is probable that the original house was chosen by the votes of all the freemen in the Colony. This seems to have been the case in 1645, but ten years later, the suffrage was restricted to housekeepers, whether freeholders, lease-holders, or ordinary tenants. Subsequently, all freemen were again admitted to the privilege, but about 1670 the rule was changed once more. The right to vote was then confined to freeholders and householders as the persons who had to bear the principal burden of taxation. The Reform Assembly summoned by Bacon conferred the suffrage on all freemen. This regulation remained in force until 1684, when the former limitation was reestablished.

At what place was the election held? In the early years of the Colony, it seems that the citizens assembled at the sheriff's home to cast their votes. Subsequently, he or his deputies visited the homes of the voters and recorded their preference. Later still, it was provided that the right of suffrage should be exercised wherever the County Court convened, which might be in the Courthouse, or in a tavern, or in a private residence. The Court's place of meeting was always accessible to the people at large; and very naturally that place was adopted as the place for the county elections. It is probable that the actual manner of delivering a vote varied at different periods. Sometimes it seems to have been by a "plurality of voices," and sometimes by "subscription," the term applied to the ballot. In 1654-55, the successful candidate was referred to as having obtained "the major part of the hands of the electors." The candidate might be a citizen of a different county from the one in which he was seeking the honor of an election. At one time, a clergyman was debarred from the right of holding a political office dependent on popular suffrage.

The members of the House belonged to the ranks of the most important men in each community. Every family of prominence was represented in that body in the course of a series of years. The allurements of the office seem to have been felt especially by young men of talent and ambition, and, perhaps, not a man who, in after life, occupied a position of influence, had not, in his youth, been a member of the House of Burgesses. Jamestown, during a session of that House, must have offered many social diversions which were only rarely enjoyed on the remote and isolated plantations.

But the representatives were not restricted to men of fortune, whether young or old. Towards the middle and the close of the century, there was in attendance a considerable number of Burgesses who possessed only narrow financial resources, and who, in some cases, had begun their active lines as indentured servants. The size of the Houses' membership was in proportion to the number of inhabitants belonging to the different communities. As the general population enlarged, the number of delegates increased.

During the time of the Company, the Burgesses convened at least once a year; and this continued to be the rule down to the Restoration, and also during many years that followed that event. This seems to have been the case even during the Long Assembly's existence, although the only elections held in that interval of fourteen years were apparently those to fill vacancies which had occurred through death or resignation. In 1677, the English Commissioners urged the adoption of biennial elections, but even if this recommendation had been carried out, it would not have been inconsistent with annual sessions.

The Burgesses, unlike the members of Parliament, received a fair amount in remuneration for their services. At first, this sum was designed to defray only the actual expenses of each delegate in performing the duties of his office, but later on, the idea of reward entered into it. The figure fixed upon by the several counties was inserted in the County levy and collected along with the other taxes. Not simply the outlay for the Burgess had to be considered in determining the amount to be paid him, whether to recoup him for all charges which he had had to meet, or to reward him for his official services. The cost of board and lodging for his servants, and of forage and stabling for his horses, had to be added to the account. In 1660-61, each Burgess received, during a session of the House, the sum of one hundred and fifty pounds of tobacco a day, but after the year 1675-76, his salary was cut down to one hundred and thirty pounds. Not infrequently a county, during a single session, would incur for two Burgesses, acting together as its representatives, as much as twenty-five thousand pounds of that commodity.

During the time a member was in attendance on the proceedings of the House, and in the intervals of recess from day to day during a session, he was not liable to arrest or legal process of any kind.

As a rule, the Burgesses convened at Jamestown, but they are known to have met elsewhere, although on very rare occasions. The first body came together in the choir of the church at the former place. In 1636-37, steps were taken to build a State House for its use, but this structure, and also the one afterwards erected, were destroyed by fire. In the intervals, the Burgesses convened in private residences. The third State House went up in flame when Jamestown was burned down after Berkeley's flight, in 1676, to the Eastern Shore. Subsequent to this event, the Burgesses were again compelled to retire to taverns and private houses in holding their sessions. By 1684, a new State House was in the course of construction; but before the end of ten years, it too had been reduced to ashes. Middle Plantation was ultimately selected as the site of the next capitol to be erected.

The principal officer of the House of Burgesses was the Speaker. The position which he held was both profitable and influential. His salary, like that of the Governor, was paid by means of a special assessment, which was included in each annual public levy. Subordinate to him was the clerk, whose duty consisted of keeping full and accurate minutes of the Burgesses' proceedings. He was considered to be the sole custodian of the records of the House. The most famous of these clerks, Robert Beverley, became involved in a violent dispute with Governor Howard because he refused to deliver them up. "I am the servant of the House," he firmly and boldly exclaimed, "I cannot, without their leave, comply with your demand to transfer the records."

The Burgesses' proceedings were modeled on the forms of the Lower House of Parliament, and were governed by its rules. The work of the body was done by three committees,—the Committee to Examine the Election Returns, the Committee on Propositions and Grievences, and the Committee on Claims. All legislation seems to have begun in the Lower House. The Council, as the Upper Chamber, apparently possessed only the right to concur, to reject, and to amend,—never to originate. The regular communications between the two bodies seems to have been restricted to the meeting of their respective committees. At one time, however, the two Houses convened in the same apartment; but afterwards, while they met under the same roof, they did not meet under the same ceiling.

No Act could be accepted as law until it had been signed by the Speaker of the House and the Governor as the head of the Council sitting as the Upper Chamber. Nor was the Act even then in permanent operation, since the King's approval had first to be obtained before it could become final.

CHAPTER XV

MONEY AND TAXATION

MONEY

Throughout the Seventeenth Century, there were three forms of money in use in Virginia in different degrees. The most important of the three was tobacco. This commodity was practically coin at the very time that the whole community was engaged in producing it as a staple crop. All debts of every nature, from the largest down to the smallest,—the annual personal tax, the common and most insignificant domestic article, the salary of the Governor, the fee of the lawyer, the doctor, and the clergyman, the wage of the hired servant, the charge of the midwife and the grave digger,*—all were paid in so many pounds of tobacco. English coin was also used, but in quantities so small as to appear to most of the inhabitants to be an object of curiosity. The bill of exchange, the third form, was less familiar than tobacco, but more familiar than coin. By means of it, large sums were transferred to England and other foreign parts. It was generally based on a cargo of tobacco sold either in Virginia or in London. Apparently, the bill was always drawn on some merchant outside the Colony.

The inconvenience of tobacco when compared with coin or bills of exchange, as currency, would, on the surface, seem to be insuperable. It was a bulky substance. How was it possible to employ it in the thousand small transactions of sale and purchase which came up hourly in the life of the Colony? There

---

* Bruce's Econ. Hist. Va., Vol. II, p. 496.

is no difficulty in perceiving that it could be used without serious
awkwardness when exchanged for the cargoes of manufactured
goods which the English ships unloaded at the planters' wharves.
The hogsheads were rolled on board and the packages of merchandise were carried on shore so soon as an agreement had been
reached as to what should be the proper rate for the mutual
transfer.   But when a horse was to be bought or a slave to be
sold on court day at public auction, or when a dozen eggs were
to pass by a private bargain, or a pair of shoes or a coat to be
purchased, at a store, the cumbrousness of tobacco must have
been extremely irksome.   And yet it was only occasionally that
the drawbacks to it as currency caused serious public complaint.

The English merchant, exchanging his goods for tobacco,
regarded the transaction as evidence of the existence of that
ideal condition which was so ardently desired when Virginia was
first established.   It will be recalled that the opinion prevailed
at that time that it was a source of weakness to a country to be
compelled to purchase foreign goods through the medium of
coin.   Such a transaction was presumed to be a drain on England's resources by sucking its metallic wealth away to foreign
lands.   Commercial intercourse with Virginia was accompanied
by no such depletion.   A manufactured article was given for a
natural product and a natural product for a manufactured article.   The balance was perfect.   There was a distinct gain to
both sides.   There was no loss to either.

The advantage of this mutual exchange was obvious, whether
the transaction took place in the Colony between a planter and
an English merchant, or whether the tobacco was transferred
to England by the planter himself and there converted into all
sorts of domestic articles, such as clothes, furniture, silver, and
the like, to be sent back to the plantation in the Colony where
the tobacco had been produced.   There was in a transaction of
this kind no inconvenience.   The real inconvenience only arose
when petty trading occurred between the colonists themselves
in the course of ordinary sales and purchases.

An attempt was made as early as 1632 to fix clearly the prices in all bargains, both great and small, by requiring that all valuations should be made in the terms of coin. A pound of tobacco was worth so many pennies from year to year. The value of that pound changed almost annually because it was a commodity which depended for its correct appraisement on changing circumstances. The value of a penny, on the other hand, was stable, and it was, therefore, entirely natural that it should have been used as an expression of value more than as a medium of value; and such was the service which it performed. Through that first use, a perfect equality was assured without those fluctuations which would have been inevitable had tobacco alone been the medium for estimating values. For instance, to provide that a public official should be paid annually a salary of five thousand pounds of tobacco would have subjected that salary to constant variations in its purchasing power; but to prescribe that he should receive one hundred pounds sterling simply meant that his remuneration was to be the number of pounds of tobacco which that metallic sum happened to represent from year to year. Any decline or advance in the price of the commodity made no real difference to him.

In spite of the convenience to the people at large which would have been subserved by the copious introduction of small coins, all attempts looking to that end apparently came to nothing practical. The General Assembly sought without success to give a fixed value to foreign coins like the piece of eight. As this computation was more or less arbitrary, the people were indisposed to handle them, and, indeed, went so far as to denounce them as "worthless counters." It was expected that the imposition of a tax of two shillings on each exported hogshead of tobacco would tend to increase the tobacco of small coin circulating in the Colony, but this anticipation seems to have proved insubstantial. Undoubtedly, however, considerable metallic money crept into the principal communities of Virginia through the annual arrival of sea-captains and their crews. But how small the volume was at all times is indicated by the insignificant amounts of such money that are to be noted in the enumerations of the personal possessions of testators itemized in the inventories of their estates.

An occasional dog or lion dollar, a Dutch coin, was found in circulation, which offered a furtive proof that trade with Holland continued during many years after the passage of the last Act of Navigation.

It is interesting to discover that certain media of barter derived from the Indians was employed at times in the Colony. Such were Roanoke and Wampumpeke. Roanoke was principally used by traders in the frontier counties in their purchases of fur from the savage tribes. It was also offered and accepted as a remuneration for services which Indian scouts had performed. The use of beaver as a currency was not uncommon among the people of the Eastern Shore.

Taxation

It was in the payment of taxes that tobacco, as a currency, played its most frequent and most conspicuous part. There is not a chapter in Virginia's colonial history which, from an economic and administrative point of view at least, is more interesting or more significant than the one which treats of the subject of taxation.

An experiment was undertaken by the London Company, in 1618, which, had it not been interfered with and balked by the recall of the charter in 1624, would have set an example in this province of the public interests that might have been followed in the same community down to our own age. A provision was adopted, and actually carried out, that each office of the local government should be maintained, not by an assessment to be borne by all the tax-payers, but by the income to be derived from a tract of land to be specially set apart for it. The area reserved for the officeholders' support embraced thirty-one thousand acres. Without laborers to till this domain, which was composed of the most fertile soil lying within the boundaries of the Colony, it would have served no useful purpose. But the Company foresaw this need, and at an early date took steps to obtain numerous tenants, who would make a return of the sum required, absolutely certain.

The dream entertained by Sandys and Southampton of founding a great free community oversea was fitly accompanied by a policy designed to relieve its inhabitants of those burdens of taxation for the local government's maintenance which had been so oppressive during so many generations in England. That policy, had it been allowed to develop uninterruptedly, might not have assured exemption indefinitely in every direction, but it would, at least, have lightened the load of public taxation to a degree unknown in older lands. Such a policy could only have been put in practical effect in a new country like Virginia, where a vast extent of virgin ground was still unoccupied.

The necessity of erecting fortifications seems to have caused the first imposition of a formal tax; and the second was precipitated by the impressment of troops to garrison them. Other demands on the resources of the public purse not provided for by the assignment of definite tracts of land would have certainly arisen with the growth of the community in wealth and population, but the new burden of taxation thus laid would have appeared light had the main expenses of local administration been met by means of the Company's farsighted plan. When that plan finally was uprooted, the whole support of the government in all its branches was shifted to the shoulders of the people at large. Thus taxation became a matter of vital importance to every person in Virginia who owned any property.

The rule was soon recognized that the House of Burgesses was to be the only body which should have the authority to originate taxes for public objects in general. A levy could be ordered by a county or a parish for local purposes, but even in this necessary step, they were looked upon as having obtained the right to act by the formal consent of the assembled representatives of the whole people sitting at Jamestown. No Governor or Council could, without the Burgesses' approval lay a tax of any kind whatsoever. One of the clauses in the Articles of Surrender agreed upon when the Colony submitted to the power of Parliament in Cromwell's time expressly stated that, without the General Assembly's consent, not even England could claim the right to impose a burden of this nature.

This attitude of determined opposition to taxation, unless it originated with the House of Burgesses, or the County and parish authorities, continued down to the end of the century. It led to dissensions with the Governor or the English Government for the time being, but it never on that account showed any tendency to weaken. On the contrary, the feeling only grew increasingly inflexible. This was illustrated in the instructions which were given to the commissioners who visited England in 1674-75 to obtain a general charter. They were specially directed to secure permission to insert in this charter a clause exempting the Colony from every form of taxation which did not have the approval of its own General Assembly. The same instructions were given to Jeffrey Jeffreys in 1691, at which time he was serving in London as the agent for Virginia.

This principle, which the people of the Colony insisted upon almost from the birth of their community, still exerted such influence over their minds in the Eighteenth Century that it drove them into war when England, with cynical indifference and incredible folly, disregarded it.

There were three tax levies in use in the Seventeenth Century. These were known respectively as the parish, the county, and the public. The parish levy was laid by the vestry of each parish; the county tax by the justices of each county; and the public by the General Assembly.

In a former chapter, we mentioned the objects for which the parish levy was imposed; namely, the building of new churches and the repair of old; the purchase of glebes, and the erection thereon of parsonages and the necessary plantation houses; and finally, the payment of the salaries allowed the clergymen, clerks, and readers. The county levy was designed to defray still more numerous expenses, such as those which were incurred for building and repairing courthouses, prisons, stocks, whipping posts, pillories, and bridges; maintaining ferries; holding inquests over dead bodies; settling the awards for the destruction of wolves; and paying the salary granted the county Burgess for service in the House. His expenses also in traveling to Jamestown, and returning home at the end of the session were always included in the amount.

The public levy imposed by the General Assembly was more voluminous. It covered all charges for building and repairing fortifications; feeding and paying the garrisons and supernumerary troops; recouping for the loss of horses in an Indian march; transporting Indian prisoners; furnishing friendly tribes with match coats; transmitting public letters; impressing boats for public purposes, and supplying the rowers with food. The public levy also provided medicines for wounded soldiers, and met the cost of conveying persons to Jamestown for trial.

The funds obtained by the public, county, and parish levies were raised by means of taxation by the poll. This was practically the only way. No tax on land was imposed because the soil was already burdened by the quit-rents. Trade was exempted because it was already subject to the duty of two shillings set upon every hogshead exported. Livestock escaped because property in horses, cows, and hogs was thought to be too difficult at times to enforce, owing to the wild habits in which they were allowed to fall by their owners, anxious to avoid the expense of stabling and providing them with forage.

At an early period, there were successful attempts to shift the heaviest taxation from the poll to the visible possessions of the citizen, such as land and cattle. The poll tax was retained, but to a moderate degree only. The charge was made for the benefit of that major class in the community whose means were the smallest. The greater the increase in the new supplementary taxes, the more the poll tax could be reduced. It is true that much land and some livestock were owned by the poor families taken as a whole, but there was a gain to them because the addition to their tax by the assessment of their little plantations, and horses, cows, goats, and pigs, which was not done before, was more than counterbalanced by the curtailment of their poll taxes.

There was an injustice to the large landowners in the imposition of the land tax, because there was such a vast area of the soil held by them in its original wild state of nature. This uncultivated ground was already encumbered with the quit-rent payable to the King. To add a land tax to that quit-rent whether the soil was under tillage or not, made the cumulative charge oppressive. Had the land tax been restricted to fields in a state of profitable production through maize, wheat, or tobacco, the new imposition would have been fair enough in spirit. But it was difficult and inconvenient to make such discrimination as this a part of a general policy.

The situation of the numerous families who were compelled to depend absolutely upon themselves as hired free laborers for a livelihood was greatly improved by the passage of the new rule, for, under the operation of taxation by the poll, which was the former law, the head of a family in this propertyless condition, paid, as was said at the time, "as deeply to the public as he that had twenty thousand acres."

When the laborers consisted of indentured servants alone, it was not they who carried the burden of the poll tax, but the master who owned them and the plantation on which they worked.

The poll tax, perhaps, tended more than a tax on land to encourage a spirit of liberal expenditure in those who carried on the administration of local affairs. A land tax depended on assessments, which could not be made annually without great cost, because they varied in degree in different counties and even in different neighborhoods. On the other hand, it was easy and not expensive to ascertain the number of tithables from year to year, for here number alone was to be considered. The persons who laid the taxes felt under the system of taxation by the poll that they had a clearer and more exact idea of the Colony's resources than if they were acting under a system of land taxation. In theory, if not in fact, this feeling on their part was justified, for it was by the poll that the productiveness of the lands was gauged. The question was: how many laborers are attached to each plantation? The number once discovered, it required only a few minutes' calculation to reach a correct general estimate of the annual income of each property, since it was measured by the number of hands that cultivated it.

The weight of both the land tax and the poll tax was lightened by the regular duty of two shillings which was placed on each hogshead exported. The original rule was to reserve this income for the payment of the Governor's salary; and should there be a surplus, this was to be expended for other public purposes. In the end, the poll tax became the accepted form of taxation in the Colony; and whenever it was in danger of being greatly swelled by unusual additions to current expenditures, that prospect was removed by imposing a duty on imported liquors.

Incidentally in the chapters on the slave and the agricultural servant, we referred to the regulation which fixed the age which was to be accepted as giving the character of tithable. The first poll tax, which was adopted as early as 1623, placed all settlers above eighteen years in that general category. The second poll tax, which went into effect at a later period, declared that every male person whose age exceeded sixteen was to be taken as a tithable. This rule was, in 1662, made pertinent also to all women who were ordinarily employed in tilling the fields.

About ten years afterwards, the limit was lowered. Negro children were to become tithables at twelve years, while all white servants reported under indentures were to be listed so soon as their fourteenth year was reached. No Indian child was to be so recorded until he or she had passed the sixteenth year. At the end of the century, the age for the male tithable was to be in excess of sixteen; for the male or female slave, twelve, if a native of the Colony, or fourteen, if imported.

The list of tithables was made up by officials appointed by the County Court; and to the justices this list had to be submitted so soon as completed. By them it was forwarded to the Secretary of State at Jamestown, by whom in turn it was transferred to the House of Burgesses for the purpose of the public levy. Before the rule was sent to the Assembly, however, it was required to be set up at the Courthouse door for examination by the people at large. If there was an error in the report of a taxpayer in giving in the list of his tithables, it was quite certain to be exposed by his neighbors. The number of tithables belonging even to the wealthiest planters of the Colony during this century was always moderate.

The assessment of the parish levies was, as we have mentioned in a former chapter, made by the members of the vestry sitting as a single body. The amount of the tax apportioned to each poll depended upon the volume of the parish expenses for that year, and it, therefore, fluctuated with each levy. This was true of the county and public levies also. The public imposition, in some years, rose to one hundred and eighty pounds for the individual taxpayers, and in others, it sank to as low a figure as nine pounds, but, as a rule, the public levy was moderate in amount. Had it been otherwise, the burden thus created, added to the respective burdens of the parish and county assessments, would have been intolerable.

The public levy was fixed by the House of Burgesses; and the county, by the justices of its court. The amounts of the three levies were collected by the same public officers; namely, the sheriffs of the several counties. The rates adopted in the valuation of the tobacco in which payment was made were governed by the contemporary prices prevailing in the English market.

Exemption from taxation was only granted to individuals specifically named. Such were the persons who had agreed to settle at certain very dangerous points on the frontier. This occurred only in the early years of the Colony's history. The privilege was often extended to persons who suffered from physical infirmities to a degree that prevented them from working in the fields. It was also enjoyed by the occupants of the higher political offices; and at one time too by clergymen who were employed for a season in preaching before the General Assembly.

By the provisions of the original charter, the future land-owners of Virginia were to hold their respective estates "in free and common soccage." It was not until the King resumed direct control of the Colony's government, which occurred in 1624, that a quit-rent of one shilling for every fifty acres was reserved in each patent granted in the royal name. It was quite naturally a very unpopular tax, for, in a certain sense, it was, if not a cloud on the title, a burden that seriously diminished its value. There was, for that reason, a feeling of the strongest objection to its payment at all; and it was evaded by every means in the reach of those liable for it. It was said, in 1631, that, had the quit-rents been collected with fidelity, not less than two thousand pounds sterling, equal in modern value to the sum of two hundred and fifty thousand dollars, would have been paid annually into the treasury. The amount actually received from that source did not, at that time, exceed five hundred pounds sterling.

The quit-rents belonged to the King, and it was in his power to assign them, if he saw fit, to private individuals. This he did in 1671, when they were granted to Colonel Henry Norwood in recompense for his loyalty; and in 1673, to Arlington and Culpeper; but this latter gift was subsequently revoked.

During the greater part of the century, the quit-rents were used for the support of the local government, with the royal consent, after they had been reported to the Auditor-General of the

Colonies in England. At times, the salary of the Governor or the Lieutenant General was paid out of this income. Sometimes, a portion of it was expended for some urgent purpose, like the erection of fortifications at an hour when an invasion was threatened; or it was given to some neighboring Colony to strengthen its power of defense against a common enemy.

The general failure to pay the entire amount of quit-rents due was attributable, after the middle of the century, chiefly to the extent of the soil in a state of nature, although the ground may have passed to private ownership. Towards the end of that period it was calculated that, of the five million acres taken up, only forty thousand had been brought under the dominion of the hoe and the plough. A vast proportion of this idle land offered on its surface not one object that could be made subject to distraint, even if the sheriff had attempted to collect in that way the delinquent dues. As late as 1692, although the population had increased so greatly, and so much new land had been patented, the amount of quit-rents turned over to the Auditors of the Colony had been augmented but little in comparison with the amount received from the same source fifty years earlier. This condition was due to laxness in making the collections.

The indirect taxes took several forms of importance. One of the most valuable was the duty imposed on all liquors brought into the Colony. Every ship captain, before he landed his cargo, was required to report the quantity of spirits which he had stored in the hold of his vessel. The only exception to this rule was in the case of a ship which had been entirely constructed in the Colony; but such an instance was so extremely rare as to be almost negligable. At first, a duty of six pennies was paid by the owner of every servant or slave disembarked. This duty was afterwards increased to twenty shillings in the case of the slave, and fifteen in the case of the servant, if imported from another Colony. A head tax of six pennies was also collected from every passenger who arrived with the intention of remaining permanently.

Another form of special taxation was the duty imposed on all skins, furs, wool, and iron before they were allowed to be shipped away. About one hundred pounds sterling were derived from this source. The income from the duty of two shillings paid on every hogshead exported was far larger than this; and as tobacco culture widened steadily each year, that income showed a proportionate tendency to increase. If the hogshead was consigned not to England, but to another American Colony, the duty was advanced to ten shillings, and later to one penny the pound weight. In this instance, also, the tax was not to be collected if the vessel which was to transport the hogshead had been constructed in Virginia.

The duty on exported tobacco was unsound from an economic point of view, as it was laid on a product which the Colony relied upon for the support of its inhabitants; but it was too profitable to be dropped, for while much of the income from the duty was transferred to the royal treasury in London and the Auditor-General there, a large part of it was reserved for the payment of the salaries of the officers of the government in Virginia. Additional revenue was secured by the acquisition of fines and forfeitures, and also of compositions for escheated plantations and chattels. Waifs and estrays were also included.

The income derived by the Colony from all these various taxes was insignificant in comparison with the annual fund which the royal treasury obtained from the tobaccoo of Virginia alone in the form of customs. As early as 1675, the revenue thus arising exceeded one hundred thousand pounds sterling.

So soon as the export tax of two shillings a hogshead was created, it became necessary to appoint agents to collect it, and these in turn were empowered to name deputies to assist them in the performance of their duties. These duties extended beyond the collection of a single tax. For instance, these officers carried out all the orders governing the plantation trade, whether coming from Parliament or the commissioners of the English customs; they recorded the arrival of every ship, and saw that

its captain had obeyed all the regulations relating to his cargo
before and after he had reached the waters of Virginia; they
obtained a certificate from him that he would convey his outgoing cargo to England in accord with the bond which he had
given before leaving for the Colony; and they also handed him
a certificate that he had conformed strictly with the law relating
to this second cargo. They were also required to send to the
commissioners of English customs an annual report as to the
condition of Virginia in the provinces of agriculture, manufactures, and ship building.

The duties of the collectors in their character as naval officers seemed to have been only small details that partook more or
less of a clerical nature, such as drawing up an account of all the
commodities brought into or carried out of the Colony; the names
and tonnage of arriving ships; the ports from which they hailed;
and the ports to which they were sailing.

Finally, there were two other high officers in Virginia;
namely, the Auditor and the Treasurer. Their duties did not
differ materially from those that usually characterize their
several positions.

III

THE COLONIAL PERIOD, 1700-1776

CHAPTER I

WESTWARD MOVEMENT. HUGUENOT, SPOTSWOOD, AND BYRD

The spread of the population of Virginia during the first century was limited to a somewhat narrow area. The foundation of the Colony was laid at Jamestown in 1607, and, from this point, it threw off new communities at a very slow rate. Seventeen years after that date, there had come into existence numerous small settlements scattered at considerable intervals from Henricopolis, on both sides of the Powhatan, down to Newport News and Isle of Wight. The Massacre of 1622, had at first proved to be a severe blow, for it led immediately to the drawing in of the people. Indeed, the sites of some of the most important plantations were abandoned entirely for the time being.

Luckily, the catastrophe left behind no bad results that were permanent. On the contrary, the vigorous retaliation which followed dispersed the Indians and broke up all the villages along the lower Powhatan and Pamunkey, which were formerly a perennial menace to the continued existence of the entire English Colony. Gradually, the valley of the Powhatan, between the falls and the mouth of the river, was subdivided into cultivated plantations. So were the banks of the Pagan, Warwick, Nansemond, and Lynnhaven rivers. Families crossed the modern York and took possession of the fertile region lying along the Pyanketank. Not all of them belonged to the ranks of the newcomers in the Colony. Indeed, a large proportion hailed from the older settlements of the general community.

307

When the valley of the Rappanannock was reached, this movement became still more active. The roll of the planters suing out patents to lands situated on the north side of that stream contains the names of many families who had already been associated with the region of Nansemond and Lower Norfolk. It required only a few years more and the valley of the Potomac was also laid off into homesteads. Many of its new inhabitants, like those of the more southern valleys, had quite lately arrived from England, but, perhaps, most of them, like their forerunners elsewhere, too, had been residents of other parts of the Colony during a considerable interval of years.

If a line had been drawn in 1690 along the western edge of the settlements from the modern Suffolk at the southern end to the modern Petersburg and Richmond in the middle, and thence as straight as an arrow to the modern Fredericksburg and Acquia Creek in the north, we would have had all that part of the present State of Virginia which was occupied by an English population at that date. Within these limits, the colonists had constantly shown a disposition to shift from section to section and place to place; never receding, but only by comparatively slow degrees advancing.

Why was it that the planters of that day, with this spirit of expansion sensibly animating them within definite barriers, reluctant to pass beyond the invisible fence that ran at their back along the western line which has been mentioned? A great mass of people are not likely in their practical life to follow a course of conduct which has no sound reason for its continuation. If the inhabitants of the Colony, through the long period lying between 1616 and 1700, persisted, as we know they did, in confining themselves to the region east of the falls in the great rivers emptying into the Chesapeake Bay, there was undoubtedly some influence controlling their action, which, for the time being, at least, was irresistible. Why did the enterprising landowners who filled the region stretching from those falls to the salt water content themselves so long with the possession of so moderate an area for settlement and tillage? Why did they not burst through that invisible wall on the western horizon, and spread out through the wide forested domain beyond until the shadow of the noble Blue Ridge was reached?

At the first view, the answer to this question seems difficult, but it is, in reality, simple enough when two facts are taken into consideration.

First, from the beginning, the desire of every one who sued out a patent was to acquire soil that hugged either an arm of the Bay or the waters of a navigable stream. There was no market in the Colony to which the tobacco produced from year to year could be conveyed by wagon or boat to be sold. The only place of disposal for that crop was to be found in Holland or England, and these countries could only be reached by sea-going vessels. Such vessels could not expect to find in one port, or even in the whole of Virginia, the cargoes which they were seeking to secure. They had to pass up and down the rivers of the Colony to procure their loads. If a plantation was not situated on a stream, the inconvenience of reaching some remote wharf overland was almost insurmountable, simply because the roads were at wet seasons impassable, and the wagons for conveyance neither strong nor enduring.

Every planter knew that these difficulties would have been increased almost an hundred fold had he penetrated the woods and established a new home far behind the back line which connected the falls in the rivers. There were no deep, wide streams in that region to carry off the tobacco even had no cataract at the head of the inward flow of the tide obstructed the descent to the sea. No shallop even could live in those shallow, rocky upper waters though it were unburdened with a cargo of tobacco. As for roads, the rough face of this outlying region made the construction of highways expensive beyond the resources of men who might have been inclined to take possession of these virgin lands.

Moreover, the growth in the number of inhabitants below the falls was not even during the last decades of the Seventeenth Century so rapid as to create in them the impression that they were overcrowding the only part of the country which possessed a sufficient number of navigable streams to assure the profit of their tobacco crops by offering easy and immediate transportation to the foreign market. In short, no pressure from an increasing population was in existence in those times to make the people forget all the drawbacks to a settlement in the wild regions above the falls in the rivers.

There was a second influence also which carried very much weight at this period. Every man who, by climbing a very high tree on the frontier at that time, could catch a glimpse of the Blue Ridge on the horizon, was perfectly aware of the fact that in the eastern shadow of those mountains there ran the trail of the fierce Iroquois, who varied the monotony of their life in their Northern villages by an annual excursion to the hunting grounds of the Cherokees and Choctaws in the South, for the purpose of trading or carrying off scalps and squaws. No home of an English settler would be safe if it was situated within fifty miles of this path of those terrible marauders. It will be recalled that, in 1676, the people who lived near the site of the modern Richmond were harried by the Susquehannocks, although this place was within the long established boundaries of the Colony. The peril of attack would have been much increased had the plantations been scattered along the upper waters of the Roanoke, James, Pamunkey, and Rappahannock.

It was not until the Scotch-Irish and Germans began to creep into the region beyond the Blue Ridge that the intervening country became really secure for occupation by families that had entered it from the east.

The first settlement of importance to be made behind the line that united the falls in the great rivers had its origin with a community of Frenchmen. In the light of the difficulties to be overcome and dangers to be faced back of that line, as already enumerated, it was a sagacious act to concentrate this settlement as far as it was practicable to do so.   There was small probability that the same number of persons of Virginian nativity could have been induced to seat themselves, like these Frenchmen, in the form of a village, either in the old part of the Colony, or in this outlying part towards the mountains, since they were accustomed to a system of separate plantations, which, whether large or small, gave a distinct character to each estate and fostered a spirit of personal independence in its master.   Apart from their love of such independence, these landowners conceived that the separate plantation, with its own new grounds and its own agricultural servants and slaves, was the only certain means of producing the only profitable crop, tobacco.

On the other hand, the Huguenots, who came over in 1700 and sat down in a considerable body in the wilderness about twenty miles above the Falls in the James River, had been familiar with a different system, either in their own lives in France, or in the lives of those of their ancestors who had halted in England after leaving their native country.   These people's mode of life had been the one still to be observed in the modern French village. This village was and is, an irregular line of houses, perhaps even of the size of a little town, with a central street occupied by a single community, which daily dispersed in the morning for the tillage of their respective plats of ground situated in the immediate surrounding country.

This system was repeated in the foreign settlement above the Falls.   Although to each family was assigned a tract of one hundred and thirty-three acres, the whole number of householders, in the beginning, seem to have resided in a magnified hamlet, in harmony with the habit which had prevailed among themselves or their forebears before their emigration from France. Doubtless, this natural disposition of the newcomers was known to the Colony's authorities at the time the choice of a site for the projected settlement was made.

Apparently, there was never any attempt on the part of these authorities to persuade the people residing in the tidewater counties to spread into the region back of the Falls. They, no doubt, were convinced that the reasons which led to the local confinement of that population were practically sound. In the Huguenots, however, they found a band of families who were, not only willing to live in a self-protective village, through the influence of their inherited instincts, but also were ready to rely for their subsistence on other products of the ground beside tobacco. Indian assault was warded off by the one condition, and the need of a navigable stream was made perfectly dispensable by the other, because these settlers really produced nothing exportable.

From the start, the French men and women at Manakin were employed in breeding cattle, expressing wine, planting maize, and manufacturing cloth. Gradually, however, the original small estates grew in number, the herds and flocks enlarged, and slaves were purchased. In other words, the economic influence which had moulded the social and agricultural system of the counties in the lower valleys of the James, Nansemond, York, Rappahannock, and Potomac, in time began to operate in the lives of these aliens, who had brought all their contrary ideas with them when they made their homes in the back wilderness of Virginia. Their village was later on broken up by their decision to seat themselves permanently on their separate estates. Most of them ultimately also found tobacco more profitable as a crop than corn and grapes, and almost before they had forgotten the use of their original French language, they could hardly be distinguished in their manner of life and employment from their English neighbors, who, by this time, were crossing the undefined back line and pushing their way westward along the upper valleys of the Appomattox, James, North Anna, and the Rappahannock.

The governor and council and the General Assembly could not have obtained more useful instruments for blazing the first stage in the journey to the mountains than these newcomers of another nationality proved themselves to be. They possessed precisely the peculiar habits and qualities called for to overcome the first obstruction facing the acquisition of that virgin wilderness.

It was in the year 1700 that four bands of these invaluable immigrants of French blood were landed in succession in the Colony, under the leadership of Richebourg, De Joux, and Latane. There were about one thousand persons embraced in the united company. The Edict of Nantes had been repealed in 1685, about fifteen years earlier, and had resulted in an enormous hegira of the French families who remained loyal to the protestant religion. It has been calculated that not less than 400,000 individuals, the flower of industrial France, had been constrained by their religious scruples to desert their immemorial homes to seek refuge in foreign countries.

The Walloons, as early as 1621, had submitted a petition to the London Company for permission to settle in Virginia. The negotiations, however, fell through. About 1629, a group of French protestants actually seated themselves there, but, in time, appear to have separated and dispersed. From the beginning, many persons of that nationality found their way into the Colony along with the annual English newcomers, but their immediate descendants, chiefly by intermarriage with the members of the English planters' families, lost their Gallic identity so far as to become indistinguishable in the ranks of the purely English population.

The settlers at Manakin, being congregated in a large body in one locality, which enabled its members to retain their native language for a generation, made all the deeper impression on the social history of Virginia by preserving so long the purity of their French blood. It is due to that sturdy stock that the state can boast of its greatest scientist, Matthew F. Maury, whose genius conferred such invaluable benefits on the practical affairs of the whole world by his discoveries in meteriology and

COLONEL ALEXANDER SPOTSWOOD

oceanic currents. That blood was also responsible for a strain
of Gallic wit and vivacity that has run through many Virginian
families, who inherited it by intermarriage with the descendants
of the early settlers of Manakin, the first large company of
pioneers to raise a formidable barrier against further Indian
invasion from the West, and also to point the way to the occupation of that fertile but isolated region which spread away to
the foot of the mountains.

Not many years passed before there appeared in Virginia
a man who was resolved to explore in person the broad wooded
plain which separated the settlements lying along the north
and south line of the falls in the rivers, from that lofty blue
chain which rose on the horizon. Governor Spotswood had obtained by patent an estate at Germanna, which was situated
some distance west of the present city of Fredericksburg. There
were forty-five thousand acres in this tract, and the owner had
been tempted to acquire it, in spite of its isolated position, by
the existence of iron ore beneath its surface. This ore he afterwards endeavored to utilize by the construction of furnaces,
and the employment of Germans skilled in iron craft to run
them. Later, these workmen became dissatisfied, and a considerable number of them founded new homes nearer the mountains. It was doubtless during Spotswood's visits to his property, while he was still the incumbent of the governorship, that
the plan of making a journey to the crest of the Blue Ridge,
plainly visible from Germanna on clear days, occurred to him.

An example of western exploration had already been set in
the seventeenth century by men like Abraham Wood, and above
all, by Loederer, who had penetrated deeper into these interminable wildernesses than any of his predecessors. These travels
had proved to be of no practical moment, and really had their
motive more in adventurous curiosity than in any desire to
show the suitability of this back country for settlement.

The conditions existing in that vast region were very different in 1716, when the expedition to the ridge was undertaken

by Spotswood, from what they had been in the time of Berkeley.
Then the endless primeval domain of stream, forest, and sa-
vannah beyond the mountains, was occupied exclusively by the
aboriginal tribes. In 1716, on the other hand, the mighty valley
back of the Alleghanies was possessed in part at least by a
race far more dangerous, in the opinion of the sagacious and
enlightened governor at Germanna, than the fiercest Indian
warriors. These intruders were the French, the immemorial
enemies of the English. Their presence would not only be a
permanent obstacle in the future to the expansion of the English settlements that far westward, but also an increasing menace to the Colony in Virginia as it then stood.

"With the forts the French have already built," he said,
"the British plantations are in a manner surrounded by their
commerce with the numerous nations of Indians seated on both
sides of the lakes. They may not only engross the whole skin-
trading, but may, when they please, send out such bodies of
Indians on the back of these plantations as may greatly distress
his majesty's subjects here. And should they multiply their
settlements along these lakes, so as to join their Dominions of
Canada to their new Colony of Louisiana, they might even possess themselves of any these plantations they please."

It is to be inferred from these words that, in setting out
to the mountains, Spotswood was not thinking of spying out
the country in the interval simply to discover whether it was
suitable for new settlements, like the one which had, in 1700,
been founded by the Huguenots at Manakin, or for separate
estates, like those which covered the whole surface of Tidewater, Virginia. His object was, through inquiry of the Indians in the Shenandoah Valley, to find out whether the English
could yet erect colonies on the lakes of the Northwest, and at
the same time, possess themselves of that series of passes in
the intervening mountains "which," as he expressed it, "were
necessary to preserve a communication with such settlements."

Swift Run Gap, by which he ascended to the top of the Blue Ridge, was not to him simply a pass which allowed him to reach the Valley beyond with comparative ease. Rather it was one of those highways which, when fortified, would keep open the road to the far West, and be always a barrier against French

THE WILLIAMSBURG CAPITOL

From an old painting in Richmond

incursions into the communities of Virginia lying between the mountains and the sea.

Spotswood, at this time, was residing in the Governor's palace at Williamsburg. On August 20th, 1716, he set out, in the company of Ensign John Fontaine, for the ferry over York River; crossed that stream, and also the Mattapony, further on, and spent a night at the home of Robert Beverley, the historian. From there, the party, receiving a few additions as they traveled, made the journey along the southern bank of the Rappahannock to Germanna, situated about eighteen miles west of

the falls. Here the first little band of horsemen was increased
in number by the arrival of other gentlemen of prominence, and
also by two companies of rangers and several Indian scouts.
It was calculated that there were about fifty persons in all taking part in the expedition; and for their ease and accommodation, they were accompanied by a string of pack-horses bearing
provisions and liquors in large quantities.

The liquors, indeed, threw a remarkable light on the variety
of spirits which were considered necessary to beguile the passage of the primeval woods.

There was no path, not even an Indian trail, to lead them
forward conveniently to their destination. It was the thick
virgin forest which they were traversing, and it was only, at
long intervals, in an opening on a hill, that they could descry
the mighty wall of the mountains that shut in the western horizon. From hour to hour, they advanced under a canopy of green
leaves, with a patch of blue sky showing here and there above
the massive foliage of the tree tops. At night, they raised their
tents to shelter their bodies from rain, or if it was clear, they
lay down on beds made of bushes spread out on the ground,
and slept soundly in the stillness of the woods, which was broken
every now and then only by the cry of a wandering panther
or the hooting of a horned owl.

They never forgot either at meals during the day, or on
retiring after dark, to drink a loyal toast to the King. Their
larder was constantly garnished with the flesh of deer and
other animals killed by the scouts for the replenishment of the
forest tables. No painful or exciting episode occurred to jar
the smoothness of the journey. The most serious event in its
course did not rise in importance above the swarming forth of
hornets disturbed in their nests, or a fall from the back of a
stumbling horse, or the rattling of a coiled jointed snake.

By the fifth of September, the members of the party had
laboriously climbed up to the entrance of a gap in the chain
of mountains. Here the waters at one end flowed eastward to

the Rappahannock, and at the other westward to the Potomac by way of the Shenandoah. Far to the west, the travellers descried the misty rampart of the Alleghanies, with the beautiful valley lying between clothed in the still green vesture of the early autumn. On descending to the banks of the river flowing through the valley, they found vast reaches of natural pasture where elk and buffalo were quietly browsing. The waters of the stream were alive with chub and perch, and the hedges near its margin were overrun with fruitful grape vines. The party celebrated the happy ending of their forward excursion with volleys of musketing, in the intervals between which they refreshed themselves with draughts of their rare and numerous liquors. The return journey was as pleasantly uneventful as the original advance. The expedition had consumed a period of six weeks, while it had traversed to and fro about four hundred and thirty-eight miles. Its romantic character was appropriately commemorated in the gift of a golden horse-shoe set in diamonds which Spotswood made to each member of the party. This bore the engraved legend *Sic juvat transcendere montes.*

During his term of office, he built a fort at a place in Southside Virginia which he named Christanna. The purpose of its construction was to obtain a stronghold in that region as a step not only towards the maintenance of peace, and the promotion of civilization among the different tribes who inhabited it, but also to protect the first stage in the road to the future settlements of the Southwest.

But as a pathfinder in the wilderness, Spotswood was to be surpassed by a man who exceeded him in polite accomplishments, but not in solid sense and trained judgment. This was the second William Byrd, the most attractive and polished figure in the colonial history of Virginia. He was the son of the first of the name, who spent so much of his life as an active man of affairs at the little settlement nestling near the falls in the James on the site of the modern city of Richmond. This

WILLIAM BYRD, II.

spot was known at that time as the World's End. It stood on the border of the vast wilderness which extended as far to the west as the mountains and also interminable beyond. Here the elder Byrd had established a trading post in the close vicinity of his residence. To this post, he invited the neighboring Indians to come, in order to dispose of their furs in return for his guns and powder, cloth and blankets. To what was more important, however, as bearing upon the interest which his brilliant son was, in after years, to take in opening up the Southwest to settlement, it was from this post that the father sent out his rough frontier agents, with their heavily burdened pack horses, to barter with the tribes occupying the villages along the Roanoke and the Tennessee. These agents came to know that fertile country, with its great streams and endless forests, as well as the natives themselves did, and from them the younger Byrd, in his youth and early manhood, must have learned much about that wild land, with its wild animals and still wilder warriors.

Seated, in his mature years, at his beautiful home at Westover on the James, where he was surrounded by every charm, comfort, and advantage to be enjoyed at that period, he had only in his mind's eye to look across a very narrow settled belt of country to detect the practically unoccupied region which lay west of the Roanoke and the fountains of the Dan and Staunton. At the death of his father, he had inherited 26,231 acres of land. Like all his contemporaries in the Colony of the same high social position, he was deeply bitten with hunger for the soil. Excepting slaves and livestock, it was the only form of investment open to them, and it offered an ownership which had its fine social as well as financial stimulus. Byrd began at an early period of his career to accumulate additional ground. His observation of the rich river bottoms which he saw while serving as one of the commissioners for running the Carolina-Virginia boundary line in 1728, only increased his original appetite for the acquisition of more virgin soil.

One of his most important purchases was twenty-six thousand acres situated on the upper Dan River in the former domain of the Saura Indians, and so fertile were they that he gave the tract the name of the Land of Eden. It was this little principality in the wilderness which led him to patent smaller tracts nearer home, so that he might have convenient plantations all the way to it to furnish him with stopping places. He bought an estate of four hundred and twenty-nine acres on the Meherrin River as the first outpost; and patented twenty-three hundred acres at the Forks of the Roanoke as the second. At one stroke he acquired the ownership of one hundred and five thousand acres on the Dan River in the vicinity of the mouth of the Hico River.

It was in 1733 that he undertook the excursion to the Sauran lands, which he has described in the most sprightly journal of exploration which has descended from colonial times. Spotswood was fortunate in possessing in Ensign Fontaine a companion who was able to record faithfully the main incidents of his romantic journey to the Blue Ridge and Shenandoah Valley. But Byrd was far more happy in finding in himself the historian of his own adventures in threading those forested uplands and reedy lowlands that lay between Westover on the James and the southern spurs of the same splendid chain of mountains. It is true that there was no great open valley at the end of his journey like the one that broke upon the astonished eyes of Spotswood and his companions from the mountain top; but his progress every where, after the passage of the Roanoke, was through a region watered by innumerable streams, both great and small, and clothed for the most part with the noblest woods, varied here and there by quiet upland savannahs and luxuriant river—meadows, which were haunted by countless flocks of birds, and great herds of deer, elk, and buffalo.

Even in the remotest quarters of this new country, Colonel Byrd discovered the presence, at long intervals, of a few squatters who had ventured into the silent fastnesses of the forests, and built cabins and opened up little patches of ground. Taken, however, as a whole, the region along the Dan and its tributaries was, in 1733, in the condition in which it had lain during unrecorded ages. To the view of the explorer, it was quite similar in its primeval aspects to the region, situated towards the north, which Spotswood had crossed seventeen years earlier.

At the time of his death, Byrd was in possession of over one hundred and seventy-nine thousand acres of land. Much of this vast area had been acquired by him in the expectation of disposing of it to advantage to large bodies of settlers. He endeavored to sell a section of it to a colony of Swiss, but this scheme came to grief. Instead of these families seating themselves, as he urged, on the land which he owned along the Roanoke and Dan, which was particularly desirable, they were diverted to Carolina. Ultimately, he was compelled to accept individual purchasers, but the process of filling up all the vacant spaces of his vast estates in the southwestern parts of the Colony had made little progress before he passed away in 1744.

CHAPTER II

WESTWARD MOVEMENTS—GERMANS AND
SCOTCH-IRISH

It was not through the advance of the English inhabitants from the plantations of Tidewater Virginia that the country lying behind the Blue Ridge, between the banks of the Potomac on the north and the banks of the James on the south, was to be permanently occupied. Before the offshoots of that population had, by following the tributaries of the Pamunkey, James, and Rappahannock, slowly crept up to the shadow of the great chain forming the eastern rampart of the valley, two peoples of different nationalities had acquired the main part of the valley itself, and had already begun to stamp their respective characters upon its practical destiny. It is true that, in that section of this beautiful region which lies within the angle between the Potomac and Shenandoah rivers, some of the oldest family names in eastern Virginia were represented among the men who were purchasing lands there of the proprietor of the Northern Neck. Robert Carter alone obtained a grant of fifty thousand acres. Here the Pages, Burwells, and their kinsmen, were to plant a social system, and as far as possible, an economic system also, which was not to differ at all from what had already so long existed in all the countries of Tidewater Virginia, and which was then spreading out westward to the foot of the Blue Ridge.

But these scions of the oldest English stock seated on the American continent were not selected by fate to become the dominant inhabitants of the Great Valley. That destiny was

324

ROBERT (KING) CARTER

reserved for the Germans and the Scotch-Irish, two peoples who differed in genius and habits to a striking degree from the descendants of the Jamestown adventurers. The Germans settled in the region that lay in the long shadow of the Massanutton Range, while the Scotch-Irish seated themselves in the midst of the varied and beautiful landscape of the modern Augusta and Rockbridge counties.

Here were two groups of people who were precisely fitted to develop the particular spots which they respectively occupied. The valley was unlike Tidewater Virginia in climate and in soil. The mighty wall of the Blue Ridge had shut off the passage of transmontane streams,—except by too wide detours, the James and the Potomac,—towards the harbors along the Virginia coast. There was no frontal natural outlet; nor was there any crop like tobacco to promote the introduction of slaves on the scale which had exerted so powerful an influence in shaping the conditions prevailing east of the ridge. Here a different social life existed, not only because the physical characteristics of the country were different, but also because the previous history of the German and Scotch-Irish settlers had been governed by more democratic influences and by more impoverished resources. In them both was found that narrower, but more thrifty, spirit which led them to cultivate their lands with their own hands, and made them, as a rule, content to confine themselves to small estates.

The first of these two people to push their way into the Valley were the Germans. There was already a considerable element of that population to be found in dispersed communities along the headwaters of the Rappahannock River. It was due to the personal solicitation of Governor Spotswood that these immigrants had originally made their homes on the great estate which he owned in that part of the Colony. They had expected to join Baron Von Graffenried after the rupture of the settlements on the Neuse and Cape Fear rivers, in North Carolina, by the murderous Tuscaroras. But their patron, dis-

COLONEL JOHN PAGE

couraged by his misfortunes, left before their arrival in Virginia, and many of them, in consequence, accepted offers of employment in the iron mines and furnaces at Germanna, whilst others scattered among the nearest counties. Spotswood erected comfortable houses for their shelter, and in return for their labor, supported them until they could obtain a more permanent situation by founding homes of their own elsewhere.

A second German immigration took place in the interval between 1735 and 1740. These last colonists had previously resided in Switzerland and the Carolinas. They seated themselves along the banks of the Roanoke and the Dan, and in time, spread to the banks of New River.

There were two important differences between these isolated communities and the later German settlements in the region of the Shenandoah. In the first place, the movements of the earliest German immigrants were made by very considerable bodies who established their homes, in the spirit of the first New England colonists, close together. On the other hand, the Germans who sat down in the Shenandoah Valley seem to have, as a rule, acted more independently of each other, after the manner of the patentees who first occupied Tidewater Virginia. In the second place, the German settlers on the Rappahannock and Dan did not continue to hold together permanently. They gradually dispersed, or were lost in the surrounding English population, with little survival of their racial identity beyond the family names. Their inherited language was even dropped.

In the Shenandoah Valley, on the other hand, the German element has, down to the present day, maintained its social and economic supremacy in the community, and in doing so, has retained all those characteristics which belonged to it in the beginning, only modified to a very small degree.

There was another difference to a certain extent. The German immigrants who found employment at Germanna or acquired lands in southern Virginia were, in the large majority of instances, natives of Europe. They had had, as a rule, no

foretaste of American life or American ideas. While the largest proportion of the German settlers of the Shenandoah Valley
were also of European birth, yet they had lingered long enough
in Pennsylvania, from which they came in their second stage,
to obtain a full knowledge of the new country in which they
found themselves after landing on the Delaware River.

The region in Pennsylvania in which these northern Germans first built their homes was marked by many physical advantages aptly calculated to make them satisfied with their
new situation in life; but there were also serious drawbacks
which tended to create among them a spirit of discontent. They
were, in the first place, very much harassed by Indian incursions, from which they could secure no protection through such
military force as was locally available; and, in the second, which
was almost as important since they had left Europe to escape
bigotted religious persecution, they found themselves oppressed
by religious intolerance, and treated, in other ways, with grave
injustice. A natural disposition sprang up among them to seek
an asylum in some region where they would enjoy a larger
degree of personal freedom in their lives and opinions.

It was known to them that the Shenandoah Valley was still
open to settlement. Reports from men who had seen it with
their own eyes represented it as possessing all the attributes
of an earthly paradise,—a fertile soil adapted to every form
of agricultural product, a wealth of perennial streams, a salubrious climate, and a natural beauty unsurpassed in the fairest
lands of Europe.

As early as 1725, John Van Meter, a Dutch citizen of the
Colony of New York, was engaged in the profitable Indian
trade as far south as the region inhabited by the Cherokees
and Catawbas. He was familiar with the Great Valley throughout its entire width and length, and was so deeply impressed
with its physical advantages as a site for white settlement, that
he persuaded his two sons, John and Isaac, to acquire title to
land lying along the lower Shenandoah River and the south

branch of the Potomac. This was in 1730. The two brothers were granted patents to tracts that, together, spread over forty thousand acres. Subsequently, they sold a part of this vast holding to Jost Hite, who, during the following year, in the company of his sons-in-law, arrived on the ground, with the purpose of making his permanent home on his princely estate. By 1734, many families had been brought by these four pioneers into the neighborhood of the modern Winchester in order to conform to the legal requirements imposed in the case of all public grants. With the exception of a few Scotch-Irishmen, these supplementary groups, were, like Hite and his sons-in-law, of German origin. Hite himself was a native of Strasburg.

These families, however, were not the first German people to sit down in the Shenandoah Valley. About 1726-27, a small company of that race crossed the Potomac and halted on the site of the modern Sheperdstown. In the beginning, they could not claim legal possession of their lands. They were simply squatters, but afterwards were able to validate their tenure.

In June, 1730, Jacob Stover acquired in his own name, and the names of his German and Swiss associates, a grant of ten thousand acres in the shadow of the Massanutton Range. This grant was later on divided into two tracts, consisting of five thousand acres respectively, and lying a considerable distance apart, but both situated on the banks of the Shenandoah River. One of these tracts passed into the hands of Adam Mueller and others, all persons of German blood. Mueller had emigrated first from Europe and afterwards from Pennsylvania. He had entered the Valley by the blazed pathway which Spotswood had used in 1716 in the excursion across the Blue Ridge; and he was so much delighted with the beauty and fertility of that region that he induced the members of his family and several friends then residing north of the Potomac, to make their permanent homes on the lands which he had already acquired from Stover. His title was afterwards disputed by Robert Beverley, but subsequently it was fully confirmed by the Virginia Council.

Mueller survived to exhibit the qualities of a gallant soldier in the French and Indian war, and also lived long enough to see the close of the Revolution.

Some of the later patents to German colonists from Pennsylvania were enormous in area. In 1731, John Fishback and his associates obtained title to fifty thousand acres in the present counties of Page and Warren; and Jost Hite and Robert McKay, in the course of the same year, took up one hundred thousand acres in the same fertile region. Intermingled with these vast tracts were separate bodies of land of almost equal area which had been conferred by public conveyance upon members of ancient Tidewater families, like the Tayloes, Lees, and Beverleys. But in spite of the distinction of the English patentees scattered up and down that region, the predominant influence in the chain of communities from Winchester almost to Staunton was exercised without interruption by the original German settlers or their descendants.

The very great majority of these settlers were satisfied to limit their purchases to such small areas of soil as they would be able to till themselves. Even in those instances in which the tracts obtained were large, the intention does not appear to have been to hold the ground undivided permanently. On the contrary, it was for the speculative advantage of selling that the soil was patented in large bodies, to be subsequently disposed of after partition into farms that rarely exceeded a few hundred acres. While some of the estates ran into the thousands, the popular disposition was not to engross the soil in the spirit which had prevailed on the east side of the mountains almost from the beginning of the system of separate plantations there. Even in the eighteenth century, there were no artificial manures in use in Tidewater and Middle Virginia to restore the fertility of the ground. A rich and fresh soil was essential to the culture of tobacco with profit, and this was only obtainable during that period by the opening up of virgin forest lands. In order to secure these new lands, additions had often to be made to the existing bounds of each plantation.

Tobacco was not cultivated in the Valley, for the reasons already mentioned. The crops which the German householder produced did not demand these constant enlargements of his estate's boundaries. The soil which he possessed, being of limestone origin, was naturally rich, and only required careful tillage to retain its fertility almost indefinitely.

The preponderating German element in the communities along the Shenandoah were people of strong religious instincts. This characteristic either they or their ancestors had brought with them from Europe, which so many of them had deserted in order to secure freedom of worship. In the settlements in the Valley, there were five distinct religious denominations of pure German origin, namely, the Lutheran, the German Reformed, the Dunker, and the United Bretheren. Besides these, the Protestant Episcopal form, which was, at that time, the Established Church of the Colony, counted many notable adherents; and even the Catholic Church had its earnest and loyal supporters sprung from immigrants who had come from those provinces of Germany where that faith had continued strong in spite of the Reformation elsewhere. The Presbyterian Church also was not without importance, owing, perhaps to the influence of the Scotch-Irish population in the Upper Valley, which was brought, from time to time, in contact with the German people seated nearer the Potomac. Some of these early German families had also been trained in the doctrines and customs of the Quakers.

It was characteristic of the Germans of the Valley from the beginning, that, while always sound and useful in practical citizenship, they failed to produce men of the first order of distinction. This fact was especially observable in the provinces of war and politics. Even in these, however, they exhibited a high sense of patriotic duty whenever called upon to defend the Colony or the state, or cast a protective ballot at the polls for the general welfare of the commonwealth. They were frugal, industrious, conservative, peaceful, and obedient to the law.

In the upper part of the Great Valley, there was found in the eighteenth century, a large community of people, who, like the Germans of the lower Shenandoah, could trace their descent straight back to a European stock that had always been remarkable for the vigor and solidity of its qualities. The Scotch-Irish of Rockridge County, the principal seat of their settlement in Virginia, had their springs first in Strathclyde,—situated in Southwest Scotland, and afterwards in Ulster, a province of Northern Ireland, both of which resembled the Virginia Rockbridge County in their varied surfaces, tall mountains, swift streams, and moderate temperature. Before emigrating to Ireland, these people,—grave in bearing and thoughtful in mind, partly in consequence of their somewhat stern environment,—had, with eager sympathy, adopted the reformed canons of religion which had been urged upon their consideration with so much intolerance, and yet with so much power, by John Knox. He also, by his teachings, confirmed the frugal disposition and the inclination to labor which had always distinguished them.

Firmly attached to the soil as they were, these Scotchmen were not unwilling to desert their native soil permanently, if, thereby, they could improve their general condition; and such an opportunity arose early in the reign of James the First. The Irish of Ulster, goaded to desperation by drastic laws affecting every relation of their lives, sprang up in revolt against their oppressors, were crushed by the merciless English soldiers, and their lands confiscated. Over three million acres were thus thrown open to resettlement. This extended surface was soon assigned to a mass of new proprietors. Scotchmen of Strathclyde made up the large majority of them, and, in the end, dominated the whole as thoroughly as if the entire mass had come from the same stock. But there were many families in that population which had emigrated from other regions,—from the north of England, for instance, which had shared the moral characteristics of Strathclyde; and from Huguenot France, which was also like Strathclyde in the firmness of its religious convictions and in its fidelity to principle, even if life had to be sacrificed. These Frenchmen had joined the community in the reign of William of Orange.

In time, this population became thoroughly amalgamated, and its qualities were summed up by one of its historians when he said that "Ulstermen had the steadfastness of the Scot, the rugged strength and aggressive force of the Saxon, and a dash of the vivacity and genius of the Huguenots."

These people, before so many of them departed for America, had almost as much religious intolerance to contend with as the Irish Catholics of the same province. They were Presbyterians in faith, and the Anglican Church of Ireland regarded Protestant dissent as being hardly less heinous than the tenets of the Roman Church. But this fact did not mollify the Irish, when, in 1689, they sprang to arms in support of the Catholic English King. They then vented a degree of cruelty on the Presbyterian Ulstermen such as has rarely been recorded in history. These Ulstermen defended themselves with desperate courage, and ultimately with success; but after the tempest had blown over, they found themselves still the victims of the same English intolerance as had oppressed them before the war began. And to add to the seriousness of their situation, the government in London adopted laws that virtually destroyed their manufacture of woolen cloth, upon which their prosperity chiefly depended.

The emigration began in 1718. Five years afterwards, it had grown to a very large volume. It has been calculated that, between 1718 and 1776 not less than three hundred thousand Ulstermen, in protest against the illiberal policy which had been so long pursued towards them by a hostile church and a short-sighted government, deserted their native country. The desire which actuated them in the mass was summed up by one of their own stern clergymen just before he sailed. It was "to avoid oppression and cruel bondage; to shun persecution and designed ruin; to withdraw from a community of idolators; to have an opportunity to worship God according to the dictates of their conscience, and the rules of His word."

Philadelphia was the principal port which received these emigrants from Ulster because Penn had given a noble reputation to that Colony by his policy of sagacious tolerance. They, after the manner of the German newcomers, established their homes in what was at that time considered to be the interior of the country. Like the Germans, too, they soon found that America as well as Europe could be narrow and oppressive in its attitude towards both the religious and the political rights of the men who had sought a refuge on this side of the ocean.

The lure of the Valley of the Shenandoah was as strong for the Ulstermen of Pennsylvania as it had been for the Germans who had also seated themselves in Penn's province first after their arrival in the Colonies. In 1726, John Peter Salling explored the southern division of the Valley as far as the upper Roanoke River. On the banks of this stream he and his only companion were attacked by Indians. Salling was captured and hurried off to the West. Subsequently, he was purchased by the Spaniards to serve as an interpreter in their trading intercourse with the numerous tribes residing along the banks of the Mississippi River. After several years passed in a life of adventurous vicissitudes, he visited Williamsburg, and meeting there his former companion, who had escaped from the Indians' clutches on the upper Roanoke, he was persuaded to accompany him in another journey to that region. Salling was so much pleased with the fertility of the lands situated in the Valley of the James River at the head of Balcony Falls, that he returned to Williamsburg and obtained a grant to a large tract in that neighborhood, and built a dwelling house on it in the midst of the forest.

The first immigrant to seat himself in the neighboring
county of Augusta was the Scotch-Irishman, John Lewis. It is
said that Lewis was influenced to acquire a large holding in
that virgin quarter by the description which Salling had given
him of its extraordinary beauty and fertility. He probably
erected a cabin there before he received his grant, since six
years seem to have passed between his first appearance as a
householder there and his actual possession, by a public conveyance, of any part of it. In this interval, numerous immigrants of the same origin as himself had settled near him.
Among them were several families who afterwards attained to
prominence in the affairs of that region.

About this time, there arrived at Lewis's home, Benjamin
Borden, accompanied by John McDowell, a surveyor. Borden
had obtained a grant to one hundred thousand acres in the
Valley. This was found to lie in the vicinity of South River in
the modern County of Rockbridge. Here McDowell soon built
a cabin. Before the end of two years, Borden had secured by
advertisement at least one hundred families; and other families rapidly followed. At this time, European immigrants were
entering the port of Philadelphia in large numbers, and many
were easily and quickly induced to accept the first offer for
settlement that was made to them. The rule still prevailed in
Virginia that every person who arrived with the intention of
seating himself there permanently was entitled to a tract of
fifty acres not already occupied; and for every person who
accompanied him, he was entitled to fifty acres in addition.
When a large grant had been obtained, like the one which Borden had secured, the next step was to gather up the number
of settlers which the law required. The patent was not issued
until the patentee had sworn to the statement that, for every
one thousand acres situated within his tract, he had planted
one family.

The head of a family was entitled to what was called a cabin
right. In return for building a cabin, he received one hundred

acres as a gift. Very grave frauds were committed in the acquisition of some of these cabin rights. The Borden grant in after years became involved in a suit at law which affected the titles of all the occupants of the soil within its limits; but in the end, the families in original possession of the different subdivisions retained their holdings.

Gradually, the whole surface of the upper and middle parts of the Valley was brought into the ownership of the class represented by John Lewis, Robert McClanahan, John Preston, James Patton, and Alexander Breckinridge. These men were the typical leaders of the movement which carried the footsteps of the Scotch-Irish from one end of that beautiful section of Virginia to the other. Their names were all Scotch. Indeed, it has been said that the list of prisoners captured at Bothwell Bridge was like a muster roll of the first settlers of Augusta County.

The general background of this sturdy population was in full accord with the original instincts of their Caledonian ancestors. Subject to the influences of a similar physical environment in Virginia, and in possession of no fortune, except what had been extracted from the soil which they occupied, they were not separated so distinctly into the classes which were then to be found everywhere in the eastern communities of the Colony. The support of the social framework that prevailed among them was derived from a social order which, in the counties of Tidewater, would have been designated as yeomen. In that day, a yeoman was the term applied to a freeholder who had a right to vote in an election and to serve on a jury. He stood not so high as the wealthy planter of the East, but far higher than the indentured servant. Indeed, he filled a part which was notable for its usefulness and respectability.

The class of the indentured servant, which was not unrepresented in the Upper Valley, varied in character. Some were men who had been convicted of felony before they left England; others had been men of honest lives, who were constrained by poverty, after they arrived in Virginia or even before, to bind themselves for a term of years to some cultivator of the ground, who needed the assistance of laborers. The system enjoyed over the institution of slavery the advantage of creating a class of individuals, who, if they should develop high personal qualities, could justly expect to reach the plane of the most respectable element in the community.

Among the first settlers were found many persons who were skilled in the mechanical crafts of the weaver, millwright, cooper, ropemaker, carpenter, and blacksmith. The blacksmith was always versed in several kinds of workmanship in iron, such as the manufacture of nails, edged tools, and farming implements.

In the Scotch-Irish settlements of the Valley, the first dwelling houses were, as a rule, very plain and simple. They consisted usually of logs cut in the nearest wood and left in their natural shape; but these were followed by houses constructed of hewn logs, with wide and airy rooms, large chimneys, and enduring shingle roofs. The hewn log-house was succeeded by the frame-house, and in time, here and there, by stone and brick houses. In many of these houses, the spinning wheel and loom were to be seen, since a large proportion of the people made their own garments from the first to the last stage in the process. The soil was tilled with care and skill, although there was hardly a product, except flour from their own mills, and also hemp, which could be sent out of the country, even by wagon, but there was an abundance of corn for domestic consumption, and fruits of all sorts were grown in profusion. The cattle, sheep, and hogs rapidly increased in number, and served the purpose of food at every season of the year. Horses were also numerous, owing to the excellence of the natural pasturage.

The great body of the people, like their forefathers in Scotland and Ulster, belonged to the Presbyterian faith. Their lives were deeply colored by religion. Even their social intercourse was said to have been profoundly influenced by their spiritual emotions. The services in their churches on Sunday lasted, with a short intermission for a frugal dinner, from ten in the morning until sunset. All the lighter amusements rested under a ban of disapproval. They were a people of stern instincts, unconquerable souls, and unyielding convictions, such as the Covenanters had been before them. They were even ready to sacrifice life itself if a question of principle was involved. The granite of their hills was not firmer and stronger than their character.

CHAPTER III

WESTWARD MOVEMENT—CONFLICT WITH FRENCH AND INDIANS

As we have already mentioned, Spotswood had, in pushing his expedition across the Blue Ridge to the banks of the Shenandoah, been largely influenced by his fear lest the aggressive advance of the French power in the region of the lakes would, in the end, not only confine the English settlements to the country east of the mountains, but not improbably endanger their tenure of the ground which they already held below the falls in the great rivers of Tidewater. This apprehension, doubtless, did not rest on a very firm basis so far as the older parts of the Colony were involved; but there was good reason for its existence so far as it related to the possibility of the French blocking every gap in the Alleghanies likely to be traveled by English families seeking new homes in the fertile country beyond. As a matter of fact, the French were resolved to dominate, by force of arms, if necessary, the immense territory between Canada and Louisiana, and they had already begun at least to consider the establishment of a chain of military posts between the banks of the Great Lakes and the mouth of the Mississippi River. It was natural enough that they should desire in a general way to widen the area under their control in the most fertile region of the continent, and thus keep away all offshoots from the older English settlements.

But there was another motive of immediate practical purport to influence them. The French colonists were as deeply

340

immersed in the fur trade as the English and as solicitious to monopolize its profits. To share this trade with the ever-advancing outposts of the English colonists was to curtail its returns to a very serious degree.

William Byrd perceived as clearly as Spotswood the significance of the French occupation of the territory watered by the Ohio and its tributaries. In 1735, nearly twenty years after the romantic expedition across the Blue Ridge had been made, he warned the English authorities of the designs of the French, and the manner in which they would be carried out. "The advantage of their being beforehand with the English in gaining possession of the mountains," he wrote in 1735, "was obvious." "For so doing," he added, "they will have the following temptations: first, that they may make themselves masters of all the mines with which those mountains (the Alleghanies) abound; second, that they may engross all the trade with the western Indians for skins and furs; which, besides being very profitable, will bind those numerous natives to the French interests so far as to cause them to side with the French against the King's subjects, just as those bordering on Canada are already employed to give trouble to the adjacent British Colonies. And, lastly, that they will be in condition, not only to secure their own traffic, and protect their own settlements westward, but also to invade the British Colonies from thence. Nor are these views so distant as some may imagine, because a scheme for that purpose was, some years ago, laid before the Sieur Croissat and approved; but it was not, at that time, thought to be sufficiently ripe for execution. These inducements to the French make it prudent for the British monarchy to be watchful to prevent them from seizing this important barrier. There should be employed some fit person to reconnoitre these mountains in order to discover what mine may there be, and likewise observe what nations of Indians dwell there, and where lie the most considerable passes, with a view to their being secured by proper fortifications."

It will be observed that Byrd, in this weighty communication, did not seem to consider the possibility of the English colonists making a settlement themselves in the Ohio Valley, and for that reason, if for no other, endeavoring to obstruct the further advance of the French. But he did clearly perceive the importance of keeping the French and Indians apart. Let the two form an alliance south of Canada, he intimated, and the safety of the English colonists would, from that time, be in constant jeopardy.

His expectation was proved by subsequent events to be too well founded. The great French and Indian war that followed at the end of a few years was exactly in harmony with the anticipations of all the English colonists of that day who gave any thought to the menacing condition which from an early date was in the course of development in the Valley of the Ohio. Only three years after Byrd's letter was written, a band of murderous Indians crept into the region east of the Blue Ridge as far as an isolated district of Orange County and put to the scalping knife nearly a dozen men, women, and children. Even after a formal treaty had granted to the colonists of Virginia the right to hold all the territory beyond the Alleghanies, as far as the banks of the Ohio River, these Indian incursions were repeated, leaving a trail of blood behind them.

But it was not in the spirit of the Virginians of that time to stand indifferently back from the opportunities which the settlement of the West was opening up, whether on the eastern or the Western side of the Alleghany Mountains. So soon as the Valley of Virginia had begun to fill up with immigrants, the possibilities of making fortunes by the acquisition of the virgin lands beyond it took possession of some of the most conspicuous men in Eastern Virginia. We have already referred to the large tracts patented by the Carters, Beverleys, and Lees, in the Valley of the Shenandoah. It was inevitable that members of the same class should reach out still further for an even larger area. There was in the Colony, in those times, but one way of making or increasing estates with some degree of rapidity. This was not by the sale of crops, nor by additions to the number of slaves, but by the engrossment of uncleared lands in those backwoods to which the tide of immigration was flowing or was certain to flow in the future.

In 1749, a band of wealthy and influential citizens, composed in part of Governor Dinwiddie, George Mason, Thomas Lee, and Lawrence and Augustine Washington, organized the Ohio Company for the acquisition of lands in the region of the Ohio River, which they proposed to bring under settlement by the introduction of immigrants from Europe as well as from the Atlantic Colonies. Christopher Gist, an agent of large experience as an explorer and pioneer, was sent out to inspect the country. He found it to be extraordinarily fertile in soil, and, in large part, overgrown with the most magnificent primeval forests. The grant to the Ohio Company embraced five hundred thousand acres.

In the course of the same year, permission was obtained by the Loyal Company, composed of such men as Dr. Thomas Walker, John Lewis, and others of equal importance in the Colony, to survey a certain designated tract in Southwest Virginia that contained within its boundaries an area of eight hundred thousand acres. Twenty-four months afterwards, the Greenbrier Company received a similar grant to one hundred thousand acres lying between the Cowpasture and Greenbrier rivers. Before a decade had passed, these enormous bodies of land had been occupied by a large number of permanent settlers, who had entered subject to the strict regulations which then governed the preemption of such public domain.

An abrupt, but more or less nominal termination to the issuance of grants was brought about in 1763 by the proclamation of the King forbidding it. The object of this document was to prevent further conflicts with the Indians until a formal treaty had been made with them that would assure the legal cession of all the territory reaching from the slopes of the Alleghanies to the banks of the Ohio. In spite of the grant to the Ohio Company in 1749, the title to this intervening territory was not as yet clearly established. In 1768, a treaty with that effect was drafted with the Iroquois Indians at Fort Stanwix.

In the meanwhile, a course of events had occurred which gave the government of Virginia practical domination over all the territory east of the Ohio River, and confirmed the possession of every settler who was occupying a homestead within its boundaries. Governor Dinwiddie had not been long in possession of his office at Williamsburg when he clearly perceived that the most dangerous condition confronting him, as the representative of the King and the Colony, was the continued advance of the French in the Valley of the Ohio. It was no longer a mere rumor that they were considering the erection of a series of forts, which would extend from the shores of Lake Erie to the upper waters of the Ohio, and thence along the banks of that stream to the Mississippi River, with an additional chain to connect that point with the Gulf. The basis of the claim to this vast territory was the explorations of LaSalle. To confirm that claim, the French had buried in the earth at the mouth of each principal tributary of the Ohio a bronze plate with an inscription asserting their right to the soil. From the head waters of such tributaries as the Kanawha and Tennessee, the Blue Ridge was almost visible. This claim, if once conceded by the English, would, as Spotswood and Byrd foresaw, and actually predicted, as we have already mentioned, confine them within a boundary line that ran along the crest of the furthest eastern spur of the Alleghanies. That spur had already been reached by the German and Scotch-Irish settlers in the Great Valley.

In 1753, Dinwiddie, under the influence of his own apprehensions, and also of specific instructions from the King, took the first practical step to halt the descent of the French from their stronghold at Vincennes, near Lake Erie, which was the initial link in their projected chain of forts. This step was the acquisition by treaty with the Indians of the right to erect a fortification at the confluence of the Alleghany and Mononga-hela rivers. His second step was still more emphatic in express-ing his determination. He despatched the youthful Washington to Vincennes, with a message to the French commander there warning him to retire from the English territory which he occupied.

The journey began in the latter part of autumn, with a harsh winter in prospect. Washington was accompanied by an interpreter, for he himself had never enjoyed an opportunity to learn the French language. Before his arrival at the Ohio River, he was joined by Christopher Gist, who, only a few years before, had explored that region as the agent of the Ohio Com-pany, and who was familiar with the principal trails that threaded it. An escort of four men were with him. No trace of a fort was found at the spot between the Alleghany and the Monongahela rivers which Dinwiddie had secured by treaty to become the site for a formidable fortification. Washington and his companions, undeterred by the formidable obstacles which apparently completely blocked their forest path, rapidly ad-vanced to Vincennes. There the French commander received them with great courtesy, but exhibited neither in his conver-sation with the young Virginian nor in his letter to Dinwiddie, any disposition to abandon the Ohio territory in deference to the demands of the English.

During the journey homeward, the difficulties of the passage were increased by the season, for winter had set in, snow cov-ered the ground, and running ice filled the flooded rivers. Wash-ington and his companions at first travelled on foot leading their horses, which were now too fatigued to be of assistance except in carrying the light baggage. Ultimately, Washington and Gist left the rest of the party and pushed forward through the woods. Overtaking a band of French Indians, they em-ployed one of the number to serve as a guide, but he soon dis-closed his treacherous character. Nevertheless he was suffered

to escape in the night. They, themselves continued their journey under the cover of darkness.

Washington and Gist were dressed in the costume of the
frontier, which consisted of an Indian matchcoat, buckskin
trousers, and leather moccasins. They had their packs slung
loosely over their backs, and bore their rifles in their hands.

While they were attempting to cross the Alleghany River by
a raft of their own construction, their frail boat was upset by
the crush of ice and sank to the bottom, submerging the two
men in the water. The second raft upon which they endeavored
to cross the river floated down to an island, after Washington
had again been thrown into the stream by catching his pole in
a floe. There was no fire to warm them when they at last landed,
and Gist, by morning, had been so bitten by the excessive cold,
that it was only with extreme difficulty that he was able, even
with Washington's help, to reach the nearest trading post. The
journey had extended over fifteen hundred miles to and fro, and
it had taken three months to complete.

The great events which followed this excursion to Vincennes
decided finally: first, that the Indians would not be permitted
to stop the advance of the English pioneer settlers to the banks
of the Ohio and the Mississippi; and, secondly, and principally,
that the French would not be suffered to retain any part of
the territory lying south of the Great Lakes which they had
claimed so vigorously.

When Dinwiddie found that the French commander at Vincennes, in reply to the letter which Washington had handed him,
had asserted his intention to uphold the French right to the
region of the Ohio, he concluded that only energetic military
measures would dislodge the enemy. A regiment under Colonels
Fry and Washington was organized and sent off through the
forests to the point where the Alleghany and Monongahela mingled their waters. Washington marched rapidly ahead, and
when, in April (1754), he reached Great Meadows, situated
not far from that spot, he was informed that, not only had

GOVERNOR ROBERT DINWIDDIE

no fort been erected there since his visit to Vincennes, in accord with Dinwiddie's instructions to the Ohio Company, but that the workingmen who had come to undertake it had been driven off by the French, the ground occupied, and a strong fortification built on the site for their own use. It was too formidable to be attacked by Washington with his limited force, and he, therefore, contented himself with assaulting, under cover of night, the entrenchments of a small body of French troops and their Indian allies who had stationed themselves a short distance from Great Meadows. The movement was successful. The officer in command and ten of his men were killed, and many others captured.

About three months afterwards, a French detachment, composed of nine hundred men and supported by a large contingent of Indian scouts, attacked Washington standing on the defensive in Fort Necessity. The siege of his position continued for some days. Each assault was repulsed, until a heavy rain having made his trenches almost untenable and hampered the usefulness of his guns, he decided that it would be discreet to accept an offer of the French commander to permit him, without interference, to abandon the fort with the full honors of war and to withdraw to Virginia. Since the arrival of their reinforcements, the enemy had greatly exceeded his army in numbers.

The alarm caused by this success of the French on the Ohio was so general in Virginia that the General Assembly appropriated twenty thousand pounds sterling for the prosecution of the war, and Dinwiddie doubled the forces already under arms. These were organized as a body which was to be kept entirely separate from the regular British troops either then stationed in the Colonies or to be stationed there in the immediate future. A considerable delay followed, as the governor and General Assembly were confident that aid would ultimately be received from England.

This expectation proved to be correct. In February, 1755, General Braddock, at the head of one thousand thoroughly drilled British soldiers, arrived in Virginia. His formal commission invested him with the command of all the troops in the Colony, to whichever of the two services they might belong. One of his first steps was to appoint Colonel Washington to be a member of his staff, an act of good judgment, as Washington was perfectly familiar with the country to be traversed in the proposed campaign against Fort Duquesne, which the French, as we have seen, had built at the confluence of the Alleghany and Monongahela rivers. This distinguished officer's knowledge of Indian methods of forest warfare does not appear to have been taken into consideration in his nomination, and yet it was in this particular that his services would have been supremely useful, had his advice during the expedition been followed.

The campaign which the British commander now entered upon was one entirely foreign to his experience. In reality, it offered no feature whatever in which his previous training as a soldier could have been employed to advantage. He had all the inflexibility of a military martinet, and he held in small esteem the apparently raw and undisciplined colonial militia who accompanied him. They might be fitted to build roads for his passage of the wilderness, but would be hardly able to cope successfully with the French troops so soon to be encountered.

But Braddock forgot that the French officers, although they had been trained in the tactics of their profession in the military schools of Europe, had associated in the American forests long enough with the Indian warriors to learn the superior efficiency of the Indian methods of resisting an enemy traversing the primeval woods. This was precisely what the brave, imprudent English commander was now on the point of doing; and the French officers laid an ambuscade for his red-coats that was nicely adapted to diminish, if not destroy altogether, the effectiveness of their courage and training. Indeed, had the

British troops been less highly disciplined, they would have stood a better chance of triumph by scattering in the adjacent woods on the Duquesne highway, and fighting the enemy, as the shrewder Virginians did, behind the trunks of trees and piles of logs, which served as breastworks.

It is not necessary to describe the course of the terrible battle that took place on the banks of the Monongahela. A more complete defeat is not recorded in history, and certainly not one in which the atrocities committed by a part of the successful army were surpassed in ruthlessness and horror. A larger number of the British forces were killed or wounded than were enrolled in the entire body of their French and Indian opponents. Of eighty-six British officers, the full complement, twenty-six were killed and thirty-seven wounded. Braddock, who, like Washington, had had several horses struck down under him, received what proved to be in the end a fatal bullet; and he was only saved from the scalping knife of the ferocious savages by the assistance afforded him by the Virginian officers to escape from the field.

When it became known that the British army, with their colonial contingent, had been decisively defeated, a wave of dread swept all along the line of the outer settlements. Thousands of families deserted their homes on the frontiers, and fled to a safer region either in Virginia or further south.

Washington proposed, in 1756, that a cordon of forts should be erected from the Potomac to the middle Carolina border. There were fourteen in all, and they were so quickly constructed and so fully garrisoned, that the people who were exposed to peril began to recover their former confidence. But this was soon shown to be delusive. The French and Indian raids were renewed with increased cruelty, and by 1758, the situation of the colonists, even when residing far within the old frontiers had become again intolerable. A second campaign was organized against Fort Duquesne, with Washington, a second time, holding one of the subordinate commands; and this expedition

Frontier Fort Chiswell Monument in
Wythe County

proved so successful that the people in Virginia were never afterwards molested by the French Power.

We have already referred incidentally to the treaty with the Iroquois Indians signed at Fort Stanwix in 1768. By this compact, which was one of the fruits of the fall of Fort Duquesne, the last French stronghold on the Ohio, that tribe surrendered to the English their title to all the lands west of the Alleghanies as far as the mouth of the Tennessee River. There was a serious interference with this settlement in a treaty which the Superintendent of Indian Affairs for the Southern District of America made with the Cherokees in the course of the same year. The House of Burgesses, in a memorial to Governor Botetourt, protested against this intrusive agreement, and insisted that the boundary line should be extended from the end of the existing line between Virginia and Carolina straight to the banks of the Mississippi River. Ultimately, the General Assembly, unable to enforce this claim, was constrained to purchase a great area of country, lying as far as the Kentucky River, from the Cherokees, who asserted their title to it.

That body was largely influenced to follow this course by a report from London that an association known as the Walpole Company had been organized to establish a great Colony in the territory which Virginia held beyond the Alleghanies. It seems that this company, which was made up of some of the first men in England at that time, had petitioned for a tract as enormous as twenty million acres situated entirely within the bounds of Virginia. A vigorous protest against the proposed engrossment of so much of her soil was promptly submitted by her agent in London. Washington, when informed of the scheme, declared that such a concession "would be a fatal blow to the interest of the Colony." He pointed out to Governor Botetourt that two hundred thousand acres of this territory had already been promised to the Virginian soldiers who had taken part in the French and Indian war.

Dunmore, who succeeded Botetourt, was opposed to the projected grant, but the Company's influence in London was too
strong to be resisted even by the Board of Trade, which was
also hostile to the grant. In May, 1773, the document was
signed. By its terms, all patents which had been obtained during previous years by individual settlers were confirmed, but
the title of the Ohio Company was completely extinguished. The
most disturbing feature of the grant was the fact that it set
up a new colony expressly intended to form a community entirely independent of Virginia. It was to be known as the Colony of Vandalia. Provision was made for the transfer of bounty
lands as promised to the soldiers of the French and Indian war
by Dinwiddie; and additional efforts were put forth to placate
other interests which had been injuriously affected.

Dunmore was zealous in diminishing the value of the grant
as far as his power reached, and he excused himself to the
English Government, when censured for his active opposition,
by advancing the ingenious excuse that he supposed that the
royal proclamation of 1763 was still in force; and that, therefore, he was led to think that grants like the one to the Walpole Company were invalid. Fortunately before this concession
of the Walpole Company could pass the last formality, the first
Continental Congress assembled in Philadelphia, and though
the Company was eager to go ahead, the Privy Council in London advised it to discontinue further action until hostilities had
ceased. This was the practical death-knell of that menacing
project.

The Battle of Point Pleasant, fought at the mouth of the
Great Kanawha, in which the Indians, in September, 1774, were
decisively defeated, was a far reaching stroke for the establishment of permanent peace on the western frontiers of Virginia. During a long series of years, there had been an almost
constant fear of attack, first by the Indians, then by the French
and Indians combined, and finally by the Indians alone. Now
for a short spell there was to be peace,—only too soon, how-

ever, to be broken by the alliance between the English and Indians in the course of the impending Revolutionary war.

In the interval, a host of settlers poured, like the waters of a mountain stream, into the fair territory of the modern states of Kentucky and Tennessee. At an early date, these lands had been explored by Dr. Thomas Walker and his companions, who were looking over the country in the interest of the Loyal Company, which they represented. They had been followed by hunters, who were drawn thither, in spite of peril at every step, by the presence of noble herds of buffalo and elk; and these intruders, in turn, were followed by traders, who were seeking to reap the harvest of invaluable furs which the Indians were ready to exchange for powder and shot and other articles of merchandise appealing to their untutored fancy.

The upper valley of the Tennessee was gradually filled up under the leadership of Virginians like James Robertson and John Sevier. About the same time, the soil of Kentucky was showing the imprint of the feet of similar intrepid pioneers. In 1769, Daniel Boone, the greatest of all back-woodsmen, accompanied by five persons of the same bold and enterprising temper as himself, pushed his way into that beautiful region, with the intention of erecting a new home there. It was not, however, until 1775 that he laid the corner stone of his dwelling house at the spot which was afterwards to be known by his name.

Other Virginians had preceded him; among them, George Rogers Clark, the future conqueror of the Northwest, and one of the founders of the United States. James Harrod arrived in 1774. The Transylvania Company was soon represented in the person of Richard Henderson, a native of Virginia, but now a citizen of North Carolina. Henderson was only satisfied with the sufficiency of his company's claims when he had asserted its right to the whole territory of Kentucky. He organized a government for his new colony, and held out many tempting inducements to families to settle within the boundaries of that fertile domain.

Virginia very naturally disputed this proclamation of independence, and when George Rogers Clark in person presented a petition for the conversion of the entire country into a new county, the Council at Williamsburg, after a moment of hesitation, consented. With the erection of this county, the era of the pioneer within the boundaries of the new state may be said to have closed.

CHAPTER IV

MATERIAL DEVELOPMENT.

We have, in the course of the preceding chapters, traced in as much detail as our space permitted, the different stages in that expansion of the territory of Colonial Virginia, which, by 1776, had brought its confines in the Northwest to the Great Lakes, and in the West, to the Mississippi River. Here was an empire in itself, which, as time passed on, was, step by step, contracted until, at the end of the war for Southern Independence, the boundaries of the state on the side of the Alleghanies were limited by the landscape which Spotswood saw from the crest of the Blue Ridge.

Within Virginia's Colonial borders, when most extensive, the greatest races of Europe were represented in its far-spread population; every religious sect found there its loyal adherents; every shade of enlightenment, as it was then judged, its exponents. The negro, the Indian, the German, the Frenchman, the Irishman, the Scotchman, the Englishman,—all were to be observed there, subject to the same government, and each pursuing the course of life which irresistible circumstances, or his own natural inclination, had prescribed. The varied physical character of that vast stretch of country, with its broad arms of the sea, its coastal plain, its lofty mountains, its great inland rivers, its fertile valleys, its apparently interminable forests,— all combined to diversify the daily existence of the inhabitants, without, however, increasing, to a remarkable degree, the number of their employments even after the possession of the face of the country was no longer disputed by Frenchman or Indian.

356

There was not even in the eighteenth century, a systematic effort to turn to account the wealth of magnificent timber that was to be discovered everywhere, even in the oldest parts of the Tidewater region. Such use as was made of it did not extend beyond the acquisition of a small quantity of lumber for the erection of a plantation mansion, a pioneer's cabin, or a hunter's lodge. The axe was directed towards the destruction of that towering growth, not for the profit of a sale, since there was no market, but for the clearance of the virgin soil for the planting of maize and tobacco and vegetables.

In the oldest as well as in the newest parts of the principality which now looked to Williamsburg as its political center, it was still the agricultural products of the land which were relied upon for the subsistence of the inhabitants. There were sections near the sea in which the fishing hook and the seine greatly helped the people to eke out a livelihood. There were others spreading out in open plain or rising in mountain spurs, where the people turned to the rifle for important assistance in furnishing forth their dinner tables. But for the vast body of the population, it was the hoe and the plough which were still trusted with the highest confidence to afford them nourishing food and comfortable shelter.

West of the mountains, with no tributaries of the tidal streams sufficiently deep or unobstructed to bear the crops to the ocean-going vessels, there was not, until the wagon came into use, any convenient means of disposing of these crops on a great scale, except through consumption under the numerous local roofs. Apparently, however, there was as little inclination among the Western Virginians as among the Eastern to turn to manufactures beyond what were practicable in a simple way on their respective farms. As we have seen, the Scotch-Irish of the Valley ground some of their grain into flour for local export by wagon, and this was also done on a much greater scale by the German people residing in the neighboring region. It was also done in a still more extensive way by the landowners of Northern Piedmont, who turning their tobacco fields into wheat fields, found at Alexandria and other towns on tidewater, a ready sale for their grain converted into flour.

During the eighteenth century, as during the seventeenth from start to finish, the English Government never ceased to discourage all enterprises directed towards the production of satisfactory substitutes for the articles manufactured in England. This policy had never altered; and so few were the facilities even in the eighteenth century for manufacture in the Colony on a scale even remotely approaching that of the Mother Country, that the thought of any real rivalry in this province with her never occurred to the Virginian people, except possibly in hours of great impoverishment. Even then the popular efforts were limited to the making of certain artificial articles of the simplest nature. There was in this intermittent action apparently only an intention to meet the wants of single householders.

As the eighteenth century progressed, the size of the Eastern plantations increased, in consequence of the introduction of a large number of African slaves. Each estate of importance tended to become more and more able to furnish itself with all those numerous articles which were required to carry on successfully the work in the fields. Indeed, the various slave artisans belonging to a planter of wealth made him, to a great extent, independent of the English manufacturer. He owned carpenters, coopers, blacksmiths, tanners, shoemakers, and even distillers. The carpenter built cabins for the slaves and barns for the tobacco, constructed the vehicles, and raised and repaired the fences; the cooper made the hogsheads; the tanner, the leather; the cobbler, the shoes; the blacksmith, the ironware; and the distiller, the spirits. All these things were constantly in demand by the master's household and by his slaves.

But these men were not all the mechanics at that master's disposal among the people who were in a state of servitude to him. There were times, which returned only too often in that day of

OLD STOVE IN CAPITOL
Made in England in 1770.

fluctuating prices for tobacco, when, for instance, it was cheaper
to manufacture than to buy of English merchants the clothes
needed by his own family and his dependents.   For this purpose,
he kept always actively at work his own spinners and weavers.
The spinning wheel and the loom were familiar objects on every
large plantation of the eighteenth century.   But their presence
was not suggested simply by convenience and economy, although
that was, of course, the chief reason for their existence in Virginia in that age.   They were there in harmony with an ancient
English custom.   Almost immemorially the production of all
sorts of goods had been carried on in the English cottages by
the hands of its humble inmates.   The factory system did not
become universal in the Mother Country until the application of
steam began after the close of the Napoleonic wars.

There was not a single raw material which the wealthy
planter of the eighteenth century could not furnish for the
manipulation of his slave artisans.   The plantation forest supplied the carpenter and cooper with the finest lumber; the grassy
uplands supplied the tanner with hides, which he prepared and
delivered to the shoemaker; and the lowland pastures supplied
the spinner and weaver with wool, which was supplemented by
flax and cotton from the cultivated fields.   In addition, the orchard supplied the fruit for conversion into cider and apple and
peach brandy.   The blacksmith alone could only be furnished
with the materials which he needed by actual purchase.

What were the facilities within the Colony for the manufacture of such articles as were required on the plantations, but
which their mechanics were unable to make?   Apparently, down
to the end of Spotswood's administration, the only means in
existence in Virginia, apart from the cargoes of in-coming ships,
of obtaining the iron which the blacksmith, for instance, called
for were the furnaces which the Governor had erected at Germanna.   Afterwards, there were other furnaces in that part of
Virginia.   We have already mentioned that he had been able to
put the first of his own in operation through the aid of the

Germans whom he had induced to settle on his great tract of
land situated along the upper waters of the Rappahannock.   At
the beginning, there seems to have been a company of forty men,
women, and children.   Many of the men were experts in mining
ore, building furnaces, and manipulating them after construction.   Spotswood had served as a soldier under Marlborough in
Germany, and, possibly, during his campaign there, had had
an opportunity of observing the process of both mining and
smelting ore and fashioning the product into finished iron.   He
had discovered traces of iron ore on his lands, and this fact, no
doubt, had had its influence in causing him to make so liberal an
offer of settlement to a band of people who were more likely to
be of aid to him in that field than the same number of English
indentured servants.

In the beginning, they apparently showed no symptom of discontent with their occupation, but subsequently, they, with the
later reinforcements, were drawn away into important communities of their own.   Spotswood was then compelled to rely upon
negro slaves in the management of the furnaces.   These did not
prove to be unsuccessful in performing the work.   The like ability has been exhibited by members of the same race in the modern South when employed in the manufacture of the cruder
forms of iron, as their predecessors were at Germanna under
Spotswood's supervision.

Spotswood did not attempt to place finished iron in the
market.   He was content to make such castings as chimney
backs, andirons, fenders, rollers, skillets, and boxes for cart
wheels.   These found a ready sale in the Colony without arous-
ing the opposition of the English manufacturer of the same
articles; probably because most of them were very cumbrous.
It may be the profit in the importation of such burdensome materials was so small that the English manufacturer did not think
that it was worth the trouble to raise a protest.   Apparently,
the bulk of the output of Spotswood's furnaces remained from
start to finish crude pigiron, which he exported, not only to

England, but also to the English Colonies. The manufacturers
of the Mother Country were satisfied to receive it, as they, in
consequence of the decline in English mining and smelting, were
compelled to look to foreign lands for their main supply.

It is not an overstatement to say that, independently of these
furnaces at Germanna and others in the surrounding country,
the manufacturing interests of the Colony during the colonial
period of the eighteenth century, or at least during the far
greater part of it, were of such small proportions, where they
existed at all, as to be undeserving of serious consideration.
Flour, it is true, was produced in many mills in Piedmont Virginia and the Valley, but this seems to have been a local and
fluctuating interest. The manufacturing development on the
larger Eastern plantations was, as a rule, no more than the
exercise of the immemorial arts of small tradesmen. In bulk,
the products of these plantation mechanics were very great, but
they were simply for local utility. One plantation did not serve
another out of its surplus. Each plantation, in fact, restricted
itself to the volume of its needs. The plantation was the beginning and the end of the economic life of the community in the
seventeenth and eighteenth centuries alike, for it was practically
to one interest, agriculture, that the thoughts and energies of the
population as a whole were limited.

In some important features, the agriculture of the Eighteenth Century did not differ at all from the agriculture of the
Seventeenth Century. Tobacco was still the principal crop of
most of the plantations, although in Piedmont a great quantity
of wheat was produced. Proportionately to population, the volume of the tobacco, however, in the Eastern counties at least,
was as great in one century as in the other. It was subject
to precisely the same influence of fluctuating prices. It was
still used as a medium of valuation. It was still the lure that
drew thousands of English families to the Colony. It was still
the chief source of wealth. It still entered into every ramifica-

tion of Colonial life. It still carried the name of Virginia to the confines of the civilized world.

But there was at least one radical difference between the agricultural system of the first century and that of the greater part of the second. In the Seventeenth, the laborer relied upon almost exclusively was the English indentured servant. It is true that there were numerous small plantations cultivated by the hands of their owners. These men were representatives of the ancient English class of yeomen. But the ambition of every landed proprietor, great or small, was to secure the assistance of as many indentured servants as he could afford to buy. The number of the helpers attached to single tracts varied from one to a dozen or more, and among them, a few negroes were detected. But not even as late as 1700 had African slaves seriously displaced the white indentured servants.

A change now began which brought about a profound alteration in the racial character of the laborers who tilled the tobacco fields, planted the maize, and reaped the wheat. The black slave rapidly took the place of the white indentured servant in practically all the communities in the eastern parts of the Colony. It is estimated that, between 1699 and 1708, nearly seven thousand negroes arrived. During the summer of 1705 alone, over eighteen hundred were landed at the wharves in the different rivers of Tidewater. Three years afterwards, there were twelve thousand slaves in the Colony as compared with a population of thirty thousand white persons; in 1715, twenty-three thousand as compared with a population of seventy-two thousand white. In 1756, the respective figures were 120,000 and 173,136.

It was noted in this year that the strong influx of indentured servants, which had been so conspicuous during the previous century, had now dwindled to a negligible number. There were several reasons for this unprecedented condition. In the first place, the price of tobacco had fallen so low that the cheapest laborer obtainable was now in demand. The negro constituted such a laborer, because, as we have already pointed out, he did not have to be periodically replaced by a substitute who was expensive to purchase. He could be supported at less outlay than the white servant. He was more enduring in the hot suns and miasmatic breezes; and finally, while he had to be rationed and sheltered in his old age, he could still perform a few simple tasks. The indentured servant, on the other hand, when his contract expired, had to be provided with numerous costly allowances.

The decline in the number of indentured servants was not to be attributed altogether to the demand for a less expensive system of labor which would enable the planter to stand more successfully the stress of the prevailing low price of tobacco. Formerly, as we have seen, the English Government used all the influence at its command to encourage the emigration of that large number of persons of the lowest social rank, who, by the fluctuations in wages and in the cost of bread, were often compelled to rely in whole or in part upon the assistance of their native parishes for a subsistence. The cue had been really given to the Government by the vestries of these parishes, owing to the fact that they were greatly burdened by the contributions which they were annually forced to make for this purpose. A solution was found for the problem of this more or less helpless population by shipping them to the plantations oversea.

Apparently, some years after the opening of the eighteenth century, both the English Government and the individual parish showed little inclination to promote even the voluntary withdrawal of the persons belonging to the most respectable division of this surplus population; and there was certainly no greater energy put forth now by either to get rid of the members of the purely criminal class.

The explanation of the change in attitude is not entirely clear, unless there had arisen in the kingdom a new demand for the services of every pair of hands in the development of local industries. England was now content to increase by every means in her power the number of African slaves imported into

Virginia. It was, apparently, no cause for concern to her that the population of the Colony, instead of being composed as formerly of a homogeneous race, however wide the gradations in social rank, was soon composed of one large element of English blood and an almost equally large element of African blood, two incongruous strains which could not be mixed without the debasement of the English. Previous to 1700, the population of Virginia was restricted almost entirely to white people, which created a community knit together by the powerful ties of a common descent. Every yeoman had a chance of becoming a wealthy planter of social and political influence, every indentured servant could look forward to the prospect of becoming a yeoman so soon as his term had expired. In each grade, the tendency was always to a higher and more prosperous platform in society.

The situation of the slaves both before and after 1700, was altogether different. The bulk of them had no prospect of a better condition. They were born in bondage; they remained in bondage; they died in bondage. Even those who were set free by the action of their masters could not hope for a higher fate than that which had fallen to the most insignificant white yeoman. It is true that he might become a small landowner, but there his good fortune ended. His social status continued to be that of the negro race. In some respects, it was less happy, for he could not expect equality in his personal association with the white race, and he was disposed to look down with contempt on personal association with the black.

The injurious effect of the introduction of negroes into Virginia in an increasing stream, while the influx of white servants was dwindling to a mere trickle, was bound to be enormous. Apparently, England did not give a thought to the evil which was foreshadowed so distinctly. She stuck with cynical selfishness to her old doctrine that the Colony was made for the advancement of the economic welfare of the Mother Country; and that the Mother Country really owed no obligation to her offspring to preserve indefinitely those social conditions oversea which had existed throughout the Seventeenth Century.

Unfortunately, the requirements of tobacco culture, always suffering from low prices, tempted the planters themselves to close their eyes to the calamities to be anticipated from the inflow of negroes from Africa as substitutes for the old class of indentured servants; but there are distinct indications that the General Assembly were not entirely blind to the consequences of this black tide in the long run. From time to time, that body passed laws imposing a tax on the head of every slave imported. The object of these Acts was to check the flood of Africans, although, in order to escape the suspicion to that effect of the English Government, the Burgesses pretended that some other object,—such as the need of raising special funds for public purposes, for instance,—was the true motive.

Not infrequently, the Assembly openly protested against the inflow as jeopardizing the social future of the Colony; as increasing the danger of slave insurrections; and as lowering still further the price of tobacco by swelling the quantity produced. But so little attention was paid to these complaints by the English Government through a long series of years, that, in drafting the Declaration of Independence, Jefferson included this offense in the long list of those which, as he declared, justified his indictment of the King.

How far did the introduction of slaves in large numbers after the opening of the eighteenth century affect the fortunes of the yeoman class, who formed so useful a part of the community previous to that period? It has been presumed that the arrival of Africans in such a multitude raised so great a desire in persons of this class to emigrate that they deliberately deserted their lands in Eastern Virginia, and left the several communities there to the possession of men who owned slaves either in large or small allotments. But this explanation is not altogether pertinent. From the time when the Indian menace,—which so long retarded the spread of population after the foundation of Jamestown,—was permanently withdrawn, the tendency of the settlers was to shift from one region to another. The Northern Neck, for instance, was largely occupied by emigrants from the plantations on the Nansemond; the valleys of the Roanoke and its tributaries by emigrants from the south and north side of the James River; and the valleys of the upper James and Rappahannock by emigrants from all parts of Tidewater.

The spirit of practical adventure which had brought these people across a wide and turbulent ocean remained even after their first settlement. The lure of the westward movement never really subsided in their hearts. The wandering spirit was always ready to take fire; and in no breast was this susceptibility stronger than in that of the yeoman. His possessions were not large enough to hold him always to the little homestead which he had carved out of the forest for himself and his family. He was sanguine that he would be able to gain more elsewhere, and as there was nothing, while his physical strength lasted, to tramel his feet, he often abandoned the old place and went in search of a new.

His disposition to do this had been increased by a practical evil with which he had had to contend as constantly as the wealthiest planter. There were no artificial manures in use in that age. When a field showed symptons of exhaustion, another, fitted to serve the same purpose, had to be carved out of the forest. A new and fresh soil was essential to the production of tobacco if that production was to be made highly profitable. A planter of large means was always able to provide against the expected loss of fertility by adding a wide area of woodland to his estate, but the yeoman was only able to add a mere fringe of forest to the narrow area which he had under cultivation. When this fringe had been used up, the impulse to move on and to sue out a new patent was naturally very strong.

In the beginning, when the Colony was as yet confined within narrow borders, these yeoman emigrants were satisfied to halt at no great distance away; but during the first part of the eighteenth century, when so much of the outlying soil was held by wealthy planters in vast tracts of forest, they were forced to find new dwelling places, in many cases, in the northern or southern colonies. The great majority of this class, however, either remained in their old homes in Virginia or settled again somewhere within its boundaries, and in time, became slave-holders themselves in a very small way. It was natural enough that they should, in order to secure assistance in the fields, follow the example of their wealthier neighbors by buying a slave or two. The fact that the small landowner had attached such a slave to his little plantation did not make him different in spirit from his yeoman father of the previous century, who had relied upon his own horny hands alone for the production of his crops.

As a matter of fact, in the course of the eighteenth century, the bulk of the slaves in most of the counties belonged to the smaller planters, and the majority of these petty proprietors owned but one, two, or three at the most. In every community, the greater proportion of the plantations were limited in area. In 1704, three of every four landowners were in possession of estates which continued less than five hundred acres, and of the three the majority owned less than one hundred acres.

Virginia, during the first part of the eighteenth century, was made up of plantations practically entirely. The influences existing in the seventeenth had, as we have already pointed out, discouraged the building, not only of towns, but even of hamlets. In vain, the English Government had endeavored by every means at its disposal to stimulate the growth of little urban communities in the Colony. Thus, each county at one time had been instructed to erect a specified number of houses at Jamestown; these houses were certainly built in part, if not in whole; but no persons came forward to occupy even those that were in condition to receive owners or tenants. Similar laws were passed at a later date, but equally without any practical result. The

General Assembly knew that these successive Acts would fail
to accomplish the purpose in view, but they felt constrained,
under injunctions from England, as announced by the Governor,
to, at least, appear to confirm to the order.

The influences most hostile to town building in the Colony
were the same in both centuries.   In the first place, there was in
the tidewater counties at least but one form of profitable employment in each community, namely, the culture of tobacco.
The production of that commodity, as we have already mentioned, encouraged, not the concentration of population, but its
dispersal over an ever-increasing width of ground.   The reason
at the bottom of this fact was the increasing need of virgin soil
to bring forth tobacco in perfection.   As the confines of the
plantations, both great and small, spread out, the inhabited
space naturally broadened instead of contracting.

There can be no doubt too, that, as the years passed, the
taste of the people came more and more reconciled to country life
in its simplest and most independent form.   In that form, it was
to be perceived everywhere in the Colony; and generation after
generation, each, in their turn, having unconsciously imbibed
its spirit, were even more disinclined than their fathers to lead
any other existence.   The town had no charm for them in the
mass.   During the eighteenth century only persons who had
emigrated from England had, in reality, ever seen a large town.
There were thousands of families in the Colony in both centuries
who had no real conception of such a community beyond the size
of Jamestown or Williamsburg.

But there was a stronger influence than an inherited liking
for country life to discourage the growth even of villages in Virginia in the early and middle colonial age.   With ocean-going
vessels anchoring up and down the different rivers at the
wharves of the planters, in order to supply them with all the
articles of manufacture which they needed, and with a store at
every cross-roads also, why should they have felt the want of
other distributing centers of even superior utility?   Even if a

center of this kind had existed in every county, it would have been too far off to subserve the convenience of the great majority of purchasers in the contiguous districts.

The wealth of Virginia, by the middle of the eighteenth century, swelled to such a volume that several places, which were mere trading posts during the previous century, began to reveal a decided tendency to expand to the dimensions of small towns, which gave them some industrial and commercial importance. Williamsburg, as the capital, was the first of these. It was carved out of the wilderness with the calculated precision which marked, in our modern age, the survey for the City of Washington in our own country and Canbarra in Australia. The State House, the Governor's Palace, the College, the Prison, were all handsome buildings. Numerous inns had been erected because here the General Assembly convened; but at a later period, the wealthy gentry added to the existing structures, houses of their own for winter residences. There were also a number of stores, which provided, like the country stores of the same period, a great variety and quantity of merchandise for sale.

In 1722, Williamsburg, was incorporated with all the rights and privileges of a city charter. It was empowered to hold market twice a week, and it also possessed a hustings court. Its first manufacturing enterprise seems to have been the paper mill erected in 1744 by William Parks, who, eight years before, had issued the first number of the *Virginia Gazette,* a weekly publication. By this time, this town was the center of the dominant business interests of the Colony, for the regulation of which the merchants there had formed what was named the Cape Company. In 1759, the General Assembly authorized a recently organized society there to offer bounties to any one who could prove that he had made valuable discoveries and improvements for the promotion of manufacturers. This included the production of fine wines, among other native commodities. The resolutions of the patriots interdicting the purchase of British goods encouraged manufacturing enterprises in the little capital. A factory was built there for the weaving of woolen and linen cloth, and also one for the construction of carriages. There was a third for the manufacture of wigs, and a fourth for the making of snuff.

Norfolk was incorporated in 1736, and at the beginning of the Revolution was the most important port in the Colony. It carried on a large trade with the West Indies in the tropical products of those islands, especially in sugar, molasses, and rum. Apparently, even as late as 1775, it possessed no manufacturers in the higher sense of the word, although the home of numerous mechanics.

Richmond enjoyed the trade incident to its situation at the head of tidewater. Petersburg was in somewhat the same position, but it also was too small a center of population to have yet acquired any importance beyond its distribution of plantation supplies in the nearest southside communities; and this was true of the other small towns, like Alexandria, Fredericksburg, Staunton, Winchester and Lynchburg.

CHAPTER V

SOCIAL FEATURES

Did the social life of Virginia in the eighteenth century differ essentially from the social life of the seventeenth at its highest mark? If so, in what details? If we omit from view the German and Scotch-Irish populations in the Valley, which, previous to the Revolution, exerted no real social influence upon the communities east of the Blue Ridge, the Virginia of the period that followed 1700 was only distinguishable from the Virginia of the period which preceded that year by two conditions of importance,—first, the possession of larger wealth, and second, the substitution of the negro slave for the white indentured servant.

The enjoyment of increased resources caused no alteration in the social spirit of the community beyond making possible a greater display of fortune by a greater number of planters. These erected more spacious and imposing mansions; they purchased a more notable quantity of household furniture, and plate; they were more lavish and splendid in their dress on fine occasions; they owned more coaches, more thoroughbred horses for the saddle, more herds of cattle and hogs, and more flocks of sheep. In short, the existence of greater affluence disclosed itself on every side of the social life of the people who occupied the highest position in each community.

The simplicity in which the fathers of these landowners had, with few exceptions, passed their lives, had necessarily been modified in the lives of the sons by the wealth which time had brought; but below the surface there could not have been any

very important change in the springs that gave character to the
social life of the two centuries respectively.

Which were the families that are most intimately associated
in history with the social distinction of the eighteenth century?
They were the Armisteads, Banisters, Bassetts, Blands, Bollings,
Beverleys, Burwells, Byrds, Carys, Corbins, Carters, Claibornes,
Custises, Fauntleroys, Fitzhughs, Harrisons, Lees, Lightfoots,

CARTER'S GROVE

Ludwells, Moseleys, Masons, Pages, Peytons, Randolphs, Robinsons, Scarboroughs, Spencers, Washingtons, and Wormeleys.
But there was not one of these conspicuous families which was
not also prominently identified with the social life of the seventeenth century.

The difference between the social life of that century and the
social life of the eighteenth was the difference between the home
in which John Carter resided, and Shirley, the home of his

immediate descendants; between the home in which the elder Byrd spent the latter part of his life, and Westover, the seat of his accomplished son. The same parallel could be extended to the seventeenth century homes of the Harrisons, Lees, Bassetts, Pages, and others in the list as compared with Brandon, Stratford, Eltham, Rosewell, and the other mansions in which they lived in the eighteenth. The roofs over their heads were more lofty in height and more spacious in breadth than those which rose over the heads of their ancestors half a century before. There was also a more striking display of plate on their sideboards, a larger attendance of servants at their meals, a more delightful variety of wines, perhaps, on their tables, and more gilt on their coaches; in short, more of those *indicia* which have accompanied wealth in all ages. But the social spirit of these famous families, so influential and so prominent in both centuries, remained equally true in each to the social traditions of their English descent. There was wealth in their possession in the seventeenth century as well as in the eighteenth.

By the eighteenth, there had been time enough for the evolution of a community that was composed entirely of persons of Virginian birth. The leading figures in the social life of the previous century had been born in England; had been educated in English schools; had been religiously trained under the influence of the English church; and had drunk in unconsciously all the various ideas and principles that governed English society. They brought these ideas and these principles to Virginia, and without any set determination or calculation, they wove every one of them into the social fabric of the Colony. It was a thoroughly English community which they founded in the valleys of the Powhatan, the Pamumkey, the Rappahannock, and the Potomac. There arose there no opposing influences emanating from any other people close at hand to modify the English characteristics, even if the tenacity and conservatism of the race had not made it really impossible to do so.

The new conditions confronting the settlers undoubtedly had its effect on the development of the social life of the colonists,

LOWER BRANDON

UPPER BRANDON

but not to a degree to alter substantially the English inherited tendencies of the community. England never ceased to be spoken of by them as "home"; and it was to England that they continued to look in spite of passing gusts of bad feeling. The Mother Country remained the model for law, for government, for society, in the eyes of all her transplanted sons of the seventeenth century. This loyalty, especially the loyalty to the race's social standards, descended to their posterity in the next century, and if increased wealth brought anything more than a superficial change, it was a change wrought by the ability which such affluence gave them to show a more impressive fidelity to the customs and principles of their fathers.

Was any alteration produced by the substitution of the slave for the indentured servant? Indentured service was, in reality, a form of slavery. In spirit, it was difficult to distinguish between the two. The servant, during the period of his contract, was as absolutely under the master's control as the slave. He performed all the tasks of the master's house, and all the labor of the master's field, with the same submissiveness as if he too were a bondsman for life.

Had not a single African been imported into Virginia in the course of either the seventeenth or the eighteenth century, the framework of its social life would not have swerved from the line which it really followed, provided that the influx of English indentured servants had continued uninterrupted. The social influence of the one institution was similiar to the social influence of the other,—a directing master at the top, and a dependent and obedient servant or slave at the bottom. The servant could be sold during his term; the slave could be sold during his life; but in both cases each was a piece of property like a horse or an ox.

Undoubtedly, there was, in the mass, a closer social tie between the master and the slave than between the master and the servant. The servant knew that the tie was temporary; the slave knew that it was permanent; and so did the master in each case. This was a social influence and not an economic one, and apart from greater fortunes, may have had its effect in making the social life of the Colony more baronial in spirit in the eighteenth century than in the seventeenth.

But this more imposing character would have come with increased wealth even if that wealth had continued to be produced almost entirely by indentured servants. The great estates in land in the course of both centuries, supported by the recollection of high social position in the Mother Country before emigration, were the real pillar that upheld the aristocratic tendencies of the foremost families of the Colony; and these tendencies would have arisen even if the slaves had been too small in number to displace the indentured servants. There were few negroes listed among the laborers of the Colony previous to 1700, and yet in every county after the middle of the seventeenth century, there was to be found the germ of that aristocratic society which was to reach its full flower during the following century.

If we consider more in detail the characteristics of the social life of the eighteenth century, we soon discover their essential identity with the characteristics of the social life of the seventeenth. One of the most striking features of the eighteenth was the extraordinary closeness of the domestic bonds. During several generations, members of the highest class of planters had been intermarrying until, by the middle of the eighteenth century, there was not a family of prominence in the Colony who could not claim the tie of blood or marriage with every other family of the same social eminence. A son or daughter of a distinguished household like the Byrds was apt to have found a wife or husband at Sabine Hall, Brandon, Mount Airy, Shirley or Stratford. A Carter or a Beverley, a Harrison or a Wormeley, a Bland or a Corbin were equally certain to have sought a bride or groom under the same roofs. There was a constant interchange of partners for life in these stately homes, one after another, until the connection became so intricate that only a skilful genealogist could unravel it.

John Randolph described precisely the result of this consanguinity among the principal families when he compared them to a bundle of fishhooks: if you picked up one, he said, you picked up all.

The Colony was so remote from other communities along the Atlantic, and so cut off by the ocean from England, that marriages between Virginians and persons residing beyond the Colony's borders rarely took place during that period. There were only a few instances of intermarriage with English women living in their own land, and those only occurred, because, as in the case of the second Byrd, the young Virginian was visting the Mother Country on business, or had entered college there for the completion of his education. Instances of marriage with persons of the other Colonies were not unknown, as the third William Byrd's choice of a Willing of Philadelphia disclosed, but such alliances were so exceptional as to give them a peculiar prominence in the history of a Virginian family of that day.

It was no smooth journey for a lover from Sabine Hall to find his way to Westover, or from Westover to Mount Airy, or from any one of those famous homes to any other. There were broad rivers to cross and there were wide forests to traverse. The only reliable means of transportation was the horse, and but for the hospitality of the people along the route, the impatient traveller would have to camp out at night in the woods. But to have looked for a wife or husband in New England would have been accompanied by more difficulties of passage in the eighteenth century than a search for a partner for life as far away as Australia would be in our own times. England was made accessible, it is true, by the regular merchantmen engaged in the tobacco trade, but the proportion of young Virginians who undertook the voyage even once was small, indeed.

There were two conspicious results of these continued intermarriages within the borders of the Colony without infusion of blood from without: first, they confirmed and increased the already intense fondness for all things Virginian; and second, they encouraged and strengthened loyalty to ties of kinship, not only within the sphere of the separate family itself, but also so far outside that family as to take in the entire circle of blood relationships. All degrees of cousinship were cheerfully and spontaneously recognized. A single drop of blood in common raised a claim that never failed to make its appeal.

This attitude gave a very kindly flavor to the intercourse of all the families within the same circle. Hospitality, stimulated by this spirit, became not simply a conventional duty, but a source of unaffected pleasure and happiness. The remoteness of the situation of so many colonial homes of the eighteenth century made the presence of a guest all the more highly relished. He brought with him the latest political news and the latest social gossip, and since all the principal families, as we have mentioned, were related to each other, this gossip carried a deeper interest than if it had been retailed about far off persons only known by reputation to the listeners.

Visitors often came for a day and spent a week, or for a week and passed a month, or for a month and remained a year. And some individuals are known never to have departed,—and that too with the family's approval,—until they were borne out of the house in death, and interred in the neighboring flower garden close to the graves of the family's ancestors.

One result of this hospitable spirit, this spirit which sought so successfully to brighten the life within the domestic walls, was a desire for the presence of a large group of children under every roof. The Virginian home of the eighteenth century, as of the seventeenth, was noisy with playing and shouting children of every age. The high esteem in which matrimony was held by the men and women of that day was indicated by their apparently irresistible disposition to remarry when death had broken the matrimonial bond. Instances of a fourth marriage were not unknown. Indeed, three at least, with offsprings in proportion, were far from uncommon in the history of that period.

It was not an idle life which the mistress of the household led. As the husband was busy with the management of the plantation, so the wife was employed in directing the affairs of the home. The fact that she possessed many servants who had been trained to every branch of the household work, was not accepted by her as an excuse for neglecting its careful supervision. In addition to the ordinary domestic duties which arose every day, with only the variation made necessary by the season, there were the clothes for the slaves to be made under her eye, the dairy to be overlooked, the garden and grounds to be inspected, the poultry to be fed, and the raw contents of the smoke house to be cured.

She also gave the first lessons in spelling, reading, and arithmetic to the young children, and she often acted, and with skill too, as the family doctor, an accomplishment always needed in a country side where the only physician perhaps practiced over an area of twenty or thirty miles.

One of the features in which the social life of the eighteenth century excelled that of the seventeenth was to be found in the superior methods of travelling on land. We have seen that, in passing from one place to another, previous to 1700, the boat was the usual means of conveyance. All the important estates were situated on the banks of streams of sufficient depth to allow even a seagoing vessel to navigate them with ease. The wide reaches which these waters offered to rowing or sailing were entirely without any obstruction, unless caused by sudden tempests, which raised the waves sometimes to menacing heights.

When members of a family on the James wished to visit their friends who resided in a mansion standing on the same side of the river, they could arrive at their destination more comfortably and perhaps, more rapidly in a boat than on horseback; and this was equally true when the inmates of a house on the Rappahannock started to call on some family whose seat stood near the margin of the same stream. The situation was precisely the same on the York and the Potomac; and so too in counties like Gloucester, which, all along its boundaries on the side of the Bay, was broken by the mouths of salt water creeks.

Perhaps, some of the happiest hours of the people of the entire Colonial age were passed on the water in these exhilarating expeditions from house to house. The young men came to learn how to manage a sail-boat with the skill of experts, and were ready at any hour of the day or night to face the chances of a storm or a calm; and equally dexterous and confident were the indentured servants or slaves who had been picked out to direct these crafts.

This means of traversing ground was, perhaps, in more common use in the seventeenth century than in the eighteenth; and so were the riding horse, for, however full of ruts and mud holes the road might be, a horse could always pursue his way along it without difficulty or delay. During the services in the parish church on Sunday, whether in the one century or in the other, a great number of horses were always found tied to the swinging limbs of the surrounding trees. Even the women used them, for they possessed a comfortable seat in the pillion which was attached to most of the saddles.

It was not until the eighteenth century had made good progress that vehicles of different kinds began to offer a brave show, not only in the church-yards, but also at the musters and balls, or wherever else the families of social distinction assembled on either public or private occasions. This fact was not due to any improvement in the condition of the highways,—the roads of the eighteenth century were hardly superior to those of the seventeenth. It was really due to the possession of larger wealth by the principal landowners, for, as this wealth increased, and became more widely distributed, the disposition of the families who made pretension to fashion to imitate their English kin who were in the enjoyment of equal fortunes, grew more constant and conspicuous. As early as 1724, Hugh Jones

records that "most people of any note in Williamsburg had a
coach, chariot, berlin, or chaise." Twenty-two years afterwards, a second English traveller was so much impressed by the
number of wheeled conveyances to be seen in the town that he
could only describe the spectacle with the word "prodigious";
and Yorktown was equally remarkable in the displays of carriages.

These carriages were not confined to the streets of the little
town. They were to be found in the stable-sheds of all the
large plantation mansions. Many of those so noticeable in Williamsburg belonged to wealthy families who passed their winters there during the sessions of the General Assembly.

The large coaches were lumbering in their movements, and
they were, in fact, only able to advance at all at a fairly reasonable speed through the vigor of the six horses which were
always harnessed to them. Three servants,—the driver, pos-
tilion, and footman,—accompanied each of these coaches on
formal occasions, and possibly lent a shoulder when the wheels
sank too deeply into the sand or mud. An Englishman of distinction, who visited Virginia in 1764, mentioned the fact that
the average coach could cover a distance of nine miles an hour,
and that, not infrequently, a guest would travel sixty miles
by this means and at this rate, in order to be present at a dinner-
party on a friend's plantation. It was to be expected that this
stranger would be impressed by the excellence of the carriage-
horses, for, with so heavy and constant a draught on their
strength, only the hardiest specimens could have endured the tax.

But not all the vehicles were of these large dimensions. The
chair, with a single horse harnessed to it between the shafts,
was generally used by professional men, like doctors, lawyers,
and clergymen, whose engagements required them to travel with
speed. The chaise, with two horses only in the traces, was also
to be seen; and so were the calash and the phaeton. The wealthy
planter ordinarily possessed a conveyance of each of these several kinds.

Benjamin Harrison

Governor Spotswood bequeathed to his family a coach, chariot, and chaise; Wilson Cary, a coach, post-chariot, and chair; and Benjamin Harrison, a chair, coach, and chariot, and also six horses.   These may be mentioned as typical instances of the testamentary gifts of this nature in the eighteenth century. All, doubtless, were painted in brilliant tints, of which yellow and pea green appear to have been the most popular.   The family's armorial bearings were invariably stamped on the panels of the doors.   The cost of the handsomest coaches ran as high as two hundred and sixty pounds sterling, a very large sum in that age.

There is an additional detail in which the wealthy planters of the eighteenth century adopted a habit different from that of their fathers in the seventeenth.   No evidence exists that the sessions of the General Assembly during the latter century allured to Jamestown families who were seeking a temporary social change in the current of their plantation lives.   The Burgesses went thither accompanied by their body servants, but not by their wives and daughters.   While the little town, apart from its few public buildings, was composed almost entirely of inns or ordinaries,—as the taverns were known in those times,—there does not seem to have been any structure,—even among these,— that was adapted to handsome entertainments.   So far from there being any residences in the town reserved for occupation in winter alone, there were few, independently of the inns, designed for use throughtout the year.   Not even Governor Berkeley himself, a man with a keen taste for social recreations, spent any part of each year at Jamestown, unless he was drawn there by the business of the General Assembly.   His days, when that body was not in session, were passed at Green Spring, which was situated not far from the Capitol.   Howard, we are told, became a frequent guest at Rosegill, whenever the press of public affairs allowed him to go so far afield.

Possibly, the more or less miasmatic air of the region contiguous to Jamestown was the reason in part why that town never obtained any social distinction independently of its political character. Williamsburg had been built on a far more salubrious site, and it also became the capital of the Colony at a period when wealth was rapidly increasing in volume under the influence of more favorable political conditions both in Virginia and England. This combination was the chief explanation of the fact that the new seat of government assumed in time the aspect of the social as well as the political center of the Colony at large.

The erection of the College there was probably not without its effect in drawing thither for temporary residence families of position who counted sons in their membership. Certainly that institution was looked upon with pride by the leading planters, and its commencements were always attended by a concourse of men of that rank. Its existence there could not have failed to give a permanent distinction to the place, apart from its association with the General Court and the General Assembly.

There is no indication that the habit which sprang up of spending several months at Williamsburg in the course of the winter extended beyond the circle of the wealthiest citizens of the country districts. Some of these must have found accommodation in the best of the inns; but there were also a considerable number who went so far as to build dwelling-houses there for their own occupation at the height of the season. As their wealth augmented, their families desired more keenly than ever to follow more and more closely the course of English fashion. This spirit was seen in their purchase of the dress that was most popular in the gay world of London; in their acquisition of the smartest chariots and chaises that could be imported; and in their display of a still larger quantity of beautiful plate on their sideboards and tables. They noted with keen interest the publication of the latest English literature, whether it was a satire by Swift, an essay by Addison, or a philosophical poem by Pope. It was more natural still that they should have kept themselves conversant with all the reported gossip of the London drawing rooms.

The next step was to imitate the London season by establishing a season of their own at their little capital between the York and the James. It is the testimony of more than one traveller of that day that the assemblages which they had attended at Williamsburg compared with conspicuous equality with entertainments of the same kind at which they had been present in the best social circles of England. The dress was as fashionable; the manners as polished; the spirit of gayety as hearty and yet as restrained. Ball after ball, musical concert after musical concert, theatrical performance after theatrical performance, followed each other in rapid and delightful sequence. Balls and musical concerts also occurred with frequency in the social life of the county neighborhoods, but it was only at Williamsburg that a play by skilful and trained actors was to be seen and enjoyed.

As early as 1702, "A Practical Colloquy" was performed before the Governor; and the taste for the drama grew so fast, after this event, that, in 1716, a playhouse, the first to be built in America, was erected by a local merchant, who promised to provide English actors, scenery, and music for the performance. These performances were to be both comic and tragic. But the venture was, perhaps, too ambitious for the time to be successful. The playhouse, however, survived, and on its boards many dramas were acted. Later, the structure was considered unsuitable for its purpose, and another one was erected in its place, which opened with the tragedy of Richard III. In 1752, a company from London presented a series of plays, which included *Othello* and the *Merchant of Venice*. This troupe remained in Virginia for a period of nine months.

The season of 1768 was long remembered in Williamsburg for the numerous handsome balls at the Governor's Palace and in the houses of the wealthy citizens, both permanent and temporary, and for the theatrical performances offered by trained actors from London. These performances began at six in the evening, and lasted to a late hour owing to the audience's demand for a comedy or a pantomime after the serious drama had ended. A play was presented every night in the season.

The gay and even brilliant lives of the members of the distinguished circle which annually enjoyed all these pleasures in the little capital of Wiliamsburg were in strong contrast to the lives of the small planters of Eastern Virginia, who rarely went further from their homes than the muster-field or the courthouse. But they too possessed their own amusements and recreations.

Still sharper was the contrast with the habits and customs of the quiet and religious German population beyond the Blue Ridge. That population as a whole avoided, it was said, "fashionable and gaudy attire," they practiced temperance in the use of liquor; they abhorred slavery; they shrank from war; they built homes for shelter and not for show; they valued thrift, and pursued it with unswerving persistence; they retired to bed at an early hour; they rose before dawn; they did all their own household work; they manufactured their own clothes; they fed their own livestock; and they forged their own nails.

In short, their existence was laborious, their recreations limited, their spirit subdued. The Bible, the hymn-book and the almanac not infrequently embraced all the volumes on their shelves. Their regard for a life apparently so narrow and so dry lay in the earnestness of their spiritual hopes; in the uprightness of their conduct; in the skilfulness of their tillage; and in the abundant prosperity which resulted from their sober industry. There were men of ability and culture among them, especially among their clergy, but the mass were content to work the ground.

As the first Scotch-Irish settlers had come from large communities of their own stock in the British Islands, they were naturally disposed to maintain all the ingrained habits of their ancient race. Indeed, in every department of their lives, they showed their unrelaxed regard for all those conventionalities

which they had known in the old environment. Their number
enabled them to do this. This conservatism, however, did not
apply to their language. At first, they retained the vernacular
speech of Ulster, but this disappeared gradually in their new
situation, just as the French tongue ceased in time to be used by
the Huguenots in the community seated at Manakin. In the way
of clothing, the hunting shirt and leggins apparently were only
worn in the Valley by persons whose days were passed in threading the forests beyond the settled area, or who took part in
guarding the frontier. Within the bounds of Rockbridge and
Augusta, there is no reason to think that there was a woodland
manner of dressing which would have attracted startled attention on the streets of Philadelphia, the most polished American
city of that period. It is even noted by one historian of the
Scotch-Irish people in Rockbridge that there resided on Jack-
son's River, which was a very remote spot in those times, a man
who wore a wig and a stock and buckle.

In the county inventories there are entries of silver buttons,
silk bonnets, and lawn handkerchiefs. It was asserted of one
well known citizen of that day that, "he wore short breeches
buttoned and buckled at the knee, long stockings, large shoes,
with heavy silver buckles, a dress-coat rounded in front, and
with its many buttons on one side only and a standing collar."
His cocked hat was three-sided and broad in the brim, and his
riding boots reached nearly to his knees.

CHAPTER VI

POLITICAL SPIRIT

The most conspicuous political characteristic of the Virginians during the interval between 1700 and the outburst of the Revolution was the clear understanding which they had of their rights as citizens. In no single particular was this characteristic so distinctly displayed as in their opposition to every form of taxation to which their consent had not, through their repretives, been formally given. This attitude of jealousy revealed itself early in the history of the community. By the terms of the original charter, the first colonists were granted all "the liberties, franchises, and immunities of English subjects." So far as these were concerned, it was as if the early settlers had not left their native shores behind. It is true that, in the actual working of the colonial system in the beginning, the inhabitants of Jamestown enjoyed no freedom of life at all. They were ruled under martial law and were deprived of the right to acquire a fee-simple title to the soil. But there was no intention to reduce them to a kind of serfdom any longer than the difficulties of the abnormal situation in which they stood required.

During the first years, the inhabitants of Jamestown were in the position of men who occupied a besieged fort; military discipline was necessary to the preservation of the garrison; but, by 1619, the demand for this discipline was supposed to have passed, although the massacre of 1622 revealed that it had not really done so. In the course of that year, the General Assembly, under the power granted by the London Company, convened; men were now building homes on plantations of their own;

389

numerous local courts, in addition to the General Court, were soon to be sitting; divisions into district corporations had taken place; and the community as a whole was organized on the basis of the system that was to continue throughout the colonial period.

The principle involved in the summoning of the first Assembly was of the most vital importance, for it signified that, in the renewed right to choose their own representatives, the people in Virginia were again in the possession of that great privilege of citizenship, which they had enjoyed in England, and which was expressly reserved by charter for exercise by them after their removal oversea. This right to elect was valued, not simply as a proof of the individual's political importance, but as a means of protection against arbitrary tax burdens. The Englishman at home in his own island had always been singularly clear sighted in his comprehension of the real meaning of taxation. The right to tax, as he had learned from history and his own experience, was the power to destroy. Carried too far, it was merely robbery in a veiled form, but it was not the less damaging for that reason to the interests of the sufferer. The Englishman's attitude became at once suspicious whenever the question of imposing this burden under a new guise arose, and he was always tenacious of his claim that he could only be required to pay by the action of his own public assembly chosen by the voice of himself and his fellows.

Fourteen years had barely passed after the foundation of Jamestown when the Virginians, in their General Assembly, following the example set by their English fathers, asserted for the first time in the Western Hemisphere the principle that there could be no legal taxation without the consent of the representatives of the people. The Governor might be the representative of the King, but not even that fact could invest him with the right of imposing a penny for the purpose of taxation. This right belonged to the Burgesses, independently of the King himself. The principle was solemnly reaffirmed by an Act passed in 1642, about the time of Berkeley's first accession to the office of Governor.

It was clearly stipulated in the Articles of Surrender to Parliament that the General Assembly should continue to possess and exercise the "sole right of laying any tax, custom, or imposition on the people of Virginia"; and this right seems to have suffered no interruption through Cromwell's Government.

In 1674, the agents of the Colony in London, who were endeavoring to obtain a charter which would protect it from future royal grants, distinctly asserted as a fact that no king had attempted to tax the inhabitants of Virginia without their approval announced in the most public way by their General Assembly. So sensitive, indeed, were the people on the subject of taxation without their consent, that they often took exception to what they considered to be an indirect tax. When, for instance, it was decided to establish a postal service in the Colony during Governor Spotswood's administration, popular opposition to the project was emphatically expressed, on the ground that the requirement of payment of postage was designed as an indirect means of taxing the people.

Not the slightest approach to the independent exercise of this power of taxation by the Governor and Council was tolerated, although it would have saved a large sum, during many years, by making the coming together of the General Assembly unnecessary. However pressing the demand for economy might be, it never influenced that body to postpone a session at Jamestown. The utmost limit to which the General Assembly is known to have gone in colonial times was to direct the Governor and Council to impose a definite tax subject to certain restrictions laid down beforehand by the Burgesses, with whom all tax bills originated. But such an incident was so rare that it did not amount to an exception,—especially as the exercise of the authority so given made the Governor and Council simply ordinary fiscal agents, without power to exceed their instructions.

Spotswood complained in 1731 that the General Assembly at that time was so unreasonable in maintaining their claim to be the fountain head of taxation that they were indisposed to make appropriations even for necessary purposes, simply because they had been urged to do so by the Governor, with impatience. Such an attitude they considered to be an interference with their right to lay or not to lay taxes just as they should decide to be best. The Governor of the eighteenth century, with the possible exception of Spotswood himself, were shrewd enough to recognize the strength of the convictions which controlled the Burgesses on their relation to this subject; and, in consequence, the cause of so much friction during the previous century rarely afterwards came into play on either side.

Such friction, however, did arise in connection with Dinwiddie when he announced that a pistole would be charged for every patent which should be issued thereafter. This pistole, small amount as it was, was taken by the House of Burgesses to be an indirect tax of a more serious character than the charge for postage under the postage law which was in force during Spotswood's administration. They protested against this addition to the expense of suing out these documents; and again asserted the "rights of the people were so secured by law that they could not be deprived of the least part of their property but by their own consent." They were not satisfied with this expression of their indignation. "Whoever shall hereafter pay a pistole as a fee to the Governor for the use of the seal to the patents for lands," they declared, "shall be deemed a betrayer of the rights and privileges of the people."

Such was the spirit of the Virginians in the eighteenth century in their attitude towards all violations of their rights by the representatives of the King.

The time was soon to arrive when they were to be called upon to confront the King himself in a struggle over the same issue. This struggle was a far more serious one than the conflicts which had so often arisen with Governors and Councils in the course of the previous periods in colonial history. However acrid and protracted these latter may have been, the Burgesses were never suspected of disloyalty or treason on account of their stubborness in upholding what they very properly looked upon as their rights. Neither King nor Parliament was involved in these legislative fights. As a matter of fact, the charge of even mild and indirect antagonism to them could not be justly laid against the Lower Chamber of the Assembly at any time throughout that long interval. Not even during the supremacy of Nathaniel Bacon, perilously near as he apparently brought the Colony to the brink of disloyalty to the English Government, was there any real hostility to the King or to Parliament. With the passage, however, of the famous Two Penny Act in 1755, the train was set for a series of events in opposition to both that was not to end until allegiance to the throne and obedience to Parliament had been completely destroyed.

During the progress of these events, there rose to view three men who were to win lasting renown for the great parts which they were destined to play: first, Patrick Henry, the voice of the Revolution; second, Thomas Jefferson, the pen; and third, George Washington, the sword. Henry was the morning star of the revolt; and he ascended from the horizon to the zenith of the political skies with the abruptness and brilliancy of a meteor.

By the terms of the Two Penny Act, every one who had a pecuniary obligation to meet was authorized to settle it at the rate of sixteen shillings, eight pence, for each one hundred pounds of tobacco which the debt included. A significant feature of the law was the fact that it contained no provision for suspension until the royal approval had arrived. On the contrary, it was to become effective immediately. No section of the community offered any objection to the new law except the clergy, who, by the Act of 1696, had been allowed sixteen thousand pounds of tobacco in payment of their annual salaries. The leaf at that time was valued at ten shillings the hundred pounds as compared with two pence the pound sixty years afterwards.

The Act fixing the clergy's remuneration at sixteen thousand pounds was readopted in 1748. As it again received the royal approval, it could not be repealed by the General Assembly except with the consent of the King. But, as we have just mentioned, the Assembly did revoke it in 1756 without any provision for suspension until this consent had been obtained. The clergymen refused to accept the measure as final because, by commuting their salaries in money, it reduced substantially the value of their stipend as calculated in tobacco; but, by 1677, the two pence

Fran: Fauquier

AUTOGRAPH OF FRANCIS FAUQUIER

a pound at which their sixteen thousand pounds of tobacco were rated had come to be the real value of the commodity. Their opposition, in consequence, quietly died out for the time being.

In 1758, Fauquier took the place of Dinwiddie, and, in the course of that year, a second Two Penny Act was passed by the General Assembly. This like the first, had no provision for suspension until the King had announced his approval. The clergy, again discontented with the prospect of a depreciated salary by estimating it in money, formally complained to Fauquier, and urged him to exercise his right of veto, but the Governor, who was a man of humor, refused in words that were distinctly suggestive of a jest.

The clergy, having held a convention for consultation, decided to send an emissary to London to submit an appeal to the King in person. At once the question arose by implication: was there some other power which possessed a higher right than the General Assembly to pass upon the justice of a local tax law?

This was the momentous issue now raised, and for the first time in colonial history, the Virginians found themselves directly confronting the throne in a matter of this nature.

In August, 1759, the King on the advice of the Board of Trade, formally disallowed the Acts of both 1755 and 1758, and soon afterwards Mr. Camm, the clergy's agent in England, instructed his attorney in Virginia to enter suit for his salary. A vigorous defense of their action was now undertaken by the General Assembly, and this was supplemented by a pamphlet written by Colonel Richard Bland, which declared that "the safety of the people was the supreme law"; and that this maxim sometimes justified a departure from the text of the King's instructions to a Governor. Nevertheless, the royal order was carried out, but its effect was small, as the Two Penny Act had now expired by limitation.

A number of clergymen followed Mr. Camm's example, and brought suit for the payment of their salaries on the basis of the then market value of sixteen thousand pounds of tobacco, which was still higher than the two pence which had been prescribed by the Assembly. One of these clergymen was James Maury. The Court decided in his favor, on the ground that the Two Penny Act was "null and void"; but the jury when summoned to assess the damages, fixed them at one penny, a verdict grossly inadequate in the amount granted.

One of the counsel for the defense was Patrick Henry, a young lawyer without any distinction until he proved in this case that he possessed extraordinary boldness and eloquence. The salient feature of his speech was the assertion that "the King, by taking upon himself to disallow the Act of the Governor and Assembly, had forfeited all right of obedience heretofore due from his subjects in Virginia." This was a more open and emphatic defiance of the royal authority than the words of Colonel Bland's pamphlet justifying disregard of the royal instructions to Governors, if plainly repugnant to the public welfare.

The first most notable event that followed Henry's speech was the publication of a second pamphlet by Colonel Bland, in which he expressed the opinion that "any law respecting our internal policy which may hereafter be imposed upon us by Act of Parliament is arbitrary and may be opposed." Laws for the regulation of trade were exempted from this condemnation, but not taxes for purposes of revenue, whether laid directly upon the Colony in the form of a stamp duty or indirectly in the form of import duties.

In 1764, the British Parliament passed the famous Stamp Act. This measure placed that body in the position of imposing an internal tax on the Colonists. This was the consummation of what had been expected since the royal disallowance of the Two Penny Act. It was very generally felt by the Virginians that the principle of the new law was full of menace to their interests, however plausible might be the justification for it which was given by the British Government when it was adopted. All that had been apprehended during so many generations by the people in the way of taxation without their own consent was apparently brought to a head by the imposition of this tax by the English authorities beyond the Atlantic.

It is quite possible that the spirit of opposition would not have gone beyond the adoption of resolutions in favor of non-importation and local manufacturers, as measures of retaliation, had not the bold and uncompromising spirit of one man stepped in to scatter to the winds the policy of only passive resistance. This man was Patrick Henry. We have seen with what courage he censured the royal interference with the enforcement of the Two Penny Act. But a more sinister question than that was now to come up for settlement: the question of Parliament's right to lay an internal tax on the people of all the Colonies.

Henry was, at this time, a member of the House of Burgesses. This body understood the seriousness of the crisis, but they decided to act patiently and conservatively, under the influence of the anticipation that the English merchants, irritated by the loss of trade, would compel the revocation of the Stamp Act. In vain Henry waited for one of the older leaders of the Assembly to rise and protest against that Act. None did so, and delaying no longer, he submitted five resolutions, which asserted in unequivocal language that the people of Virginia were under no obligation to pay any taxes that had not received the approval of their own General Assembly; and he supported these resolutions with a speech that, near the end, was so defiant that it was interrupted with cries of treason all over the House.

The fifth of the series was so outspoken that, after its adoption, it was expunged from the minutes. The significance of Henry's action, however, was not lost, and the substance of his fearless words was soon reported in all the Colonial newspapers, and served to strengthen the influences which led to the convening of the Stamp Act Congress in New York City in the following October.

The opposition had now crystallized into the clearly defined principle, "no taxation without representation, and no legislation without representation." This was the momentous cry which had been given by Henry; and it was this cry that most powerfully sustained the spirit of the impending Revolution, until, becoming irrepressible, that spirit broke out into a conflagration.

In 1766, a new doctrine found voice, which was to serve, in the minds of many, as a justification for revolt. This doctrine had its earliest exposition in a third pamphlet by Colonel Richard Bland, who, as we have mentioned before, had, in a previous document in the same form, argued so vigorously in support of the validity of the Two Penny Act, irrespective of the royal approval or disapproval. He now asserted that Virginia was no part of the kingdom of England in the sense that it was subject to the laws of Parliament. It was a province of the crown alone and subject to the crown alone. This position was in exact conformity with the action of James I in 1624, who, when revoking the charter in that year, angrily and successfully for-

bade the Parliament of that day, who wished to intervene, to interfere, because, he said, they had no constitutional authority to do so in the case of a Colony. It is true that Virginia had acknowledged Parliament's right to enforce the Navigation Acts. But why? Only because, argued Bland, she was too feeble to resist.

Bland himself, in a previous pamphlet, had been compelled to admit that Parliament did have the right, whether by prescription or not, to regulate the external trade of Virginia. He seems also to have drawn a line of distinction between the Colony's allegiance to the crown, which he granted, and the Colony's obligation to submit,—which he denied,—to a royal refusal to approve a law passed by the General Assembly of Virginia relative to its internal affairs.

Bland was not only supported in private by many persons who accepted his view of the Colony's independence of Parliament, but he also found in one of the county courts,—that of Northampton, on the Eastern Shore,—a public body so bold as to proclaim that the Stamp Act was contrary to the English constitution; and, therefore, entirely without validity. This Act was subsequently repealed, but the revenue measures which succeeded it were quite as galling in the impression which they made on minds of the people of Virginia.

At this time, Thomas Jefferson, the pen of the Revolution, was a young man. He came of age in 1764, the year when the peace of the Colonies was so rudely shaken by the British policy that followed the signing of the treaty of Paris. Fresh from the liberal companionship of Small and Wythe at the College of William and Mary; deeply versed in the interpretation of the law by Coke and Lyttleton: remembering the Whig principles of his father; and inspired by the freedom of his native mountains, he, youthful as he was, instinctively resented the reservation of the British Parliament, after revoking the Stamp Act, that it possessed the right and the power to tax the American people, with or without their consent.

The substance of Henry's famous resolutions probably did not go as far as Jefferson wished, if the tenor of his own later *Summary View* can be taken as proof; but how thoroughly he approved of their spirit was shown by his course just so soon as he began to take an active part in the political affairs of the Colony. It was not until two years had passed that he became a member of the bar, which brought him into intimate relations with the most influential public men of the community; and it was not until two years later still that he was elected to a seat in the House of Burgesses. Now, for the first time, he was able to utter his opinions from a political height that was bound to draw attention to them. He had not hesitated to express these opinions in private, and with such vehemence that he had become alienated from all the conservative members of his mother's family, the Randolphs, many of whom remained loyal to Great Britain throughout the Revolutionary war.

During Jefferson's first session in the House, Botetourt dissolved that body because of its sympathy with the action which Massachusetts had recently taken in opposition to the measures of the British Government. Jefferson was one of the members who retired to the Raleigh Tavern and drew up articles of association recommending to the people of all the Colonies the policy of refusing to buy British merchandise; and he was also, at a later date, one of the signers of a series of resolutions in favor of the appointment of a committee of correspondence in each Colony whose duty it should be to promote unity by constant intercommunication. These resolutions also recommended the summoning of a convention, in which all the Colonies should be represented, and which should lay down the course which all should be urged to pursue.

In 1773, the freeholders of Albemarle County gave instructions to their two newly elected Burgesses, one of whom was Jefferson himself. These instructions were undoubtedly drafted by him, and they offer a remarkable statement of his convictions touching the rising controversy between Great Britain and her

American dependencies. The note which he now struck runs through all his Revolutionary documents of a subsequent composition. The people of the Colonies, he declared, possessed, not only the charter right to be governed by the laws of their own assemblies alone, but also what he termed the "common right of mankind" to be so governed, independently of all charters. It was these combined natural and constitutional rights which had been invaded by Parliament in numerous instances in the course of recent years, and in doing so, that body had impaired the natural and constitutional rights alike of the British Empire as a whole.

The doctrine of natural right,—which was simply an abstruse idea of the philosophers of the eighteenth century,—was now heard for the first time in the controversy. Hundreds of resolutions were adopted by the Virginian counties in this crisis in presentation of their views, but in Albemarle alone was the justification for resistance based primarily on natural law and natural rights. Jefferson admitted in after life that he was upheld in this extreme opinion by one man of influence in the community; namely, George Wythe. All the others, however liberal and outspoken, while denying Parliament's right to tax the Colonies without their consent, acknowledged its right to impose duties in the regulation of external trade.

It was not long before there opened up to Jefferson a much more conspicuous opportunity to reiterate the same radical principle by action. The celebrated *Summary View of the Rights of British America* was drafted by him for the Convention which met at Williamsburg in August, 1773, only a few weeks after the passage of the resolutions of Albemarle County. Jefferson himself candidly acknowledged at a later time that his radical pamphlet was not at that period beneficial to the Patriot Cause. In fact, not even the boldest spirits in the Convention were then ready to assent to his cool statement that Virginia, Hanover, and England stood on a footing of political equality, because all three were simply provinces of the British Empire;

27—Vol. I.

and that the only ligature that joined these provinces to each other was their common allegiance to George the Third. Virginians, Hanoverians, Englishmen,—all he asserted were fellow-subjects of the King, but all were independent of each other. Upset the monarchy, as in Cromwell's time, and the last political tie between them would at once be loosed.

In the present four great divisions of the British Empire apart from the British Islands,—Canada and South Africa,

SEAL OF VIRGINIA DURING THE REIGN OF GEORGE III.

Australia and New Zealand,—we perceive the exact relation which he affirmed had existed from the beginning between Great Britain and her American Colonies, a relation of practical independence in every way except in allegiance to the throne. But this relation in our own time has been brought about, not by a clearer conception of the presumptive natural rights of people, but simply by the growth of those former dependencies in wealth and power.

A copy of the *Summary View* found its way to London; was warmly approved by Whigs like Edmund Burke; but was looked upon by the Government as so seditious a document that the name of its author was included in a bill of attainder. This, however, was afterwards suppressed.

The Declaration of Independence, the next great state paper
drafted by Jefferson, based, after the manner of the *Summary
View*, the right of separation from the Mother Country on the
natural right of a community to govern itself, but at the same
time he recognized that what he described "as a decent respect
for the opinion of mankind" required that he should detail the
practical motives which justified the exercise of that natural
right.

The Americans as a people put very slim reliance on the
political philosophy of the opening paragraph of that great
document as a really acceptable reason for a revolution,—the
right of self-determination was even more of a glittering theory
then than it has proved itself to be in our own day,—but supported by the long array of grievances which Jefferson mar-
shaled, that philosophy assumed a practical complexion; and
this practical complexion had only deepened with the progress
of time, for what was more or less idealism in the eyes of his
contemporaries, has, in the eyes of later generations, become,—
largely through the constant recital of the doctrines of the Great
Declaration,—the accepted principles of the American people,
although not as yet of the whole world.

What are these principles for which we are so much indebted to the author of this document? First, the equality of
all men, if not in the eyes of nature,—as Jefferson asserted,—
at least in the eyes of the law. Second, the right of all men to
life, liberty, and the pursuit of happiness; third, government was
instituted to protect this inalienable right; and fourth, the exercise of the powers of the government without the consent of the
governed is tyranny, and only the governed can legally prescribe
what those powers should be.

The voice of Henry, the pen of Jefferson,—profound and
splendid alike as were the political truths which they proclaimed
and illustrated,—how far could they have prevailed, had it not
been for the backing of Washington's sword? In time, without
this sword, the principles, announced by that voice and that pen

GEORGE WASHINGTON

might have crept quietly and gradually into the convictions of mankind, which are ever growing more and more enlightened from century to century, and even from decade to decade, but they would not have found confirmation so soon in the success of the Revolution, for, without the sword of Washington, it is altogether probable that that great movement would have ultimately ended in failure, to be followed by the at least temporary obscuration of the great political doctrines which it had sought to vindicate and permanently enthrone.

Washington's task called for a greater variety of qualities than the respective tasks of Henry and Jefferson in the mighty struggle for Continental independence. It was his part to act, and not to talk or to write, and action is the severest of all the tests of character and capacity. That he was able to close the war in triumph was due primarily to his patience, fortitude, and skill; but back of him stood the American people, who had caught, not only the flame of his own indomitable spirit and inflexible resolution, but also the soul of those lofty political principals, and that intense love of freedom, which had found such vivid expression in the voice of Henry and the pen of Jefferson, and the voices and pens of thousands of other American patriots, equally loyal to the cause of independence.

CHAPTER VII

CHURCHMEN AND DISSENTERS

In studying the history of the Established Church during the long period from the close of Nicholson's second administration to the reduction of that church to the footing of a dethroned religious denomination, at the end of the eighteenth century, one is impressed with the harsh fate that overtook it without that fate being really deserved. The Established Church was, in the light of all the circumstances, more sinned against than sinning. In more than one emergency, it was, treated without equity, and in the end, when it had been severed from the state, it was grossly wronged by an act of confiscation for which no tenable defense can be offered. Its clergy were, as a body, victims of the democratic spirit which had been steadily spreading after the middle of the eighteenth century. The church was an aristocratic institution, supposed to be tainted with the odor of England, and it finally went down before the storm.

But long before the eighteenth century began, the clergy had suffered their first injustice, which was destined to leave an unwholesome impression on their order. In England, during the seventeenth century, as before and after, the benefices were, as a rule, in the gift of what were known as patrons, who might be either a wealthy and powerful individual or an educational or ecclesiastical foundation. When a candidate for a vacant pulpit had been properly presented, he was inducted into his new office, and, thereby, acquired a permanent right to it, independent of his vestry or his congregation. The reason which lay behind this custom was that the rector of a parish would

406

be more disposed to act and preach impartially and disinterestedly, if relieved from all pecuniary dependence on the caprices of those whom he was spiritually serving.

The system of vested tenure had its drawbacks, as the lax conduct of many an English clergyman of those times only too clearly revealed. Once entrenched in his pulpit, it was difficult to prize an incumbent out, even when he had subjected himself to merited censure. Under the English as well as under the Virginian law, the parishioners were liable to considerable penalties should they fail on Sunday and holy days to be present at religious worship. They were, therefore, unable to show their disapprobation of a dissipated rector by refusing to listen to his sermons, or to receive the sacraments from his hands.

Numerous parishes were laid off in Virginia at an early date in its history, but as the community was new, there could be no local patrons to present to the livings thus created. That right was assumed by the vestries in the absence of any other rule to meet the situation. Properly, if the Anglican law had been followed, as it should have been under these circumstances, the vestry of a vacant parish would have offered a candidate to the governor, who would then have proceeded to induct him into his office, thereby giving him, as in the Mother Country, a permanent fee-simple title to his benefice. Should the vestry wilfully neglect to present within six months, then the governor, as the Bishop of London's representative, possessed the right to collate a minister to the vacant pulpit.

Such was the regulation which was supposed to exist in Virginia as late as Nicholson's time, when the English attorney-general, Sir Edward Northy, delivered the opinion that the Colony was subject to precisely the same ecclesiastical laws as the Mother Country. But as a matter of fact, the ecclesiastical system there had been perverted by the action of the vestries. Among these bodies, the almost universal custom had sprung up of employing a minister without presenting him for induction, as they were unwilling to give him a permanent tenure

which would be practically independent of their control. It was
this illegal custom that led to so much controversy with various
governors, who, as the representatives of the King and the
Bishop of London alike, were required by their specific instructions to enforce the ecclesiastical laws in both letter and spirit.

BRUTON PARISH CHURCH, WILLIAMSBURG
Built in 1710

These governors had not only to contend with the calculated
neglect of induction by the vestries, but also with the jealousy
of the commissary, who vehemently and pugnaciously asserted
his primacy, on the ground that he was the only real representative of the Bishop of London.

It was the vestries' claim that they were justified in appoint-
ing ministers by the year without offering them for induction,

by the fact that, in this way, they were able to protect their
parishioners from the incumbency of unworthy clergymen. Why
were the Virginian pulpits more open to occupation by that
type of men than the English pulpits? The reply of the vestries
to this was that little could be learned about the antecedents
of the English candidates before their arrival in Virginia, owing to the fact that they came from so great a distance.

Now, there was, undoubtedly, some soundness in this reason
for the vestries' action in refusing to observe the strict Anglican
rule in filling the parish pulpits. On the other hand, there could
not have been adopted a more effective means of reducing the
average moral and intellectual quality of their pastors than by
depriving their incumbency of all permanence by making it
absolutely dependent on the decision of a small body of men
from year to year. The clergymen who came out from England
were perfectly well informed as to the uncertainty of the tenure.
Would any young minister of great abilities be willing to leave
England in the teeth of such a risk? At the very best, he was
aware that he would have to cross a vast ocean and establish
his home in a half settled country, where he could hope for no
clerical advancement whatever. The only cause for surprise is
that any divines at all, old or young, unless disadvantageously
situated could be found who would consent to go.

The action of the several vestries was not only a violation
of the law as it really existed, but it was a violation that went
far to defeat its own ends. England, during the seventeenth
and eighteenth centuries, did not offer high remuneration to its
clergy in the mass. If there had been stability in the tenure of
the Virginian benefices, the Colony would have drawn to its
parishes many young incumbents of talent, learning, and energy. Divines of that type very sensibly preferred to await
their chances of promotion in the Mother Country, where, at
least, the ecclesiastical law was rigidly enforced in their favor.
It was natural that they should have distrusted parishioners
oversea who insisted upon the adoption of an ecclesiastical law

of their own, for the existence of which there was, in reality,
no more justification than there would have been in England
itself.

In the previous chapter, we pointed out the damage which
was suffered by the clergy in consequence of legislation by the
General Assembly which tended to lower their salaries. There
had always been some difficulty in collecting these salaries to
the limit allowed. Again and again, individual ministers complained of the deficit in the payment of the amount due, of which
they were too often the victims. In 1727, the General Assembly
was so much impressed with the justice of these complaints
that they passed an Act which they anticipated would remove
the evil that was causing so much discontent. The salary was
again fixed at sixteen thousand pounds of tobacco, and each
vestry was enjoined to appoint officers for its collections, and to
see that they performed their duty. Two hundred acres were
to be reserved as a glebe for each parish, and the clergyman in
possession was to be permitted to sue in case of trespass,
whether he had been formally inducted or not.

These provisions were calculated to improve the pecuniary
condition of the ministers, but it was not long before a reaction
set in, and the General Assembly, under its influence, began to
curtail the advantages which had been bestowed. In 1753, an
Act of that body required that the salaries of the clergymen in
two parishes,—which were designated,—should be paid in pounds
sterling instead of in tobacco. This was ostensibly done to
lighten the burden of the tithables in these two parishes, but
as the Act aroused suspicion, it is possible that the amount allowed fell short of the real value of the original sum as stated in
the form of tobacco.

Reference has, in a previous chapter, been made to the
subsequent Act of 1755, which permitted a parishioner to discharge his debt to his clergyman, among other creditors, in
a fixed sum of money instead of in tobacco as formerly; and the
possibility of injustice was increased by the fact that the Gen-

eral Assembly fixed the price of the commodity. This destroyed
all chance of substantial benefit to the ministers from the rise
in the value of their original sixteen thousand pounds of tobacco. Their loss might be small or it might be great, according to the condition of the market. The Act was not designed
to extend beyond a period of ten months, but it was easily renew-
able whether it was to the advantage of the debtor class in the
Colony for this to be done.

The practical result of such a policy, so far as the clergy
were involved, was, they claimed, to impower the General Assembly to pay them "in tobacco or money, or something else as
any of them should happen to be least profitable."

To cause the law to be more censurable in its moral complexion, it was declared to be retroactive in its operation, for it was
held to apply to salaries overdue as well as to salaries yet to
mature. The result of the new law was to reduce the renumera-
tion of the clergy, according to their estimate, to the level of
that of an English curate who was in the receipt of only forty
pounds sterling by the year.

The Composition Act of 1755 did not call forth any protest
from any section of the community affected by it, except the
clergy, who, from the special nature of their situation, were the
only persons,—being all creditors,—who were seriously damaged. As we have mentioned in a previous chapter, they made
an appeal to the throne itself against both the Act of 1653 and
the Act of 1655. It was only in the instance of this last appeal
that the King lent an attentive and favorable ear; and steps
were soon taken by many of the clergy to recover by suit the
amounts due to them after the nullification of the Act of Composition.

The most famous of these was the suit of Rev. James Maury,
in which a verdict by the jury of one cent damages confirmed
the justice of his claim, which was in no sense lessened by the
trivial sum awarded him. That sum was in itself a true gauge
of the wrong which had been done him and his brethren of the

same cloth throughout the Colony. The jury had been bent by the persuasive powers of the eloquent Henry, who, blinded by the broad colonial view which he took of the significance of the cause under argument in its relation to the constitutional powers of the King, inflamed the minds of twelve men to a point where, out of resentment against that King's interference, they committed a palpable injury in refusing to uphold, in a more impressive way, the rights of the plaintiff.

There can be little doubt that the clergy had a perfectly good reason for declining to submit to the diminution of their salaries by the action of the General Assembly. But was their course a wise one from a practical point of view? It was not, however much we may admire the indomitable spirit of Camm, their bell-wether. In the first place, the Composition Acts, while they hurt the clergy the most, and the wealthy planters the least,—because taxation was temporarily shifted from the latter's tithables,—were yet really designed by the General Assembly to give relief to the whole community at an hour when every family was restive under the burden of hard times. Had the incomes of the clergymen been insufficient to support their households, their action in declining to submit to composition would not have been selfish at all; but in the General Assembly's eyes, their salaries were ample; and when they protested against a reduction by payment to them in money, a general impression was created that they were unwilling to share the difficulties of the hour on an equality with their parishioners. In other words, they were looked upon as acting unpatriotically, not only in the broadest public sense of the word, but in its narrowest private sense.

Was it possible for any real advantage to accrue to the clergy, if they were to reap at the same time a harvest of alienation by their attitude of stickling too firmly for their just rights? Such a harvest they did reap in the course of a few years.

But the popular feeling against them as a body was not attributable entirely to their action in 1653 and 1655 in declining to put themselves, in the matter of their salaries, on the level of all the other creditors in the community at large. What was far more inadvisable, they appealed to a power enthroned beyond the sea to interfere with the enforcement of laws passed by the local Assembly for the purpose of advancing the welfare of the Colony as a whole. This was an ominous attitude for any body of men who were citizens of that Colony to assume. In spite of the prevailing loyalty to the King, there had been steadily growing in Virginia a feeling of impatience with every royal attempt to intermeddle with the administration of the affairs of the community. This feeling was disclosed in the limitation of the Composition Act to a period of ten months. The General Assembly, by this provision, aimed to make it impossible for the throne to interpose before the practical objects of those Acts had been attained.

In spite of the increase in wealth, and the presence of a still more powerful landed class, the democratic spirit, as synonymous with a desire for self-government, was rising rapidly. By their action in protesting against the composition of their salaries, the clergy offended this sentiment, because they virtually demanded that they should be treated more favorably than the rest of the creditor community, who had consented to be paid in money and not in the more renumerative form of tobacco. They stood squarely on their rights, but the temper of their parishioners, being what it was, made it a tactical mistake for them to do so. Indeed, there was never a period in the history of the Established Church of Virginia when it was so necessary for the clergymen of that church to act with discretion as during the years that followed 1745 down to the opening of the Revolution, for it was during this interval that the dissenters were able to obtain a firm foothold in the Colony, in spite of the obstructions which they had to face on every hand.

During the previous century, the Quakers had made up the chief personal element of opposition to the enforcement of the ecclesiastical laws. Persecution served only to inflame their zeal and swell their numbers, but notwithstanding this fact, their influence was crippled by the impracticable character of some of their doctrines, which appeared to bring them very close to the border line of treason to the community. It was not simply that they rejected the requirements of the Prayer Book. They also refused to take up arms when the Colony was in danger of invasion. It was due to characteristics of this peculiar nature that they were looked upon by the people at large with a feeling of mingled alarm and contempt. So soon as the sect secured immunity from persecution, it seemed to lose ground in numbers, and also in its power of popular appeal, and gradually sank into obscurity.

From several points of view, the Quakers represented with close fidelity the spirit, which, in the next century, through the Baptists, and to a less degree, through the Presbyterians also, was to undermine the foundations of the Anglican Church in Virginia. Like the followers of Whitfield and the Westleys, the great English religious reformers, they went out into every corner and by-way of the plantations and labored and preached among the poor with the self-sacrificing ardor of the Apostles themselves.

The Puritans, whom Berkeley detested with as much vehemence as he detested the Quakers, did not raise the same tumult or excite the same personal antagonism. Indeed, the largest proportion of the members of this denomination ended by conforming or by emigrating to Maryland, in which province religious freedom prevailed.

At first, the Presbyterians' foothold was feebly maintained, although, in 1699, the General Assembly acknowledged in their favor that the English Act of Toleration was in force in the Colony. The extent of the sufferance seems to have been restricted, in the case of this denomination, to the right to hold religious services every other Sunday, and to remain away from the parish church without being liable to a fine. When the Scotch-Irish, who were of this faith, began to pour into the

southern part of the Great Valley, the Presbyterian congregations in Eastern Virginia, having lost the powerful leadership
of Mackie and Mackemie, who were now dead, had virtually
fallen into dissolution. Gradually, under influences brought in
by the Valley immigrants, the denomination was revived in the
region east of the mountains.

In 1743, a permanent congregation was established in Hanover County, and, from this nucleus, the Presbyterians spread
into the country below the James. Here several of their
preachers soon made themselves notorious by public criticism
of the clergymen of the Established Church and condemnation
of its doctrines. This attitude led to the resuscitation of the
hostility and petty persecution of a former day, and that action
would have been pushed to a further point had it not been for
the arrival of Samuel Davies from Pennsylvania, and his early
assumption of the leadership of his church in Virginia. He was
a man of extraordinary eloquence, but what was of more service to his sect at this difficult hour he was conciliatory and diplo-
matic in his relations with the Governor and Council and clergy
of the Establishment.

Nevertheless, Davies found it impossible to break down the
narrow interpretation of the scope of the Toleration Act. For
instance, there was vigorous opposition to granting a license to
a Presbyterian minister to preach in more than one meeting-
house; and this feeling did not disappear until the congregations
became so large that they could afford to provide a permanent
minister for each of these bodies. They had also drawn to
their pews many persons of social and political influence in the
community, and were soon to lay the foundations of a college
that was destined to rise to a high rank in the province of education. It was fortunate for the tranquility of the Established
Church that the spirit of the Presbyterians, after they had once
obtained a secure foothold, was not aggressive and irritating, but
the blow which they had struck by merely acquiring this foothold
was full of significance, because they had demonstrated that a

dissenting denomination could spring up and flourish within the boundaries of every parish.

It had always been asserted by the enemies of the Established Church that its severe religious restrictions were a serious impediment to the Colony's growth by immigration. Not many families of other denominational fealty were ready to come into the older communities when they knew that they would have to face, from the hour of their crossing the border, the keen aversion with which all dissenters were regarded. Indeed, it was not until the middle of the eighteenth century that the Baptists began to defy this sentiment and seek homes in the Colony. The first contingent to arrive proved themselves to be quiet and unprovocative, but so soon as the second, composed of persons known as "separatists," appeared, an agitation arose that was not destined to end until the Established Church was abolished.

These Baptists were provincial representatives of the great evangelical movement in England which had caused so extensive a secession from the Anglican fold. Their English forerunners had declaimed against the cold religious spirit of the English Establishment of their day, and also against the selfish aloofness of so many of its clergymen from the spiritual life of their congregations. They had gone even further than this: they had attacked the personal character of the majority of these clergymen as demoralized by worldly, if not by grossly vicious indulgencies. Such was the line of assault now pursued in Virginia by the fierce and bitter propagandists of the local Baptist faith.

Was there sound reason for their censure? From the point of view of rigid sectaries and fanatical contemners of all the pleasures of life, undoubtedly there was. Had the Anglican clergymen in the Colony started out, under the influence of the evangelical and democratic spirit of the hour, to denounce an innocent dance, a pleasant game of cards, an exciting horse race, a dram of whiskey, or a glass of wine, as sins of a very black dye, they would have pleased the Baptists of that day, but they would have alienated their own more rational congregations by such spiritual narrowness. A stricter standard has been justly required of the ministers of the Gospel in all periods of modern history than of members of the laity, but there is no reason to think that the clergymen of the eighteenth century, either in England or in Virginia, taken as a body, outraged, except in exceptional cases which never escaped condemnation, the moral sense of their congregations by following the liberal social customs which were characteristic of the most highly placed society of that age.

In Virginia, every vestry had the power to terminate the services of the clergymen of their parish, should he be open to serious censure. It is much more reasonable to infer that these men in general behaved with the propriety called for by their cloth than that the congregation quietly submitted to the ministrations of persons not worthy of respect or toleration.

Never probably was a large body of men exposed to fiercer or more prejudiced denunciation than the Anglican clergymen of Virginia in the eighteenth century. The Baptists, their most unsparing critics, were aroused to uncontrollable bitterness against them; first, by the recollection of the unpardonable persecution to which the dissenters had been subjected; and secondly, by the consciousness of the social inferiority of their congregations to the congregations which assembled weekly in the parish churches. Above all, they were animated by that kind of religious zeal which burns in the hearts of so many reformers unaccompanied by either the wish or the ability to judge their opponents with moderation and fairness. Undoubtedly, the sermons of the ministers of the Established Church failed to inflame the breasts of the mass of the common people in their parishes simply because they had been trained to make no appeal to the more violent religious emotions of their auditors. It was here that the Baptists, like the Quakers before them, seized their opportunity, and in pushing their missionary labors, they heroically defied the persecution which their unrestrained fervor so often provoked. As a result, they came,

not without truth, to be considered by large bodies of men in the
Colony as martyrs in the cause of religious freedom.

This attitude led to an attempt by the General Assembly to
modify the strictness of the rules that were applied to all the
Dissenters. This more liberal disposition would undoubtedly
have continued to grow had it not been interrupted by the arrival of the Revolution.

The principal event in the religious history of that great
episode was the adoption by the convention of May, 1776, of the
sixteenth article in the Bill of Rights. This was most probably
drafted by Mason, but its authorship is still a subject of dispute.
It declared that "all men were equally entitled to the free exercise of religion according to the dictates of conscience." In
spite of its character as simply a general statement, its practical
effect was at once conspicuous. There was no persecution inflicted thereafter; no disabilities for religious opinion were
again recognized; and the members of every sect, and persons
of no sect at all, were granted the benefit of every civic privilege
on a footing of perfect equality with each other. It is a singular fact that the Catholic, the Jew, and the Evangelical looked
upon this famous sixteenth clause as signifying a permanent
and absolute divorce between Church and State, while the Anglican congregations looked upon it as only giving authority for
a more liberal union between the two.

At the moment, the suspension of the annual salaries paid to
the clergymen of the Old Establishment was really of more
practical importance, since it relieved the Dissenters of the burden of taxation for the benefit of that Establishment. This provision was renewed several times, and in the end, it exerted a
powerful influence in destroying the Anglican organization,
which had always depended upon State tithes, in largest degree,
for a maintenance. The conservative sympathizers with that
organization refused, even under these discouraging circumstances, to abandon its defense, and they took heart from the
fact that the tie with the State was still not completely broken,

since the Anglican clergymen were alone authorized to perform the marriage ceremony, and their vestries to assess taxes for the benefit of the poor.

The year that saw the adoption of the Bill of Rights also witnessed the inaguration of Jefferson's various measures of religious, political, legal, and educational reform, all of which were inspired and sustained so largely by the democratic spirit which the progress of the war was doing so much to strengthen and expand. In January, 1777, the General Assembly passed an Act that provided for the complete exemption of dissenters from payment of taxes designed for the support of the old Church Establishment; and from this date, no imposition by the Commonwealth for the support of religion in any form has ever been adopted.

When the exemption was first debated by the General Assembly, the question arose: was it not the duty of every community to require every householder in its confines to contribute to a general State fund for the maintenance of religion? That fund, it was proposed, should be divided among the denominations in proportion to the number of their communicants. This scheme of assessment had later on the vigorous advocacy of Patrick Henry, who, by that time, had begun to be guided in his public course by a more conservative spirit. It was strongly opposed by Madison, who, like Jefferson, was keenly hostile to every measure which seemed to uphold, however remotely, the union of Church and State. Ultimately, the scheme of enforcing by law popular support for religion was abandoned. The partisans of the Old Establishment had encouraged it, even though they could no longer hope to be the sole beneficiary.

At the beginning of 1779, the condition of the Anglican Church was one of almost complete disruption. The salaries of the clergymen were no longer paid; the vestries on their own motion were more or less dispersed; while the parish system had been fatally damaged. In the end the vestries were formally disbanded by an Act of Assembly. In the course of 1779, a bill

for religious freedom was drafted and submitted to the Assembly
and ultimately passed.

The new Protestant Episcopal Church, the name which the
Old Establishment assumed after the Revolution, petitioned, in
1784, for an Act of Incorporation, by which it expected to re-
organize its affairs in harmony with the public conditions which
now prevailed. A change in its government and its liturgy
had been made necessary by its severance from the Church of
England. This petition reveals, that, in spite of the sixteenth
clause of the Bill of Rights, which was supposed to have left each
denomination to the exercise of its own judgment in adopting
its own rules, an impression prevailed that the former Anglican
laws were still in force; and that the General Assembly alone
could modify them. Moreover, without incorporation, the new
Protestant Episcopal Church would be able to retain possession
of the property which it had held as the Anglican Establishment.

The bill for incorporation passed in December, 1784, largely
because those who were opposed to it in principle were afraid
that, unless it was granted, the popular demand for an assessment for the support of religion in general would be greatly
increased. The Act, however, raised a feeling of apprehension
among the members of the other denominations, because it gave
the new Episcopal Church an advantage by allowing it to retain
a large amount of property, which, it was claimed, belonged to
the tax-payers at large, as this property had been purchased with
the money of the whole community in the past.

Afterwards, the Act of Incorporation was repealed, and the
glebes were appropriated by the State, a step that completed the
confiscatory policy that, in one form or another, had been pursuing the Anglican Establishment, and its heir, the Protestant
Episcopal Church, from the rise of the democratic spirit in the
years that preceded the Revolution down to the end of the eighteenth century. The Establishment had found its most successful enemies in Jefferson, a speculative deist, and Madison, a

ratiocinative dissenter. Behind the movement that over-
whelmed it, there were certain personal and sectarian influences
that were more radical and selfish than patriotic or just.

CHAPTER VIII

EDUCATIONAL INFLUENCES

It has been asserted by some students of the colonial age that there was a very great difference in character between the seventeenth century, even in its closing years, and the eighteenth. This difference has been attributed by persons of that opinion to the supposed destruction of many of the original social conditions by the rather abrupt substitution of slave labor for indentured white labor.

As a matter of fact, this substitution really intensified the spirit of the social influences already in a state of activity. It enlarged the scope of all these influences, with the simple exception that it diminished the number of indentured whites who previously had been brought in from England. The real effect of this practical cessation did not come to the surface in the colonial age at all. Indeed, it did not fully show itself until the negroes had been emancipated nearly a century after the close of the Revolution.

How did the presence of persons of that race in Virginia in a greater multitude after 1700 accentuate the conditions inherited from the previous century? It may be said, in a general way, that the seventeenth century was simply the eighteenth in embryo. The plantation framework of the eighteenth was the same as that of the seventeenth—only it was more solid and permanent, because the negro was not, like the indentured servant, a slave for a term of years, but a slave for life. The production of crops was the same,—only on a more voluminous and productive scale. The economic spirit was the same,—only the

422

field in which it exhibited itself was wider in its dimensions. The political organization was the same,—only the public men of distinction were more numerous and of greater influence in intercolonial affairs. The religious establishment was the same, —only it was more compact and powerful, owing to the growth of population and the consolidation of the parishes. The social system was the same,—only the manifestations of its spirit were characterized by more imposing mansions, greater abundance in the general style of life, more brilliant display on special occasions, a more liberal hospitality, and, doubtless, too, a broader intellectual culture.

In no respect was the life of the eighteenth century more plainly an extension of the life of the seventeenth than in the province of education, whether solid or embellishing. We discern in every aspect of this province simply an enlargement of the conditions which had prevailed previous to 1700.

In an earlier chapter, we gave some description of the free schools that had been founded in the seventeenth century. The same public spirit was exhibited in the eighteenth. Numerous proofs of this fact might be offered. For instance, the parish of Christ Church in Middlesex County was the recipient of two legacies for the support of schools of this character. Mrs. Mary Whaley, of York, founded a free school in 1706 in Williamsburg in memory of her son, and bequeathed it a large sum under the terms of her will, which enabled it to be of substantial service for the tuition of the community's children. William Stark, also of York, followed her example. He seems to have been associated in this benefaction with sixteen gentlemen of his vicinity, who were highly distinguished in the affairs of the Colony.

In the same spirit, Mrs. Elizabeth Smith, of Isle of Wight County, left by will an amount sufficient for the purchase of a lot in Smithfield and the building of a school house thereon. She also provided in the same instrument a handsome endowment for this useful establishment. Among other generous and far-sighted benefactors was Joseph Royle, who directed, that, in case his son should die before he came of age, the estate descending to him was to pass to trustees, to be invested by them in a free school, in which numerous courses specified by the testator were to be taught. Colonel Landon Carter, William Robinson, and Humphrey Hill, residing in different divisions of the Colony, set aside large amounts for use in educating the poor of their respective parishes in the rudiments.

Common private schools for the children of parents in the enjoyment of fair pecuniary circumstances were to be found in each Eastern County, and every facility was granted by the public authorities to increase their usefulness and to advance their prosperity. There are several instances in the history of Princess Anne County, the home of the notorious Grace Sherwood at an earlier date, in which the justices permitted this ordinary class of school-masters to assemble their pupils in vacant rooms in the Court-House until the carpenters should complete the erection of their school-houses. One of these county dominies, whose only really valuable possession was, perhaps, his learning, was granted the privilege of building such a house on public land,—doubtless, with the contributions obtained from the parents of his pupils.

Famous in their time were the two academies over which the Rev. James Marye and the Rev. James Maury presided. These establishments, as we learn from the biographies of their most celebrated pupils, Jefferson, Madison, and Monroe, were on such a scale as to be able to afford board and lodging for numerous pupils who had been drawn to them from a distance. It was at such a school that George Mason also received his first important lessons as a student; and there, too, like his distinguished contemporaries under similar roofs elsewhere, he acquired a valuable training in independence and self-reliance.

A school of as high character as the Marye or Maury was founded by the Rev. Jonathan Boucher in Caroline County, and owing to his reputation for scholarship, it was patronized by the parents of thirty boys belonging to the most conspicuous families

RICHARD HENRY LEE

in that region. These pupils lodged and boarded in his home, and thus enjoyed, not only the benefit of their headmaster's learning, but what was, perhaps, still more fruitful, the moral training which his example conveyed. All that was expected of an instructor even of this calibre at that day was that he should teach the English, Latin, and Greek languages, English composition, arithmetic, mathematics, and ordinary accounts. Sometimes the principal landowners of a neighborhood would agree to take it by turns to supply a tutor for the older children of them all. These children would reside for the time being under the roof where the tutor happened to be stationed. This custom seems to have prevailed most generally in the rather sparsely settled counties lying towards the mountains, where distance probably made it difficult to support numerous independent private schools for the young living in that part of the Colony.

At this period, though the danger of Indian invasion appears to have lingered as late as 1766, there were isolated country schools in the Upper Valley, where the Scotch-Irish had founded a large community. These people had brought with them from their original homes across the water a strong sentiment in favor of giving their children as much education as their situation on the border made possible. The private teacher here, in consequence, obtained a liberal patronage. In most cases, the pupils received tuition until their sixteenth year, and were then bound out to one of the crafts. We find this provision for sons sometimes inserted in the wills of wealthy planters who resided in Eastern Virginia. Such was a clause in the testament of Thomas Lee, of Stratford, the father of Richard Henry and his brothers, all of whom won distinction during the period of the Revolution.

The custom with a very large number of parents of ample fortunes was to complete their sons' education, either in the College of William and Mary, or in the Universities of England.

By 1729, the seat of learning at Williamsburg had acquired the scope and dignity of an institution of ripe scholarship. Every department contemplated in the original charter had, by this time, been added to the course of study by the surviving trustees, and as empowered by that instrument, they had trans-ferred all the College property, real and personal, to the Presi-

WILLIAM AND MARY COLLEGE IN 1723.

dent and the Faculty. When this important ceremony had ended, the new officers subscribed to the Thirty-nine Articles of the Church of England.

By the statutes now in force, four years were required to be devoted in the grammar school to the mastery of the Latin tongue, and two to that of the Grecian. The same text-books were used in the acquisition of these tongues as had long been employed in the University of Oxford. At the conclusion of their sixteenth year, the pupils of the grammar school, having first passed a successful examination in the ancient languages, were permitted to don a cap and gown and were then enrolled under the name of "students" in the School of Philosophy.

There were two branches of study in this school, one of which was confined to the themes of rhetoric, logic, and ethics; and the other to the topics of physics, mataphysics, and mathematics. The two teachers in these several branches were known respectively as the Professor of Moral Philosophy and the Professor of Natural Philosophy and Mathematics.

In order to win the diploma of bachelor of arts, it would appear that the student, following the English rule, had to remain in the School of Philosophy two years; but, on the other hand, if his object was to acquire the diploma of master of arts, he had to remain there four. In 1729, the professor in charge of the division for rhetoric, logic, and ethics was William Dawson, who was a graduate of Queen's College, Oxford. In addition to the schools of languages, moral philosophy, and natural science, there was a school of divinity. In one branch of this school, the Hebrew language was taught and the Old and New Testaments expounded, while, in the other, a second professor was employed to explain "the common-places of theology and controversies with heretics." Unusual attention was paid by the students in all these schools to "disputation," with a view to cultivating the art of debate.

The school for the Indian children seems to have been attended also by boys from Williamsburg, whose parents were in indigent circumstances.

The chief function of the President, apart from a weekly lecture on some theological topic, was to overlook the students and the members of the faculty, and to guard the revenues. He also presided at every meeting of the College Council. Besides a salary of one hundred and fifty pounds sterling, he was furnished with a mansion and garden. This house had been the official residence of the President of the College down to our own times.

The College of William and Mary was so far modeled on the English University scheme of education during the eighteenth century that lectures were delivered on the subject of the rights and duties of the State. The continued competence of the teachers was assured by the appointment of Oxford graduates. In 1744, William Preston, a master of arts of Oxford, filled the professorship of moral philosophy, and, in 1749, Richard Graham, a graduate of the same University, the chair of natural philosophy and mathematics.

Perhaps, the most acute and most versatile of all the professors was William Small, whom Jefferson, his pupil, held in such high esteem for scientific knowledge, that, in after years, he said that his "destinies in life," by which expression he probably meant his tastes, had been fixed by his old preceptor's instruction. Small introduced in the College of William and Mary a rule which was to become one of the most remarkable features of the courses in the University of Virginia in the next century; that is to say, as a teacher he imparted his lessons by oral lectures, and not by text-books. Small, who was a Scotchman by birth, had been educated in his native country, and was the master of a broad, deep, and varied erudition, which made his colleagues disposed to overlook his lack of conservatism on several subjects of moral importance. He was unquestionably influential in increasing the radical bent of Jefferson's mind in early manhood. Characteristically, he was keenly interested in Watt's scheme for utilizing steam, and after his return to England, he assisted that great inventor in carrying out his experiments.

The Presidents of the College, though not men of equal aptitude for the duties of their office, were all persons of ability and learning. Dr. Blair, the most conspicuous of them all, died in 1743, after an incumbency which had lasted during half a century. He was succeeded by Dr. William Dawson, the former professor of moral philosophy, who also received the appointments of Commissary and Councillor. His occupation of his post terminated in nine years. The next President was Rev. William Stith, who will be recalled as the author of a valuable history of Virginia. He like, his predecessor, Dawson, was a graduate of Oxford University. His incumbency was remembered for the sympathy and active support which he gave to the successful movement to provide a fund for the widows and children of the deceased clergymen of the Colony. A similar scheme has only, in recent years, been adopted by the Protestant Episcopal Church of the United States at large.

Rev. Thomas Dawson's tenure of the Presidency, which followed Stith's, was remarkable, like that of the Rev. James Blair, for the number of other offices which he filled at the same time. To the Presidency, he added the Commissaryship, a membership of the Council, and the rectorship of Bruton Church. His compensation for the increased load of duties which he was called on to carry was a salary of two hundred pounds sterling, instead of the one hundred and fifty which had been previously allowed.

His term was agitated by events which caused him severe personal harrassment. Among these was the Two Penny Act of 1755, by which the salaries of the clergymen were reduced in value in consequence of their computation in money, and not in tobacco, as had previously been customary. Dawson declined to take any step to alter the situation in the clergymen's favor, since he saw clearly that this could only be done by an appeal to the King, a course which was certain to create a general feeling of hostility against the Established Church in the Colony. By this sensible refusal, he made himself very unpopular with the members of his own calling. They declared that he was simply a tool of the Governor; and that he was really influenced by a desire to retain his salary, which would have been jeopardized had he assumed a decided position on the opposite side. They charged him also with over-indulgence in liquor. "No wonder that he has taken to drink," remarked the Governor, in his defense, "since he has been teased to desperation by persons of his own cloth."

The Visitors of the College followed the example of Dinwiddie and Fauquier in openly showing their sympathy for Dawson;

but the only result of their removal of several opposing professors from their chairs was to cripple the institution to the point
of practical suspension for the time being.   One of the curious
sides of the controversy, so far as it involved two of the faculty
who were dropped, was the allegation that they had married,
and "contrary to all rules of seats of learning," kept their wives,
children, and servants in College. "This," it was said, "occasioned much confusion and disturbance."   Afterwards, it was
expressly provided that the marriage of a professor should be
interpreted as his resignation in fact.   There was an impression at this time that the teachers in an important institution had
no moral right to wed at all, as there was a sacerdotal aspect to
their calling.   This idea would not have gained such a foothold
at the College of William and Mary had not the professors there
been almost without exception clergymen.

One of the vacancies was filled by the election of Rev. Gor-
onwy Owen of Wales.   Mr. Owen was the "premier poet" of
that minstrel-haunted land, and he had also graduated at Jesus
College, Oxford, which was a proof of his knowledge of the ancient languages that he was now called upon to teach in the
grammar school.   Unfortunately for himself, he recalled with
so much pleasure the conflicts of town and gown in the streets
of his alma mater that he now took them as his justification for
leading his scholars in a similar excursion against a gang of
Williamsburg boys.   This was an Oxford custom which the visitors failed to approve, and in spite of his learning and his
prowess, he lost his position in the College, but found some compensation in his nomination to a living in Brunswick County, a
parish so close to the backwoods that he would run little risk
of being deprived by a rival there of his old primacy as a poet.

Fauquier, a man of remarkable acquirements, intellectual
and social alike, had presented Owen with this living.   The
Governor had shown a violent hostility to the clergymen in the
squabble over the Two Penny Act, and his partiality for Owen
was probably first aroused by the Welshman's opposition to the

course in that matter which the other professors had pursued. Perhaps, too, he did not consider the accusation of intemperance to be more objectionable in Owen's case than it had appeared to him to be in Dawson's. Fauquier was of a convivial turn himself, and it is not likely that he thought any worse of either because they were inclined to drink. He was a sceptic, and, therefore, no great stickler for the dignity of the Church. Moreover, Owen was a man of extraordinary learning, which always appealed to this ripely cultured official. Small was still more to his taste, although a temperate man in his habits. The jovial meetings of Fauquier, Wythe, Small, and Jefferson, then youthful students in Williamsburg, were among the most celebrated traditions of the ancient College.

In the case of Bartholomew Yates, who was warmly esteemed for his piety and learning alike, the mantle of the Presidency fell for the first time on the shoulders of a graduate of the College itself. He had previously enjoyed a useful experience as the rector of a large parish and the headmaster of a school of wide reputation in the Colony. In the meanwhile, several of the professors who had been removed from their posts during the wrangle over the Two Penny Act, were restored to their old places in the College. One of these was Mr. Graham, who had filled the chair of natural philosophy; and another was Mr. Camm, who had filled the chair of divinity. Mr. Preston, who had been suspended on the same occasion, had returned to England.

It had become a custom with the respective incumbents of some of the chairs to preach in the pulpits of surrounding parishes. To this the Visitors objected as diverting these professors' attention from their regular duties. Apparently, too, the men who occupied outside pulpits from Sunday to Sunday quietly assumed the right to reside beyond the local jurisdiction of the College. This also was put an end to by the Visitor's action.

The President at this time was Rev. James Horrocks, a young man of great talent and energy, who had, before his elec-

tion to that office, won unusual distinction as the master of the
grammar school. His term was marked by numerous disputes,
which he, if not the cause of them, at least was unable to allay.
A very fierce flame was lit when he summoned a convention of
the clergy of the Colony to pass upon the advisability of petitioning for the establishment of an American Episcopate. Horrocks, being young, determined, and aspiring, was, perhaps, correctly suspected of a desire to be chosen to this great office, no
unworthy ambition on his part; but so little interest was taken
by the clergymen in the proposed innovation that only ten
appeared at Williamsburg when the day appointed for the meeting arrived. The project failed to secure sufficient support, in
spite of the inconvenience that had always accompanied dependence on a Bishop who resided three thousand miles away, and
whose representative in the Colony was only too often, like Rev.
James Blair too contentious, or like Rev. William Dawson, too
weak, to exercise any real control over the clergy. Jonathan
Swift is said to have been a candidate for the office of Bishop of
Virginia. Had he succeeded in obtaining it, the world might have
been indebted to the Colony for another chapter in the Voyages
of Gulliver.

In 1772, James Madison, a man of extraordinary qualifications, was elected to the chair of natural philosophy; and three
years later, he visited England to secure ordination.

Rev. John Camm had, in the meanwhile, been appointed
President in succession to Horrocks. Unlike most of the professors under him, he had been educated at the University of
Cambridge. The first chair which he occupied at the College of
William and Mary was that of divinity. We have already described the resolute, if not pugnacious, spirit which he displayed
in his appeal to the King to disallow the Two Penny Act. Born
in England, his sympathies, after the Revolution opened, were
naturally enlisted on the side of Lord Dunmore. He began by
censuring James Inglis, the usher of the College, for the active
partisanship which he had shown in raising a patriot company;

29—Vol. I.

and later on his Tory leanings became so unrestrained that he was displaced, in the teeth of his vigorous refusal to recognize the Visitors' right to pursue such a course.

His successor was Rev. James Madison, a near kinsman of the future father of the American Constitution. Madison, as we have already mentioned, was a member of the College faculty. The new President was heartily in accord with the Patriot Cause. Indeed, it was said of him that he was never heard to speak of Heaven as a Kingdom, although he would have been justified by the language of the Bible in doing so, but as a "Great Republic, where there was no distinction of rank, and where all men were free and equal."

During several years, the faculty was reduced in number to three professors, but these, with Madison at their head, were men of extraordinary talent for instructing as well of the ripest training and culture as scholars. Never in the College's history was more fruitful work done in its lecture-halls than now. Tuition, in spite of the exigencies of the Revolutionary Period, was suspended only during a short time. This occurred just before the siege of Yorktown, when Cornwallis established his headquarters in the President's house; and just after that event, when the surrounding country was still in a state of confusion from the recent military campaign.

Jefferson, who was deeply interested in the creation of a really great seat of learning in the Colony, recommended, as a member of a committee of revisors appointed by the General Assembly, that the charter of the College should be altered with a view of widening the scope of its studies to a degree which would enable it to fulfil the purpose of a true university. He was unsuccessful in changing the charter by legislative action, but as a member of the board of visitors he used his influence to bring about a substantial alteration in the curriculum. As he was an accomplished classical scholar himself, it is strange to find that he was willing to advise the discontinuation of the grammar school, in which such effective teaching had been done in the several ancient languages. This school seemed to be as necessary then as formerly, if a thorough education was to be imparted at the College of William and Mary. It was through this college chiefly that Jefferson had acquired his own profound knowledge of the classics, a source of solace to him throughout his life.

The scheme of a university which he had been carrying in his mind called for a series of subordinate institutions to serve as tributaries to the reservoir of an advanced seat of learning at the top. It was only in these minor colleges, as he planned them, that the ancient languages were to be taught. As a substitute for such colleges in the scheme which he actually submitted and persuaded the visitors to adopt in 1770, three schools, namely, modern languages, municipal law, and medicine, were established. The two schools of divinity, on the other hand, were dropped. In the abandonment of the grammar school, and also of the two schools of divinity, the most characteristic features of the original College of William and Mary were erased; but the new institution was undoubtedly nearer than it had been before to a university in a modern sense.

A faculty of a remarkable acquirements was appointed, composed of James Madison, president and professor of natural philosophy and mathematics; George Wythe, professor of law and police; James McClurg, professor of anatomy and medicine; Robert Anderson, professor of moral philosophy; and Charles Bellini, professor of modern languages. Wythe resigned to become a chancellor and was succeeded by St. George Tucker, one of the most accomplished men, and one of the most learned lawyers of that day. The whole of America at this time might have been searched with unbiassed care, and no seat of learning could have been found that offered, in proportion to number, a more highly trained or an abler faculty naturally than was formed by these five men.

As late as 1785, Jefferson, an excellent judge of academic merit, writing to Mr. Banister, expressed the high esteem in which he held the instruction obtainable at the old college. "What are the constituents of a useful education?" he asked. "Classical knowledge, modern languages,—chiefly French, Spanish, and Italian,—mathematics, natural philosophy, natural history, ethics, and civil history. In natural philosophy, I mean to include botany as well as other branches of those departments. It is true the habit of speaking the modern languages cannot be so well acquired in America. But every other article can be as well acquired at William and Mary College as at any place in Europe. When college education is done with, and a young man is to prepare himself for public life, he must cast his eye for America either in law or physics. In the former, where can he apply himself so advantageously as to Mr. Wythe? The medical class is the only one which need come to Europe."

Although the College of William and Mary offered, certainly from the middle of the eighteenth century to the close of the Revolution, an opportunity to secure an excellent training in many of the branches of a higher education, through the instruction of graduates of the English universities, nevertheless there were many parents of wealth in the Colony who were not content until their sons had enjoyed the advantages of this English tuition in England itself. So numerous were the young men in Virginia who, before the Revolution, had been educated in English schools and colleges that this fact drew the attention of English travellers who visited the Colony. The names of these young men included the names of most of the distinguished families. A full list is not available, but some of the most prominent of the matriculates may be mentioned and also the colleges of the several universities in which they had been students.

There were four colleges at Cambridge which were the first in the esteem of the Virginians: namely, Trinity, Christ, Caius, and Pembroke. In these, between 1714 and 1772, representatives of the following families were entered: Carter, Ambler, Beverley, Wormeley, Spencer, Corbin, Nelson, Lee, Baylor, Burwell and Clayton. At Oxford, on the other hand, the colleges that showed the largest attendance of Virginians were Oriel, Queen, Saint John, Balliol, and Brasenose. In them were enrolled members of the Wormeley, Robinson, Yates, Lee, Stith, Page, Fitzhugh, and Burwell families. In the Middle Temple, the list embraced the names of Byrds, Randolphs, Blairs, Corbins, Fauntleroys, Balls, and Lees.

Eton school enjoyed a large Virginian patronage also. In the roll of its scholars are found the names of youthful members of the Page, Burwell, Lee, Wormeley, Grymes, Spotswood, and Randolph families. So well known to English headmasters was the disposition of Virginian parents in the course of the eighteenth century to enter their sons in English public schools that these schools, in some instances, were advertised in the *Virginia Gazette*. The most popular of them all, after Eton, were Woodend Grammar School in Scotland, Putney Grammar School in London, and the Schools of Dalston, Harrow, Appleby, Winchester, and Leeds in England at large.

In our description of the libraries of the Colony, during the seventeenth century, emphasis was laid upon the size and value of many of these collections. The increase in the planters' wealth in the course of the following century was in no respect more conspicuously indicated than in the large additions which were made to them from time to time. The inventory of the volumes belonging to Ralph Wormeley in 1701 discloses the fact that the number of titles alone mounted up to five hundred; and that it was rich in such of the English classics as had been published previous to that date. The library of Richard Lee, which contained two hundred and eighty titles, included works in the Latin, Greek, French and Italian tongues. Robert Carter of Corrotoman bequeathed by will five hundred and twenty-one titles. There were in this collection, and also in that of Daniel McCarty, numerous books relating to theology and history as well as many volumes of the ancient classics. The library of Robert Beverley contained all the prose works of great contemporary fame: the *Spectator, Tatler, Hudibras,* the *Beggar's Opera,* and the rest. This was equally true of the library of John Parke Custis, whose collection also contained the works of all the principal English poets. This was true too of the libraries of John Waller, John Herbert, Augustine Washington, and William Cabell. Cabell was not content unless he added fifty books to his collection annually. Robert Carter of Nomini possessed a library that numbered over a thousand titles, and it was especially rich in works of English poetry. But the largest and choicest collection of all was the one which adorned the shelves of Westover. This had been gathered up by the purchases of three generations.

The *Gentleman's Magazine* counted many subscribers in Virginia, and the *Virginia Gazette* was also widely distributed among the members of the landed gentry. As early as 1736, a book store was established by William Parks in Williamsburg; and a second store of the same kind was opened in that town at a later date.

IV

THE FEDERAL PERIOD 1776-1861

CHAPTER I

INSTITUTION OF SLAVERY

The Revolution closed in 1783, when the treaty of peace was signed. Virginia, which had organized an independent state government early in the progress of the war, and adopted a Bill of Rights and a Constitution, which reflected faithfully the new principles by which her people were now guided, had suffered severely, during the conflict,—especially in the course of the closing campaign within her own borders. Cornwallis invaded a large section of the new commonwealth and left behind him a scene of devastation. Many thousands of slaves were carried off; livestock were killed; and crops consumed. It required many years to remove the destructive effects of this ruthless incursion.

There was after Yorktown a bitter wrangle over the settlement of the debts due to British merchants by the planters, and it continued with serious injury to the prosperity of the new community, until payment was finally made in 1802.

An additional damaging influence during several years sprang out of the uncertainty created by the weakness of the Confederation. This was removed in the end by the adoption of the national Constitution, which served to strengthen the position of the states as a whole. In the meanwhile, the machinery of Virginia's local government had been in full operation.

In some details, the character of this government remained the same as it had been in colonial times. The House of Dele-

441

gates, like the House of Burgesses, numbered two representatives from each county. These had been elected on the basis of the former qualifications. The Colonial Council was converted into a Senate, which, like the Colonial Council itself, was denied the right to bring in a money bill. Its power in fact was limited to the proposal of amendments, which .could be accepted or rejected by the House as it should decide to be best. The Council of colonial times survived in the State Council, which, however, possessed only executive capacity. Its members were elected by the General Assembly. The governor was chosen, not by a direct ballot of the people, but by the vote of the Senate and House of Delegates.

The new judicial system was composed of the County Courts, a General Court, a Chancery Court, and a Supreme Court. The common law canons of descent were discarded in January, 1787, and the land of a decedent, in the absence of specific provision by will, was distributed equally among his children or their descendants in the same proportions. The number of capital offenses was reduced to two.

We have already described the course of events which led to the abolition of the Established Church, and the adoption of the Statute for Religious Freedom. Unfortunately, it was not as easy for the General Assembly to alter the material conditions of those times as it was to alter the framework of the government, the organization of the judiciary, or the curriculum of the college, or to put an end to the enjoyment of exclusive religious privileges. The changes made in every one of these departments of community life in Virginia by the Revolution were varied and comprehensive, but the system of labor in the state did not depart from the system which had prevailed in the Colony. Indeed, it continued to prevail under the commonwealth until the emancipation of the negroes was brought about by the upshot of the war for Southern Independence. Nor was there any marked alteration in the general methods of agriculture during the same period. The number of manu-

facturers increased, but so slowly that the commonwealth was
compelled to rely almost exclusively on the products of the fields
for the income of its people.   Facilities for transportation grew
larger, but the horse and carriage were still the main dependence
in travelling to a distance.   The villages expanded in some instances into towns, but hardly one of these towns became a city
of any importance.

In short, the Revolution precipitated a change in the political, religious, and social life of the Virginia people, and, to a
definite extent, in their educational life also, but in their economic situation it produced no substantial difference, although,
during the long interval that elapsed before slavery was abolished, there was a steady growth in population.

In 1790, the size of this population, including the inhabitants
of the County of Kentucky, was estimated at 747,610. This number, at the end of ten years, had expanded to 880,200, although,
by this time, Kentucky had been organized into a state. It was
not until 1810 that the federal census began to be taken. By
that year, the total population had increased to 974,622 individuals. Of these, 392,518 were slaves and about 20,000 free
persons of color. In 1840, the relative proportion were 790,710
whites, 449,087 slaves, and 50,000 negro freemen. In 1860, the
corresponding figures were 1,047,411, 548,907, and 58,000.
This growth in numbers was due exclusively to the laws of natural increase within the boundaries of the state. There had
been no addition as in the North, by European immigration.
Moreover, as we shall see, there had, throughout this period,
been a heavy outflow to the South and the West of natives of
Virginia who were attracted by the prospect of acquiring more
fertile lands in those regions that they possessed in the communities which they were leaving.

Although the largest proportion of the small landed proprietors were not interested in slave labor, since they cultivated
their ground with their own hands, the institution of slavery
continued, after the Revolution, to enter deeply into the spirit

of the economic life of Virginia, as a whole, especially in that part of the state which was situated between the falls of the rivers and the seacoast. We propose now to examine the main aspects of that institution as they presented themselves in the long interval before the war for Southern Independence began.

In a former chapter, we described very briefly the resolute and vigorous efforts of the House of Burgesses to block the stream of Africans which England persisted in pouring into the Colony. It was not until 1778 that the new state was in a position to carry her earnest wishes on this point into effect. In the course of that year, her General Assembly passed an act that prohibited the importation into any of her harbors of a single cargo of negro slaves; and the penalty for the violation of this act was a fine of one thousand pounds. Every slave brought in, in disregard of this law, was to be entitled to his freedom so soon as his foot should touch the shore.

It was Mr. Jefferson who inserted in the bill for the Ordinance of 1784 a clause which would have prevented the introduction of slavery, not only into the five states of the Northwest, but also into the present area of Kentucky, Tennessee, Alabama, and Mississippi. The later bill of 1787 finally saved the Northwest from the presence of the institution by confining its colonization to freemen, a clause which had the approval of all the influential Virginians who were members of the committee that framed it.

It was in the teeth of Virginia's protest that the Federal Constitution deferred the interdiction of the external slave trade for a period of twenty years. Her opposition to the proposed delay was voiced with emphasis by one of the greatest of her citizens, George Mason, and it was most fitting that he should have been supported in the debate by one even greater than himself, James Madison. When the date to which the importation of slaves had been limited arrived, Mr. Jefferson was President, and he warmly congratulated Congress on the termination of a traffic so repugnant to "the morality, reputa-

GEORGE MASON

tion, and best interests of the country." It was due to the influence of two Virginians in the House of Representatives, Charles Fenton Mercer and John Floyd, that an act was passed which required that armed American cruisers should patrol the African coast in order to intercept all slave-ships which should appear in those waters; and this continued to be the federal policy until slavery was abolished in the United States.

During the first years that followed the Revolution, several measures were adopted in Virginia which looked to the strict enforcement of the rights of negroes who could claim that they were really free. In 1785, it was declared by the General Assembly, for instance, that all slaves brought in thereafter should be entitled to absolute liberty at the end of twelve months; and three years subsequently it was enacted by the same body that any one who held in bondage the child of a negro freeman was to be considered guilty of an offense punishable by death. Registers were ordered to be kept of all blacks who were born free, or had been manumitted by will, so that any infringement on their liberty could be quickly detected.

By the end of 1810, the census disclosed that the free negroes had increased in number to thirty thousand. The presence of so large a body of persons in the community who possessed no status as citizens, and at the same time, could not be controlled as bondsmen, created a situation so perplexing and dangerous that the General Assembly, in harmony with public sentiment, decided that no slaves were to be manumitted thereafter without provision for their removal from the state within a period of twelve months. The advisability of such a regulation was emphasized by the Turner Insurrection, which occurred in the course of 1831, and resulted in the murder of fifty-seven white people. This event was made more atrocious by the fact that the large majority of the victims were women and children. Moreover, it was a cause for additional alarm that the principal lieutenant of the leader was a free and educated negro.

JOHN FLOYD

During the session of the General Assembly a few months afterwards, the subject of emancipation was earnestly and exhaustively discussed. A resolution which provided for the removal at once of every free negro domiciled in the state, and every negro to become free in the future, was adopted in the House by a vote of seventy-nine to forty-one, but defeated by a narrow margin in the Senate. The desire for the destruction, by one means or another, of the institution of slavery was felt by most of the members of either body. The difficulty of finding a feasible plan alone confused the movement in the two chambers; and a second reason for their uncertain and feeble action was the expense which was expected to accompany any scheme of liberation which should be followed.

The sentiment in Virginia in favor of general emancipation reached its high water-mark at this session of the General Assembly. The failure of that body to grapple with the question and to settle it properly, very naturally led thousands of people in the state to conclude that the problem was beyond the power of the commonwealth to solve. A determination was now reached by the majority of them to endure the existence of slavery in their midst indefinitely, in the hope that time, by means then unforseen, would uproot the institution from the soil. This attitude became more emphatic so soon as the campaign of the Northern Abolitionists against the Southern Slaveholders began to be pushed without regard to the feelings or the interests of the southern people at large. Slavery, these intemperate and fanatical advocates declared, was an institution that was criminal in itself. The slaveholder, therefore, possessed no rights that were entitled to the respect of mankind or the protection of law. Slavery should be abolished at once without compensation, and the region where it had existed left to shift for itself, and if unavoidable, to go to pieces on the rocks of complete bankruptcy. All attempts, open or concealed, to incite the negroes on the plantation to kill, to burn, and to ravish, were deemed by these fire brands to be perfectly justifiable if universal emancipation could be hastened by that inhuman method of assault.

The earliest consequence of this attack on the character and safety of their communities was to create a sense of outrage in the breasts of all Virginians, whether they favored the liberation of the slaves or not. The second was to harden the great majority of them permanently against all proposals to destroy the institution even by gradual emancipation, as recommended by Mr. Jefferson originally, and by his grandson, Thomas Jefferson Randolph, in the General Assembly at the memorable session of 1831-1832.

While the people of Virginia as a whole, subsequent to that session, showed themselves to be more and more determined to resist the aggressions of the Northern Abolitionists, they had not ceased to hope that the worst evils of slavery would be removed by the adoption of a policy of gradual colonization, in place of a policy of gradual emancipation, to which they had looked during the period that followed the Revolution. The first suggestion of the colonization plan is said to have been submitted by Mr. Jefferson to the General Assembly in 1777. Twenty-three years afterwards, that body was so much interested in this farsighted suggestion that it instructed Governor Monroe to propose to the President of the United States the purchase by the National Congress of a domain beyond the borders of Virginia on which all free negroes, or negroes to be freed, could be settled. It was even recommended by the same body in 1805 that a part of Louisiana, then recently acquired, should be reserved as a region suitable for such occupation. It was not until 1861 that the west coast of Africa was mentioned as a place well adapted to the establishment of a colony of the kind desired.

In January, 1817, largely through the active interest shown by influential Virginians in the scheme, the American Colonization Society was organized under the Presidency of Bushrod Washington, a nephew of General Washington, and a member

James Monroe.

of the Supreme Court of the United States. At the end of thirteen years, Justice Washington was succeeded by Charles Carroll, of Carrollton, and he, in turn, by James Madison and Henry Clay. The money needed to pay the expenses of two agents, who were dispatched to Africa to inspect the west coast, was obtained through the subscriptions of Virginians. Finally, the Colony of Liberia was founded, and, in 1824, its capital received the name of Mr. Monroe, at that time the President of the United States. Thirty-one auxiliary societies were soon organized in different parts of Virginia, in city and county alike; and these subordinate associations were composed of a membership which embraced the most distinguished citizens of the commonwealth at large.

In 1828, the Virginia Colonization Society was founded, John Marshall was elected to the post of President, while at least three former Chief executives of the United States were counted in the roll of its subordinate officers. In 1853, the General Assembly granted this association an annual appropriation of thirty thousand dollars for a period of five years to carry out its purpose of transporting to Liberia all free negroes who were willing to immigrate thither under its protection. This appropriation by the state was supplemented by large sums subscribed separately by benevolent citizens.

Philanthropic and farsighted as the scheme of colonization in general undoubtedly was, it had to face a vigorous opposition from proslavery men in Virginia and also from antislavery men in the North. The latter thought that colonization would postpone the hour of universal emancipation; the former thought that it would gradually lead up to practical emancipation through forced emigration to another hemisphere.

While many Virginians were endeavoring to plant the Virginia Colonization Society on a highly useful footing, numerous citizens of the state were seeking to solve the problem in their own case by manumitting their slaves in the testators' lives or by will, and providing the means for their settlement on lands beyond the borders of the South. Several instances may be mentioned in illustration of the steps taken in cases of this kind. In 1819, Samuel Gist, by will, directed that two hundred and sixty-three slaves belonging to his estate should, after his death, be transferred to trustees, with specific instructions for the purchase in the Northwest of a sufficient area to furnish each family with a small farm. These negroes, it is said, were coldly received in their new community, and, within a few years, appear to have lost their holdings through bad management in tilling their ground.

Edward Coles, of Albemarle County, was even more generous. He had, in early life, come to have a strong distaste, if not abhorrence, for the institution of slavery, as it exposed its evil sides under his own eyes. He determined to remove from his conscience the twinge of reproach which his possession of slaves caused him to feel more and more keenly as he grew older. In 1819, he collected them all about him, and at their head, set out for Illinois. Selecting a large tract in a fertile part of that state, he subdivided it into farms that embraced respectively one hundred and sixty acres. To each head of a family, he conveyed one of these farms, after equipping it with implements and livestock, and erecting, at some convenient spot on its surface, a snug farm house.

All these improvements called for large expenditures, and yet Mr. Coles did not shrink from supplying the necessary funds for their creation. His act was not only one that entailed extraordinary financial loss, but also one that called for personal temerity, for he was indicted by the State of Illinois for introducing his freed-men within her bounds, and for a time, he also suffered socially for this course of philanthropy. Subsequently, he was elected to the governorship, and took an energetic part in preventing the introduction in the constitution of that commonwealth of a clause that would have legalized the institution of slavery on her soil.

It is a fact of significance, as throwing light on the spirit of these private emancipations by Virginians, that Governor Coles's son volunteered promptly on the Southern side so soon as Virginia seceded, and perished at the Battle of Roanoke Island.

A still more conspicuous instance of the liberation of slaves was that represented in the case of the celebrated John Randolph of Roanoke. But the spirit exhibited in his instance was not as generous as that exhibited in Edward Coles's, for the statesmen waited until he drafted his will to give substance to his intentions. His executors, however, carried out these intentions with fidelity. Thirteen thousand dollars had been set aside by Randolph to defray all the charges of his four hundred negroes' removal to Ohio, and the cost of acquiring the land which they would need after their arrival there. A concerted effort was made by the white people in the vicinity of this settlement to disrupt it by forcing the freedmen to abandon their holdings and take refuge elsewhere. It is said that, having many other obstacles to success, besides the one just mentioned, to overcome, the transplanted community retrograded rather than progressed; and that its presence left a perceptible mark of decay on the face of the particular area which it occupied, as compared with the highly cultivated lands of their white neighbors.

In 1848, John Warwick, of Amherst County, emancipated his slaves by will, and provided for their settlement as one body in Indiana; but that state, in 1851, before these slaves' removal thither could be completed, prohibited the immigration of African freedmen; and the Warwick negroes were subsequently established in Ohio. They were seventy-four in number. Sampson Saunders, of Cabell County, followed Mr. Warwick's example. Under the provisions of his will, his slaves were set free, and the sum of fifteen thousand dollars reserved for the cost of transporting them to the Northwest and purchasing

JOHN RANDOLPH OF ROANOKE

lands and erecting homes for their occupation. They found an asylum in Michigan.

The examples which we have given are typical of all that occurred during the years that preceded the formal abolition of slavery by the impact of national power. Many other instances might be brought forward.

When a former master, like Edward Coles, led the way to the West, his freedmen offered no opposition. Apparently, this was the case also when the master had died after making a will that struck the shackles from the limbs of his slaves and ordered their deportation. But there were cases in which a Virginian liberated his bondsmen in his own lifetime, and provided for the expenses of their emigration without intending, like Edward Coles, to accompany them. If he had been kind and considerate in his treatment of them, difficulty was always found in persuading them to leave and take possession of the farms chosen for them in a free community. A typical instance of this kind occurred in Culpeper County. A tract of land had been purchased in Pennsylvania for the occupation by a large band belonging to a planter of the county who was conscientiously opposed to holding slaves. When the first volunteers for the long journey, under the temporary direction of the planter's son, were called for, only a few responded, and but one of these was suitable for the purpose of encouraging the rest to go. There were eighteen in all to be sent. Forced against their will as a body at last to depart, two of the band, before the end of two weeks, deserted the place of settlement chosen, and by the close of twelve months more, the rest, like the first two, had returned to the home of their former master.

Beginning with the adoption of the Treaty of Peace in 1783, the records of all the County Courts, down to the middle of the following century, are found to contain numerous wills, the makers of which had liberated their slaves with ample provision for their support. They were expected to remain in Virginia and there merge in the already large body of freedmen.

The influence of the Declaration of Independence was very perceptible in the expression of the earliest of these wills. "Freedom," asserted Joseph Hill, of Isle of Wight County, "is the natural life of all mankind." Charles Moorman, of Campbell County, repeats these words. "No law, moral or divine," he adds, "has given me a property in the persons of any of my fellow creatures." Richard Randolph, Jr., in his last testament, refers "to the lawless and monstrous crime of slavery," from which he hopes to exculpate his memory by the manumission of his bondsmen. George Washington, by a similar instrument, emancipated all the negroes in his possession, with a generous provision for those who were infirm or advanced in years. Jesse Bonner, of Dinwiddie County, in setting his negroes free by will, devised for their support the plantation on which he had resided. Charles Ewell, of Prince William County, arranged in the same way for the liberation of all his younger slaves at the age of twenty-five. John Smith, of Sussex, after a testamentory declaration of his conviction that freedom "is the natural right of every person," provides for the manumission of all his slaves so soon as his widow should die. John Ward, of Pittsylvania County, in 1826, imitated his example; so did Mrs. Peyton, of Prince William County, in 1831, and Aylette Hawes, of Rappahannock, in the course of the following year. William H. Fitzhugh, the uncle of Mrs. Robert E. Lee, provided for the liberation of all his slaves who should survive to the year 1850.

After 1833, when the activities of the Abolitionists had begun to threaten the safety of every community in the older parts of Virginia, the testators who freed their bondsmen were less frank in expressing their disapproval of slavery, since this would have put them in the position of encouraging indirectly those northern aggressions which were now causing so much bitterness. But emancipation by will continued. In 1838, Carter H. Edlow, of Prince George County, manumitted all his slaves by this means; so did Thacker V. Webb of Orange County, in 1843; so did Thomas Eppes, of Henrico County, in 1848. After

1850, provision was made in numerous testaments for the transfer of the makers' emancipated negroes to Liberia, but in others, the former rule of liberating without provision for removal was still frequently followed. Such was the case in the wills of Philip Lightfoot, of Culpeper County, in 1855, William Smith, of Orange, in 1857, and George Washington Parke Custis in the course of the same year. Indeed, the like testaments were placed on record until 1860.

These instances of liberation by the act of individuals,— of which we have only given a few characteristic examples,— are significant as showing that there was no vigorous sentiment in each community in favor of completely balking the generous impulses of citizens who had recourse to this means of emancipating their bondsmen. When the serious obstacles in existence to discourage this form of generosity are recalled, the only cause for surprise is that so many owners of slaves were ready, under the influence of their consciences alone to defy them.

There were three impediments which exerted a peculiarly strong influence on the action of individuals. First, the rights of creditors. Slaves were property, and subject to sale for debts. Second, doubtfulness as to whether the bondsman's happiness would be increased by freedom, if they had to remain among a great multitude of persons of their own race who were still in a condition of servitude. Thirdly, could any country really prosper which was overrun by thousands of former slaves, who possessed no civil rights, and were naturally antagonistic to the white people, and, perhaps, even inclined to incite insurrections in the plantation quarters? Political and civil coelescence was morally impossible, and physical amalgamation would mean simply the practical destruction of both races, by reducing them both to the status of mongrels, who would lack the virtues of either race.

The impression of the evils of the institution of slavery was softened in the minds of the majority of the Virginians by their knowledge of its finer and gentler aspects. There is no reason to question the general fact that the system was, to a large degree, a patriarchal one. Affection and conscientiousness on the side of the master, a blind fidelity and devotion on the side of the slave, often made the relation one of genuine nobility and beauty. But in the shadow of every slaveholder, however high-minded, lurked the shadow of the negro trader. Many planters often passed their whole lives without buying or selling a single slave. It was at the death of these men, if there was more than one heir, that the evil of division and separation always arose, even if they had left no debts. This condition was still more poignant, should the master, in his lifetime, have fallen into a slough of liabilities from which he could only be extricated by the sale of the whole or a part of his roll of slaves.

There is little reason to doubt that many negroes were carried out of Virginia to the plantations situated in the far South. Many of these slaves had been purchased at auction by professional traders, and led away to their remote destination in sullen gangs. But a large number yet accompanied their masters, when the latter, with their families discouraged by the agricultural conditions prevailing in the older parts of the state, emigrated to the cotton regions of Mississippi and Alabama, in the hope of recuperating their fortunes by the cultivation of a newer and richer soil. We shall discover in a subsequent chapter the powerful influence which this lack of agricultural thrift exerted on the well-being of slavery in its oldest seat.

The existence of this unprosperous condition on her plantations was in itself a disproof of the assertion that Virginia had become simply a slave-breeding community, which found a ready and profitable sale for her human cattle from year to year on the great cotton estates. Had the income from this source been as considerable as affirmed by hypercritical historical writers of the past, Eastern Virginia would have been in as flourishing a shape as Kentucky was, owing to the latter's similar traffic in horses and mules. On the contrary, its impoverishment during a long period before 1850 was, as we shall see, one of the most patent facts in its agricultural history.

It should always be borne in mind that the number of land-owners in Virginia who could not claim the possession of a single slave far exceeded the number of those who held that form of property. In 1860 the white population of the state was set down by the census of that year at 1,047,299 persons. Of these, 52,128 were slaveholders, one third of whom owned one or two slaves, while one half owned less than four. Only one hundred and fourteen landowners in Virginia then possessed one hundred slaves respectively.

CHAPTER II

AGRICULTURAL CONDITIONS

Perhaps, the most remarkable general feature of the history of agriculture in Virginia during the Federal Period, 1775-1861, was the unfavorable contemporary impression which its condition made on the most thoughtful citizens of the state itself. Not until the last decade of that period, or, to be more accurate, not until the last half of that decade, was reached, that is to say, the interval between 1855 and 1861,—was there any brightening in this cloud of pessimism to be noted; and the revival of hopefulness then was really due, not to any permanent improvement in the agricultural condition of the commonwealth, so far at least as the productiveness of the soil alone was involved, as to a more profitable market in Europe, which unexpectedly increased the demand for one of the important crops of Virginia, namely, wheat. The influence of the Crimean war was felt at once in the state, not only in the augmentation of the volume of the exports of this commodity, but also in the advancement of its value.

The agriculture of Virginia, like every other department of its industrial life, had also responded to the rise in all prices which had followed the discovery of gold in California in 1849.

The failure of Virginian agriculture to make the progress during the Federal Period which was observed in the North and West during the same interval, had at the time been attributed chiefly to the influence of the institution of slavery. How far was this impression correct? There can be no doubt that the slaves served a more useful purpose in the colonial age than they

460

did after the close of the Revolution down to the opening of the
war for Southern Independence. And why? Because, during the
whole of the colonial age, there was a demand for an extensive,
as opposed to an intensive, system of cultivation.

Not only on the great coastal plain spreading from the falls
in the principal streams to the seacoast, but also on those uplands which ran back to the Eastern spurs of the Blue Ridge,
the task of each year that taxed the laborers' power of endurance most was the removal of the natural growth of forest from
the surface of the land. This task fell as heavily on the yeoman
dependent on his own hands, who owned a small estate, as on
the class of the wealthiest planters. It is true that the muscle
of the African bondsman was not entirely indispensable even
in the colonial age, since the same work had been done almost
exclusively by the English indentured servant during nearly
the whole of the seventeenth century; but there can be no doubt
whatever that the ever-increasing importation of negroes after
1700, until they came to take the industrial servant's place, had
an enormous influence in widening the area of cultivated ground
after that date.

It is quite possible that, had this extension of soil under tillage been left to the diminishing number of indentured servants
after 1700, when a new disposition in England to discourage
the emigration of persons of the working class became so conspicuous, it would have been more remarkable for the slowness
of its progress than for the rapidity. The greater the number
of slaves introduced, the more quickly fell the woods before the
axe, not simply on the frontier, but within the boundaries of
each of the oldest plantations of that day. Jefferson summed
up the character of the agricultural situation both in the seventeenth century and in the eighteenth, when he said that it cost
less to acquire a fertile field by destroying the forest than it did
by manuring previously used ground which had begun to show
the first symptoms of exhaustion.

During that period, the same influence was at work on an old plantation as on a new. The owner of the new had to cut away the timber to secure any tillable soil at all, and the owner of the old had to follow his example if he wished to obtain a substitute for the additional overworn acres which confronted him at the end of every year. In this process, the labor of the negro was invaluable for the time being, however injurious his presence, from a social and political as well as from an economic point of view, might become after the whole face of the country had been cleared of the original forest.

By the beginning of the Revolution, this work of denudation had been carried by no means to the limit possible, since the aspect of the rural districts was still that of a land heavily wooded, but it had at least reached a point which made the slave no longer indispensable, since the need of new grounds on each estate was not now as urgent and as constant as it was formerly. One reason for this fact was that the culture of tobacco had declined in volume, not only throughout the region of Tidewater, but also in the districts lying nearer the mountains. That crop had, by this time, found a partial substitute in wheat, a grain which could not be grown to the greatest advantage in forest mould, a substance so essential, as we have seen, to the production of tobacco in the absence of modern manures. To make the cultivation of wheat equally profitable, a large area of ground was required, and this fact tended to encourage a disposition in the landowner to turn to a better use of his old cleared fields than to allow them to spring up in broomsedge and stunted pines.

The falling off in tobacco culture, both before and after the Revolution, diminished the economic value of the slave because it signified a slackening in that demand for heavy labor which alone had given him his superiority over the average white field-hand. From the hour when the chief plantation task ceased to be the destruction of the virgin forest, the real importance of the institution of slavery dwindled. Slave labor was no longer more valuable than indentured white service. Its primary usefulness had ended.

If every slave living in Virginia at the close of the Revolution could have been withdrawn from the state under some conservative plan that would have been equally just to the white people and the black, the welfare of the commonwealth would have been enormously advanced. It is true that after the long training which the negroes had received in the fields, they had come to possess great skill in the production and handling of crops. They worked faithfully and effectively under continuous supervision, and they were probably less expensive, owing to their greater power of endurance, than the same number of white laborers would have been. These facts, however, no longer made them indispensable. No doubt the influence of the Revolution, by introducing new ideas as to the natural rights of men, had much to do with the readiness of persons of that day to adopt a general system of emancipation, had one been found to be practicable; but below this spirit of philanthropy, there must have lurked a feeling that, in the agricultural conditions then prevailing, the value of negro labor had declined to a point where its loss would inflict no serious damage beyond what is apt to follow a change in any economic system.

The shrinkage in the prosperity of agriculture during the Federal Period was, on the whole, to be attributed, not to the malign impression of the institution of slavery, but to certain influences which would have come into operation even if slavery had not existed. These influences were undoubtedly aggravated by the presence of that institution, but were not really created by it, as was so generally believed by the Virginians themselves. If slavery had been the cause of the decline in agriculture, the thousands of yeomen without slaves who constituted the great majority of the population would not have felt the stringency as acutely as the large landowners, who were so badly injured by the prevailing depression. There is ample proof that these yeomen suffered as much damage as their wealthy neighbors.

In other words, the discouraging influence at work touched them equally as closely and directly.

What were these influences which left so distinct an impression on the prosperity of the agriculture of that day? They arose from two causes, namely, emigration and an impoverished soil,—in most of Tidewater at least. To some degree the two acted on each other. The impoverishment of the soil, on the one hand, stimulated the impulse in many landowners to set out for some region lying beyond the borders of the state which would offer more advantages in the possession of fertile lands. On the other hand, the withdrawal of a great number of citizens who belonged in most cases to the younger and more enterprising element of the population tended to defer the rehabilitation of agriculture in Virginia by decreasing the number of persons who followed it, or, under other circumstances, would have followed it, as a means of earning a livelihood.

It would be a mistake, however, to infer that the emigration of so many Virginians between 1800 and 1850 was due exclusively to the pressure of unprosperous conditions on the plantations which they were leaving. The instinct which had led thousands of Englishmen to abandon the Mother Country, in the seventeenth century, was attributable as much to a spirit of enterprise and adventure as to a shrewd practicality, which found the circumstances of their situation in the English town and country intolerable because so unpromising. The lure of the life which Kipling in our own age held out as lying beyond the ranges on the horizon, made the like irresistible appeal to the breasts of the young Virginians in every period of their community's history, apart from a mere hope of material gain, although that expectation too, naturally enough, had its reflection in their motive for seeking a new domicile beyond the Alleghanies or in the far Southwest.

It was an untrammeled life of movement which the Virginians led on their plantations, a life, that, in all its varied activities,—especially in the open air, where most of it was spent, cultivated in them a manly, self-reliant, and sanguine temperament, the very temperament, indeed, which emboldered them to strike out for new scenes in search of new fortunes. It was this spirit which had made their English ancestors the greatest colonizers of their times; and it was this spirit also which drove so many of their descendants in Virginia far from the scenes of their birth.

Below it all, there were in the cases of thousands some special personal reason at work in addition. Virginia, throughout the Federal Period, remained a plantation community, in spite of the existence of numerous small towns like Richmond, Norfolk, Lynchburg, and Staunton. But there was not room enough in these towns, and at the courthouses, to offer an opening for all the young men who desired to follow some intellectual profession. The career of the planter-father would not have been satisfactory to all his sons, even if the condition of agriculture had been highly prosperous. It was perfectly natural that many young men of ambition, like Henry Clay, and hundreds of others of great talent and destined to high distinction, should have directed their footsteps to the new communities beyond the borders of the state, where the prospects for professional aspirants were so much more promising than the prospects which were held out to them in their native communities in Virginia.

There was another influence stimulating emigration which was not necessarily brought about either by slavery or by the impoverishment of the soil. Among the notable features of the Virginian's family life in those times was the number of children who daily gathered about the domestic hearth. The Virginian father, like the English father of the seventeenth century, might well have been perplexed to decide what was the wisest step that he could take for his sons' benefit as they grew to maturity. Was there room enough on his own plantation for the accommodation of them all, when sufficiently old to leave the threshold of home? Could new plantations be bought for

them in his own neighborhood when they came of age? Did
Virginia at large offer a favorable opening in the pursuits of
agriculture? It was under these circumstances that the de-
pressed condition of that industry was influential in determining
the fate of many families in Virginia, not only by encouraging
the emigration of their younger members, but also by prompting
numerous fathers more or less advanced in years to sell their
lands, and accompanied by wives, children, and slaves, to set
out for the cotton regions of the Southwest or the park-like
uplands of Kentucky.

In 1786, the population of the latter, then a county of Virginia, numbered twenty-five thousand persons. Before four
years had passed, this population had increased to one hundred
thousand. It is estimated that at least two-thirds of these people
had come in from the Mother State. In 1850, the census revealed
the fact that, of 1,260,982 persons born in Virginia, not less
than 388,059 were residing permanently beyond its borders. In
other words, at least one third of its natives had cast in their
fortunes with other communities lying as far away as Pennsylvania and New York in the North, Iowa in the West, and
Alabama and Mississippi in the South.

The loss in intelligence, energy, and capital which these figures indicate would be almost enough in itself to explain the
general unprosperity of Virginian agriculture during the
greater part of the Federal Period. The full economic force of
this loss is only clearly taken in when we recall the second fact
which had also so much to do in bringing about the prevailing
depression. This second fact was the natural thinness of the
soil as a whole in the counties of Tidewater, which were the
ones that felt most acutely the effect of the emigration. If the
state, during the Federal Period, had been a country,—like
England, for instance, in the past and present,—full of large
cities, and thickly inhabited throughout, and in possession of
great wealth, this emigration would not have been damaging

at all. On the contrary, it would have been as wholesome as a blood-letting in the case of a man with a tendency to apoplexy.

Virginia was no such over populated community as this. The withdrawal of hundreds of thousands of her citizens, instead of relieving a mere plethora, drew upon her vital resources, and to that extent, made her more unable to go forward as fast as so many of her sister commonwealths were doing.

During this time, the plough had been depleting her soil, especially in all that area of country which lay east of the Falls. The first impression of the voyagers of 1607 was that the virgin region which they saw on all sides, as they made their way slowly up the waters of the Powhatan, was one of extraordinary productiveness. This impression was not entirely inaccurate. The low grounds along the banks of the Powhatan have, down to our day, been justly celebrated for their fatness. This was revealed as early as the first settlers' arrival by the enormous growth of timber which covered the general face of the country, and by the rich abundance of the crops which were noticed wherever the Indians had removed the trees and planted the ground in maize and vegetables. A more critical examination of the soil, in after years, however, modified this first impression of the region's extreme fertility.

The country earliest occupied was capable of three divisions. First, there were the lands situated on the ridges. These were always poor in quality, as they were in part sandy, and in part clayey. As late as 1833, a large proportion of these lands remained in cut-over woods, and, when fully cleared, hardly justified tillage, since in the clayey section they brought in a return of only five bushels of corn or wheat per acre, and in the sandy, only twelve bushels of corn, and practically no wheat at all. The slopes that led down from the ridges to the level of the bottoms along the streams were generally composed of a sandy surface, which easily yielded to disintegration by rain. These slopes were not adapted to the culture of wheat, and when abandoned, quickly sprang up in small pines.

The only soil that was naturally fertile was the area of low grounds adjacent to the streams. In a few places only, this area was very extensive in width, while in others it was simply a narrow strip.

The system of cultivation pursued from the beginning was as follows: first, the bottom lands were stripped of wood and brought under the hoe and plough. They stood the annual drain on their fertility with fair success. The next step was to clear the slopes, and put them under tillage, and to continue this, at first every year, until an obvious depletion in productiveness set in. This was a warning to allow the ground to lie fallow every other year until the reduction of the crops to five bushels of grain per acre should compel the abandonment of the land to pines. At the end of twenty years, the soil had recovered sufficiently to justify its second clearance,—only to revert in time, however, to its previous condition by the ruthless resumption of the same exhaustive methods of using it.

Edmund Ruffin estimated that, during the first four decades of the nineteenth century, the extent of the land denuded from year to year almost exactly balanced the area of land abandoned to the regrowth of forest. According to his calculation, the region lying east of a south and north line drawn thirty miles back from the falls in the rivers and extending to the sea-coast, would not, for nine-tenths of its surface, in consequence of long abrasion by hoe and plough, yield more than ten bushels of grain per acre. How was this condition of practical exhaustion outside of the area of the different oases of low ground, which embraced the rest of the country, to be remedied? It was his theory that this could only be done by supplying the calcareous ingredient which was so largely lacking when his experiments began. By combining sand, clay, and marl in the same soil, the defects of each, when left by itself, could be removed. The result would be a soil precisely adapted to the production of such a crop as wheat, to which the agriculture of Tidewater had, dur-

EDMUND RUFFIN

ing the Napoleonic wars, been turning as a substitute for to-bacco.

It was a matter of urgent importance to that section of the state that the production of this crop should be enormously increased, and until marl, as a fertilizer for the restoration of the exhausted fields, began to be used, there appeared to be little hope of any profitableness from that branch of tillage.

Ruffin's observations led him to certain definite conclusions which may be presented substantially in his own words. The natural sterility of the fields of lower Virginia, he said, was caused by the fact that they were destitute of calcareous earth, and at the same time, they were full of vegetable acids. The virtue of calcareous earth consisted of its ability, by neutralizing these acids, to produce a perfect combination between putrescent manures and the soil to be tilled. This combination meant a high state of fertility; and a state of fertility signified abundant crops where before no crops could be coaxed into growing. Where was this calcareous earth to be obtained? Ruffin pointed out that there were few tracts of land of any size in Lower Virginia which did not contain a natural bed of marl.

He reached his conviction as to the beneficent effect of this substance on agriculture by a long series of experiments of the most minutely observant nature, which took in the special quality of each field and the exact amount of fertilizer which it called for to be productive. He proved that, with marl, the farm-yard manures would improve soils which were not susceptible of improvement with the farm-yard manures omitted; and that soils of a sandy character required a different sort of treatment with marl from soils that partook chiefly of the nature of clay. He discovered that there was a limit to the advantageous use of marl, and that its virtue might be practically destroyed by running beyond that limit. The quantity per acre which he employed fluctuated between three hundred and six hundred bushels.

Ruffin took a higher view of his experiments than to look on them as being purely agricultural. He rightly regarded his work of experiment in the spirit of the humanitarian and the statesman also. "Unless we can feed our slaves," he said again and again, "we must continue to export them like so many cattle from the state." "Nothing," he added, "can check this forced emigration of flocks of blacks, and this voluntary emigration of whites, except an increased production of food, which is only to be obtained by enriching our lands. Wherever our land is so improved as to produce double its present supply of food, it will also hold and retain double its present population."

In a petition to the General Assembly, he stated,—and there is reason to think, with perfect accuracy,—that the value of the soil in Eastern Virginia had been augmented to the extent of eighteen million dollars by the use of calcareous manures. His principle had been adopted at an early day by the most thoughtful and enterprising farmers in all the counties of Tidewater, and their example had been imitated in time by the large body of persons who followed that calling, whether on a large or a small scale.

It would be an error to suppose that, even when severe depression prevailed in Virginian agriculture during the Federal Period, there were not many individual landowners who endeavored, by every enlightened means in their reach, to improve the condition of their soil with a view to making it more productive. The eagerness of those residing in the region of Tidewater to utilize, as we have stated, Ruffin's experiments indicates the quickness of the response of the planters at large at that time to every device which promised even a moderate increase in the return from their lands. To picture all these men as being in such a state of hopelessness as to accept emigration, or the sale of their surplus slaves, as the only way of maintaining the fortunes of their respective families would be to misinterpret the situation, in spite of its admitted drawbacks.

John Taylor, of Caroline, the author of the *Letters of Arator*, the greatest single contribution ever made to the history of Virginian agriculture, with the sole exception of Ruffin's *Calcareous Manures*, did not stand alone even in his own day as

ONE OF VIRGINIA'S RICH GRAIN FIELDS

a student of agricultural methods. Along the alluvial banks of the Dan, Staunton, Roanoke, James, Rappahannock, and other streams, there were to be found large plantations which, whether devoted to maize, tobacco, or wheat, or to all these in equal proportions, offered as fine examples of thorough tillage, abundance of product, and skilful management, as the whole face of the United States at large at that period could furnish. Estates like Mount Airy and Kinlock on the Rappahannock,

Claremont, Curl's Neck, and Brandon on the Lower James, Elk Hill and Dover on the Upper, Prestwould on the Roanoke, Staunton Hill and Green Hill on the Staunton, Berry Hill and the plantations of the Hairston family on the Dan,—to give the names of only a few of the large number that existed,—all these and hundreds besides lying in the interval between the Chesapeake Bay and the Blue Ridge proved unmistakably that neither the art of tillage nor the art of management was lost in Virginia.

It should not be forgotten that the state, throughout the Federal Period, was a series of rural communities to which the play of the highest talent of its people was restricted. It is true that much of this talent was directed to the pursuit of politics, but what remained unemployed in this manner was devoted to the administration and cultivation of the plantations, on which, with small exception, the population depended for a support.

The great body of the owners were men of excellent education, since they had, in their youth, been sent to superior academies and colleges, not all of which were local. They adopted agriculture as their calling because it offered them the most congenial field for the gratification of their chief interest in life which was in the tillage of their lands; and the sons followed in their footsteps, not in a perfunctory or conventional spirit, but with their entire heart fully embarked in their occupation. If, at any time, the agricultural condition of their several communities showed signs of languishment, it was not due to negligence or ignorance on their part as a body, but to reasons, such as low prices, which they could not control, because governed by influences of world-wide scope.

One of the means which they adopted, as early as 1811, for the advancement of their calling was the organization of an agricultural society for the commonwealth at large, with auxiliary societies in numerous counties. These subordinate associations found presiding officers in the most influential men in the state. In 1836, a great agricultural convention was held in

CYRUS H. MCCORMICK

MATTHEW F. MAURY

Richmond, and five years later, the General Assembly established a State Board of Agriculture. But it was not until 1853 that the first State Fair opened; and it was repeated annually until the breaking out of hostilities brought all activities of this kind to an end.

After 1850, when the salable value of the products of the Virginian farms and plantations increased, in consequence of the discovery of gold in California, and of foreign wars, the agricultural scene in Virginia assumed a new aspect. The prosperity which prevailed among all classes of landowners down to the beginning of the war of 1861 was never surpassed, and perhaps never equaled in the history of the state. All this occurred before the lure of the West and Far South had started to decline, and when the necessity of halting the impoverishment of the soil was still as urgent as ever.

It was during the Federal Period that Virginia produced two sons whose work for the advancement of agriculture reached out, in its beneficial effects, far beyond the confines of the state. The one was Cyrus H. McCormick, who perfected the reaper, and the other was Matthew Fontaine Maury, who initiated the use of the science of metereology for agricultural purposes.

McCormick, perceiving clearly the wide field for his invention which was opening up with the spread of population over the Western plains, left his native Rockbridge County, where his experiments had been successfully made, and settled ultimately in Chicago, which, at that time, contained only ten thousand inhabitants. Stage by stage, he increased his machine's efficiency until he had brought it to the point of binding the sheaves with wire and afterwards with twine. It was estimated that one of these harvesters possessed the capacity of eight men who were working with the old-fashioned cradle in cutting wheat, and gathering it up and shocking it with their hands.

It was asserted that, after the reaper came into use, the line of frontier was thrust back as rapidly as twenty miles a day in excess of what had previously occurred. This was due simply to the saving in labor which resulted from the operation of this ingenious piece of mechanism. Seward went so far as to say that the reaper had been the principal means of bringing about the final triumph of the Federal arms, since it had made possible the use on the battle line of a great body of stalwart men, who, if the blade and cradle had been still the only implement employed in cutting wheat, would have been compelled to remain in the harvest field to provide food for the soldiers at the front.

In 1855, Maury began the delivery of a series of addresses before many Western and Southern agricultural societies, in which he urged them to make a record of their observations on the temperature of the atmosphere and the force and direction of the winds. He recommended that they should submit a petition to Congress to influence that body to establish a central office in Washington for the reception of daily reports on the weather. The substance of these, he said, might be telegraphed from all over the country, so as to hasten the means of protecting the crops in time against the ravages of storms and frosts. One of the most familiar departments of the National Government in our own age is the Weather Bureau, which subserves, by its vast organization of stations and observers, the very purpose which the great Virginian had suggested with such keen foresight, and such profound wisdom, long before the plan was actually carried out by the United States,—to be afterwards imitated by all the nations of the civilized world. Maury was thus directly instrumental in securing for the toilers of the land the same enormous advantages which he had previously secured for the toilers of the sea.

CHAPTER III

INTERNAL IMPROVEMENTS

If we examine a map of Virginia as it stood at the beginning of the nineteenth century, it would be hard to imagine an equal area of country, the development of which would be more likely to be hampered by obstructions to travel and transportation than the Western and Central regions of the state, owing to the presence there of mountain chains. There was no difficulty of this nature within the boundaries of the Tidewater territory, which ended on the west in the line than ran south and north across the falls in the rivers. Most of the plantations situated on the surface of that restricted area had, from the first settlement, followed the banks of the navigable streams. The possession of the site for a wharf was, in the colonial age at least, almost essential to the value of land, for, without it, access to market was rendered toilsome and expensive. The public roads connecting the back plantations with the nearest warehouse on the nearest river were always inferior in character, and at certain seasons, barely passable; but still, by rolling the tobacco hogsheads, the river was ultimately attainable. Even when a large body of water flowed some distance away, the merchantmen achored there could generally be reached by sloops of a sufficiently light draft to navigate the numerous shallow creeks that led from the interior down to the main stream.

Taken as a whole, Tidewater Virginia was a section of country which at no period of its history suffered seriously from a lack of means for removing to market the products of the soil. The enormous economic influence of the natural channels for transportation which it possessed is revealed by the fact that, previous to 1700, the advance of its population westward was completely halted by the existence of the cataracts in the great rivers. These rivers ceased to be of use when they came to offer a barrier of rocks to the passage of boats. It was in harmony with this condition, that, throughout the seventeenth century, the little outpost on the site of the modern city of Richmond was known as the World's End.

As the population seeking the fertile valleys adjacent to the same streams west of the falls gradually made their way towards the foothills of the Blue Ridge,—which they reached before the middle of the eighteenth century,—they continued to employ the larger streams for transportation so far as it was practicable to do so. The James River, in spite of its dangerous channels, was, before the close of that century, the principal artery for the transfer of crops to the markets in the East, and for the conveyance of articles to supply the needs of the interior regions. A long and slim batteau was in use for this purpose, which was exactly suited to its shallow yet turbulent current.

There were two important *entrepots* west of the Ridge. The one was situated at Scottsville on the James; the other at Milton at the head of navigation in the Rivanna. These little towns, which were the seats of a bustling commercial life, retained their conspicuous position in trade until the construction of the Central Railway and the James River Canal had been completed to points beyond them. The wagon drawn by teams of four horses was a very necessary accessory to the prosperity of these inland ports. Long caravans of these canvassed vehicles crossed the Gap at Rockfish with their heavy loads of country produce, and descending the eastward slopes of the Ridge, made their way either straight to Scottsville by the southeast public highway or to Milton, some miles beyond the town of Charlottesville. Many of these wagons did not halt in Albemarle, but journeyed steadily on to Richmond, where the drivers drew rein, after probably spending a week on the road between Staunton and the Capital. There was a regular tariff for the various articles which they carried.

Throughout the Valley of the Shenandoah, the wagon played the chief part in transportation at this time, although the Shen-

APPLE BLOSSOMS IN THE SHENANDOAH VALLEY

In the growing of commercial apples Virginia ranks third among all States

andoah River had been improved. The horse and the mule, and the rough teamster and his vehicle, were the most reliable agents and instrumentalities for that purpose in one of the most fertile regions to be found, not merely in the United States, but in the world. Upon them alone the people who resided among the Alleghany mountains, and the counties just beyond that chain, depended for the acquisition of the household articles which they could not manufacture with their own hands, or for the conveyance to market of such of their crops as would stand the wear and cost of removal.

These people, unlike those inhabiting the Valley and Piedmont, were not reached by a quicker means of travel and transportation until nearly an hundred years later, when the first railways penetrated those remote scenes. The building of turnpikes at first improved their situation, without, however, entirely relieving it. Beginning at the first passes of the Alleghanies, the country has continued to be, independently of the railroad and turnpike lines, one of the most difficult in the Southern States to enter or to traverse.

When we recall the character of the roads which, at the beginning of the nineteenth century, were in use, not simply in the western parts of Virginia, but in the Central and Eastern also, it is hard to understand how they ever fulfilled the purpose for which they were designed. There was in all the counties, it is true, a system of road preservation, but it was of the most primitive nature, except where the turnpike had been introduced. In summer, even the important highways were drowned in dust, made all the more aggravating when long strings of wagons and their four-horse teams were passing. In winter, a spell of rain or a fall of snow reduced them to a state approaching complete impassability. The difficulties of transportation were increased by the fact that the line of highway so often run over the crest of mountains, great or small, through high foothills, and almost everywhere, down to the edge of the coastal plain, over a country of great inequalities of surface.

The obstacles which impeded the progress of the covered wagon also confronted the stage-coach patronized by travellers. With a full complement of passengers and baggage, these coaches, in spite of the number of horses that drew them, could only move forward at a very slow rate. The sole condition in existence to console the weary and fatigued occupants was the

presence of many taverns along the main road, where a draught
of good liquor, and an old fashioned meal, were always obtainable during the day, and at night, a comfortable bed. It very
often happened, however, that the passenger was compelled to
leave his seat in the coach to assist in prizing out of the mud
a wheel which had sunk to the hub, or it may be he had to
remain exposed to the cold winds of winter until a blacksmith
could be brought from his stand at a cross-roads many miles
away to patch up the damage to the tires until the nearest town
could be reached.

In considering the physical character of Virginia in its
relation to transportation, we have seen that there existed on
its surface great ranges of mountains running, not eastward
towards the sea, which would have left open wide valleys for
a comparatively easy traversal by railways and canals, but running north and south, which created enormous barriers to be
surmounted by both the railway locomotive and the canal boat
when they were reached. There was hardly a state in the Union
at that time in which the engineer of a turnpike, pushing his
way towards the banks of the Ohio River in the far West, had
so many natural obstructions on a vast scale to overcome.

These obstructions towering to the skies assumed a more
regrettable significance when it was recalled that, so far back
as the time of Washington, the most farseeing Virginians had
formed a just impression of the benefits that would flow to the
state, if easy and direct means of communication could be established with the empire in the West, destined, as they could
already discern, to an unexampled expansion in wealth and
population. If Virginia could be made the highway from those
vast plains to the seaboard, she would inevitably become, thereby, the most opulent community in America. Her inland towns
would increase in number of inhabitants, while its seaport,
Norfolk, would draw to its wharves from year to year, the largest commercial fleets in the Western World. Here the principal
imports into the United States by foreign nations would be

32—Vol. I.

unloaded, and here the bulk of American grain conveyed overland from the Western States would be placed on board for
transfer to the harbors of other continents.

Agriculture also, under the nourishing influence of this ever
expanding commerce, would take on a new aspect of prosperity,
and local trade would grow to an unprecedented volume.

In other words, the prospect which rose before the eyes of
these thoughtful Virginians was precisely the one which, in our
day, has been fully realized in the history of New York State
and New York City.

Fully aware of the possibilities of wealth which lay in building broad, straight, and substantial highways to the West, and
equally clear in their recognition of the physical obstructions
which stood in the path, why was it that the people of the state
east of the Blue Ridge so deliberately, and apparently so fat-
uously, turned their backs on all the inducements held out to
them to give their ardent support to the eminently sensible and
practical principles of the American System, so earnestly advocated by Henry Clay and other public men? There was not
a state in the whole sisterhood of states that would have derived greater advantage at that period from accepting unre-
servedly the Doctrine of Internal Improvements at the national
expense, in part or in whole, than Virginia would have done.
She was now in no financial position to carry out all these
improvements at her own charge exclusively, if this was to be
accomplished on a scale commensurate with the difficulties which
her mountain chains presented. Nor could she, under the most
favorable circumstances, acting alone, expect to finish the task
within a time that would disconcert all rivalry on the part of
the states north of the Potomac. Speed in undertaking and
carrying through that work was the vital element. The first
in the race would bear away the prize permanently, as the completion of the Baltimore and Ohio Railway and the Erie Canal
was soon to demonstrate.

It is no overstatement to say that the institution of slavery was the most powerful practical influence that led Virginians of the East to take so unwise a view of the doctrine of internal improvements with national aid. That view undoubtedly had its origin, theoretically at least, in the principle of strict construction of the Constitution, a principle which would have come into existence in the older part of the state had there not been a single negro within its borders. It arose largely at first from the jealousy which Virginia and her sister southern communities felt for the maintenance in their new character as states of the practical independence which had prevailed among them as colonies before the Revolution. The Constitution had been adopted by them in a spirit of more or less compulsion created by fear of external invasion rather than in a spirit of unreserved approval. And the tendency towards consolidation was encouraged to an extreme by the Virginia and Kentucky Resolutions of Madison and Jefferson.

With the growth in the North of the sentiment in favor of abolition, it became clearer to the public men of Eastern Virginia that the only bulwark that was likely to protect the institution of slavery was continued loyalty to the principle of strict construction of the powers and limitations of the Constitution. Unfortunately for the material development of the state as a whole, the doctrine of internal improvements was considered in the East to be a departure from the spirit of strict construction, and, therefore, to be rejected as practically heretical.

It was not unnatural that the people of the Eastern part of the State should have looked upon the adoption of a tariff as damaging to their welfare. It necessarily fell heavily on their agricultural interests at a time when these interests were the only source of income in the possession of the great majority of its people. The tariff raised the prices of all the articles which they had to purchase, without assuring any compensation by broadening the foreign market, which, on the contrary, tended rather to shrink with the increase in the American import duties. The domestic market for Virginia at least failed to expand to any substantial extent. But there was no such serious objection to the American System, so far, at least, as it related to the doctrine of internal improvements, unless the preservation of the institution of slavery and its corrollary, State Sovereignty, was more important than the development, with national assistance in part, of the enormous natural resources of the State, which only in our own day have begun to be adequately exploited, but too late to snatch the primacy from other States on the seaboard, although none of these really surpassed Virginia, even if they equaled her, in the like advantages.

Regarded from the point of view of our own times, Eastern Virginia's opposition to the Nation sharing in the building of the Cumberland Road appears to be trivial and parochial in spirit. This spirit was to prove very damaging in its remote consequences to the State as a whole. In its apprehension of encroachment by the National Government, Eastern Virginia at least was always prepared to refuse all national aid in a matter of this kind, on which its welfare really turned in a far more comprehensive way than on the preservation of the institution of slavery.

Let us consider what steps were taken by the State at large to furnish the internal improvements which the people in the mass perceived were now indispensable, but which, at that time, the Eastern Virginians at least were unwilling for the National Government to undertake even in part, although, in our own age, no demur to appropriations for this purpose is ever heard on the score of their being in conflict with the Constitution.

In 1833, the State Government held in reserve a separate fund of $2,415,586, the annual interest from which, amounting to $144,934.00, was to be devoted chiefly to the construction of improvements of that nature. The immediate custody of this fund was assigned to a Board of Public Works composed of thirteen directors, and numbering among its members the Governor, the Treasurer, and the First Auditor, *ex officio*. This Board had been organized in 1816, with the power to take possession of all the stocks owned by the State in companies which it had chartered in recent years. This was the capital of the Board. The rule which it followed was that every survey for any proposed internal improvement was to be completed under its supervision, and should the conclusion be favorable to the expediency of its construction, the Board would be always willing to provide two-fifths of the money that would be required, on condition that the remaining three-fifths should be subscribed by private individuals.

It was not long before it was discovered that the funds of the Board were going into small enterprises only, which were of no lasting public utility. The expense of carrying out larger undertakings of permanent value was too great for that body to bind itself to supply its customary share. A broadening of the original plan resulted. The State now assumed all the cost of completing certain internal improvements which were on a great scale, while the Board of Public Works continued to assist, under its former rule, enterprises of smaller importance, and therefore, ones calling for no extraordinary outlay on its part.

It soon became necessary for the Commonwealth to issue bonds to prevent a drain on its financial resources, in consequence of the extensive projects which it endeavored to carry through alone. It was expected that the stock acquired by the State in these projects would meet the interest and principal of the bonds; but if it did not do so ultimately, it was understood that the funds in the hands of the Board of Public Works were to be diverted to their payment; and should these funds too prove to be insufficient, then the contents of the State Treasury were to be liable. In the end, bonds for loans obtained by the State came to be employed even in those enterprises for internal improvements to which private individuals had subscribed. There was always great danger from the start that the Treasury, in assuming the whole burden of these larger enterprises, would be compelled to have recourse to the imposition of new taxes, which the people would be certain to resent. Prudent management of the finances of the State, therefore, required that the policy of making great public improvements should not go forward uninterruptedly, but by successive advances, with intervals of complete abstention.

By the middle of the fourth decade of the nineteenth century, the improvements of this character which had been completed, or were in the course of construction, were considerable in number. As early as 1825, a canal along the James had reached a point about thirty miles beyond Richmond towards the West. There was also, in continuation of navigation by river, a short canal that had been dug to remove the difficulty of passing Balcony Falls, in the Blue Ridge. In order to prolong the highway to the west, a large sum had been spent in building a turnpike from Covington to the Kanawha River; and an additional sum had been appropriated to facilitate the navigation of that stream to its mouth.

Naturally, this mixed system of communication and transportation was unequal to the demand upon its resources, and in 1831-32, a charter was granted to the James River and Kanawha Canal Company, with an authorized capital of five million dollars. This company was the successor of the James River Company, which had been organized as early as 1784, with the object of making that stream navigable for batteaux, either by clearances of the main channel, or by the construction of canals in the neighborhood of impassable falls. By the opening of the war in 1861, the James River and Kanawha Canal had been pushed as far as Buchanan. Had the State possessed the means to press construction rapidly from the start, this canal would have reached the Ohio in time to have converted Virginia, previous to 1861, into one of the wealthiest commercial communities in the Union. Nay more, it might have worked such a revolution in the general sentiment of her people at large as to have destroyed after a few decades the institution of slavery in their midst, and with it the disposition of the majority to support the South in Secession.

A second internal improvement in existence in 1832 was the Dismal Swamp Canal, which connected the waters of the Chesapeake with those of Albemarle Sound. The Roanoke Company had cleared the channels of the Roanoke, Dan, and Staunton Rivers for navigation by batteaux, and these frail boats carried down to Weldon annually a great quantity of tobacco and grain. The Rappahannock had, for the passage of similar boats, been opened to a landing situated forty miles above Fredericksburg. This work had been accomplished by locks, dams, and canals; and through the same means the use of the Shenandoah had been made practicable for a distance of two hundred miles.

An act was passed in 1831 to bring about the construction of a turnpike from Winchester in a north-western direction to some place on the banks of the Ohio. Among the other turnpikes projected as early as 1833, were those which aimed to make various towns more accessible to the State at large. Among these were Lexington, Warm Springs, Warrenton, Danville, Staunton, Fincastle, Charlestown, Fredericksburg, and Millborough. The funds that were to be expended in their construction were estimated at five hundred and fifty thousand dollars, of which the Commonwealth was expected to contribute about two hundred and twenty thousand. The railways in actual operation at this time were the Chesterfield,—which connected the Midlothian mines near Richmond with the head of Tidewater in the James,—and the Petersburg and Roanoke, which extended to Weldon. The Winchester and Harper's Ferry Railroad was not yet fully finished, and the Richmond and Fredericksburg was in the same stage of incompleteness.

Whilst all these public improvements were in contemplation, or in one of the stages of construction or extension, the political association of the people of Western Virginia with the people of Eastern was constantly embittered by the disputes which grew out of them. The Western region, beginning at the eastern spurs of the Alleghany Mountains, unlike the region between the Blue Ridge and the sea, could point to but one great river that served as a highway; and unfortunately for its people, that highway, which was very defective in itself, was turned in the wrong direction. What they needed most was a means of easy communication with the seaboard, and not with the Ohio. Omitting the Kanawha River and several turnpikes, they were cut off from a convenient outlet in every quarter. Naturally, the majority of them were not hobbled by any theory of strict interpretation of the Constitution in their desire to secure this outlet by the most powerful instrument in sight, namely, the National Government. Moreover, they owned no slaves to make them apprehensive of the consequences of the Government's going beyond its constitutional powers in giving aid in the construction of roads and canals, leading, on the one hand, to the valley of the Ohio River, and on the other, to the Atlantic ports.

Western Virginia at first was disposed to sympathize with the principles of the Federalist Party, and later its leanings in the way of internal improvements became distinctly nationalistic. In the Assembly of 1814-15, delegates from the Valley, Alleghany, and the counties beyond, were able to cast a majority vote in favor of national appropriation for the removal of obstructions from the western rivers. Their spokesmen took the ground that Congress was impowered to interpret the Constitution in harmony with the practical need for such assistance,—an expression of opinion which was approved even by the Republicans who had been elected from the western counties. These latter men, contradictory as the fact may seem, however natural, were perfectly willing to accept a strict construction of the Constitution provided that it was not made to apply to national appropriations for the benefit of internal improvements.

The nationalistic preferences of the Western Virginians, had, by 1819, undergone some modification in the light of promises by the East to inaugurate, with the State's assistance, a system of internal improvements independent of the National Government. But the hope born of these promises faded, owing to the fact that the enterprises demanded in Western Virginia were on such a scale, in consequence of the physical character of the country, that the fund of the Board of Public Works was entirely inadequate to carry them out even in association with private subscriptions.

All the representatives in Congress for the counties west of the Blue Ridge favored the grant of additional appropriations for the benefit of the Cumberland Road, then a bone of contention; and there were bills and petitions submitted which asked the National Government to aid the Virginian Government in financing the most important schemes for internal improvements in the State. This aggressive feeling of the Western Counties was temporarily quieted by the State's purchase of the rights of the James River Company, with the view of continuing, with its own resources, the improvements looking to the consolidation of the James River water-highway with the water-highway of the Kanawha, by means of an intervening great turnpike. This scheme seemed to have been pursued with a fair degree of energy, but the people of Western Virginia again became dissatisfied when they compared this limited work designed for their benefit with the great system of roads and canals that was fast coming into operation in the communities situated beyond their northern borders. Their own Commonwealth, they declared, did not possess the financial ability to follow in the footsteps of her sister commonwealths in that quarter, and the Western Virginians began, in their discouragement, to look again for aid to the National Government. This feeling was further embittered by the attacks of the Eastern Virginians on the principles of the American System, which was now regarded with increasing favor in the Western region, because the people there were anxious, not only to obtain the National Government's cooperation in the construction of roads and canals, which would remove their isolation, but also to enjoy the benefit of its tariff rates for the protection of their salt and iron manufactures.

Eastern Virginia offered a vigorous opposition to the Congressional bill for a General Survey because it empowered the President of the United States to order the survey for any highway that would promote the commerce, and strengthen the military defense, of the whole country.

When the Federal Government undertook to contribute to the cost of the Chesapeake and Ohio canal, interest in the completion of the James River and Kanawha was revived in Eastern Virginia, as a counterblast to the principle of national appropriations for internal improvements. It was noted that the western counties interested in such improvements cast their votes for Adams and Clay in the Presidential election of 1824; and the same fact was recorded in the Presidential election of 1828. These counties obtained no comfort from the proceedings of the Convention of 1829-30, nor from the defeat of the bill to charter a turnpike which was designed to extend from Buffalo in New York State, through the Valley of Virginia, down to New Orleans. All the representatives in Congress from the Alleghany region had voted in support of this bill.

It discloses the spirit of the majority of the General Assembly, which was drawn from the Eastern Counties, that, when the Staunton and Potomac Company was chartered, the Act provided that its privileges should be forfeited should it receive aid from the National Government.

One of the notable proposals of this period was that the canal project to unite Richmond with the Ohio should be abandoned, and a railway line substituted for it, a suggestion too much in advance of the times to be accepted. During the period between 1835 and 1838, a strong impetus was given to the construction of new railways and turnpikes, while the James River and Kanawha canal was more or less neglected in the State appropriations. It was urged in 1845 that it should not be pushed beyond the town of Buchanan, where it was to be joined on to the heads of two railways yet to be built,—one, to run to the Tennessee border; the other, to the Ohio River.

These, however, were not constructed at that time, nor afterwards in the manner proposed.

A more liberal policy was now pursued by the General Assembly in providing new lines of turnpikes for the western region; and its people, in consequence, became better satisfied for a time. A railway from Covington to the Ohio was proposed, but was not laid down during that period. In the meanwhile, the Western Virginians enjoyed the advantage of the Baltimore and Ohio railway in their northern counties, and of the Virginia and Tennessee in their southern.

Nevertheless, when Virginia seceded in 1861, the feeling that the western counties had not received their proper proportion of the internal improvements had its influence in causing the people of that region to disapprove of the Convention's action. Apparently, it was thought by them that the economic and material aspirations of Western Virginia would be better and quicker promoted by the principles which governed the development of the North than they would be by those which governed the development of the South.

CHAPTER IV

MANUFACTURES AND BANKS

There has always been an impression that the former plantation system of Virginia, under the influence of the institution of slavery, was inimical to the growth of manufactures. In a general way, this was not inaccurate. Manufacturing interests are fostered by the spirit of cooperation, and the cooperative spirit was not very vigorous in the more or less isolated, and the absolutely independent, life of the plantation as it was formerly organized. Each plantation, if of considerable area, was a small world in itself, which tended but slightly to promote the expansion of the community spirit, which is always at the root of cooperation.

The same plantation influence which, in Virginia, previous to 1860, discouraged an increase in the number of its towns, and kept more or less stationary the size of those already in existence, was precisely the influence which discouraged the establishment of a great system of manufactures. That influence operated to spread the population out and not to bring it together. It diminished the independence of men subjected to it, and to that degree lessened their desire to work together in those joint associations which are essential to the success of manufactures. But there was another feature of that old plantation life which was depressing to this branch of enterprise—certainly if it was to be conducted on an important scale. That life fostered a deeply conservative spirit, which was hostile to novelty. This spirit indirectly promoted ignorance of every economic employment but one. A man entering active life became a planter generally because his father, his grandfather, and even his great-grandfather, had been a planter before him. It was land that he had inherited, and land only, and it was natural that he should wish to manage it.

During many generations an immense majority of the Virginian people in the country had followed agriculture as a calling. It was the one pursuit which they really understood, and it was the only one which appealed to them at all. They regarded all other employments, with the exception of the intellectual professions—which were really dependent on agriculture for their prosperity—with sincere misgiving, if not with genuine aversion. If they came into the possession of money for investment, it rarely occurred to them to convert it into stocks and bonds. Their disposition was to use it in the purchase of more land and more slaves. And this disposition was confirmed when they saw that nearly every man who accumulated a large fortune in trade in town was not satisfied until he had bought a fine mansion and a fertile plantation in some district that was entirely given over to the cultivation of the soil.

This controlling taste which the people of Virginia had always exhibited for the pursuit of agriculture was the more remarkable in the light of the fact that the English stock from which they were sprung had, as time progressed, developed the greatest genius of modern times for the creation and management of all forms of manufactures, and at the same time, they had showed equal skill in the utilization of the ground. But it would be a grave mistake to conclude that there were practically no manufactures of importance in Virginia between the close of the Revolution and the opening of the War for Southern Independence. What manufactures did exist assumed various forms. The most numerous of these were naturally enough the products of purely manual trades. Taking them as a whole, they may be divided into, first, the products of the slave artisans on the largest plantations; second, the products of the white and free negro artisans in the villages scattered about the districts of each county; and third, the products of the numerous mills and factories that were to be found principally in the towns and cities.

We have pointed out, in our description of the economy of the plantation during the colonial era, that every estate that possessed many slaves found it expedient to obtain the mechanics needed by it out of their ranks. The whole round of the ruder arts was represented among this picked set of men, such as the craft of the blacksmith, the mason, the carpenter, the shoemaker, the weaver, and others previously enumerated by us. When it was clothes that were called for, there was the plantation seamstress to cut them out and sew them in their proper shape; there was a tanner to supply the leather for the shoes; there was a harness-maker to make the saddles and the harness; there was the blacksmith to fashion the horse-shoes and repair the tools; and finally, there was the miller to convert the wheat and maize into flour and meal for the hands.

All these artisans were also found on each large plantation in the course of the Federal period. Such a plantation was, during that period, fully self-contained outside the mansion of its owner. Not a thing for consumption or practical use in the cabins or in the fields, with the exception of the plough and some of the farming implements, was imported. All had been produced under the roofs of the plantation itself. The area of that plantation was a scene of manufacture in its most primitive forms, it is true, but forms that served their purpose quite as well as if they had come out of some great factory where machinery, and not human hands directly, had brought them into a condition to accomplish the various ends which they were designed to perform.

In the course of long years of practice, the plantation artisans were often able to acquire a high degree of manual skill. Their value from a pecuniary point of view was very much greater than that of the average slave. Indeed, many of them were hired out by their owners at a very handsome rate of wages.

When emancipation came as a result of the War of 1861-65, not all these highly trained artisans continued to live on the large plantations to which they had been attached as slaves. A disposition to break away from their native scenes and abandon their old employment was shown by nearly all the younger mechanics. They did not feel that they were really free until they had put it to the actual test by leaving their homes, and having no native preference for their respective trades, they objected to pursuing these even in their new places of settlement at a distance. Such callings as those of the blacksmith and mason were taxing to their strength, while those of saddler, shoemaker, cabinet-maker, and the like, were very confining. Old business could not be kept, or new business obtained, unless these young mechanics had been willing to remain steadily at their stands, and this few of them could be persuaded to do. In the majority of cases their skill was lost by their drifting into temporary employments which made no demand beyond the use of their hands in crude forms of work.

The plantation mechanics who found themselves advanced in years when Appomattox released their bonds stayed on, as a rule, with their former masters or opened little shops at the nearest cross-roads. The old plantation system, as a whole, did not begin to break up until a decade had gone by after the close of the war. This fact redounded to the advantage of these older negro mechanics, whose habits of steady labor had been formed under the inflexible discipline of slavery. Those habits still governed them in their general course of action, even when, like the younger mechanics of their race, some preferred to reestablish themselves at a distance. Gradually, as time passed on, they died off, only to leave few, if any, successors in their place. A group of plantations, which, under the former system, had each possessed numerous slave craftsmen, came, after the death of the elderly men who had remained loyal to their original homesteads and callings, to possess hardly one artisan among them all. Nor did the erection of negro mechanical institutes tend to make any alteration in this situation. The graduates of these schools preferred to settle in the towns.

When we consider the number of planters who were living in Virginia during the Federal period, those among them who were able to rely on their own negro craftsmen for all the work of that nature which was needed in the round of the seasons, formed, as might have been presumed, a comparatively small proportion of the whole number. There were many planters who could not afford to train more than one or two artisans of their own for their own use exclusively. There were numerous others whose operations were on such a limited scale that they could not afford to train any at all. There were still more who possessed no slaves to train. Upon what artisans did this great majority rely for the erection of a cabin, the fashioning of a horse-shoe, the making of a bridle, or the production of those other articles which they needed from time to time in the management of their plantation business?

In every county of Virginia, during the Federal period, there were to be found villages or hamlets in which all the principal crafts pertinent to agriculture were pursued by white or free negro artisans. They had settled in these little centers, which often did not contain more than two or three dozen houses, or a population in excess of an hundred persons, in order to meet the demand for their skill, which was constantly arising among the proprietors of the lands in the adjacent neighborhoods. We have a full record of all the crafts that were pursued in 1832-33 within the limits of the counties left in the present State of Virginia when the new State of West Virginia was formed during the War of 1861-65. Our necessarily concise survey of these trades is confined to that area, but its results were, in a general way, true of Western Virginia also. In all these counties, there were numerous stores in the different villages and hamlets which were perennially ready to supply the various articles which were called for in the rural economy of that day; but the patronage which they enjoyed does not appear to have seriously interfered with the custom of the mechanics who had their shops almost under the very eaves of these rural emporiums.

Among the various artisans who were to be found in each settlement, however small, were tanners, harness-makers, saddlers, cabinet-makers, blacksmiths, watchmakers, hatters, milliners, tailors, shoemakers, carpenters, wheelrights, tinners, and distillers. Coppersmiths and silversmiths were not unknown; nor were confectioners. Very frequently two persons of the same craft would be found working in shops standing side by side; and sometimes even three or even four were close together, an indication that the demand for their respective services was constant and profitable.

The case of the little Town of Washington, in Rappahannock County, which had a population of 350 persons, was not as exceptional as might have been inferred. In that population were included a silversmith, four blacksmiths, two saddlers, one hatter, one tanner, two wagonmakers, one cabinetmaker, four carpenters, one plasterer, one bricklayer, three tailors, three milliners, and four shoemakers. Washington was the seat of county justice, and this fact drew to the town every month a concourse of people who wished to be present at the sessions of court. The patronage of these visitors was, perhaps, larger than the inhabitants of the town itself could furnish, and it was equally as constant and reliable. The same prosperous condition was perceptible in the vicinity of every courthouse, and for the same reason, the planters of the surrounding country in each instance took advantage of a day's sojourn at the county seat to have much important work done for themselves by the various craftsmen established there. At Woodville, also in Rappahannock County, which was a village of 200 people only, without the advantage of court sessions, there were one tanner, three blacksmiths, one saddler, one boot and shoe maker, one cabinetmaker, one carpenter, one house-joiner and one tailor.

Turning from Piedmont to the Northern Neck, and selecting only a village, we find that Heathsville, the seat of justice for Northumberland, numbered, in a population of about 200, one tanner, one gigmaker, one hatter, one saddler, two tailors, two boot and shoe makers, and one confectioner.

Across the Rappahannock River, in Essex County, Loretta, in a population of fifty persons, could count one shoemaker, one blacksmith, one tailor, one bricklayer, one painter, and several carpenters. Westville, the seat of justice for Matthews County, nearer the sea, had, in a population of 150, one tanner, three boot and shoe makers, one tailor, two blacksmiths, one saddler, and one carriagemaker. Among the inhabitants of Yorktown, in York County, were to be found one tanner, one cabinetmaker, one carriagemaker, one carpenter, and three blacksmiths. Its population did not exceed 280 persons.

Lawrenceville, in Brunswick County, situated south of the James River, included, in a population of 350, two tanners, one saddler, two tailors, and three blacksmiths. Other trades were also represented. Maysville, the county seat of Buckingham, in a population of 300, could count one tanner, two saddlers, two boot and shoe makers, one silversmith, one watchmaker, one milliner, two wagonmakers, two cabinetmakers, three tailors, one tin-plate worker, and one miller. Meadsville, in Halifax County, with a population of seventy persons, could count one iron-founder, one plough manufacturer, one cabinetmaker, one tanner, one tailor, and one blacksmith, and also mechanics familiar with the manipulation of flour mills, cotton gins, wool carding machines, and tobacco factories.

Rocky Mount, in Franklin County, possessed two tailors, a saddler, a cabinetmaker, two blacksmiths, a shoe and boot maker, and several printers. New Castle, in Botetourt, included in its population of 105, one iron-founder, one blacksmith, two boot and shoe makers, one tanner, two cabinetmakers, one hatter, one wagonmaker, one saddler, one tailor, one house carpenter, and one boat-builder. Fincastle, in the same county, in a population of 700, numbered a printer, a confectioner, two clock and watch makers, one gunsmith, four blacksmiths, four boot and shoe makers, two tailors, two hatters, two tanners, five cabinetmakers, two wheelwrights, one chairmaker, one coppersmith, four saddlers, four wagonmakers, and one saddle-tree maker. Mount Crawford, a town of minor importance in Rockingham County, possessed two tailors, two saddlers, two boot and shoe makers, one blacksmith, one tin-plate worker, one cabinetmaker, one wheelwright, one cooper, one potter, two milliners, one gunsmith, one wagonmaker, and several millers and sawyers.

We have selected at random from the records of the older divisions of the state, namely, the Piedmont, Northern Neck, Peninsula, Southside, and the Valley, typical instances of the number and kind of craftsmen who were seated in the numerous villages, which ranged from 50 inhabitants to 500. If we were to include the towns of the size of Williamsburg, Winchester, Charlottesville, Staunton, Wytheville, and the like, the number of local craftsmen could be easily increased to very large proportions. We have given enough examples, however, to show that the planters everywhere had an opportunity to enjoy the services of ordinary artisans, even if their respective counties had within its bounds only a few villages and hamlets.

So far, we have been treating of the achievements of the fundamental mechanical arts. We come now to those forms of production which were carried out on so great a scale, with the use of machinery in part at least, as to fall under the head of general manufacture. For instance, the barrel could be made by a single workingman in a small shop, a purely manual act, or it could be made as one of an hundred thousand in a large factory, employing very many workingmen, and using machinery in principal degree. This was also true of other articles in constant demand.

Let us first direct our attention to one of the commonest of these articles. We find that boot and shoe factories were, in 1833, in operation in all parts of the state. They had been erected in villages like Maysville, in Buckingham County, where there were two at work, or like Brookneal, in Campbell County, where there was one. Not far off at Leesville, in the latter county, there were two such establishments. In Caroline County, there were also two; in Charlotte County, three; in Culpeper, four; at Cartersville, in Cumberland County, one; at Lawrence-ville, in Brunswick, one; in Fairfax, four; in Fauquier, also four; at Columbia, in Fluvanna, three; and at Palmyra, in the same county, one. At Rocky Mount, in Franklin, there was one; in Gloucester and Goochland counties, there was also one respectively; in Halifax, four; at Nottsville, in Lancaster, two; at Middleburg and other villages in Loudoun, six; in Louisa County, five; in Madison, two; in Matthews, three; in Mecklen-burg, one; in Suffork, in Nansemond County, three; in Norfolk County, two; in Northampton, three; in Northumberland, two; in Orange County, one; at Danville, in Pittsylvania, two; in Prince Edward and Prince William, one respectively; and in Richmond County, two.

Many of these boot and shoe factories were on a very small scale, no doubt, but their manner of production, if not their volume, gave them substantial importance in the economic life of the community.

The carriage and wagon factories, like the boot and shoe, varied in the number of their operatives, but they too served an indispensable purpose in the plantation communities of those times. We find factories of this character established as fol-lows: One at Gholsonville, in Brunswick County; one at Mays-ville, in Buckingham; one in Caroline; and four at the county seat in Charlotte. These factories employed respectively from eight to ten operatives. There were also two at Keysville, in Charlotte County, which gave work to numerous hands. In Culpeper County, there were two factories of the same kind; at

Petersburg, in Dinwiddie County, four; at Rectorstown, in Fauquier, two; at Salem, in the same county, one; at the county seat of Gloucester, two, and of Halifax, one. In Loudoun, there were five wagon and carriage factories. Two of these were situated at Middleburg, two at Hillsborough, and one at Leesburg. There were three in Louisa County, which had a wide reputation for the excellence of their output. In Madison, there were two; in Matthews, one; at Boydton, in Mecklenburg, one; and at Clarksville, in the same county, one; in Middlesex County, one; in Northampton, one; in Northumberland, one; in Orange, two; in Prince Edward, one; and in Southampton, one.

Flour mills were still more numerous, as their output was often distributed by wagon or boat far beyond the particular region in which it had been produced. In Richmond City there were four large mills. These were the Gallego, Haxall, Rutherford, and Mayo, which consumed annually an enormous quantity of grain. There were several mills also in the vicinity of Charlottesville. One of the most famous of these was the Shadwell. The Finney mill, in Amelia, also possessed a state reputation for the excellence of its brands. It consumed about twenty thousand bushels of wheat each year. There were three flour mills in Bedford, and two at Diuguidsville, in Buckingham. There were also several in the City of Lynchburg. In addition, there were three in Campbell County at large. There were also mills in Caroline and Charlotte counties, and also two in Cumberland. One of the latter consumed about thirty thousand bushels of wheat each year.

There were five large mills in Culpeper, six in the City of Petersburg, and two more in Dinwiddie County at large. At Barnetts, in Fauquier, there stood a mill five stories in height, and producing annually 4,000 barrels of flour. A second mill belonging to the same county consumed 30,000 bushels of wheat. There were five other mills in operation in Fauquier. In Fluvanna there were two similar mills of large capacity; in James City, at Williamsburg, four; in King and Queen, two; and in

Loudoun, four at Hillsborough, and one at Oatlands. This latter mill produced forty barrels of flour a day. There were five mills in the vicinity of the Madison County seat, and there was also one in Nelson County; one in Northumberland and Nottoway, respectively; in Patrick, one; in Pittsylvania, three; in Powhatan, two; and in Rappahannock, three.

The number of cotton mills in Virginia in 1832 fell very far short of the number of the flour mills. There was a large factory in Lynchburg engaged in this branch of manufacture which had a capital of $100,000, used 2,500 spindles, and gave employment to seventy men. Manchester possessed a mill that had been organized with a capital of $70,000. In Petersburg, five cotton mills were in operation. One of these worked over 2,000 spindles, and another over 3,500. This mill counted about 200 operatives on its roll. At Union Mills, in Fluvanna, there was a cotton factory of 1,500 spindles, with twelve power looms in addition.

But the most important cotton mill in the state was the one that belonged to the Richmond Manufacturing Company. Here 70 white operatives and 130 black were employed. It worked nearly 3,800 spindles and 80 looms, and consumed 1,500 pounds of raw cotton daily. The capital in its possession amounted to $120,000 in volume. There was a cotton factory at Verdun, in Hanover County, and two at Smithfield, in Isle of Wight. There was also one of 1,000 spindles at Occoquan in Prince William County, and one of 200 at the county seat of Surry.

There were few woolen mills situated in the state at this time.

The number of tobacco factories almost rivaled the number of flour mills. In Manchester, there were eight, and in Lynchburg and Richmond, a still larger group. There were also factories of this character at Rocky Mount, in Franklin County; at Danville, in Pittsylvania; at Farmville, in Prince Edward; and at Meadsville, in Halifax. In short, they were found in all the towns of importance in the region still busy with the tobacco plant as the principal crop.

Iron foundries and forges, in which a large quantity of pig-iron, bar-iron, and castings were manufactured, were in operation in Richmond City, and also in Rockbridge, Halifax, Mecklenburg, Pittsylvania, and other counties.

So far, we have only considered the volume of the manufacturing interests in existence in 1832-33. Let us now advance our study to 1860, and at first still limit it to the counties embraced in the modern State of Virginia. We have only space to present these interests in the mass. The amount of capital invested at that date was $17,718,188.15 approximately; the value of the annual products, $39,151,544 approximately; the number of establishments, 4,209 approximately; and the number of hands employed, 29,661 approximately. At this time, about thirteen cotton mills were in operation; also about fifty-five tobacco factories; about nine woolen mills; and about twenty-five iron mills and forges for bar, pig, and cast iron. If we include the manufactures of Western, Central, and Eastern Virginia combined, in other words, the entire original state, we find the aggregate figures to be as follows: Number of establishments, 5,885; amount of capital invested, $26,935,560; number of hands employed, 36,174; and the annual value of the products, $50,652,124.

It will be perceived from these figures that about one-third of the capital of the then undivided State of Virginia was invested in manufactures carried on within the confines of the present State of West Virginia. About one-fourth of the proceeds from the products of these manufactures belonged to those counties; and also about one-seventh of the hands employed. The same counties could also claim about 1,600 of the 4,200 manufacturing establishments of the entire original state.

It should be borne clearly in mind that the Census Report for 1860 includes in its enumeration of manufacturing interests every possible product of hand and machine, from the product of each simple mechanical art, like the art of the carpenter and blacksmith, for instance, to the art of the weaver, the milliner, the glovemaker, the hatter, the shoemaker, the ironmaster, the distiller, the glassmaker, the marble and stone worker, the millwright, the papermaker, the pumpmaker, the silversmith, the coppersmith, the wagonmaker, the woolcarder, the sailmaker, the soapmaker, the shipbuilder, the maker of musical instruments, and the nail and spike maker. The list, in fact, embraced 107 different lines of business, each of which was engaged in the actual production of an article of some kind.

What were the financial facilities enjoyed by the various forms of business—mercantile, manufacturing, or agricultural—followed in Virginia during the Federal period? After the Revolution, there were organized a large number of private voluntary associations to serve the purpose of banks. These were not chartered, but, at the same time, they possessed and exercised the right to issue currency notes. Still the state had no part in their transactions. The General Assembly, in fact, endeavored, by the passage of crippling acts, to force them to close their doors. By 1820 this had been accomplished.

In the meanwhile, the Bank of Virginia had been incorporated and chartered. It owed its existence to private subscriptions. It was a central bank only, in name, for it conducted its practical business through offices in every large town in the commonwealth. In authorizing the erection of this bank, the state bound itself to purchase 3,000 shares of its stock so soon as the required number of private subscriptions had been obtained. The Bank of Virginia was empowered to issue notes limited in volume to the total amount of its average deposits. These notes were accepted as legal tender in the payment of all taxes collectable by the commonwealth. The transactions of this bank were so successful from the start that the Farmers Bank of Virginia was incorporated, with a capital of $2,000,000. This capital also was obtained by subscriptions. The state agreed to buy $334,000 worth of its stock. It was not many years before the Exchange Bank of Virginia also was chartered on a scale of equal importance.

Virginia suffered as severely as her sister states from the frequent suspension of specie payments and the periodic occurrence of panics.

The following statistics show the volume of the assets of the three principal banks of the commonwealth in October, 1859: The Farmers Bank of Virginia, $7,142,697.85; Bank of Virginia, $6,024,177.43; and Exchange Bank of Virginia, $6,356,507.85. The deposits were in proportion for each of these banks in the following order: $1,736,159.48, $1,480,921.86, and $1,150,630.48. Their capital was respectively $3,150,900, $2,651,250, and $3,088,600.

Additional capital and deposits were represented in the resources of the small banks at Berkeley, Charleston, Fredericksburg, Fairmont, Howardsville, Pearisburg, Philippi, Rockbridge, Rockingham, Scottsville, Danville, Fincastle, and Wheeling. There were also other banks that were known only by general names, such as the Central, the Merchants, the Southwestern, the Northwestern, the Monticello, and the Valley of Virginia. There is reason to think that the financial facilities furnished by all these banks, large and small, were ample for the transaction of the business of the state.

CHAPTER V

INTELLECTUAL INFLUENCES

Probably, no single mind ever conceived a more comprehensive, and at the same time, a more minute system of public instruction than the one which we owe to the philosophical intellect of Thomas Jefferson. It is not an over-assertion to say that his native state has not yet fully carried out the far-sighted educational scheme which he, a century and a half ago, so clearly formulated as a revisor of its laws. It is doubtful, indeed, whether his native country as a whole has caught up with the final stage of that scheme, since few of the American Universities have even yet dropped the courses for undergraduates. But every decade has seen a closer approach to his ideal.

During nearly one hundred years, his principle of division into primary, secondary, and higher education, with the aid of the public purse, was quietly and consciously overlooked by the people of Virginia, who were willing only to follow his recommendation to provide to a certain degree at the public expense for higher instruction. They paid no serious attention to his equally important recommendation to provide for primary and secondary. It is true that there was a meagre public expenditure for primary education, but in such a form as practically to penalize it. There was no aid of any value offered for the advancement of secondary. Jefferson's great plan called for equal public assistance to each grade of popular instruction. It is only in our own day that this plan has even approximated the complete realization to which he so eagerly aspired.

What was that plan? First, the erection of elementary schools in every community, to be maintained by local taxation.

Second, the erection of a series of academies and colleges in general harmony with the character of our modern secondary public schools. These were to be supported partly by state appropriations and partly by tuition fees. The subjects to be taught in these institutions were to be the ancient and modern languages, the physical sciences, moral philosophy, mental philosophy, and political theory. Thirdly, the erection of a university, in which the whole field of human knowledge was to be surveyed and fully mastered.

Jefferson, on more than one occasion, declared that no single feature of his scheme was, in his eyes, less important than any one of its other features; that all, indeed, were equally essential to its complete success; and that to omit one, or slur over another, was to weaken the whole structure from its foundation to its roof. If he appeared in the end to give more thought to the introduction of means for the advancement of higher education rather than of primary and secondary, it was because he soon perceived that the line of least resistance to appropriations was along the path which led to the acquisition of facilities for advanced education. On the other hand, the path which led towards the acquisition of facilities for primary education was blocked by innumerable obstacles. Not even individual enterprise, which secured, by means of denominational colleges and private academies, a large number of secondary seats of learning, was ready to establish primary schools at private expense. These schools, however, were not left, as we shall soon see, entirely to their fate, for the public conscience, backed by the schemings of politicians seeking votes, did recognize a certain degree of educational obligation to the indigent. That degree was really so small as to be a reflection on the sense of public equity.

Let us first consider the rather melancholy history of such primary instruction as the children of this class in each community was able to secure.

Again and again, the adoption of Jefferson's plan for public primary tuition was pressed on the General Assembly's attention as a beneficent policy calling for immediate action. But that body was always disposed to balk when this question came up before them. In the first place, the public school was repugnant to that spirit of individualism which the independent plantation life did so much to foster and encourage. The education of the members of each family was looked upon as the private concern of that family alone. Public interposition in its behalf carried the idea of personal degradation even in the minds of the pupils to be helped. Their parents felt this so keenly that it was often said that their pride was the greatest obstruction to the success of the state-assisted primary schools, such as they were.

In the second place, a selfish motive played a part in crippling public primary education. The members of each county court were reluctant to increase the taxes of the landowners by imposing this additional burden on their shoulders. The Act of 1796 authorized each of these courts to appoint the year in which a system of primary schools was to go into operation, but this scheme was defeated by their failure to name a year. A bill for the creation of such a system in 1817 only obtained the support of the House.

In 1846, a third Act provided for a system of free schools, but the preliminary conditions to be fulfilled unfortunately prevented its success. It was not a general scheme to go into operation all over the state as soon as it was approved by the General Assembly. On the contrary, the several counties were permitted to accept or reject the plan separately by a two-thirds vote of its citizens. Only a few of the counties took advantage of this Act. An important additional obstacle to its fruitfulness was the necessity of obtaining the funds needed by local taxation alone.

It is questionable whether Virginia as a whole would have contributed one dollar out of the state's treasury for the support

Governor of Virginia

of primary schools had it not been for the providential establishment of the Literary Fund in 1810. This fund was an
accumulation of moneys accruing to the commonwealth from
the receipt of escheats, confiscations, fines, forfeitures, and penalties. It was very much increased by the repayment of the
principal of the loan which the state had made to the National
Government during the War of 1812-1815. Another important
addition to the fund began in 1853, when the annual capitation
taxes were ordered to be turned over to it without any deduction.

By an Act of the General Assembly, passed in the course
of the year 1811, it was provided that the income should be
used in founding or assisting schools in every county of the
state for the benefit of the resident children of the indigent.
The management of the fund was left to a board, which, however, could only disburse the interest in accord with the Assembly's particular directions. Commissioners were appointed in
each county to select the teachers for the new charity schools,
as they soon came to be known, and it was the duty of these
officers also to pick out the pupils who were to enjoy the advantages of these schools. Whenever a school house was needed,
the state agreed to contribute a certain percentage of its cost,
on condition that the rest of the amount required should be
raised by local taxation. In such a case, the children of the rich
as well as of the poor were to have the right to attend.

In some communities, it was often impossible to find teachers
who would consent to give their services for so small a sum as
was payable to the head of a charity school; and when this was
the case, the commissioners had no alternative but to enter the
indigent children under their care in any private school in the
neighborhood which would receive them. The number who were
able to obtain a smattering of tuition was unexpectedly large.
For instance, in 1851, over sixty-five thousand boys and girls
of impoverished parentage were enrolled in schools in Eastern
and Western Virginia combined, and of these, about one-half

JAMES BARBOUR

enjoyed the benefit of at least three months instruction each year. By 1859, this number had sunk to fifty-four thousand.

Eight years before, the expense of teaching indigent children averaged about four cents a day for each individual child. Eight years later, the charge fluctuated between two and six cents. The total amount paid by the state on this general account reached, in the course of each year, a very large figure. The statistics for a period as early as 1832 and 1833 have been preserved. The sum appropriated by the commonwealth during these two years for the counties embraced in the present State of Virginia alone closely approximated fifty thousand dollars, an expenditure that averaged twenty-five thousand dollars each year.

Permission was subsequently granted the several counties by the General Assembly to organize what were known as District Free Schools, should the local demand really justify it. Under special Acts, schools of this character were opened and maintained in the counties of Elizabeth City, Henry, King George, Northampton, Princess Anne, Washington, Albemarle and Augusta, and in the cities of Norfolk, Lynchburg, and Petersburg. Only the district school of Norfolk survived down to the beginning of the War of 1861-1865.

While most of the public schools for the primary and secondary grades languished, even when a vigorous effort was made to sustain them, the system of private academies flourished. This system fitted in perfectly with the convictions of the upper classes in the community. It was self-sustaining; it covered the ground of the principal sciences; it ensured, in almost every instance, a careful training in the ancient classics, which was considered in Virginia then, as it was in the contemporary England, the basis of a sound education.

The private academy offered an ample field for the exhibition by numerous instructors of a special talent for teaching. Some of these instructors had been successful in carrying off the highest honors in English and northern universities. The principals of the academies themselves were often men of extraordinary ability, apart from their profession, and exercised a wide influence in the general affairs of their communities.

After the opening of the University of Virginia, the largest proportion of the head-masters were graduates of its courses, and had brought to their selected calling in life those high ideals of scholarship and personal bearing which had, from the beginning, been so earnestly inculcated in that institution. The aim of each academy was to approximate the standards of this seat of learning; and there was a noble rivalry among them in the preparation of their students for the work to be done in the future in its different lecture-halls. So thorough was this preparation in the academies belonging to such men as Frederick Coleman and Franklin Minor, who were only *par inter pares* in their great profession, that many of their pupils took, immediately after entrance, the high position of graduates of the most advanced colleges.

It would be hard to overstate the moral influence of the best of these private schools. The boys assembled within their precincts belonged, as a rule, to the highest social class in their respective communities. Under parental vigilance they had already been taught all those lessons of personal honor and courage which justly entitled the Virginians of that earlier day to unusual social distinction. They had been brought up amid surroundings which instilled a love for the occupations of the open air and a taste for manly sports; and, at the same time, they had been trained not to be indifferent to the claims of the cultured intellect. The atmosphere of the academies to which they were transferred from the teachings of the home tutor or the clergyman in the "Old Field School" was precisely the one in which all the virile precepts of their native hearths would be most warmly encouraged. The headmaster was an exemplar, like the father, and his discipline, like the father's also, was directed as much to the moral character of his pupil as to his mental.

34—Vol. I.

The influence of the Virginian academies during the Federal period was deeply stamped upon the contemporary history of Virginia, for it was these academies that had given the earliest lessons of scholarship to her foremost political leaders, her eminent lawyers, her distinguished clergymen, her trusted physicians, her skilful agriculturists, and her successful merchants of that day.

The public school system of our own times offers all the advantages of primary and secondary education to a greater number of persons in each community than the academies formerly did. To that degree, and to that degree alone, its superiority is undeniable. On the other hand, the old system of academies, contracted as it was in its scope from a social point of view, nourished a spirit which was not simply intellectual in the pedagogic sense of that word, but a spirit that reached deep into the whole moral fibre of a great people, and gave that fibre additional vigor and beauty. They were more than schools. They were scholastic homes in which the quality of the soul as well as the powers of the mind were fostered with discriminating care and unsleeping vigilance.

It is calculated that, previous to 1800, there were at least twenty-five excellent academies in Virginia. Some of these early foundations grew into colleges of high reputation. Such were the Prince Edward Academy, the foremost institution of its kind south of the James, soon to be converted into Hampden-Sidney College; Liberty Academy, the future Washington College; Fredericksburg Academy, the future Fredericksburg College; Albemarle Academy, the future Central College; Richmond Seminary, Princeton Theological Seminary, and the Austin Theological Seminary were established. Washington College owed its ers of almost equal prominence.

In the interval between 1800 and 1860, about two hundred and fifty academies in all were incorporated, but only a small proportion of them permanently survived. The number founded

President of the United States 1841-1845

in the part of the state now known as West Virginia, was about one-twelfth of the whole.

The various religious denominations were very zealous and successful in encouraging the growth of secondary and higher education by building up institutions of that grade for a more or less sectarian purpose. Hampden-Sidney College was administered, to a large degree, under Presbyterian influence; and it was principally through the instrumentality of this College's early or later officials and alumni that Union Theological Seminary, Princeton Theological Seminary, and the Austin Theological Seminary were established. Washington College owed its origin to the vigorous Presbyterian spirit of the Scotch-Irish population controlling the region of the Upper Valley; Richmond College, to the Baptists; Randolph-Macon and Emory and Henry to the Methodists; Roanoke College, to the Lutherans; and the Episcopal High School, to the Protestant Episcopalians.

But the most powerful influence in operation in Virginia in support of higher education during the Federal period arose from the work of the State University. This institution was the sole division of the great educational scheme which Jefferson inserted in the Bill of 1779 that became a reality in his own day. Only one other division of that scheme was carried out even in part, and this in a manner so meager and so feeble, indeed, as to amount to a travesty of this feature of his original plan. Reference has already been made to the charity schools which furnished rudimentary instruction to the children of the indigent. These schools were an inferior substitute for the primary schools which he was anxious to see established by local taxation.

The colleges which his plan called for, in order to assure a series of secondary schools, were not undertaken at all in his own life time. The denominational institutions to some degree filled their place, but their sectarian influence was repugnant to the spirit of the system which he proposed; and besides this drawback, they were not closely articulated, a fact which made them independent of each other and of the university. Jefferson was compelled to content himself with the attainment of the main feature of his scheme; that is to say, with the creation of a university; and he indulged the hope that, through this instrumentality, he would be able to spread abroad in the various communities of the commonwealth such a thirst for education in general, that, ultimately, his entire design would be adopted and enforced.

He recognized, from the beginning, that the resources of the state government were not sufficient to bear the entire expense of maintaining the system of public instruction which he advocated, but he anticipated that the burden could be made light by means of joint state and local taxation. Fortunately, the creation of the Literary Fund in 1810 went far to assure a definite income for the advancement of education in general in Virginia; and the fact that this income, owing to prevailing prejudices, was only used in small part for the support of schools for the indigent left a considerable amount to be annually appropriated for the benefit of a seat of higher learning, should one be established in the course of time.

In February, 1818, Jefferson was gratified by the General Assembly's vote in favor of the incorporation of a state university. Chiefly through his influence, Central College, which he had already founded at Charlottesville, was accepted as the nucleus of the new institution. But it was not until April, 1824, that the buildings had made such progress towards completion that the Board of Visitors felt that they would be justified in adopting a formal scheme of studies. This scheme was precisely the same as the one embodied in the report which their rector had submitted to the Legislature after the meeting of the commissioners at Rockfish Gap a few years before. It comprised the following table of studies: I. Ancient Languages, which also included belle-lettres, rhetoric, and ancient history and geography; II. Modern Languages, with modern history and geography added; III, Mathematics; IV. Natural Philosophy;

V. Natural History; VI. Anatomy and Medicine; VII. Moral Philosophy; and VIII. Law.

This general scheme was distinguished for three practical features of an uncommon character: first, the division into schools; second, the ability of each school to expand more or less as the funds of the institution increased; and third, the untrammeled right of election which the students enjoyed, instead of being bound down to an inflexible curriculum. Each school was restricted to a single subject. Each school also was entirely independent of every other school. Now, time was an essential element in all the curriculum colleges. Each year of every four years in seats of learning of that character had its set course of studies, and all four sets had to be mastered before the matriculated could win his diploma of graduation. In the University of Virginia, on the other hand, the matriculate selected such courses as he preferred, pursued them for as long or as short a time as he wished, and if industrious and successful, was awarded a diploma in each course. He was under no compulsion in choosing his grades. He could, during the same session, be a member of the senior class in Latin, the intermediate class in Greek, and the junior class in mathematics. And if he was disposed to do so, he could continue a student in the university for a period of ten years or even more, or only one, if his means were insufficient for the expenses of two.

As we have already pointed out, the number of schools, at the beginning, did not exceed eight, but Jefferson's scheme was of such an elastic nature that, not only could the course of each existing school be enlarged from time to time, but new schools could be gradually added. He anticipated that many subjects not then lectured upon at length, or even at all, in the different seats of learning, would come to be of so much pertinence to practical life as to call for a full presentation by the academic instructor. He foresaw, for instance, the importance of technical philosophy, manual training, agriculture, horticulture, veterinary surgery, and military science, as themes for University exposition. The day was rapidly approaching, he declared with correct prescience, when the field of knowledge, especially in the sciences, would become so broad and so varied that it could not all be covered by a single scholar, however diligent, unless satisfied with a mere smattering. One student might prefer to concentrate his principal attention on the ancient languages; another on history; another on the sciences; and still another on certain provinces in all three. The elective system gave each one ample room to pursue with great particularity any of these separate themes, without hampering him with the necessity, as in the curriculum, of pursuing them all at the same time.

It was special culture, and not general culture, which the founder of the University of Virginia had primarily in view, although the system permitted also of general culture in the highest measure, should the student succeed in passing through all the classical and scientific schools.

In spite of the increase in the facilities for the acquisition of a higher education which resulted from the establishment of so many academies and colleges, there does not appear to have been any corresponding growth in the literary productiveness of the Virginia people, taking them as a whole. It is true that there did arise among them, in their largest city, the most original literary genius whom the United States has given to the world, Edgar Allan Poe. All the social influences surrounding him in his formative years, with the exception of a sojourn of some length in England during his childhood, were distinctly and comprehensively Virginian; and yet, so far as the special character of his literary work was concerned, he was thoroughly alien to the soil of the state. There was no flavor in his writings of the people in whose midst he had been reared. Indeed, there was no more trace in those writings of the University of Virginia in which he had been educated than there was of the University of Paris or of the English Cambridge. The kingdom of the supernatural alone could claim him. Not even the world, much less Virginia or America, could call him its own.

EDGAR ALLAN POE

There were authors of local distinction in the state, during the Federal period, like John R. Thompson, Philip Pendleton Cooke, and John Esten Cooke, but they were hardly of a calibre in the province of fiction or poetry to confer a far reaching celebrity in their birth places.

What was the explanation of this comparative literary barrenness, when there was so much attention paid in the local seats of learning to the ripest scholarship, and when there was so much genuine culture among persons of the higher planter class? A very keen appreciation of the Greek and Roman classics, and of the modern English and American also, was observable in many of the country homes. The libraries under these roofs most frequently revealed the existence there of an unusually discrimnating literary taste. Very often, those collections of books reflected a soundness of literary judgment which had descended through two centuries in the same family. The works of Shakspeare, Johnson, and Milton, Addison, Swift and Pope, Gibbon, Goldsmith and Gray, Byron, Scott and Wordsworth, Dickens, Thackeray and Macaulay, were found on the shelves in close proximity to the volumes of Poe, Simms, Hawthorne, Emerson, Cooper, and Longfellow.

The printing press, during the Federal period, was not pouring out a continuous stream of books of merely casual interest. There were then few bursting circulating libraries to enable readers to fill up vacant hours with the perusal of literary rubbish, only to be returned when once finished and never taken out again. The prevailing taste was for a small number of books, and those of a permanent quality. Many of these were known by heart, and, like the romances of Scott, for instance, left a deep imprint on the spirit of the community at large.

And yet during all this long interval but one periodical published on the ground was able to maintain its footing for any considerable length of time. This was the *Southern Literary Messenger*. Perhaps that periodical too would have quickly perished, like so many of its predecessors and successors, had it

JOHN R. THOMPSON

not acquired almost from its birth a wide reputation through the contributions to its pages by Edgar Allan Poe, which were the first draughts from the fountain of his marvelous powers. And it also enjoyed another extraordinary advantage, at a somewhat later date, which had a powerful influence in enabling it to continue its first prosperous flight. John R. Thompson was, perhaps, the most accomplished editor of his time. A trained litterateur, an accomplished citizen of the world, and a careful business manager, he was successful in securing for the *Messenger* a very respectable position in a field where few of the numerous similar aspirants for public favor survived the vicissitudes to which they were there mercilessly exposed.

Eager as Thompson always was to encourage literary talent among the Virginians through the medium of his periodical, its pages did not again usher into the world a second genius worthy even to unloose the latchets of Poe's shoes. The names that rose, through contributions to that magazine, to some distinction, passed ultimately into obscurity. The educated Virginians could fully appreciate good literature, but they could not produce it; or if they were able to do so, they hid their light under the proverbial bushel.

The most striking form which the literary talent of the Virginians in general of that day assumed was exhibited in politics and journalism. Among the great state papers of America there are none superior in learning, in lucidity, in vigor, or in logical reasoning, to those which we owe to the pens of Jefferson, Madison, and Marshall. Where can the reader find such pungency, such sparkle, such incisiveness, as lurk in every paragraph of John Randolph's public addresses? The debates in the great Convention of 1829-30 were the last brilliant intellectual rays of a civilization that was already sinking fast to the western horizon. They have probably never been equaled in knowledge, in cogency, and in clearness, in the proceedings of any similar body which has assembled on our continent.

The same extraordinary quality is perceptible in many of the speeches of the Virginians of that period who were members of Congress, and in the messages of many of the ablest governors of the state submitted annually to the General Assembly. It was equally palpable in the best editorials of famous journals like the *Richmond Enquirer,* which commanded thoughtful attention throughout the Union, and powerfully influenced the policies of parties. These journals were not simply newspapers in the modern sense of the word. They were something more than this. They were the organs of great political principles, which were advocated in their columns with a force and dignity that were in complete correspondence with their importance in the affairs of both the state and the nation.

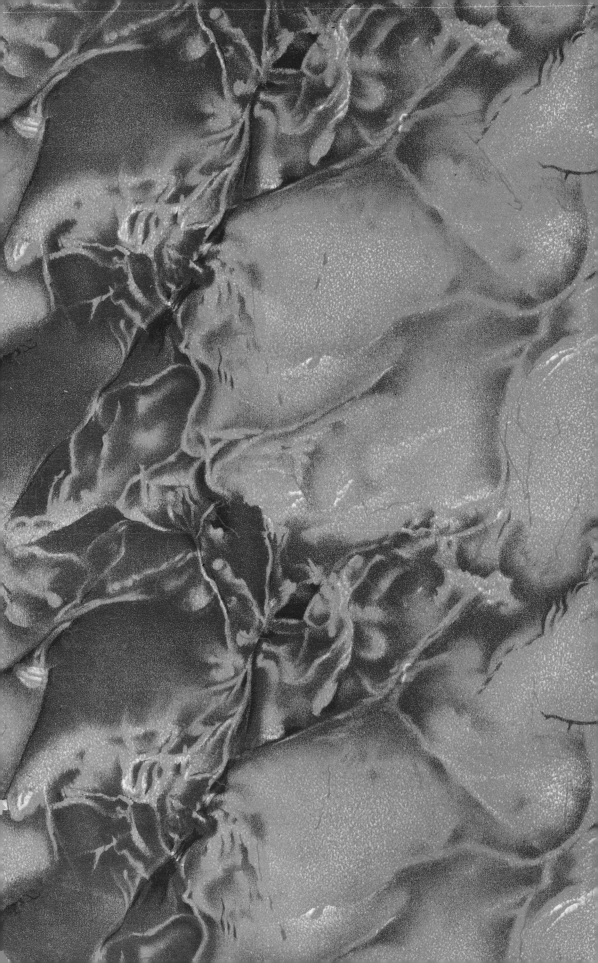